JAN MYRDAL

Report from a Chinese Village

With a new introduction by the author

Photographs and line illustrations by Gun Kessle
Translated by Maurice Michael

PUBLISHED BY PAN BOOKS LIMITED

First published 1963 in Swedish under the title
Rapport från kinesisk
This translation first published in Great Britain 1965
by William Heinemann Ltd
Translation © William Heinemann Ltd 1965
This Picador edition published 1975 by Pan Books Ltd,
Cavaye Place, London sw10 9pg
© Jan Myrdal 1963, 1975
Printed in Great Britain by
Richard Clay (The Chaucer Press) Ltd,
Bungay, Suffolk

ISBN 0 330 24257 1

Contents

Part IV
The Labour Group for Vegetable Cultivation

Part V
Liu Ling Labour Brigade

Part VI
Women

Part VII
The People's Militia

Part VIII
Liu Ling Labour Brigade's Supervisory Committee

List of Illustrations

(between pages 106 and 107)

(between pages 234 and 235)

Explanation of Terms Used

1 yuan — Roughly 20 pence or 50 U.S. cents. Contraction: Y.

Silver dollar — In principle corresponds to the silver value of the Mexican dollar.

Tael of silver — 20 or 24 dwt. of silver.

String of cash — These coins, tsien, are small round copper coins with rectangular holes. They are intended to be threaded on a string. A string of 1,000 tsien used to correspond to roughly 20 dwt. of silver.

1 li — 550 yds.

1 chi — 13¼ in.

1 jin — 1 lb. 1½ oz.

1 liang — About 1 oz.

1 mu — 0·9 rood.

Ganbu — Originally a professional revolutionary—hence the expression 'join the revolution' when one took a job in government service—now a civil servant or functionary in state industry, the party or some mass organization.

Hsiang — Smaller administrative unit, now done away with. Its area corresponded roughly to that of the present people's communes.

Hsien — Larger administrative unit, often translated as 'county'.

Kang — The domestic clay bed that is heated from underneath.

K.M.T. — Kuomintang, formed in 1912 by Sun Yat-sen as a middle-class democratic national party. Later joined the Comintern, when China's Communist Party became a part of the Kuomintang. Sun Yat-sen died in March 1925. Finally, when the Kuomintang seemed to be victorious all over the country, Chiang Kai-shek carried out his long-planned attack on the communists and leftish elements in the so-called big 'April Massacres' of 1927. The ultimate result of this action was Chiang Kai-shek's flight to Formosa in 1949 together with the remnants of the Kuomintang.

Loess	Layers of wind-blown yellow soil. Fertile. Forms huge deposits in which the rain cuts deep ravines.
Ming tuan	'People's force', defence corps, 'white bandits'. Armed free corps mainly organized as a defence against peasant revolt during the Kuomintang period.
Yamen	A mandarin's official residence, his offices.

Introduction

THIS is a book about people. A description of the villagers of Liu Ling in northern Shensi. I have attempted to reproduce as accurately as possible how these villagers, these individual men and women, portray their own reality; the experiences they remember and the role they believe they have played during one of the great social and political upheavals of modern times, the Chinese revolution. Thus it is not a study of the Chinese village in general and in the abstract, neither is it an account of the different agricultural policies during different periods of that revolution. And this I want to make very clear: the book is meant to be exactly what the title says: 'Report from a Chinese village'.

That also means that the individual interviews in this book can be read as independent stories; *contes;* human documents from a crucial period. I have not sought to write a smooth and easily read book on China where the reader is presented with all the material in a premasticated state and only needs to swallow in order to get his conclusions. I wanted to provide the material that I had found I lacked during my travels in Asia. I want the reader to doubt, to think, to utilize my work in order to understand and interpret what is happening in China, to make it one of the instruments he will use when he tries to arrive at conclusions.

Therefore I have tried to provide all the information on this village that is obtainable, without leaving anything out. I have not compared individual statements with official pronouncements made at government or party level. (That material has been published many times and is easy to find. To have included it in this volume would only have added to its bulk, not to its information.) Nor have I tried to reconcile the statements of the various witnesses, though different individuals gave mutually contradictory and incompatible accounts of the same event. I did this because my conception of the role of a writer is that he should be an interpreter of reality, not a corrector or censor; his duty is to report, not to distort.

I will later return to the question of sources of error, but here one important thing remains to be said: the usefulness of this book to the reader in his search for realities and the validity of my whole argument rests, of course, on my honesty. That goes for any book or study, though many writers try to hide the fact behind an objectivization that is misleading. No writer is as mechanically accurate as an electronic computer; but even a computer is programmed and one always has to ask how was the programming done? What was the bias of the programmer?

Very few writers are subjectively dishonest. The real question is thus not honesty or dishonesty, but what is the code of honesty of this specific writer, i.e. his bias? No human being can be an unbiased observer of other humans. The reader thus has to take my honesty, i.e. that I'm not wilfully changing the facts that I report, on trust. But he has at the same time to remember that I'm biased.

My bias is primarily that of an intellectual and humanistic tradition. My premise is that human beings are, in the last analysis, rational, that they respond in a rational manner to an existing social and material reality. Historical and cultural differences are a part of this reality, but even so the differences between villagers in Sweden, Latin America, China, Great Britain and the United States are not ones of quality. Not only in fiction, but also in fact, are we all brothers under the skin. Thus it is possible to form a judgement and hold opinions and act on these opinions on the basis of facts. The pride of this tradition is that you change your opinions as the facts outgrow them, as the snake changes his skin. You are constant not in your opinion, but in your receptivity to factual information.

I have also a strong social bias. To a large extent it has been formed by the historical tradition of my country, Sweden, a small country where free peasants during the centuries have managed to keep their own power and held off the gentry and the officials that plagued most of Europe, both the British Isles and the Continent: a tradition that even now, in industrialized modern Sweden, makes for an intense distrust of officials. I cannot express this tradition better than did the Peasant Estate of the Swedish Parliament on 9 April 1720 during a grave national crisis in a grim war:

Give us no more officers to the utter and unavoidable disaster of the country, we will not receive them or give ourselves under their orders or leadership, but we promise and honestly ensure that we, following the honourable example of our forefathers, if the enemy enters the country and highest necessity demands it of us, will go every man from his house and spare neither blood nor life for the defence of the country and the fatherland.

This bias does not make me change what people told me; but it probably makes me a more sympathetic listener to plebeian, peasant, democratic and puritan remembrances than it would a man whose ideals had belonged to the aristocratic tradition in Europe. This peasant bias was also one of the motivations behind the decision to try to write a book of this kind. The revolution in China was a peasant revolution, and the most striking aspect of the whole underdeveloped world is peasant unrest and hunger for land.

But there was also an identification on a deeper level. Not until the book was written and published and I held the volume in my hands did I become conscious of what had been the strongest emotional impulse behind it: a personal, emotional and sub-conscious drive towards identification, which has to be taken into account by a reader whose identifications and responses are different. On my father's side, the family comes from the village of Solvarbo in Dalecarlia, a province that, throughout Swedish history, has been the home of peasant freedom and peasant insurrection ('Oaks and noblemen never pass the Dala river'), and is also, in one way, the most conservative and traditional in the country. (When mentioning me in the provincial press in Dalecarlia they never fail to write: 'Jan Myrdal of Solvarbo lineage'.) Like several other villages in Dalecarlia Solvarbo refused to follow the land reform (unification of holdings) that broke up the Swedish villages during the eighteenth and nineteenth centuries. The reform had to be implemented if one peasant in a village demanded it. But until this day no peasant in Solvarbo has demanded it and during nearly two centuries of convincing arguments from the officials of the Swedish government—they still try—the Solvarbo peasants have refused to be convinced.

As my parents were abroad, I spent my early childhood with my paternal grandparents. Later on I spent nearly every summer with my paternal grandmother. During the war, when my parents were in the United States, she lived with us children. I also spent quite a long time in Solvarbo and met the old people there. During all these years my grandmother talked about our village. And, when I was young, I never quite knew whether the Slott Anders Andersson she talked about was the one that lived in the seventeenth century or the one that lived during her childhood. There was a genealogical consciousness pervading everything she said. Though she had moved from the village, she still existed inside the village framework. When, at the age of ten, I said that I was going to be a writer, she took this to be a writer about Solvarbo, describing village and family. I never became that writer; I never will. That village is dead and gone. Though the peasants refused to conform, Swedish society has changed so fast that the village has lost its meaning, even though it has not physically disappeared. Even our names have disappeared, the Myres, Knuts, Perers have all lost their names through an act of Parliament, so that I'm not Myres Jan Gunnarsson, I'm Jan Myrdal. The law of the land demands it. I knew the old ones and they are dead, I never go to the village. I never even go to the province.

But now I understand that the reason that I identified myself so strongly with these Chinese peasants and this village, Liu Ling, was because they were so close to my own family and tradition. My grandmother telling me of Myr Erik Eriksson as she remembered him, a poor and stubborn petty peasant walking barefoot through the village holding his Sunday shoes, which he never used except inside church; his two oxen, one white and one brown. The ox-driving song from Solvarbo village:

> 'The earnings are small and the days are long,
> Go slow, dear oxen, go slow.
> You don't amount to much and neither do I,
> But we'll keep on a-struggling with all our might.
> Go slow, dear oxen, go slow.'

With this book on China I unburdened myself of my debt to my ancestors. Only afterwards did I become fully conscious of this emotional drive behind my work. So, in a way, I did write the book about our village, even though I wrote of a village in China. During the time I sat in Peking and wrote the book it seems that I—according to what the then Swedish chargé d'affaires in Peking, Stig Brattström, has told me—spoke more about Solvarbo village than about the Sino-Soviet conflict.

I do not believe that this emotional motivation behind my work invalidates my findings; quite the contrary, I hold that no intellectual work can be of any value unless there is a very deep personal and emotional involvement in the issues. In my case, this involvement makes it impossible for me to see the peasants of Liu Ling as mere pawns in a game. And so I cannot see the world as a gigantic chessboard where White plays Red, the 'Free World' plays the 'Socialist Bloc' for checkmate and final supremacy. Of course I see my bias not as prejudice, but as rationality and sanity; the reader might see it differently, but in any case, knowing my bias will make my work more useful to him.

The method I have used to transmit an Asian reality to a 'Western' public is the outcome of my own experiences while travelling in Afghanistan and India in 1958–60, and in Burma and India in 1961–2. During those years I came to experience a frightening gap between the reality that surrounded me and the description of that reality as I read about it. The published material I had to use when trying to draw my own conclusions eventually proved to be unreliable, much too much was speculative, mere 'impressions'. The clarification and formulation of my ideas about social reality and the description of that reality, the problem of what source material could be available and the way to handle it was a long process. It took place in New Delhi during the winter of 1961–2 in discussions that lasted day in and day out for several months. The individuals who in these discussions influenced me deeply were Mr Bertil Mathsson, who at that time headed the regional I.C.A. (International Co-operative Alliance) Study Centre for Asia in New Delhi, and Mrs Kusum Nair, whose book *Blossoms in the Dust* about the Indian villagers made a deep impression on me. My parents Alva and Gunnar Myrdal also influenced my outlook—it would have been strange if they had not, considering that we share several fields of interest and have had an intermittent debate going on for two decades. That these discussions drove me to become conscious of what principles are tenable for an approach to the problem does not, of course, in any way mean that anybody else is responsible for the way I have worked or necessarily agrees that this method of presenting a peasant revolution in an Asian country is the most appropriate.

When, during the four months in China that preceded my stay in the village, I struggled to obtain a clear picture of the tremendous change that has taken place, I found that I lacked certain material that would make it possible for me to have a concrete picture of what happened and how it happened. Not that I lacked literature: the literature on China is enormous. If somebody had the misfortune to request—in a fairy-tale moment when all wishes are granted—that he be given everything published about China, then that poor student would immediately be crushed to death by an avalanche of books. If not a mountain, at least a hillock of excellent and scholarly tomes would mark his resting place. Even so I lacked the one book I had most wanted to read. And as the Chinese development is of such a character that it demands of each of us not to take a stand, but, much more important, to understand clearly why and how, the problem was not just a personal problem. So I decided to try to write such a book that I would have liked to read. A book that was to be concrete and factual, and about one specific village, thus making the question of the 'village in general' understandable. The formal concept behind this book—to try to be the mouthpiece of Asian villagers—is thus the outcome both of my deepest personal needs and my experiences during several years of travel and study in Asia.

When I decided to write on Chinese villagers, I knew that my formal qualifications were nil. That never disturbed me. I left school when I was seventeen, because I found that it hindered my studies. I have never cared for degrees and formalities, they are ladder steps in a career; they can be stepped upon, if you are interested in that kind of career, otherwise you don't need them. My main aim during the short life that is given any of us is to work; study, travel and write. But what really disturbed me was, of course, that my specific qualifications were not large enough. I would have wanted to be a scholar of Chinese as Dr Karlgren, to know the history of science and implements in China like Dr Needham. I don't. This lack of knowledge is a limitation. For some time, therefore, I doubted whether it really was up to me to try to do this work. But when I spoke to young sinologists, I found that they usually were both uninterested in and unfeeling for peasant problems. Their knowledge of Chinese could not help them, as they had no common language with peasants. The best works on Chinese village life, like Martin C. Yang's *A Chinese Village*, were about another period than that of the peasant revolution. Books on the peasant upheaval like *New Earth* by Jack Chen to me read too much like a Red Sunday-school tale: 'Hsinteng county will be more beautiful than ever—a land without want, without ignorance, a land of science, abundance, democracy and peace.' I did not and do not doubt that in the very long run this will prove correct both in Hsinteng county and every other county in the world. But it is not a picture of the hungry, sweating reality of today or in the next generation. My real qualification I found to be that no one else seemed to want to do what I wanted. I might qualify this statement by adding that I have later met some people who would have liked to do something similar—but they were either not allowed by their own government to go to China or not allowed by the Chinese government to enter China. In this, as in many other situations, I'm happy to be a Swede. Sweden is such an insignificant country that it does not have any mission in the world and thus its government can retain a 'nineteenth-century liberal' attitude towards their intellectuals, and no foreign government needs to see us as 'representatives'. Which brings me to the question of visas and permissions.

When I visited Sweden in the winter of 1960–1, I had preliminary discussions with the embassy of the Chinese People's Republic in Stockholm on the possibility of obtaining a visa for a protracted stay in China. At that time I had been writing about Afghanistan and I was planning a journey to the north-eastern provinces of Burma. I wanted to link this up with China, and thus I asked for permission to go to Sinkiang, which was immediately refused, Inner Mongolia (nomadic culture), western Yunnan (the tribes on the border to Burma) and a village in China proper. Already at that time I was, of course, conscious of the village problem, though I did not see it as clearly as I did a year later after the discussions in New Delhi.

In the spring of 1962, I and my wife, the artist Gun Kessle, received our visas for China and left from New Delhi for Peking. We had been granted visas for one year. Three factors probably played a part in our receiving this permission, apart from the general easiness with which we as Swedes travel around the world: the rather good diplomatic and trade relations between Sweden and the People's Republic; the fact that I was to write for the most influential weekly magazine in Sweden; the general opening-up of China for 'Western' writers and tourists as a strange result of the Sino–Soviet conflict. (While I'm writing this introduction to the English translation, news has come that agreements have just been signed that will send 300 Swedish tourists to China in the spring and summer of 1964.)

Financially the trip was made possible through two large grants from the Swedish State Writers' Fund, advances from my Swedish publishers, Norstedt & Söner, and the weekly magazine *VI*, the organ of the Swedish Consumers' Co-operative and Wholesale Society, plus diverse other magazine and book publishers. And we borrowed. Thus, we financed our journey to China and our travels in China with our own resources. We probably could have become 'invitees'; the Chinese suggested this to us on several occasions, when we spoke of reducing our expenses, and that we did not do so was less because we thought that we would be corrupted—I have never believed myself to be easily corruptible and I don't think that I change my opinions because of small economic gains—but I intensely dislike the international junkets, the pleasure trips at public expense. The big powers, the Soviet Union, the United States, China, France, Great Britain, are all subjecting the writers of small countries like Sweden (and of each other) to well-intentioned economic pressure through different forms of free travel 'with all expenses paid'. Even if I don't think I would be corrupted, I'm against the whole tendency. It has a perverting influence on the intellectual morals of the writer, it runs counter to the free expression of ideas. I can't stop this tendency, but I can at least say no for myself. I distrust free-loaders whether they are capitalists, communists, liberals, conservatives, anarchists or just plain sellers of words. I have never liked being grateful to anybody. And I can't under-tand how the public—that after all pays for it—can put up with this spectacle of politicians, writers and sundry 'public figures' banqueting their way around the world on a spree of phrases.

But as my funds were by no means unlimited and as there were, and are, few facilities in China today for the tourist with a slim pocket-book, this led to certain conflicts. Our status was that of 'short-time guests' who were supposed to stay a long time and pay their own expenses. We had brought along our bicycles and as that was not quite up to the status of a 'guest' (who ought to ride in a car, which we could not afford) it took some time and discussion before we were granted permission to go on bicycles. We tried to save on living expenses in order to be able to spend the money on travel. (For instance when we wanted to go up the Burma Road from Kunming to the border, we had to hire a car. This cost a thousand dollars. The price was quite normal in that part of the world and, if we had not paid it, we could not have gone the six hundred miles to the border. When travelling, there is always the choice between sleeping up your money or using it in a rational manner.) In Peking we first lived in a good hotel, the Hsin Chiao; it was not too expensive, but it still was too expensive for us to live there for months. Then we succeeded in getting permission to live in a small and inexpensive Chinese hotel, the Beifang, but as the food situation in China was becoming better, this hotel was converted to a restaurant and we were forced out. That was at the time when we left for Liu Ling. When we came back to Peking, we were given the choice of living in a good hotel—at a price we could not afford to pay—or becoming the honoured guests of the Chinese People's Association for Cultural Relations with Foreign Countries. There simply was no third way. Inexpensive lodgings for foreigners did not exist. Still, I succeeded in finding a third way. A Swedish journalist, Sture Kallberg, who lived in the Wai Djau Da lou, the 'Diplomatic Building', had a room I thought he could spare. We moved into it and shared the household expenses and I started to work. Unfortunately, the 'Diplomatic Building' came under the 'Diplomatic Service Bureau' and it seemed that I had contravened all regulations concerning foreigners' residence and this led to strained relations with the Chinese authorities for some time. We had no ration cards and there were interminable discussions with different officials that went on day after day. I can understand the Chinese officials who were responsible for us; I undoubtedly created great difficulties for them, broke all their regulations and tangled up the different bureaucratic organs, but at the same time, I pointed out that I was only interested in having peace and quiet and being allowed to work. In the end we reached a compromise, and even the 'Diplomatic Service Bureau' agreed to let me stay on. It was to be clearly understood that my behaviour in regard to lodging, as in regard to bicycles, was in no way to be construed as a precedent. I'm not criticizing the Chinese; in every country in which I have lived I have had to take up a discussion with the bureaucracy in order to be left in peace to do my work. The Chinese officials were reasonable and it took rather less time to convince them than it has taken in many other countries; also there was no question of corruption. They followed their regulations and I wanted to have these regulations changed. To conclude this section on my economic situation and the way it influenced my work: the final ironical twist to the story was given by the Swedish 'establishment' after this book was published in Sweden, when I was selected to be one of those writers who were to be 'freed from material cares' by being given monthly 'salaries' through the Swedish State Writers' Fund.

Our journeys to Inner Mongolia, at the beginning of our stay in China, and western Yunnan, our last trip during the stay, were interesting. Partly because it is always interesting to travel in an area like eastern Inner Mongolia, which has been closed to strangers for a long time. Just getting somewhere can be a pleasure, if that somewhere is difficult to reach. I have experienced that pleasure several times; when we arrived at Khiva, when we managed to get to the Wakhan corridor, when we went up the Bashgul valley in northern Nuristan. It might be a tainted pleasure, because it is so purely personal (though the pleasure often makes the writing pleasurable to read). But the journeys also were a part of that larger work I had tried to get a grip on for several years: what is happening to the minorities (we visited the same tribes on both sides of the Sino–Burmese border); what is happening to the nomadic cultures; what the conflicts are between the nomads and the agriculturists.

I got much material during these journeys, some of it I have used for articles, some I am planning to use in a larger context. But during our discussions in New Delhi the emphasis shifted to the village. Nomadic cultures still fascinate me, but I have come to see the Asian village and the Asian peasant revolution as the most important aspect of the journey to China. Thus, except for the journeys, I concentrated on getting permission to go to a village and live there for some time. That seemed to me the most important.

One of the prerequisite conditions for travelling in China today is that you accept interpreters and guides. We were given ours by the Chinese People's Association for Cultural Relations with Foreign Countries. I will come back to the question of interpreters, but I just want to point out that you either accept this condition or you don't travel outside Peking, Canton, Shanghai—and more often than not, not even there. I don't like this. But it is a tendency that is spreading from country to country. Even in Sweden we are starting to take in 'invitees', give them guides and see to it that they keep looking at what we want to show them. I'm disturbed by this tendency. It gives strength to my fears that we, all over the world, are moving towards a more 'supervised' form of existence. But in this case I could not just say no, find a third way out or shift the emphasis. Either I have my travel supervised—or I stay at home, quite probably supervised in one way or another even there. However much I dislike it, I have to accept this condition.

We were to be given a free choice of a village to stay in, though there were limitations to this free choice. All military areas were barred, so were the 'closed areas'. No areas in China were in general open for foreigners at that time. But some were much less open than others. We also had certain wishes of our own. I wanted a village that had been part of 'the old liberated areas', a village where the first agrarian revolution had been carried through on a local basis (i.e. not one where the change came as a result of civil war, but one where the change had been a factor leading up to the civil war). Added to this was the purely personal wish of both my wife and myself that, after five summers spent in deserts and on the hot plains of India, we should go somewhere with a slightly better climate. Accordingly, on these grounds I chose the area immediately south of Yenan. Permission for this area was granted. When I reached Yenan the local authorities had a number of villages to suggest, and of those I chose Liu Ling for a number of reasons. In the first place it was a typical village of northern Shensi, not in the sense that it was average—that I doubted—but because it presented certain features of the modern Chinese peasant revolution in their purest form; the leading communists in the village were old peasant revolutionaries, who had carried through their revolution before Mao Tse-tung came to Shensi. Then the village had been the scene of some of the earliest experiments in collective and co-operative farming. Also Edgar Snow had visited it a couple of years previously, and this meant that by choosing a village of which mention already had been made, the reader would have certain leads both to the different perspectives on the village and to the old question of how a description of people and life in a country like China changes with the degree of intensification, i.e. the validity of extensive and impressionistic reporting. Anyone interested in this would do well to read Edgar Snow's *The Other Side of the River*, pp. 475–89 (New York, London, 1962).

I have repeatedly stated that this book is not the *final* truth about China. It is an instrument. No book is more. It is necessary to read other material in order to get a clear picture. For instance, just as I have been writing this introduction I have been reading O. Edmund Clubb (last U.S. Consul General in Peking), *Twentieth Century China* (New York, 1964). It contains among other things a very good section, 'Communist leadership turns to the peasantry', pp. 186–94, that has a direct bearing on what the old peasants of Liu Ling tell about the beginnings of the agrarian revolution. This advice to read further ought to be self-evident. Unfortunately it is not. Too many people—especially students—take the words of *Ecclesiastes* much too literally: 'Of making books there is no end; and much study is a weariness of the flesh.'

We had been given permission to spend one month in a village, and we spent one whole autumn month, from the middle of August to the middle of September, in Liu Ling. The authorities in Yenan were very eager that we should not sleep in the village. They promised to arrange for us to be ferried there and back every day. We wanted, of course, to live in the village, we even demanded to be allowed to do so. The 'Old Secretary' of the village strongly supported us. To him it was a point of honour. After some discussion the Yenan authorities were (with some reluctance) convinced of our point of view. (The reluctance can be interpreted in many ways, one of them is that the Yenan authorities wanted us to be as comfortable as possible. They probably wanted to be kind. It is not their fault that their kindness would have made this book impossible.) We then lived in a stone cave (normally the party secretary's office) and I worked in another (the brigade's conference-room). Since we lived in a cave in a village of caves and ate the village food and the whole time associated with the villagers, it would be easy to say that we lived as one of the people. But that would be a romantic and thus mendacious description of reality. We were the first foreigners to have lived in the village, and the village honour required that our cave should be whitewashed and that we should eat well. We lived considerably better than the villagers. This way of treating strangers and guests is no specific Chinese trait; you meet it in every village in all peasant societies. In the evenings, when we had finished the day's work, the peasants came with gifts from their private plots, melons, corn-cobs, fruit, nuts. It was kind of them; they gave out of their poverty. But it was also pride. I have stayed with peasants in villages in Afghanistan and India and Europe and it has always been the same, the pride of the household, the pride of the village demands that the guest is given the best there is. As a guest in a village you eat well, you also eat with a certain reverence, because you know that you are eating the fruits of the toil and sweat of the people around you. But you never say so to your hosts. There is pride in toil. There is nothing 'objective' about food in a poor peasant village. It does not come out of a tin, neither is it something you carry with you from the city. But I was not one of the villagers. And I was not living like a Chinese peasant.

I spent the first few days visiting all the fifty families in the village, thus obtaining a certain picture of the village and its inhabitants. These first days in the village were rather difficult. Suddenly, after two years, I really was there in the village I had asked for. I had made a thorough nuisance of myself, pulled every string I could, demanded, written, asked, suggested, organized finance, promised to write, and now I was there and it was up to me; if I didn't do what I had set out to do, there was no one but myself to blame. During these first visits I felt depressed; it was difficult to get a grip on the work.

This feeling of uncertainty was increased by the fact that the Chinese authorities seemed to have quite another picture of my function in the village than I had. They thought that I was to work with the peasants in order to get a close understanding of their life. This I had also thought—even written in my visa application—but only if I could stay for many months. When I had only one month I could not do it, no time would have been left for the interviews; the resulting book would have been one of sentiment and description of personal experiences and I did not want to write that kind of book. (It was suggested to me later on in Peking that the permission for me to live in a village probably had been based on the assumption that I was to take part in agricultural labour.) This slight conflict was solved in a practical fashion by the 'Old Secretary'. He pointed out that he himself was doubtful about the value of middle-aged intellectuals for manual labour.

The first fifty interviews had been short. Only on the evening of the second day, when I looked over my notes, was I able to visualize the scope of the work. I found some threads that I could start winding. The material from these first interviews is not published in this volume. They were rather pointless and only gave me a background. The information they contained was later either duplicated in the statistical tables or deepened in the long interviews. On the third day, I selected the first of those people I wanted to interview. After that we worked all the time in the same fashion. My wife, Gun Kessle, walked alone in the village and the surrounding area, sketching and taking photographs, while I interviewed from eight a.m. to noon and from two p.m. to six p.m. In the midday interval and in the evenings I collected material for the 'People say . . .' sections, in general conversations, mostly with the women of the village. In the evenings I arranged my notes, prepared the following day's interviews and discussed the day's work with Gun. (Before falling asleep in the evenings we read. The day before we left Peking I had been to the Dung An bazaar and bought some books in the second-hand bookshop. While in the village I read Goethe's *Italian Tour*; *Water Margin*, the Jackson translation of the Chinese classical novel about the robbers of Liang Shan Po; and Thomas Wolfe's *Of Time and the River*.)

I did not select the people to be interviewed according to a pre-arranged plan. Some people (the economic and political personages of the village) were planned from the beginning, the others I chose one by one. Either because their names cropped up in other interviews, or because I found them interesting in one way or another. Thus even a figure such as Li Hsiu-tang, 'the counter-revolutionary', became clear to me only after ten days. This limits my previous statement that I collected *all* the material I could collect: I collected all the material that I could collect in a month of intense work. I deliberately left the final selection of people to be interviewed open as long as possible. I don't trust rigid plans; they lead to abstractions. But I did *speak* with everybody.

The decision to have an upper limit to the interviews, i.e. not to continue far up in the bureaucratic structure above the village, was contained in the idea of the book itself. But first I had thought of including at least some representative from Yenan, who could give the slightly larger picture of the village in its setting. I even tried to make that interview and spent one morning in Yenan interviewing the local party secretary, a young man. Unfortunately he was too dogmatic, too official to be of any value. (And this is a typical problem all over Asia: the middle echelon of bureaucracy is mostly young and dogmatic and narrow-mindedly inexperienced. The old experienced peasants are illiterate, the bright young administrators are already high up and the old intellectual generation of revolutionaries or 'national figures' are slowly fading away.) I don't blame the young bureaucrat from Yenan. He ran true to type, but when he flatly stated: 'We have here in our part never had any difficulty, never committed a mistake, never made a fault and we have no problems today', I broke off the interview with a few nice, pleasant phrases, and decided that he was not to be included in the book and that I had better go back to the village and talk with the peasants.

During our stay in China I met several higher functionaries, but only once was this of any value as far as Liu Ling goes. That was when I talked with Mao Tse-tung. During the National Day celebrations in Peking (drinking tea, eating sweets and looking at fireworks) my interpreter for the evening suddenly came to fetch me. I was to be presented to Mao Tse-tung. We were a long line of foreigners and each one in the line had his hand shaken by Mao. As I had the chance I did not move on according to protocol after the handshake, but tried to converse. It ran like this:

I: I have just come back from a trip to the Yenan area.

Mao: That is a very poor, backward, underdeveloped and mountainous part of the country.

I: I lived in a village, Liu Ling. I wanted to study the change in the countryside of China. [I meant historical change; Mao seemed to understand it as just economic.]

Mao: Then I think it was a very bad idea that you went to Yenan. You should have gone to the big agricultural plains. Yenan is only poor and backward. It was not a good idea that you went to a village there.

I: But it has a great tradition—the revolution and the war— I mean, after all, Yenan is the beginning——

Mao [interrupting me]: Traditions—[laughing]. Traditions— [laughing].

Then I was pushed onwards and the conversation ended. It was just that kind of surrealistic and inconsequential conversation of which diplomatic reports are made. The only concrete result was that I had my photograph taken with a laughing Mao Tse-tung.

I also set myself another limit from the beginning. I left out the folklore aspect. Not because I'm not interested—I'm deeply interested in folklore and a large part of my library is devoted to it—but having so little time I had to make a choice and that choice was easy; the folklore has been recorded, the story of the peasants in upheaval has not.

When I say that my wife and I settled down in a village and started interviewing the people, sketching them and taking photographs of them, I know that this immediately makes the reader suspicious. In our societies, the highly industrialized countries of north-western Europe and North America, we are fed up with questionnaires and scientific interviews. When your doorbell rings, you often feel a strong resentment at knowing that outside that door stands a young man with rimless spectacles and a leather briefcase (initials in gold, leather black) who will present some kind of credential and then start asking you how often you wash your feet, what you know of your neighbour's sex life and how you would feel about Malcolm X as President of the U.S.A. And we are all tired of filling up forms (name, date of birth, nationality at birth, maiden name of mother, particulars of education, where first employed, etc. etc.), filing photographs (full face and profile, twelve of each, with signed statement as to when taken and if beard has been grown since then). It might be sampling and scientific social study, but we don't like it, and we don't trust it.

I have never worked that way. I have always worked as I was taught to do, when I started as a cub reporter twenty years ago and was given my first assignment, to interview a hundred-year-old lady: 'Just get her to talk about her life, what she experienced, what she remembered. When? How? And then? That's all there is to it.' (It was not quite all there was to it; the old lady declared that she had lived to a hundred because she had taken a glass of spirits, akvavit, every morning ever since she was ten years old. This, of course, was immediately struck out by the editor. 'Boy! You can't offend the readers; in a newspaper you must know what not to write.' That's why I prefer writing books.)

To interview in this fashion is not a less scientific way of working, but it is a more human way. You don't interview 'subjects' or 'samples'; you get people to talk about their lives and you treat them with the respect that is their due as people. This is also what I meant by saying that I have tried to reproduce these peasants' 'self-portraits', I have not tried to dehumanize a human story, a story that I experienced as epic in the true sense of the word. I also believe—without wanting to start a discussion on the fundamental ideas of sociology at this point—that you give a truer 'profile' of a peasant revolution in this way, than by subjecting the peasant samples to a questionnaire and then converting the answers to algebraic notions and ending up with a symbolic line-drawing of 'the structure of peasant unrest'.

We had two interpreters with us. Apart from these there were no outsiders in the village. The fact that there was no 'politically responsible ganbu' in the village checking on our activity, I then, and now, guess to be because of the personality of the 'Old Secretary', who very much was *the* responsible man in the village.

Our chief interpreter was Pei Kwang-li. She had come with us from

Peking. She was the most flexible, the best linguist and the most hard-working of the interpreters I had come across in China. I had tried several interpreters before getting hold of her, and we had been working together for about two weeks when we arrived at the village. She was supposed to go back to Peking from Yenan and it was only after some quite hard discussion that I managed to take her with me to Liu Ling. She was of great help to me in the village. She was friendly and cheerful and interested in the work. I gathered that she was afterwards criticized for her work with me. When we came back to Peking, she went away on vacation and after that she was not so friendly, natural and relaxed as she had been during the month in Liu Ling. She later on—when the book was finished—interpreted for us during our trip to Yunnan and during that trip she was cold, formal, dogmatic and even (which in China says much) quarrelled violently with us on the grounds that we showed 'anti-Chinese' opinions. As our 'anti-Chineseness' was our opinions about toil and sweat and peasant hunger that she had understood so well in Liu Ling, I cannot explain this change in her behaviour otherwise than that she had through 'criticism and self-criticism' come to evaluate us and our work in a different way and change her opinions about our way of working. Because of this I got rather less information in Yunnan than I had hoped for. But in Liu Ling she was a good companion, hard-working and cheerful.

My other interpreter was Ching Chi, who had been in Liu Ling before. I brought her from Sian. She was talkative, but wanted to improve her English; I managed to put in about a half-hour's lesson each day with her. (I took her story as typical of lao dung, pp. 321-8.) Her duties were mainly those of a secretary—she collected statistical material and made arrangements with those I had selected for interviews, and she also acted as auxiliary interpreter when Pei Kwang-li was asleep. Both girls did a good job. As our time in the village was limited we didn't take any free days, neither could the girls have their accustomed midday rest. We were a small enough group to be able to work without friction, and once I had drawn up the schedule and we had discussed our problems and agreed that time was too short for us to afford to lose even a single hour, they both did their utmost. I am grateful to them that they never asked for time off, even when they quite plainly were ill, or protested at what they were asked to do, however onerous. In principle, I cannot help feeling that in work like this the result achieved is in exact inverse proportion to the number of those taking part.

It is of course clear that the very fact of the arrival of four strangers in the village changed the atmosphere there. That is unavoidable; measuring changes what is measured. Or, as Pei Kwang-li put it, she had been on lao dung and lived in villages, but she had not heard peasants say that much about their lives; she supposed it was because I was a foreigner and put questions in a foreign manner. One of the aspects of Chinese civilization that I like most is the respect it gives to work. Intellectual work is also work and highly respected. This trait is also to be found in other cultures. To be a poet in Iceland, a professor in Germany, an academician in Russia, an intellectual in China means holding an honoured position in society. (This needs to be pointed out because one of the strange features of Anglo-American culture is of course that an expression such as 'to live by one's wits' is condemnatory, while in most other languages the literal translation would be laudatory.) I was a writer and an intellectual, the girls were students, thus the relation between us and the villagers was one of mutual respect. But the girls were women, young women, and in China old men are still the most respected. Judging from the way the girls and the old men behaved to each other it seems to me utterly unlikely that the old men would in any way change what they were saying out of respect (or fear, or what have you) for the girls. But I do think that the fact that they were students made some of the younger and 'literate' peasants want to prove that they too were becoming 'learned'. I don't think it changed their stories, but I believe it strengthened the emphasis on being 'new and learned peasants'. This strengthening is no distortion of the process now taking place in China.

The fact that I worked through interpreters was in itself a source of possible error. I would have preferred having an absolute command of Chinese and living all alone in the village for a year. But because of political and social conditions in China today (in most of Asia, by the way) a 'Westerner' would not be allowed to live absolutely alone and on his own whether he knew Chinese or not. Thus, to hope to collect the story of the Chinese peasants without somebody sitting beside you is unrealistic.

One pre-requisite of this method of working is that the interpreter used must be able to interpret; that is to say, have an absolute command over the language into which he, or she, is translating. All too often one comes across interpreters who have only a limited knowledge of one's own working language and then it is impossible to work with them. My chief interpreter, Pei Kwang-li, had an almost perfect knowledge of the language and—what is even more unusual—was sufficiently acute to follow my way of thinking. She was to me a good interpreter and that was why I guarded her so jealously. To work with an interpreter is like being married; you have to have an absolute mutual rapport. (Not to cause misunderstanding: I don't mean marriage as a form of sex life, but as a form of intense intellectual communication. It does not matter if the interpreter is male or female.)

It is sometimes said that a clever interpreter can systematically suppress or distort information. If she is a bad interpreter, i.e. has but a poor command of the language, she can. But over the years I have worked quite a lot both as an interpreter and with interpreters, and I am convinced that in work such as this, where the interpreting has to be kept up without pause hour after hour, day after day, any such systematic distortion is impossible. It would require a superhuman intellectual effort, as any experienced cross-examining lawyer can tell you. And I certainly never had the shadow of a suspicion that it was being attempted.

The major source of possible error in interpreted material lies in the fact that all the information has to pass linguistic frontiers (*traduttore, traditore* is not just a question of bad translations, but of the impossibility of translation); thus, despite all my precautions, I must have lost certain nuances, maybe also misunderstood information. Obviously I should have preferred it if I had known Chinese like my own language.

But against this one has to set the definite advantages of working through an interpreter. This provides a calm rhythm throughout the interview and makes it possible to concentrate on the main questions. Both the interviewed and the interviewer have time to think. The use of an interpreter also creates an almost 'clinical' atmosphere. If I had been using my own language and working within my own cultural area, I should have found it difficult—or impossible—to ask certain of the questions, both political and personal, that I put to those I interviewed.

In general, I prefer to work with an adept interpreter, even when the language used is one of which I have a reasonably good command. Doing this makes the work matter-of-fact, and emotionally charged questions are cooled down and 'estranged' without becoming impersonal. If I had been Chinese, I should not have been able to ask certain questions; partly because I should not have been able to phrase them, as I should have been so impregnated with Chinese culture that I should see that culture from inside its own value-judgements, and partly because the person I was interviewing would have objected.

There is another possible source of error which the use of interpreters enabled me to reduce. It is inevitable that one feels emotional sympathy for some people and antipathy for others. In ordinary human intercourse this does not matter; in my general literary work, it is one of my—or any writer's—great driving forces, but if I had been submerged in these personal relations to different people in Liu Ling, it could have caused complete shifts in perspective unbeknownst to the reader. As I have already stated, I had a general emotional drive behind my work, but by keeping the interviews 'clinical', as I did (white-washed room, an interpreter and the calm rhythm of interpreted conversation), I believe I am correct in saying that there was never any emotional contact in this sense between myself and those I interviewed. At all events I tried to suppress any such reaction.

When I received answers that seemed doubtful or palpably incorrect, I rephrased the question so as to make sure that I had not misheard or misunderstood. I also made lists of questions to be asked in various connexions, as a result of which most questions were checked by the different people I interviewed. This, of course, led to disparity between answers. (I did not say: 'You say this, but X said that. . . .' I did not want to push the answers in any direction, I wanted to bring out as many aspects of the story as I could; the different ways in which the happenings were seen.)

But, though I certainly must on occasion have misheard or misunderstood, or been misunderstood, or got something wrong because of the interpreting, I believe that I am entitled to claim that, within the limits of my ability, I have succeeded in reproducing what these people really said, and that the interrogations were conducted in such a way that their answers are of real value.

It is another question to what extent those who told me their stories gave correct accounts of the events they had experienced or in which they had taken part. Obviously they are not 'true' accounts, if you define this truth as a 'scientifically objective account', as of an experiment. Such objectivity does not exist when living people are talking

about their lives. What is given here is the evidence of the actual participants in the events. It is notorious that no two witnesses give exactly
the same account of what happened in even the simplest traffic accident
(unless they are perjuring themselves). The evidence in this book is not
concerned with a traffic accident, but with a great revolution of profound significance for the lives of each one of the participants.

It is also obvious that the older and illiterate peasants are story-tellers,
tellers of tales. They have a life to talk about and what they say often
deviates considerably from the 'official line'. The younger and more
literate tend to verbalize their experiences in words they have read.
Incidentally, this is nothing peculiar to Chinese villagers. Also the
general tendency for these accounts is to approximate to the social conception of the events, in this case, the official Chinese interpretation of
the history of the revolution. I'm not saying that this history is necessarily wrong, only that the official interpretation influences the individual memories in different degrees. This state of affairs is in no way
specifically Chinese. A similar investigation made in Sweden—on the
break-up of the village and the origin and development of the farmers'
co-operative movement—would give the same result. In assessing these
statements, therefore, the same reservations must be made as in assessing
any other evidence. But, though every lawyer knows that witnesses'
statements are always subjective, none has yet concluded from that that
such evidence should be dispensed with and the courts fall back on
speculation instead. I want to emphasize that what is self-evident to the
lawyer does not always seem so to the social scientist. There has been a
tendency both in the 'East' and in the 'West', largely owing to the cold
war, to abandon oneself to speculation about 'the other'.

If this book were read as a novel, it might be called a parade of
'positive heroes'; but it is no novel. Here people plead their own cause.
They are trying to be honest, but they also want to present themselves
as they think they ought to be seen, which naturally means in a positive
light. The same thing goes for the village gossip, which I have used, for
example, in the 'People say . . .' sections. In this village people do not
speak really ill of each other, at least not to younger people or outsiders.

That the peasants in this book do not speak about the famine and
the agricultural catastrophe after the 'Great Leap Forward', does not
mean that that famine did not exist. Even when I and my wife arrived
in China the food situation was precarious. But for several reasons, both

climatic and political, these years were not so catastrophic in northern Shensi. One must always keep in mind that China—like India—is a vast country. Conditions can be extremely different in different parts of the country at the same time.

There are many people and many institutions in different countries that made it possible for me to write this book. The organization that was 'responsible' for us, the Chinese People's Association for Cultural Relations with Foreign Countries, had a lot of trouble with us. I am glad though that during the nine months we were in China, although they did not always share my view of the way the work should be done or of what 'reality' was (a long discussion was kept up on this question, 'objectivism' being harmful, etc.) and though we had different views of how the world was developing and argued sharply over practical questions, they never once went back on what they promised to do when we first arrived.

But there is one man I must thank personally, I didn't do it verbally as it would have interfered with the work, and that is the 'Old Secretary', Li Yiu-hua. I respect him as a person and without his understanding of what my work required, this book could never have been written.

J. M.

Fagervik
1964

Introduction to the 1975 Edition

That this is a book about people is not only a statement; it was the result of a conscious choice to make the Chinese revolution understandable to myself as well as the reader. I am interested in political theory. I am fascinated by statistics. Theory is necessary and statistics is a tool. But theories that make history are theories formed by people making history. Thus this is a book about people in North Shensi in China, not one of the main economic areas of China, but one of central significance for the Chinese revolution. It was an early revolutionary base. Then, after the Long March, it was from here that Mao Tse-tung led the struggle against the Japanese invaders and against the K.M.T. Thus this is one of the main political areas of China, and when the people of Liu Ling describe their lives from the early part of the century to 1962 they also describe the tremendous upheaval in which they took part. They lived the revolution. They caused it.

This is the book I wanted to write when I and Gun Kessle left India for China in the early spring of 1962. Other books could have been written from Peking that year. 1962 was a difficult year for China; the economy had been hard hit, and the Soviet leaders were struggling to secure political and economic control. Their economic warfare was ruthless. The Peking of diplomats and foreign correspondents was a bee-hive of rumour.

Gun Kessle and I were going to stay in China for a year. Peking was a fascinating city. The friends we had in China were intellectuals. I had known some of them for many years—left-wing writers, communists for whom the defence of the Soviet Union and the struggle for the rights of the Chinese people were one and the same. Now they were grievously shocked and hurt by the policies of the Soviet leaders towards China.

At that time I knew nothing about the two lines in China. But I wondered what was happening when a Western communist who had close contacts with the Soviet embassy suddenly said: 'Liu Shao-chi is after all an old communist. He is a true Marxist-Leninist. As long as he holds a responsible position, there is hope.' There was much to write about from Peking. But already when we had discussed the visit to China with the Chinese authorities a year earlier we had asked for permission to stay in a people's commune. Peking was interesting; a city filled with 'well-known public figures'. But what was decisive were the events taking place in the thousands and thousands of villages in the country.

Our decision to go and stay in Liu Ling was correct, as was proven some years later when the speculations and rumours of 1962 in Peking were swept away, together with many 'important people' and 'well-known public figures', by the Great Proletarian Cultural Revolution.

The people in this book were not swept away by that revolution. Their problems gave rise to it. This book was written in 1962-3, but it became truly readable some years later when many of the problems that were central to the people of Liu Ling found revolutionary solutions that changed China. In this Liu Ling of 1962 the two lines were forming in practice.

This book consists of interviews with different people in Liu Ling during the autumn of 1962. These interviews were not done by tape-recorder; I took notes. The reason was that I wanted to keep to my role as a writer and not be tempted to believe in a false objectivity. (In itself, the question of tape-recorder or note-book is immaterial.) I wanted to write stories about living people, not to cut slices out of life. Except for possible mistakes the stories are 'true'. They are not fiction. But the interviews were structured in such a way that they should give readable images of these different individuals.

The statistical tables in this book are incidental. These figures were given me. It would be wrong to see them as the central theme of the book. The stories in this book focus on the people of Liu Ling, this collective of individuals. The central theme is the one that old Mau Ke-yeh expresses when he says: 'Revolution is not a thing you can let others do for you.'

Fagervik   J.M.
1974

Report from a Chinese Village

Part 1
Liu Ling Village

36° 34' North, 109° 28' East

LIU Ling is a small village lying buried among the loessial hills west of the River Nan, immediately south of Yenan in northern Shensi.

The easiest way of getting there is from Sian. You first go to Tungkwan, either by branch line train or by bus via Hsienyang. In either event, you continue northwards from Tungkwan by bus up the old Hsienyang–Yulin highway, spending the night at the inn at Hwangling. A couple of hundred yards north of this inn is where the 'Yellow Emperor', Hwang-ti, the mythical founder of the Han people and culture, is reputed to have been buried 4,000 years ago. At all events you can visit his tomb and the temple, recently restored, that was put up in his honour. In 1959 the government had a new stone plaque put up there, inscribed: 'Father of the Han people . . .'

This is the heart of China. The first day of your journey takes you through the river country, where China's classical agricultural civilization took shape and the people of Han developed their individuality. It was here that the early forms of the Chinese state came into being, and it was from here that China was united. The second day takes you northward across the loessial plateau with its deeply etched ravines, muddy rivers, treeless bush and cultivated fields. This is a poor part of China, a borderland through which, during long dynasties, the imperial levies marched on their way north to the frontier fortifications at Yulin. Sian was the big capital city of this huge agricultural province, Yulin its border with the realm of the nomads in the north. Yenan is 600 li north of Sian and the same distance south of Yulin. Northern Shensi is bare and barren, its climate hard. The crops fail there every other year, and its people are famed for their toughness, industry and rebellious nature. All through China's long history, northern Shensi has been one of the hotbeds of the unrest that has repeatedly flared up among the peasantry, and a hinterland for the peasant armies of many a

3

civil war. In 1628 the peasants of northern Shensi rose, and the rising spread over the Empire. In 1636 their forces combined under the command of Li Tse-cheng and four years later it was announced that 'all land shall be divided equally between the poor and the rich', while at the same time all taxes were declared abolished for five years. In 1644 Li Tse-cheng rode into Peking at the head of the victorious peasant levies and, as they entered the city, Se-tsung, last emperor of the Ming dynasty, hanged himself to atone for his sins. This victory was soon turned into defeat, however, for the generals of the Ming dynasty preferred to let in foreigners and be conquered by the Manchurians than allow their own peasants to seize power.

In the early 1930s the peasants of northern Shensi rose and drove out the landowners and tax collectors, set up their own soviet republic and formed their own Red Army, which was led by the now legendary Liu Chi-tan. It was to northern Shensi that Mao Tse-tung and the Central Committee of China's Communist Party led China's Red Army of workers and peasants in the Long March, its great 25,000-li retreat. It was 19 October 1935 when the survivors reached Wuchichen in Kuyuan hsien. Then the 'Shensi–Kansu–Ningsia Border Region' was set up with Yenan as its administrative capital, and from there their struggle against the Japanese was directed, and it was from there that the Chinese People's Liberation Army eventually conquered all China.

You leave the bus after Ten-mile Village—before it reaches Yenan—and turn off to the left down a side road leading to the river. You are now heading west. You cross the River Nan by the ford and, as you climb the opposite slope, the white caves of Liu Ling's basic school will be on your right and, above them, the caves of the village itself, dug into Naopanshan. Paths wind up the hillside and the caves lie in rows, one above the other.

The village lies 2,500 feet above sea level, on the loessial plateau with its great hills of loess with their vast eroded slopes. Where the ground is not cultivated, the hills are covered with scrubby bush. The landscape is predominantly ochre in colour. Loess cannot easily absorb large quantities of rain. It can suck up a gentle rain, but here the rain is seldom gentle and so, when it comes, torrents of yellow muddy water gush down across the fields, digging deep furrows in the layers of loess.

Loess is rich and, if it gets water at the right time, can give big yields; but the climate here is a continental one and the rain refuses to come at the right time. The average annual rainfall in Liu Ling is about 20·72

4

in., 54 per cent of which falls in July–August–September. The snowfall is not great, only 3·85 in. of the above total falling in the form of snow. The ground is frost-bound to a depth of 4·2 in. for three months of the year. The winters are cold, dry and dusty, and, the ground being bare, the frost often damages the winter wheat. Spring is also a difficult season with its drought and high winds. Then they have to burn brushwood on the headlands between the fields at night to protect the young corn from the frost, and the smoke hangs heavily over the yellow earth. April and May are months of sunshine and great heat and in them no rain falls. Out of three years they reckon on one good, one middling and one bad harvest. To them there is nothing unusual about crop failure; drought, frost and hail are a constant menace.

The variation in temperature during the twenty-four hours is considerable: up to 20° C. or more. The maximum recorded temperature is 39·7° C., recorded on 29 July 1952, and the minimum —25° C., recorded on 23 January 1956. The year's average is 9·3° C.

Mean temperatures are:

January	7·2°C.	July	23.0°C.
February	2·4°	August	26·6°
March	4·5°	September	15·9°
April	11·4°	October	9·2°
May	16·8°	November	2·6°
June	21·1°	December	4·8°

Sitting on Tashiai, the Old Secretary, Li Yiu-hua, talks about the countryside, farming and women as workers

WHEN I came here twenty-five years ago, only the valley was culti-vated. All the fields you see up there on the hillside have been cleared since then. It is good soil down there in the valley. It yields ten times as much as that on the slopes. Down there we are able to use a tractor. We hire one from the tractor station at Yenan. We have only a couple of hundred mu which can be tilled by tractor, but the Liu Ling People's Commune has plans to buy one and a couple of lorries; but that cannot be till the commune has made a bit more out of its factory for agricul-tural implements. It's only on the actual floor of the valley that there is any tractor land.

Every member of the labour brigade is given a private plot down there. We reckon 0·4 mu per head, and everyone is included, even infants. The plots are allocated every other year, and people can grow what they like in them. The private plots run from the threshing floor to the melon field, where the temple, shiwa, used to be. You can tell that the plots are private from the way they are all such bits and pieces. It is good land, but not really right for tractors. We try to keep the private plots separate from land that we are going to use the tractor on.

Here, in northern Shensi, we are badly off for temples. We have been liberated a long time here and many of the temples have disappeared. This was a Buddhist temple. They say that the K.M.T. blew it up, before they withdrew in 1935. At all events, more and more of it collapsed after that and we used the stones for other things. You'll find stones from the temple in every cave in Liu Ling. In 1958 there were only a few caves left and we used them as store- and work-rooms, while we were building the Jenhuei canal, which we did that year. Last year we turned everything over to melons. That pays better. But we're going to take the stones with carving on and put them in the school, so that the children have something to look at. The tent on the melon field down there is for the nightwatchman. The fields have to be guarded at night now that the melons are beginning to ripen. There are different kinds of foxes, you see. If you hear music among the melons at night, it will be the nightwatchman. He plays to make the time pass and keep the foxes away.

Up here on the hillside is where we cleared the new ground, and are still clearing. You can see that the fields are of different shapes. The big ones are the collective ones. They are worked by the labour groups. Big fields are more economic than small. You have to have big fields if collective working is to pay better than individual. But there are smaller fields too. There is a lot of ground that is not really suitable for big fields and which, because of that, it would not pay to clear for the collective, so we let ganbus from the town come out and work it on Sundays. We tell them where they may till and in those places they grow what they like. Of course, we don't grant any title to the land. We couldn't do that; but they are allowed to grow what they like and take it home. You can see there are quite a lot of those plots.

In their free time our members are allowed to clear where they like on the hills. That is to say, they may not clear where we could make a big field, but otherwise where they like and as much as they can. Usually, there is never any cause for argument. They are all farmers,

you see, and themselves know where they can break new ground. The
only occasions on which we have had to interfere were when someone
tried to till the actual track. Wang Chen-chia did that this year.
He is not from this village. He began digging down there by the track.
Then he began planting vegetables till there was only a narrow foot-
path left in the middle, and so Li Hai-kuei had a word with him:
'That's the way we take our animals. Our goats go that way. If you
think we are going to try and stop them eating your vegetables, you're
very much mistaken. You had better move your vegetables and put
them somewhere else, unless you want to feed our goats with them.
You must just stir your stumps and climb up the hillside and clear some
ground there.' Li Hai-kuei considered that what Wang Chen-chia was
doing was inadmissible, because it did not leave room for our oxen any
longer. Well, you don't need a meeting to solve that sort of problem.
It solves itself. Wang Chen-chia had to go up the hillside and dig up
there.

Of course, lots of people have had their eye on the ground down
there by the track along the stream, for it's good soil. Ma Hai-hsiu also
dug a plot there right beside the track; but he chose cleverly and was
able both to get water from the stream and yet leave room for the
oxen on the track. You get ten times the yield there that you do
up on the hillside. Then the herdsman told him that his plot was too

near the path. Ma Hai-hsiu replied that he had remembered the oxen and left room for them; but the herdsman said that it wasn't enough and that the oxen would walk on to his plot and eat what was growing there, so Ma Hai-hsiu ought to go elsewhere. But Ma Hai-hsiu did not want to do that. He thought it a pity to give up the good soil he had, so instead he built a high wall round his plot. It's so tall no one can get over it. And that's all right.

Ever since we began co-operative farming in this district, we have had this system of five kinds of plot: collective plots in the valley, private plots in the valley, collective plots on the hillside, privately cleared plots on the hillside and ganbu plots on the hillside. We have never given up the principle of having private plots. Here, in this hilly country, work is hard and people need to eat a lot. It is mostly millet we eat. That's filling. Wheat is more of a luxury. There's no strength in it. We eat potatoes sometimes, but they won't keep longer than April. No, millet of various kinds, buckwheat and maize, though we use the maize mostly as fodder. You can eat oats too, but that's really a fodder crop. This has been a dry year, as you can see. The harvest up on the hillside will be a bad one. Down in the valley the weather does not make such a difference as it does up here.

Over there on Loushan we are ploughing for winter wheat just now. We grow wheat two years running, then we take a crop of buckwheat

9

and after that one of millet, and then it's wheat again for another two years. The leader of the labour group selects the best ploughers; they work in teams: three ploughers and a clod-crusher and four ploughers and a clod-crusher, and, in addition, there are five men with mattocks who turn the soil in the places the oxen cannot get at. A man with a wooden plough ploughs one mu a day on the average. He has either one strong ox or two smaller ones.

We go in a lot for goats here. People prefer goat's meat to mutton. Mutton has a rank taste. We usually castrate the billies; that makes their meat tender. We don't use milk. We aren't accustomed to it. Milk is harmful to others than infants. Our women make wine of maize and millet. But we only do that in the winter; in the summer it won't ferment properly, so, if we want anything, we buy spirits in the shop. No, we don't distil ourselves. Of course, we would be allowed to do so, if we wanted. Who could forbid us? But it is simpler and just as cheap to buy our spirits in the shop.

You can see that we have started weeding the fields down there. The women work well. In the old days they weren't worth anything. Women were oppressed then, and people used to say: 'An incompetent man can get about in nine countries, but a competent woman can only get round her cooking stove.' When we began making our revolution, thirty years ago, the emancipation of women was one of the main points in our programme. We sang songs about it. I can still remember them. We had a slogan: 'Free their feet!' Now their feet are free and women can work in the fields, so now, both men and women share in cultivating the land. Thirty years ago we were saying: 'Let both men and women take part in our revolution', and now that has come about. Marriage is free now, too. It's only those directly concerned who have any say in it. That's a good thing. Women are hard workers. Do you see that the women down there have baskets beside them as they weed, but the men don't? That's because the women aren't only weeding, they are also collecting grass for the family's pig.

Since 1960 we have had a loudspeaker in every cave that has electricity. Families pay five yuan a year for them. Everyone wants a radio and this is the cheapest way. We usually have a big loudspeaker outside the cave you are living in, but we took it down so that you should be able to work. Lo Han-hong thought you would find it difficult to write, if the loudspeaker was there. He ought to know. He lives in the cave next to yours and he sometimes writes to the newspapers himself.

The ox-driver there is employed by the labour brigade. He has to cart out manure, when he has time. Otherwise he carts our timber. He fetches it from a place four days' journey away, some 200 li from here. He sleeps in inns on the way. They are all right, not too wonderful and not too awful. Every place of any size has an inn and the ox-drivers foregather there in the evenings. Ai Kou-ming has been an ox-driver since he was quite young. He likes it. We have several big horse carts too.

The graves over there on Loushan are quite new. They belong to the family of Wang Fung-li's father-in-law, Li Yü-teh. Naturally, we don't till that land. One has a right to choose one's own grave, after all. Why should the collective interfere? One doesn't select good arable land for that, if one can help it.

Cave-Building, *Mau Ke-yeh*

PEOPLE in our part of the country prefer living in caves. This is largely because our loessial soil makes cave-building easy and the result is a nicer and better insulated dwelling than an ordinary house. I must have built a good forty caves in my day. My father taught me how to build them, but I'm no specialist. Anybody can build a cave.

There are two kinds of cave: earth ones and stone ones. The earth caves are dug into the hillside. The first thing to do is to find a place with the right kind of soil, hard yellow loessial soil. You cannot build a cave where the soil is sandy. There are lots of places in this valley suitable for building caves. But you can make a mistake. Li Hsiu-tang made one this year when he began building a big cave down at the bottom of the eastern side of Naopanshan behind Chang Chung-wen's pigsty. The earth was damp there and all he achieved was a big hole. The higher up the hillside you dig your cave the better the earth usually is; but it means you have a longer way to the well.

You don't need so many people to build an earthen cave. An ordinary cave of normal size, 18–19 chi long, 9–10 chi high and 8–9 chi wide, including making the kang and cooking stove and chimney, takes about forty work-days. A house of the same size takes the same or a little less, but it isn't so practical and costs more to heat.

Having selected a place where the earth seems to be of the right kind, you smooth the hillside so that you have a vertical face. In doing this you will see what the soil is like to work with. Next, you make a first hole of two by seven chi and dig in for roughly three chi before you start enlarging. As you dig, the kind of soil will show you how large you can make the cave. The harder and closer the soil is, the larger you can make your cave, and vice versa. Having dug out your cave, you polish the earth walls to make them smooth, then you plaster them with mud made of loessial earth. All this time, you leave the outer wall untouched, using just the little opening that you made at the beginning, but once the cave is finished you open up this wall so that you have a door and a window. The window is a lattice frame with paper stretched over it. This makes a good window that lets in the light, but keeps out the wind. Nowadays we also use glass a bit; but glass is expensive and it is seldom one sees a piece more than two by three chi. Besides, glass is not always practical, and it calls for a considerably more complicated structure for the lattice.

At first, caves are slightly damp, but they dry out after three or five months. If the soil is of good quality and hard and firm, you can then build additional caves and store-rooms leading off from the first cave. But if you do that, you make the passages between them rather narrow, roughly two by seven chi.

You cannot build this sort of a cave by yourself. It needs several of you. We usually exchange work and help each other. Up here in northern Shensi people prefer, as I said, to live in caves, because they are warmer in winter and cooler in summer; but down in central Shensi people prefer to live in houses.

But earth caves don't last well, and they can also be dangerous. Even if the soil is of good quality, an earth cave seldom lasts more than two or three generations. Often only thirty years. If the soil is poor and you have help enough to be able to build a whole stone-cave, you can build one that is half and half: half stone cave and half earth cave dug into the hillside. But that is not a good solution. You can tell when an earth cave is nearing the end of its days, because then small pieces begin falling from the roof. You have to be careful when that happens; but you can still use the cave, if you strengthen it.

There are two ways of strengthening. The best method, though one that can only be used for smaller caves, is to take six-inch planks that you soften and bend in steam and fix these up under the curve of the roof one chi apart. These make a good support and the cave can be used for a long time yet. The other method—you saw it used in Yen Chi-yung's cave, he's a carpenter and knows how to do it—is to build a framework with support pillars and stretchers and cross-beams to hold up the roof. But this isn't very practical and it doesn't last either.

Stone caves are better. I have built a number of them. Twenty years ago I planned all the stone caves of Liu Ling's basic school and was in charge of building them. I also was in charge when the three caves we are sitting in now were built. A stone cave calls for more careful planning and considerably more work. You can take it that each stone cave takes roughly 400 work-days. The three caves in this row took the work of seventy men for a whole month. They are thus considerably more expensive to build than both earth caves and ordinary houses; but, while an ordinary house won't go more than thirty years without major repairs, a stone cave will stand for four or five hundred years and not need a thing doing to it. In theory stone caves are indestructible. The only thing requiring maintenance is the paper and woodwork of the windows, for wood will rot in time. But in an ordinary house there is a lot that can rot and fall and need replacing.

In principle, it is best for a cave to face south, because then it will be warmed by the winter sun, which hangs low, and the summer sun, which stands high in the sky, won't reach in; but you cannot pay much attention to that, where earth or stone caves are concerned, for they have to be sited according to the condition of the ground. I have built caves facing all quarters of the compass, but, wherever I could, I have avoided making them face east or west.

Caves, of course, are built with cooking stoves and chimneys, but with both earth and stone caves we usually make an additional outside kitchen for use in summer. That helps to keep the cave cool in summer and the women consider it an advantage to be able to work outdoors. When we do this, we site the outside kitchen in a shady place.

In many places you have to be careful about drainage when building stone caves, but here with us the subsoil water is fairly far down and we have good stone. We have not needed any special drainage either at the school or for this row. We begin by digging the foundations. We excavate ten chi down. The hole corresponds to the outside measurements of the cave-to-be. Then we make a foundation of tamped loess. If this is done carefully, it becomes almost as hard as concrete. On this foundation we build two stone walls, which are the inner long walls of the cave. We make a stone floor. Whèn these inner walls reach a height of six chi above the stone floors we build the inner short walls. Then we reckon out the vault. This has to be a semi-circle and rest on the two inner long walls. We don't calculate with paper and brush. We are farmers and we cannot write or calculate on paper; but we know how it has to be. The inner short wall is a measure for the vault. We put up a frame in the cave and build the vault with stones. This calls for a lot of work, for each stone has to be cut so that it fits exactly. But you soon learn to tell from looking at a stone how it has to be done.

Once the vaulting is finished the cave will stand for hundreds of years. After that we build the outside walls. The smallest distance between the inside of the outer wall and the outside of the inner wall is five chi. The same goes for the distance between the outsides of the inner walls, if one is building several caves one beside the other as in this row. This intervening space is filled with tamped loess. The outside walls of the cave are built up six chi, plus the height of the vault, plus five chi, because the vault has also to be covered with trodden loess. Here too, five chi is the smallest permissible distance between the highest point of the vault and the top of the layer of beaten loess.

Built in this way, the roof needs no maintenance; and, although grass grows on it and we let our goats graze there, no damp can get into the cave. For the sake of drainage we make the roof slope inwards and make a gutter of baked clay there to take the water away. Neither rain nor frost nor weeds can crack the roof. Up in the north, however, where they build similar caves, but of sun-dried bricks, which aren't strong enough to bear the load, the clay roof has to be trodden every year.

We have good stone here. We took some from the old temple when it collapsed; and the rest we quarried over there where the latrines now are. You can see from the look of the hillside that we have used it as a quarry. You build several stone caves at a time, if you can; because it is cheaper to build them in a line, since that saves outer walls.

The last thing to be done to a stone cave is to plaster the walls with fine wet loess mixed with chopped straw and then whitewash them. After that, with the trellis for the window in place and the paper over it, and the door made, it is a good dwelling and one that is easy to keep warm in winter, while it is always cool in summer. And you never need to think about maintenance.

We are planning to rebuild the whole village with stone caves down here; but that is a long-term plan. We haven't yet decided exactly where we are going to build. That also depends on whether we are to get a better water supply. The well here is not as good as it might be. But we have decided in principle to start building the first range in 1963 and 1964. In a few years the whole village will consist of stone caves and they will stand for 500 years without needing repair. That is what makes stone caves the most economical.

The Rhythm of Life

Long talks with Ching Chi and the Old Secretary, Li Yiu-hua, and shorter ones with practically all the women of Liu Ling

THE mothers of Liu Ling suckle their babies until they are two or three. Many go on even longer, especially if it is the last child, or if the mother wants to avoid having any more children for a time. If a mother does not herself have milk, she does not get another woman to suckle her baby. Here, in northern Shensi, a woman does not suckle another's child. In these cases the baby is given goat's milk. Some children drink milk up to the age of seven, but never after that. 'Milk is bad for your health.'

A baby starts being given other food than breast milk when it is seven months old. It then starts being given a thin gruel of millet and rice and water; then a thin porridge of millet and water. At one year old, the child starts getting thicker porridge, then noodles and steam-baked bread soaked in gruel, but no vegetables at that age: 'Vegetables are too difficult for children's stomachs to digest.'

At three, when a mother normally stops suckling her child, it starts being given steam bread with bean stuffing, eggs and vegetables. While I was talking with Tuan Fu-yin's wife, she had her youngest daughter on her knee, and there the child sat, clutching its mother's right breast in one hand and a tomato in the other, and taking alternate sucks and bites, while we talked. This was unusual, though.

After three, a child starts to eat with the family. It is given soft, easily masticated food without strong spices. All members of the family help to feed it. Then it begins trying to eat with chopsticks, after which its diet becomes progressively that of the others in the family.

Up to the age of six all children wear trousers open behind. There is no flap or fall arrangement, but the actual fork of the trousers is hemmed on both sides, where in adult garments there is a seam, so that when the child squats or sits, this gapes, forming a large opening through which the child can relieve itself. People reckon that a child ought to be 'house-trained' by the time it is eighteen months and able to walk properly; by three, it should be able to keep itself dry, and by six it is considered to have sufficient control of its bladder to wear trousers with the seam sewn up.

On the whole, boys and girls are treated alike at this age. If a child is an only one and consequently has a lot of people helping look after it, it will be strictly brought up, but otherwise it will be able to play all day and its parents won't bother about it or what it does. In wintertime children stay indoors during the morning and afternoon, playing on the warm kang with their brothers and sisters or, perhaps, the neighbours' children. The kang is the children's place, too, when it rains.

Boys and girls start being treated differently at the age of seven, when boys will be sent by their mothers to collect wild grass for the pig. Girls are not made to help much in such ways, but they are expected to help with the housework. At ten, a girl ought to be able to help her mother unpick quilted jackets and trousers and wash them, and she should also be able to wash vegetables and cook a meal. At this age boys start fetching the water from the well, not by themselves with a carrying pole over their shoulder, but in pairs with a bucket slung on a pole carried between them. The girls mend clothes and help their mothers do the washing in the river. Normally they use nothing but the water. Soap is seldom used, but they do occasionally use soda.

It is not easy to keep the children clean. They are washed in water, and, if very dirty, given a scrub with river sand. Their parents wash when they get back from work. The children are washed in the morning and, if dirty, at night as well. Children go to bed at about half past eight in summertime and at eight in the winter. In the morning they are allowed to lie longer than their parents, not usually waking till seven, and half an hour later in winter, by which time their father is already at work in the fields and their mother busy with the housework. After that they lie on the kang playing and chattering till it is time to go to school.

Between seven and twelve, little girls play hopscotch, and in the afternoons you can see them skipping, either holding their own rope or skipping over one held by two others. They sing counting songs: 'One two two one, one two three three two one, one two three four four three two one, one two three four five', etc., and there is great rivalry to see who can go on longest. They also dance round-dances and sing. Nowadays they are said to sing mostly songs that are 'in tune with the times', like 'Chairman Mao has come to our village to visit us'. Girls 'grind salt' and 'make covers'. Girls and boys do not play together after the age of seven except in school, where the teachers make them play and dance and sing together, but the moment the teacher's eye is off them, they split up into separate groups of boys and girls. Boys of this age play with balls, hoops, diabolo and hopscotch. In wintertime they go sliding. They will sing, but they won't dance unless they are made to.

Most of the children go to school, but not all. The younger parents do send their children to school: 'I want my child to be a ganbu.' Nowadays most people consider that children ought to be taught to read, write and do arithmetic. Even the older women want their children to go to school. It's the grandparents who spoil them. It is always they who are closest to the children. They have the most time for them and talk with them most. If a child goes to its granny and says: 'It's horrid at school', 'I'm so tired', 'It's so cold in school', or 'It's so hot in school', granny will get into a state and say to the child's parents: 'It's too much for the poor child to go to school.' Whenever a child wants to do something its parents won't allow, it has only to go to its grandparents and weep; then the grandparents go to the child's parents and read them a lesson.

Last year a girl called Hu Yen-ching grew tired of school. Her father, Hu Shen-chu, didn't let that disturb him and just told her that she had to go, so then she went to her granny, Ching Chung-ying's wife, and said: 'I don't like school. I don't get good marks. The teachers criticize me. I won't go there any more.' Her grandmother was very upset and said: 'Poor little girl, working so hard! There's no need for you to go to school. Just you stay at home.'

After that, Hu Shen-chu's wife told the school-teachers: 'There's nothing I can do. My mother has made up her mind and I cannot make her change it.' Then Hu Yen-ching moved to her grandmother's, because she thought her parents nagged her about school. She refused to do what her parents said and stuck to her grandmother. It took a year for the party, the school and the collective to convince nine-year-old Hu Yen-ching that she ought to go back to her parents and start going to school again.

At twelve or thirteen girls stop skipping and playing hopscotch and such games, and play cat's-cradle instead. And there is far less talking and joking with boys. After their first menstruation, which may be any time between twelve and sixteen, they become more and more shy and bashful. They talk less, play the fool less often and sing less. They are shy when talking to strangers, especially if they are men. They stay mostly at home and devote themselves to domestic work instead of playing. When they reach eighteen, girls begin getting their trousseau ready, whether they are engaged or not. They make shoes and clothes and bedcovers. At that age they will also have begun helping with the farm work.

There is no corresponding change in boys at this age. They begin playing ball games and ping-pong; then they start working in the fields; but boys are considered to stay childish into their late teens. They are shy if they meet a girl of their own age; but otherwise they are not bashful, not even with married women. People say that a boy always gives the impression of being younger and less mature than a girl of the same age.

There is no special ceremony to mark entry into youth or manhood. The only outward sign of sexual maturity is bashfulness and the end of giggling and chattering. Girls marry at a younger age than boys. There is a shortage of girls in Liu Ling, in fact in all northern Shensi, and so girls often are able to choose between several suitors. The Old Secretary, Li Yiu-hua, said this of the shortage of girls: 'I don't know why it is, but it is a fact. Just look at my family. I have nine grandchildren: six are boys and three are girls. In Liu Ling there are thirty-six boys and twenty-two girls. There have always been far more boys born here than girls; and with us a girl child has never been an unwanted burden, as in other parts of the country. In the old days in Szechwan, in the old society, they used to kill girl babies, because they were just a burden on the family; but with us here in northern Shensi girls have always been precious. We have never looked down on girls so much as people have in other parts of the country. In the old days, parents here in northern Shensi used to get a lot for their daughters when they married them off; thus a girl did not deprive her family, but added to its possessions. That's an important thing to remember. So there was never such a great difference between the way girls and boys were treated here in the old days. We have always been short of manpower and at the same time always had more men than women. That is one of the reasons why widows always marry again here. But I have never been able to fathom why it is that so few girls are born here.'

There are three principal ways of arranging marriages:

(1) The boy and the girl live in the same village. They work together in the fields and they talk together. He likes her and she admires him. They fall in love and, as they know each other, they tell each other and they marry, if their parents agree. They marry of their own free will.

(2) They live in the same village and see each other occasionally. The boy likes the girl and the girl likes the boy, but they dare not tell each other; so each asks some older person to act as go-between and tell the other: 'So-and-so is in love with you.' That's what Lo Han-hong and Li Chin-wa did. He had a job and she was studying. They could not talk to each other and so could only gaze at each other. She noticed that he came out of his cave-office every time she walked past on her way home from Liu Ling school, and he noticed that she walked by, whenever he was looking for her. Then Lo Han-hong asked Li Kuei-ying to talk to Li Chin-wa, and afterwards Li Chin-wa asked Li Yang-ching to talk to Lo Han-hong, and in that way they learned that they loved each other. Then they met and went into Lo Han-hong's cave and talked alone together, and after that they became betrothed. It's mostly boys who get an older person to speak for them.

(3) A person with a son over twenty and not yet married grows anxious lest his son become an old bachelor. He happens to have a relative in another village, who has a neighbour with a daughter who is not yet engaged, so the man takes his son and they go together to visit this relative. The boy and the girl cannot meet otherwise. Things are arranged so that the two can see each other, and afterwards they are asked: 'Did you like him?' 'Did you fall in love with her?' After that, the two young people meet again and perhaps they do fall in love, become engaged and get married. When Chang Chung-liang's younger brother, Chang Chung-wen, was twenty-two and still unmarried, he went to Chitan hsien, where he had an uncle, and his uncle introduced him to a very young girl. They got married and she now has a child of four, though she herself is only twenty-one.

When a girl considers the boys with an eye to choosing one to marry, she looks for one who is strong and healthy and able to work well. Girls attach great importance to behaviour: the boy they choose must be even- not quick-tempered. Appearance is less important. As the girls say: 'We have a long life to live together. He may look handsome now, but his looks will soon go. But if he is faithful and kind and hard-working, we can have a good life together.' Boys who are known to be lazy seldom get married.

When a boy considers a girl, the first thing he asks himself is: 'Can she look after a home?' Next in importance is that she should be even-tempered. Appearance plays a certain part, but not a great one. In Liu Ling no one will say that a girl is ugly or plain, just that she 'looks well enough in her way'.

'In the towns the girls will tell you the same as those in the villages, but they will only do that because it is the thing to say. In reality, town girls want smart, dashing-looking boys.'

The person with the most say in the matter of a girl's marriage is her grandmother, then her grandfather, then her mother; what her father thinks is of least importance. What they all want for the girl they are marrying off—and what the boy's parents are also looking for—is a 'good marriage' to someone who is 'rich', strong and able to work well.

Once they are engaged, the boy and girl meet often. Li Chin-wa and Lo Han-hong spent hours sitting together in his cave. They were always alone then and no one would disturb them. 'We aren't so feudal in Liu Ling that we won't leave them alone together.' But when Lo

Han-hong goes to see Li Chin-wa, he has to sit with the whole family. Sometimes the two would go to the cinema in the town together.

There is no intercourse prior to marriage. That is held to be immoral. 'No girl in Liu Ling has ever had a baby before she was married. That happens very seldom up here with us in northern Shensi.' The age at which girls normally marry is such that there is no large group of sexually mature but unmarried women.

Later on, when they are to marry, the two young people go to the authorities and register. They have to say how old they are and they are asked: 'Do you love each other? Do you want to marry? Are you doing this of your own free will?' Only after that are they given a marriage licence. Having got that, they are legally married, but it has never yet happened that a couple have begun living together as man and wife after just this legal marriage. There has to be a ceremony as well, and for various reasons there can be an interval of anything up to six months between the legal marriage and the wedding.

A bride's trousseau usually consists of three or four changes of clothes, two new coverlets, one mirror, one or two chests, one cup, one soft cushion, one pillow, and one wash-hand basin, and the bridegroom should have furnished the bridal chamber with one mattress and one thick coverlet. The thicker this coverlet is, the richer and happier the bride's life will be, or so they say.

The wedding is in the bridegroom's home and it will be well attended. There can be more than a hundred guests. All relations, neighbours and friends are invited. There will be wheaten bread, buckwheat noodles and cakes of 'sticky millet' to eat. Altogether there ought to be eight courses; four is the minimum. There should be meat and wine and spirits, and everyone will eat and drink and sing and joke. At the start of the ceremony the guests are seated, gathered round the couple, who stand in front of the table, the bride on the right, the bridegroom on the left. There should be wine and a dish of sweetmeats and melon seeds and cigarettes and a looking-glass on the table; and there should be a picture of Chairman Mao hanging on the wall in front of the couple. The bride takes some flour and puts it in a porcelain bowl. Bride and bridegroom bow low to the portrait of Chairman Mao; then they turn to their parents and bow to them, then they bow to the elders and lastly to their guests.

Then the guests ask them to tell how they fell in love with each other, to tell 'the story of their love', and they both become very embarrassed and look at each other and urge each other to do the telling. And the people call out: 'Quickly! Quickly!' Then the bridegroom will mumble something in a low voice. Some just say a word or two like: 'We met and so we married.' Then all the guests ask lots of questions. They pretend that they have seen the two together and say things like: 'We saw you! You were walking very close together down by the river.' Everyone jokes and tries to make them blush as much as possible. Both bride and bridegroom wear big red paper flowers, which they exchange, and after that they drink wine. Then the guests ask the bride to sing. The couple eat a few sweetmeats from the dish, then they sit down and everyone starts eating and drinking.

Now, the bride and bridegroom are congratulated and everyone drinks. After that, good friends conduct the couple to the bridal chamber. There the bride has to wait on the bridegroom and all their friends. She must light their cigarettes and fill up their cups with wine. Bride and bridegroom sing and everyone drinks wine. About midnight the couple are left alone in the bridal chamber and the guests depart.

On the third day, the couple go to the bride's family with gifts. They take cakes and sweetmeats, dried noodles, handkerchiefs and stockings. Then the bride's mother invites some of her good friends and relations to a dinner with meat and wine and all sorts of good things. After that the couple go back to the bridegroom's family. 'This is our new way of celebrating a wedding. Everyone's wedding has been like that for many years now. But the old people say that it was done differently in the old days.'

The old women say that in the old days you were not allowed to choose whom you married. A young couple were not allowed to meet before the wedding. When a girl was sixteen or seventeen, the marriage-broker would come and say: 'I have seen a young man in such-and-such a place and he does this or that and he is healthy and strong and of good family, and he is rich and even-tempered.' If the girl's mother was interested in the offer, a day would be fixed for the young man to be presented. On the day appointed, the marriage-broker and the suitor would arrive with presents of wine and meat and other good things, as well as cloth for the girl. The girl's mother would take the meat and cook it and warm the wine, and then they would eat and drink. Meanwhile the girl would be kept hidden. She was not meant to meet her suitor. If the mother was satisfied with the suitor after she had seen him, she would say: 'It is well', and then they would settle the financial arrangements.

That done, a propitious day for the wedding would be decided on with the assistance of a wise man. This had to be at least one month away in order to allow the girl time to get her trousseau ready. She had to have four baskets of embroidered shoes, quilted trousers, pieces of cloth, socks, needle and thread, and foot-bindings for her girl-children. All her relations would have to help her get the things ready in time. After this the suitor and marriage-broker would bring the girl's mother all the things the suitor had agreed to give for the girl: money and cloth and meat and wine. The mother would cook the meat and warm the wine and accept the suitor's bride-ransom.

A girl had to weep properly on her wedding day. To begin with, she was decked out with lots of red flowers and ornaments, and then her pigtails were unplaited. Next, she was placed in a palanquin carried by two or four men and taken to the bridegroom's home, her brother going with her. When they reached the bridegroom's home, the bride's brother gave her away. Bride and bridegroom then knelt in the big room in front of a table. The room had to be decorated with flowers and ribbons, and there had to be two red candles on the table and also fruit and sweetmeats. The couple then bowed first to heaven and earth, then to the bridegroom's parents and then to the bride's brother and the marriage-broker and all the relations. After that everyone ate and drank.

In the old days, the main dish used to be wheat-flour noodles, and throughout the ceremony some men sat by the door to see that no widows, cats or dogs got into the room, because in those days these always brought bad luck, especially at a wedding. After everyone had eaten, the curtain before the bridal chamber was pulled aside. At that moment the bride had to look desperate, otherwise people said: 'Look how avid she is!'

The first three days after the bridal night, the bride had to spend sitting on the kang all the time. She was given no more to eat and drink than was necessary for survival, and if she wanted to relieve nature she could do so only at night, creeping out when everyone else was asleep, because if anyone discovered her going out she would be jeered at. During the day she had to hold it in however much it hurt. On the third day the couple went to the bride's mother with gifts. The bride's mother would have invited some close relatives and they would eat meat and drink wine, and afterwards the young couple would return to the bridegroom's home. For the first three years of her marriage a bride was not supposed to go beyond the gate. Some of the old women said that they were allowed to go a little way beyond, but they must not go far and only when it was necessary. 'Well, that was the old way of marrying. It is not practised any longer. It hasn't been employed for many years and it's a long time since anyone bowed to heaven and earth.'

Nowadays, when people marry, they are usually very loving for the first year. Not that they show it in front of others, we don't do that, but you can see it by the way their clothes are better and their shoes whole, and they look happy. But otherwise brides behave in the same way as before. People don't consider a bride properly married until she has had a baby. Until then she is still a girl, even though she is married. She won't dare talk and joke with the others; but everyone will joke with her and her husband. People will stop her on the road and ask: 'Well, are you in love with your husband?' And if the bridegroom is coming back from the town, he will be stopped and asked: 'What have you bought your bride?' They will blush, but they won't joke back till the bride has had her first child. Of course, she will be less bashful than she was before her marriage, but she isn't yet one of the married women. If they don't have any children, people usually adopt a son. That is what Tien Kuei-hua did. Her husband is a ganbu at the coal mines in Yenan. He was deputy party secretary of Liu Ling's People's Commune up to 1961, then he was moved. When they did not have any children, they adopted one. People would rather adopt the child of some close relative with lots of sons, than let their family die out. The adopted son has to be treated well, because he is the family's future. Such adoptions are quite common.

Nowadays divorce is very rare. There having been no free choice of partner under the old system, there was a sudden rush of divorces when the new order began. But that is a thing of the past. If there are children, people think it immoral and wicked to leave them. Even if the marriage is childless, people still consider divorce immoral, because now that people can choose whom they will marry, they will have chosen each other and should put up with the consequences. One can always adopt a child. If, in spite of all this, they still want a divorce, the various organizations, the party, the League of Youth, the women's group, try to instruct them and explain what is the decent thing to do and the one consistent with socialist morality. If they persist, the matter is taken up by the mediation committee of the people's commune, which goes into it thoroughly with them and explains to them why they ought not to divorce, but should live together and agree. If, after all this, they refuse to give in and still want a divorce, they are, of course, entitled to go to the court in Yenan and start proceedings for a divorce; but that has not yet happened in Liu Ling, nor have any divorces been heard of in the neighbouring villages for many years, for it is a long time now since women have been granted equality and marriages have been entered into voluntarily.

Brawling and fighting were said to be unknown in Liu Ling, nor had anyone heard of anyone suffering from jealousy. Infidelity was unheard of in the village, and they had not had any great dramas of passion, let alone *crimes passionnels*. 'It is all due to the fact that we in northern Shensi are different to people from Hopeh and Canton and Shantung and Kiangsu and Fukien. We aren't like they are. Down there, those sorts of thing do happen; but not with us.'

Eye diseases were not common, but stomach disorders were. Most children suffered from tummy-ache and diarrhoea right from infancy till they started going to school, after which the teachers saw to it that they did not sit right on the ground and that they stopped drinking water from the river, with the result that they became healthier. Children's trousers being open meant that they, especially the little girls, were susceptible to inflammation of the bladder. All that the mothers had to say about this was: 'What can we do? The children just run about as they like.' Among the older generation, the women especially suffered from rheumatic pains in their hands and feet, but aches and pains were typical of all old people.

Adults did not drink water that had not been boiled, and they did not eat raw vegetables. 'Raw food and cold food have a nasty taste.' Melons and tomatoes were the exception: they were eaten raw. Tea was a luxury. On the rare occasions when they drank it, it was the cheapest black tea they had.

Meat was party fare and when an animal was slaughtered, they ate everything, even the blood and stomach; but they never ate horse-flesh or mule-flesh: 'It tastes of vinegar'; though they would at a pinch eat donkey, even though they didn't really like the taste. They did not eat sucking-pig or chickens: 'Immature meat is harmful.' Goats, sheep, cattle and pigs were butchered and eaten. If a pig showed signs of being ill, it was butchered and eaten. If it died before it could be butchered, it was buried. If a donkey died of old age it was eaten; if it died of disease or foundered on the road, it was buried. If it fell down the hillside and broke a leg, it was slaughtered and eaten. But horse and mule were never eaten, though some people are said to have eaten even horse-flesh in the great famine.

Almost every household had its cat. Cats were the rat-catchers, but also the children's playmates. There were only five dogs in Liu Ling: two owned collectively and three privately. The collectively owned dogs were the herdsman's dogs. They were fed on millet porridge, vegetables, pumpkins and maize-flour bread. At the slaughtering seasons they got some bones, but otherwise they were vegetarian dogs. They were not used for hunting and did not hunt on their own. The three dogs in private possession were owned by Wang Fung-li, Fu Hai-tsao and Chi Pei-fa. They were not so well fed and got fewer bones. They were watchdogs and pets, mostly pets. But they also acted as guards against foxes and wolves. Foxes took a lot of the villagers' hens.

Only one person in Liu Ling had been in his country's capital; this was the Old Secretary, Li Yiu-hua. One or two had been in Sian, capital of Shensi province. On two or three occasions in the last ten years, they had had foreigners in the village, come out by car from Yenan: 'But you are the first foreigner to have spent the night here or stayed here.' A couple of years before, some young people from Sian had been in Liu Ling doing voluntary agricultural work, lao dung. (Ching Chi was one of them.)

When a couple have their first child, whether boy or girl, their relatives send them presents of dried noodles, wheaten flour, bean flour and eggs. When the baby is a month old, its mother invites their immediate relatives and best friends and all who have sent them presents to a celebration. The celebration consists of two meals, the first of which is eaten at ten in the morning and consists of buckwheat noodles and four other dishes, salted and pickled vegetables. After a noonday rest there is a second meal, which starts at four and consists of steamed wheaten bread, 'sticky millet' cakes and four courses, including mutton and fish. With all this they drink hot spirits out of small cups. The guests bring all sorts of presents: little shoes, baby clothes, etc. But this is only done for the first baby in the family. There is no celebration for the others that may come, and birthdays are not kept.

When a man reaches the age of fifty, he starts getting his coffin ready. He may even have bought the wood for this years before, and it has to be good thick wood; but having reached the age of fifty he can ask a carpenter to make up the coffin, and when it is finished and ready, it is stored either in the labour brigade's store, or in the store-room in the person's own cave. Once they are fifty, men let their beards grow and they also start smoking and drinking spirits. Some younger men smoke and drink spirits, but that is unusual. In wintertime the older men usually have a couple of small cups of hot sixty per cent spirits every day; but they do not need this in summertime.

The great day of a man's life is his sixtieth birthday, for then he has completed his span. If he dies before sixty, it is an unhappy death, but after sixty he can die happy. The next birthday celebrated is his seventieth, then his eightieth and so on, and each is a happy and honourable occasion.

One invites all one's friends and relations to one's sixtieth birthday; so that in the case of a respected man, the entire village will be there. He will regale them with noodles, eggs, meat, wine and spirits. There is a first meal at ten o'clock in the morning and this should consist of buckwheat noodles with meat gravy and four dishes of pickles and vegetables. The second meal is about four o'clock, after a midday siesta, and should consist of thirteen dishes, 'thirteen flowers', eight dishes of pork and mutton and vegetables and that sort of thing, and five dishes of pickles and suchlike. Everyone drinks and makes speeches, saying lucky and luck-bringing things to their host; in fact you eat and drink as much as possible, and talk a lot.

There is no definite age at which a son takes over responsibility for the family from his father. As long as a father can work in the fields, he remains head of the family, but once he is no longer able to do a full day's work, it is usual for the eldest son to take over from him. Big family decisions are not taken by the head of the family alone. On such questions as whether or not to build a new cave, buy a bicycle or cart, and questions of the children's schooling, all the older members of the family confer and reach a joint decision.

In principle, work done in the labour groups is calculated per person and it can also be paid for to the individual; for example, when Li Yang-ching bought her husband a bicycle as a big surprise present, she signed the receipt for her pay herself; but usually all money earned is given to the head of the family. Whichever way is used, it will go into the joint family purse.

When there are several grown-up children in a family, it is normal these days for the children to set up their own households when they marry, thus splitting up the family. Yet, even though split in this way, the family will stick closely together. For example, Ai Ke-liang, who is forty-nine and lives alone, being a widower, has his own cave and is counted as having his own household, yet he lives and eats with his sister, Ai Lan-ying, and her husband, Li Hai-kuei, and he shares all the corn and cash he gets with his sister, Ai Lan-ying, and his younger brother, Ai Ke-kao: 'My wife is dead. I have no children. Whom else have I to give it to now?'

Chen Chung-yuan's wife had had three sons by a previous marriage. (She was first married to Tsao Chen-kuei's uncle.) The eldest, Tsao Chen-yung, married and set up his own household; thereupon the middle son, Tsao Chen-hua, moved across to his newly married brother's cave. The third son, Tsao Chen-yi, had already been accepted for the Chinese People's Liberation Army, being able to get in only because the family at that time had three unmarried sons all over the age of eighteen. Chen Chung-yuan's was the only family in the village that had ever fulfilled that condition and thus Tsao Chen-yi was Liu Ling's only soldier. He had already been three years in the army and had spent all the time in Tibet. He was just a private, but he had been to school and could write. He often wrote to his mother and whenever she got a letter from him, she would take it to someone who was able to read and have it read out to her, weeping all the time as she listened, because she yearned for him so much and was so anxious about her youngest son, who had become a soldier and gone so far away. He had a lot to do in the army, he told her, and was getting on well; also he was hoping to be transferred soon to some other place, from where he might be able to come and see her, for he had been in Tibet ever since the autumn of 1959.

When an old person dies, his or her sons put on white mourning clothes and go and inform all the relations. Then they all discuss when and where the dead person is to be buried. A 'knowledgeable' person is invited to come and say which day will be most propitious and which burial place the best. There used to be one of these 'knowledgeable' men in Liu Ling itself, but he died in 1961. He was called Tung Shi-hai and his widow later moved to Yulin, while his granddaughter has gone to Sian, so that his family is not in Liu Ling any more. He was the last one able to pronounce on such matters and who used the old traditional methods in the search for what would be propitious and bring luck. Now, if there are many members of the older generation in a family, they will insist that a 'knowledgeable' person be fetched from another village, though these are getting more and more difficult to find. The young people do not bother so much about this, but the older generation still think it matters a lot how they are buried.

When a good place for the grave has been found and a propitious day for the funeral decided upon, invitations are sent out to all the relations, who then send gifts of food and money to the sorrowing family, anything from three to five yuan per household. Then they come, even from long distances, to take part in the mournful ceremony. On the first day of the funeral there are three meals: one of buckwheat noodles with meat gravy and pickles at eight o'clock in the morning; then, at midday, they have steamed wheaten bread and eight dishes of vegetables, pork and mutton. After this they all weep until the evening, when, at six o'clock, they have more buckwheat noodles—these being considered lucky—with meat gravy and pickles. After that they weep and talk about the dead man. Then they all go to bed.

Early the next morning the corpse is taken to the grave, the coffin being carried by four good friends. The eldest son heads the procession, holding the dead man's name plaque in front of him; then comes the coffin and then the members of the family in order of generations. They have with them wine and steam bread for the dead person. Everyone weeps as the dead man is being buried.

Our graves are built more or less like potato cellars. First, a perpendicular shaft is dug into the ground and from the bottom of this a horizontal grave chamber is excavated. If a wife dies first, she is buried outside the family's burial place in a temporary grave and moved to join her husband when he dies. In these cases, the wife's bones are collected and put in another coffin, smaller than the ordinary ones, which is then placed beside the dead man's coffin. If the husband dies first, the grave is made large enough for two coffins.

After the coffin has been placed in the grave, the entrance to the grave chamber from the shaft is closed up with stones and the shaft is then filled in, a mound built over it and tombstones placed on this. Then one burns paper money and other things and sets out offerings of wine, steam bread and meat for the dead person. After that everyone returns to the village, and when they get back to the cave, they have

31

another meal of 'sticky millet' cakes, after which the relations disperse to their homes.

On the third day after the funeral, the younger members of the family go to the grave and make offerings of paper money, meat, wine and steamed wheaten bread, weep a lot and then go home. One hundred days after the funeral, they again go to the grave and make offerings. After that, offerings are made once a year. Everyone in Liu Ling, both communists and those not in the party, go to the graves of their ancestors and make offerings. Each family has its burial ground.

As a general rule, widows re-marry unless they are old, that is to say getting on for sixty or more. Tung Yang-chen's mother, for example, Tsao Fong-ying, married Chang Shi-ming and that was considered right. A woman ought not to live alone. But a widow must not marry again until at least a hundred days after her husband's death. If she gives birth to a posthumous child, it is called having a 'moon child'. This happens. Women in mourning must not wear patterned materials, but must dress in white, black, grey or light blue. They must not wear ornaments. If the person who died was under sixty, people will prefer not to talk about him: 'He died an unlucky death.' But if he died after attaining the age of sixty, people will gladly talk about him: 'He died a lucky and happy death.'

Children under twelve may not be buried in their family's burial ground. The older people say: 'Children under twelve have not got fully developed souls. It would bring bad luck to bury them in the family grave.' So they are buried without ceremony up on the hillside. Children under seven are buried without coffins. They are thrust into some natural crevice or hole in the rocks near the village and covered with earth and stones to keep wild animals from getting at them. The older people say that any other way of burying those who die so young is unthinkable. 'It would bring great misfortune upon the entire family.'

The most serious thing one can say about anyone is: 'He has been so bad and behaved so immorally that he has no young generation.' To die without anyone to continue the family is the most dreadful thing that can happen to anyone. That almost happened to Li Yü-teh. He has his family grave on Loushan, for he belongs to the old land-owning family. He never had a son of his own, only two daughters and they, of course, would leave the family as soon as they married. His elder daughter is Li Kuei-fung and she is married. She married Wang Fung-li. Only, instead of her leaving home, Wang Fung-li moved to her home. That was arranged when the marriage was being settled. Li Yü-teh wanted Wang Fung-li to come and live with him and give him a young generation. You can do that if there is no son in the family, in which case sons-in-law can act as sons. Li Kuei-fung's first two babies were girls, so they were called Wang; but her third was a boy and so it was named Li. In this way Li Yü-teh has a grandson who bears his name and will continue the Li family. Thus Li Yü-teh's family will not die out; but if Wang Fung-li's son had been given the name of Wang, the Li Yü-teh family would have died out.

Fu Hai-tsao has saved his stepfather's, Tsao Shen-hung's, family in the same way, partly by bearing both his father's name of Fu and his stepfather's name of Tsao, and partly by giving his child the name of Tsao.

Tables

Prices of consumer goods in the shop in Seven-mile Village

In China the basic unit of currency is the yuan, the rate of exchange for which is, at present, about fifteen pence or thirty-six U.S. cents, but all calculations based on this are quite valueless in assessing the economic situation of these families. Thus, as in all other cases where one has to try to compare countries which have different social and historical assumptions, the prices must not be viewed in relation to those in the United Kingdom or United States, but to China's own reality. Material for doing this is provided in different places in this book. There is no coin for a thousandth of a yuan, but, as in other countries, prices in China are often expressed in thousandths of the currency unit.

Cotton wadding	jin	1·005 Y
Cotton material, simple	chi	0·295
Knitting wool	jin	8·05
Sewing thread	skein	0·15
Handkerchief	each	0·435
Galoshes (rubber shoes)	pair	4·59
Salt	jin	0·16
Sugar	jin	0·80
Sweets	jin	1·32
Vinegar	jin	0·09
Cooking oil	jin	0·72
Biscuits	jin	0·70
Spirits, 60 per cent	jin	1·34
Washing soap	2 cakes	0·435
Electric light bulb, 15-watt	each	0·63
Earthenware jar holding 80 jin of grain	each	9·91
Water cauldron, iron, holding 20 litres	each	7·82
Enamel basin	each	2·10
Enamel mug	each	0·74
Alarm clock	each	16·30
Hand-cart with bicycle wheel	each	125·50
Bicycle	each	178·00
Thermos, 2½ litre	each	2·62

The planned supply of goods

These particulars refer to the position in Yenan hsien in September 1962 and were provided by Lo Han-hong and Liu Hsin-min.

Quite a lot of consumer goods are rationed. This, however, is not called rationing, but 'planned supply of goods', since the main object is 'not to restrict the individual household's consumption to a certain maximum, but to guarantee a certain supply of the goods'.

The country people buy very little of their food. Each family receives its quota of grain from the labour group to which it belongs and, in principle, they produce on their own private plots all else that they require. In theory, a family that considers it requires more grain can buy extra from its labour group after the matter has been put to a meeting of the labour group. This, however, has never yet been done. Families can always grow their own vegetables, tobacco and the like; and they are free to buy in the market vegetables, pork, sweetmeats, everything you eat and drink, except salt and sugar. Many industrial goods are also unrationed: books, paper, earthenware, bicycles, hand-carts, electric light bulbs, man-made materials, washing powders (not soap).

Each household has a ration book in which the number of persons in the family is entered. This permits the purchase of one jin of salt per person per month, one jin of paraffin per paraffin lamp per month, one cake of washing soap per person per month, and one skein of sew-ing thread per household per month.

The department for trade and economy in the people's commune also hands out cotton coupons. The quota for adults for six months was one jin of cotton wadding and 3·7 chi of cotton material, and for chil-dren one jin of cotton wadding and 5·2 chi of cotton material. Extra can be obtained after special application has been made to the depart-ment for trade and economy.

In addition, there are four other forms of planned supply:

(1) Extra distribution consequent on the planned production of grain having been exceeded. In 1961, after the harvest had been brought in and the grain sold, Liu Ling Labour Brigade received extra permits for 417 chi of cotton material, 120 packets of cigarettes and 24 pairs of galoshes.

These extra amounts were divided up among the labour groups in accordance with their totals of days' work. The distribution was decided on by the authorities of Yenan hsien after all the corn deliveries from the district had been made.

(2) Extra distribution for deliveries of goats. Every goat delivered entitles one to coupons for six chi of cotton material or one sheepskin or goatskin. In this way, in 1961, Liu Ling Labour Brigade received coupons for 192 chi of cotton material and 70 sheepskins or goatskins.

(3) When private goats, pigs or eggs are sold to the state, the household concerned receives, as well as a cash payment, permits to buy, for one goat, six chi of cotton material or one goatskin or sheep-skin; for one pig, one set of cotton underclothes *and* one pair of gal-oshes *and* one or two handtowels; and for one jin of eggs, half a jin of sugar.

(4) Through Liu Ling People's Commune, Liu Ling Labour Brigade receives from Yenan hsien extra permits to buy industrial goods in addition to those already mentioned. This extra distribution depends on the size of the distribution of industrial goods made to

Yenan hsien, and between 1 January 1962 and 1 September 1962 there were eight of them. They comprised blankets, thermos flasks, enamel basins, thick woollen sweaters, wool yarn, galoshes and brocade bedcovers. The total value amounted to 1,443·56 Y.

Prices paid by the state for animal products sold privately

(If sold in the market, animals fetch the market price for that day, but the seller does not receive a permit to buy consumer goods as given above.)

Pigs per jin live weight	0·43 Y
Goats per jin live weight	0·43
Eggs per jin	0·795

Prices paid (per jin) by the grain office in Yenan hsien

Wheat	0·10 Y
Millet	0·06
Millet, 'sticky millet' (*glutinosa Bretsch* or *effusum Alet*)	0·065
Maize	0·065
Black beans (*Vicia faba*)	0·08
Soya	0·08
Long beans (*Phaseolus vulgaris*)	0·075
Green beans (*Phaseolus mungo*)	0·10
Buckwheat	0·065
Kaoliang	0·065
Jute seeds	0·15

Births and Deaths in Liu Ling village, 1 January 1961–1 September 1962

1961
BIRTHS: five sons (to Chang Chung-wen, died at three days; to Li Hai-fu; to Kao Yü-kuei; to Wang Fung-li; and to Tsao Chen-kuei); and two daughters (to Yang Kuei-ying and to Li Hai-ching).
DEATHS: Chang Chung-wen's son (see above); Tung Shi-hai, 71, old age; Fan Yu-lien, 27, heart disease.

1962
BIRTHS: two sons (to Chiang Hao-lu (the day we left Liu Ling); and to Li Hai-kuei; and two daughters to Tung Yang-chen and to Li Hai-fa).
DEATHS: Li Hai-kuei's father, 73, old age; and Mau Ke-yeh's wife, 54, abdominal cancer.

Households in the village of Liu Ling

50 households, 212 persons.

Listed and numbered according to the register as at 15 August 1962. The name of the head of the family is in heavy type. Age is reckoned in the Chinese way: one year at birth and then one year for every calendar year, counting from the new year of the lunar calendar. The households are numbered according to the position of the caves. The first cave is in the bottom row, farthest to the left on the south side. Then follow the caves in the second row, then those in the third, all taken from left to right.

Households in the main village on Naopanshan:

(1)	♂	**Li Hai-yuan**	48
	♀	Chia Fu-lan	50
	♂	Li Te-chua	15
(2)	♀	**Kao Chin-Lan**	26
	♂	Li Ai-ping	8
	♂	Li Chao-ping	2

(The husband, Li Hai-chang,. works at the mill in Yenan.)

(3)	♂	**Li Hai-Kuei**	38
	♀	Ai Lan-ying	34
	♂	Li Yun-shen	12
	♂	Li Shan-hsin	5
	♂	Li Chao-hsiu	1
(4)	♂	**Li Hai-fu**	50
	♀	Tu Juei-chen	35
	♂	Li Shi-wa	21
	♀	Ma Ping	21
	♀	Li Ai-ai	7
	♂	Li Lao-hu	2
(5)	♂	**Tu Yi-chen**	43
(6)	♂	**Ching Chung-wan**	48
	♀	Tu Fang-lan	56
(7)	♂	**Ai Ke-Liang**	49
(8)	♂	**Ai Ke-kao**	37
	♀	. . . .	33
	♂	Ai	14
	♂	Ai	11
	♂	Ai	8
	♀	Ai	3
(9)	♂	**He Huang-ho**	25
	♀	Chia Ying-lan	53
(10)	♀	**Li Kuei-ying**	32
	♂	Li Ho-ping	10
	♂	Li Shi-ping	6
	♀	Li Ai-ping	5

(The husband, Li Teh-chiang, is a ganbu and visits her once a month.)

(11)	♀	Chia Ping-fong	76
	♂	**Li Hai-Ching**	32
	♀	Yuan Fon-ching	26
	♀	Li Shan-ling	7
	♀	Li Chao-ling	1
(12)	♂	**Chang Chung-liang**	33
	♀	Chi Mei-ying	29
	♂	Chang	8
	♂	Chang	5
	♂	Chang	1
(13)	♂	**Kao Pin-ying**	37
	♀	Liu Kuei-ying	38
	♀	Kao	3

(14)	♂	Tsao Yiu-fa	53
	♀	Tung Kuei-ying	48
	♂	**Tsao Chen-kuei**	28
	♀	Chiao Kuei-lan	27
	♀	Tsao Shi-lien	17
	♀	Tsao Ai-ping	7
	♂	Tsao Ma-chuan	4
	♂	Tsao Chu	1
(15)	♂	**Tsao Chen-yung**	28
	♀	. . . .	22
	♂	Tsao Chen-hua	21
(16)	♂	**Chen Chung-yuan**	44
	♀	. . . .	48
	♀	Chen Nü	11
	♀	Chen	7
	♂	Chen	4
(17)	♀	Li Fong-lan	76
	♂	Kao	58
	♂	**Tung Yang-chen**	35
	♀	Kao Kuei-fang	32
	♀	Tung Yuan	12
	♀	Tung Er-wa	10
	♂	Tung Hong-hong	8
	♀	Tung Chiao-wua	1
(18)	♂	**Mau Ke-yeh**	59
(19)	♀	**Fung Yü-lan**	27
	♂	Mau Ying-shin	8
	♂	Mau	6

(The husband, Mau Pei-chin, works in Seven-mile Village as deputy director of Liu Ling People's Commune's Agricultural Implement Factory.)

(20)	♂	**Li Yü-hsin**	46
	♀	Li Shang-wa	16
	♂	Li Shung-chen	11
	♂	Li	7
(21)	♂	**Li Sha-chang**	50
	♀	. . . .	56
	♂	Li	14
(22)	♂	**Chang Chung-wen**	27
	♀	. . . .	21
	♀	Chang	4

(23)	♂ **Li Hung-fu**	33
	♀	24
	♂ Li	10
	♂ Li Shi-ming	7
	♀ Li	4
(24)	♀ **Tung Chi-lian**	49
	♂ Chang Shun	9

(The husband works as carpenter in Kanshuan hsien and visits his family once a month.)

(25)	♀ Wang Yü-lan	62
	♂ **Liang He-yiu**	33
	♀	32
	♀ Liang Yen-ling	9
	♀ Liang	3
(26)	♂ **Li Hsiu-tang**	38
	♀ Li	39
	♀ Li Chin-wa	18
	♀ Li Ai-liang	17
	♂ Li Ta-min	15
	♂ Li	14
	♂ Li Shuei-ming	12
	♂ Li	8
	♀ Li	6
(27)	♂ Tsao Shen-yung	69
	♀	64
	♂ **Fu Hai-tsao**	39
	♀ Li Tsuai-ying	35
	♀	18
	♂ Tsao Ming-wa	15
	♀ Tsao Shan-nü	9
	♂	7
(28)	♂ **Chang Shi-ming**	58
	♀ Tsao Fong-ying	51

(Mother of Tung Yang-chen by a previous marriage.)

	♂ Chang Niu-Ming	14
(29)	♂ Ma Chen-hai	65
	♂ **Ma Juei-ching**	34
	♀ ...	24
	♂ Ma	8
	♀ Ma	5

(30)	♂	**Ching Chung-ying**	54
	♀	....	51
	♂	Liu Ching-tsei	31
	♀	....	26
	♂	Liu	6
	♂	Liu	2
(31)	♀	**Jen Huai-ying**	22

(Her husband works in the coal mines in Tingshuan. He visits her two or four times a year.)

(32)	♀	**Tien Kuei-hua**	38
	♂	Liu Yuan	8

(Her husband is party secretary at the coal mines in Yenan and comes home every week.)

(33)	♂	**Jen Teh-wan**	59
	♀	....	59
	♀	Tuan Fong-ying	29

(Tuan Fong-ying's husband, Jen Teh-wan's son Jen Huai-wan, is party secretary at the pottery in Yenan. He comes home every week.)

	♀	Jen Chiu-yen	8
	♂	Jen	5
	♂	Jen	2
(34)	♂	Li Yü-teh	50
	♀	....	50
	♂	**Wang Fung-li**	31
	♀	Li Kuei-fung	26
	♀	Li Shung	12
	♀	Wang	8
	♀	Wang	4
	♂	Li	2
(35)	♂	**Hu Shen-chu**	33
	♀	Liu	28
	♀	Hu Yen-ching	9
	♀	Hu	3
(36)	♂	**Liu Chen-yung**	30
	♀	Li Yang-ching	29
	♀	Liu Lan-shuan	10
	♀	Liu	5
	♂	Liu	3

(37)	♂ **Yen Chi-yung**	46
	♀	34
	♂ Yen An	17
	♂ Yen	14
	♀ Yen	10
	♀ Yen	8
	♀ Yen	3

Households on the Shiwan side of Liu Ling village:

(38)	♀ **Chang Chu-liang**	20

(Her husband, Tuan, works at the mill in Lochuan. He had visited her twice during 1962.)

(39)	♂ **Tuan Fu-yin**	54
	♀	48
	♂ Tuan Shao-tang	11
	♀ Tuan	8
	♀ Tuan	3
(40)	♂ **Ma Hung-tsai**	29
	♀	25
	♂ Ma	7
	♀ Ma	3
(41)	♂ **Chi Pei-fa**	36
	♀ Tung Chi-fu	29
	♀ Chi	7
	♂ Chi	3
(42)	♂ **Ma Hai-hsiu**	51
	♂ Ma Tsuei-chang	22
	♀	18

Household connected to the cattle-sheds:

(43)	♂ **Wang Hsin-wang**	63

Households on the Shiaoyuanchihou side of Liu Ling village, not yet given electricity:

(44)	♀ **Kao Yü-kuei**	29
	♀ Li Ho-ping	10
	♂ Li Shin-ming	4
	♂ Li Choa-ming	2

(The husband, Li Hai-chun, is in charge of Liu Ming's People's Commune's loan department.)

(45)	♂ **Li Yiu-hua**	57
	♀	51

43

	♂	Li Hai-fa	30
	♀	She Shiu-ying	26
	♂	Li Hai-tsai	28
	♀	Chang Yü-ying	25
	♂	Li Shuan-tsai	12
	♂	Li Yen-shin	8
	♂	Li Ming-shen	7
	♂	Li Shi-shin	5
	♂	Li Chiao-ming	3
	♀	Li Mei-li	2
	♀	Li Chiao-mei	1
(46)	♂	Li Ying-teh	60
	♀	....	54
	♂	**Li Hsin-chen**	39
	♂	Li Chi-shen	17
(47)	♂	**Shi yü-chich**	58
	♀	....	52
(48)	♀	**Yang Kuei-ying**	30
	♀	Yang	8
	♀	Yang	7
	♀	Tuan	2

(Her husband, Tuan, works in Yenan. Her former husband, Yang Yung-chien, died in 1959.)

(49)	♀	**Yang Fu-Lien**	37
	♂	Li Ai-shen	9
	♀	Li Kou	6

(Her husband, Li Hai-chen, works in Seven-mile Village. He is director of Liu Ling People's Commune Agricultural Implement Factory. He bicycles home every week.)

(50)	♂	**Chiang Hao-lu**	43
	♀	....	39
	♀	Chiang	9
	♂	Chiang	6

Part II
The Road to Power

Pai Yu-teh, veteran ganbu, aged 60

now director of Yenan's Water Regulation Board

THE way the revolution took—well, that's many years ago now and I may have forgotten a lot, but I'll try and tell you what I can remember. I was never able to go to school as a child. What I've learned, I've taught myself in my spare time or at the party school. Now, I can read newspapers and letters, but no more. I am a farmer's son, so perhaps it won't all be as clear as if I had been able to study more.

I came from a peasant home. My father had 100 mu, but it was not good land. It was rocky. I began working when I was seven. I herded cows and goats until 1918, when I began working in the fields. In 1921 I took a job as hand with a farmer called Liang Hung-en in Yenchang, but went back home the next year. I had then been married for several years and we already had three children. I began working on the

47

family's land. The thing was that Father had been adopted by a farmer called Tien, who wanted to prevent his family dying out, and Father had taken his name and so inherited 100 mu in a village called Tien Family's Corner. But, as I said, it wasn't good land, and with us there in Yenan 100 mu was not much. In other parts of China it was only landowners who had so much, but in Yenan there was lots of land and too few people.

In 1927 a peasants' organization was set up here and that was when I first heard of communism. 'Destroy the landowners and do away with taxes,' was the cry, but I wasn't 'aware' at that time, of course. That year we refused to pay taxes. We heard that in the towns the students were fighting against imperialism. The leader of our peasants' organization was Chu Cheng-chiang, a big, strong man known for his integrity and honesty. I don't know if he was a communist. The party was illegal then, of course, and I wasn't a member, so I wouldn't have known about that. Then the K.M.T. came and suppressed us and all our activities stopped. Chu Cheng-chiang had to fly. He died later in Yenan, in 1949.

In 1931, 1932 and 1933 I kept hearing about Liu Chih-tan and how there were revolutionaries in Suiteh and Tsechang who had destroyed the landowners and done away with taxes. That made a deep impression on me. I especially liked the idea of the landowners being destroyed, because landowners lived in luxury, while the people suffered. As I said, the fact that I owned 100 mu myself did not mean that I was a landowner, because it all depends on what sort of land you own. There's land down in the valley and there's land up on the hillside. There are peasants who have 200 mu and are poor. Down in the valley, yields are ten times as great for less work, so you can work it out yourself.

In 1935 Liu Chih-tan was operating in Nanliang and in Wuchi. There was a lot of talk then about the Red Army. In April that year Liu Chih-tan sent a guerrilla group to Thirty-mile Village to wipe out an armed landowner group. The Red Army's slogan was: 'Down with the local landowners! Down with the local despots! Down with imperialism! Divide the land equally! Free the women! Abolish taxes!' Thirty-mile Village was not far away, of course, and I talked about what had happened with my best friend, Han Pei-hsin. He and I worked together and we had already been profoundly impressed by what we had heard of the happenings in Suiteh and Tsechang. Now, we told each other that we ought to go across the hills and see what they

48

were doing in Thirty-mile Village. After all, we wanted everyone to be equal and all bureaucrats and landowners to be destroyed. So, one night, Han Pei-hsin and I set off across the mountain to see if we could find the Red Army. It was chilly and we had only one quilted coat between us, and that was seven years old. Han Pei-hsin later became party secretary in a liberated hsien and died in 1942 of tuberculosis and undernourishment.

When we got to Thirty-mile Village we talked with a propagandist, who wore civilian clothes and was called Wang Shen-hai. He was about thirty, a dumpy chap with a round face. We told him about ourselves and he gave us the job of organizing the poor peasants in the neighbouring village for the cause of the revolution. Later on, I used to meet Wang Shen-hai now and again. He died of high blood pressure in Sian in 1960.

It was now my job to organize the people of the neighbouring villages. I had to find leaders who could help the Red Army and see that it was given food and information and was kept up-to-date with the landowners' plans. In the district there were two detachments of the landowners' armed forces, Ming Tuan, and also a dozen or so police, so I had to work in secret. They used to cut off the head of any of us they happened to get hold of. When I went to a village, it was in disguise. Once there, I visited the poorest villagers, the farmhands and daily labourers, and talked with them. I spoke about the revolution with those I thought I could trust and gave them the job of giving the Red Army all the support it needed.

In the end, the landowners no longer dared stay in the villages at night, but made fortified places for themselves up on the hillside and withdrew to those. After I had organized twenty villages, one of the Ming Tuan detachments fled, but the other remained. Wang Shen-hai then started a guerrilla action. We went to Chaochia, where there was a moneylender and landowner called Chen Chin-ho. We allowed him to escape with his life, but we confiscated all his possessions and all his land. The peasants said to us: 'Don't leave us, because if you do, perhaps he will come back with the Ming Tuan.' We agreed that we would send a 'feather-letter' round the villages. This is a letter with a feather. As soon as it reaches one village, it is sent on to the next, and so everyone knows what is going to be done. By the next morning, six hundred farmers had arrived, and we arranged a mass meeting and elected a revolutionary committee.

That, then, was our new government. There were various departments in the committee: a defence department and a land department and a grain department and a department for women's affairs and a department for young communists. We elected Wu Pao-tang our chairman and I was chosen brigade leader for the Red Guard. That was in May 1935.

We had now seized control in both valleys on this side of Yenan and the second Ming Tuan detachment also took refuge in the town. There were five brigades of us and I was leader of one of them. But we had no arms. Not all the landowners had been able to escape with their arms, but it wasn't much they had left behind. So the village blacksmiths took the surplus agricultural implements and made spears out of them; but as there were not even enough of these to go round and we weren't all armed, we made dummy ones. Each of us had three wooden hand grenades. Our uniform was a red armlet. At a distance it looked as if we were heavily armed. We got hold of some silver paper in a shop and used it to cover our wooden bayonets. They glinted in the sun. We frightened the landowners.

The women and children went and kept guard along the roads and outside the villages, and we did not let anyone pass who did not have a permit from our revolutionary committee. Each Brigade had a big red flag, and we carried these in front of us when we marched against Yenan. By June 1935 we had taken the far bank of the river and Yenan was surrounded. There were shortages of food and fuel in the town then. Here, in the Nan valley, we got into contact with Mau Ke-yeh. He and I met in Matan that June, and we discussed what was to be done. He said: 'Ought we not to establish contact with each other?' And we in our brigade thought that we ought and after that we kept in touch.

After this the Red Guard in the hills was increased. We got proper guerrilla detachments. The Land Department and the Trade Unions and Poor Peasants' Association decided to investigate the state of the classes in the villages. We were to find out who were exploiters and who weren't. We were to take away the exploiters' possessions and give the exploited their land. We were very strict and energetic, and we destroyed the landowners as a class. When we turned our attention to a certain Chang Pei-yi, six hundred of the people on his estates came to the meeting and told us how he had oppressed them. It was a long meeting. We found that he had 300,000 jin of grain, 400 goats, 6 donkeys and 21 oxen. He told us that he only owned 10,000 mu, but he really owned more. He had more than 20 villages under him and received 60,000 jin a year in rents. Well, we parcelled up his land and distributed his corn and his animals and his tools and implements. We kept back part as public property to cover the expenses of the Red Army, but the rest we divided up. Chang Pei-yi himself had fled to Yenan, for he knew what his tenants would do with him if they got hold of him. But when we liberated Yenan in 1936, there was the united front against Japan, so he was able to go on living there, and later his daughter joined the revolution and now she's a leading ganbu in Szechwan. Chang Pei-yi lives with her there now.

After each such fight against a landowner, we valued all his possessions. Everything had to have the people's support. We had to divide the man's land up and take his possessions, but we also had to take off part as public property. Everything had to be done publicly and openly. Had we worked in any other way, the people would not have supported us. In each village we would set aside ten mu or so for common needs, the amount depending on the size of the village and quality of the land.

It was at this same time that we heard that Mau Ke-yeh, using cunning and red flags, had succeeded in disarming the whole of one of the landowner's forces and made the landowner fly. You see, there were many ways of defeating the landowners.

After we had surrounded Yenan, the grain, vegetable and fuel situation in the town got worse and worse. As no supplies were being sent in, the enemy had to send out soldiers to plunder the villages, and this of course strengthened the peasants in their hatred of the enemy, making the blockade more and more effective. The peasants joined the guerrillas and fought too.

I became a member of the party in July 1935, the same month that Liu Chih-tan led the Twenty-sixth Army in an attack on Kaochia village, sixty li away. The enemy there sent to Yenan for reinforcements from the 'Peace-conserving Brigade', a special landowners' force, the main task of which was to root out communists. But before the reinforcements could get there from Yenan, the Twenty-sixth Army had taken Kaochia. We knew that reinforcements were on the way, so we laid a trap for them. Leaving only a few Red Army men in the village, the main force withdrew into the broken country round about. When the Peace-conserving Brigade arrived, it was enticed into the village by the thought of an easy victory. After that, we surrounded them and destroyed them. Lo Ting-chen, commander of the Peace-conserving Brigade, was killed and we took twenty prisoners. For three days we reformed the prisoners. 'Our fight is with the landowners,' we told them. 'You are poor people like us. We don't wish you any harm.' Then we gave them a silver dollar each and told them to go home. They went back to Yenan and spoke well of the Red Army. They told how we had control of all the villages, how we were well armed with modern rifles, how we had many flags and many soldiers, though actually we had neither many soldiers nor many rifles. They said this just as an explanation of why they had been defeated. At all events, in this way the fame of the Red Army spread in Yenan and the enemy's morale deteriorated.

On the death of Lo Ting-chen, Li Han-hua took over as commander of the Peace-conserving Brigade. He shrank from nothing and was our most serious opponent.

The Twenty-sixth Army now freed Yenchang, Anting, Chinchien, and thus a large area round Yenan was liberated. The people were in control in Kanchuan and Fuhsian, and then in August of that year, the North-eastern Army arrived under Chang Hsueh-liang, the Young Marshal, and their slogan was 'Root out the communist bands in a month'. That made the landowners happy. They sent messages to their villages: 'Every goat stolen shall be paid for with a head. If anyone has been eating my corn, his whole family shall pay with their lives', and people were terrified. Then the North-eastern Army marched in with its modern weapons. People were afraid and asked us: 'How can we be expected to fight them? How can we save ourselves?' The North-eastern Army had sent to the villages, telling them to send corn to Yenan; so we sent round our propagandists who told them: 'Don't be afraid. When the troops come, we shall hide in the hills and they won't venture there.' We organized peasants on whom we could rely to take grain to Yenan. Every day we sent some people with corn and fodder from the villages, just enough to keep them quiet, but not enough to meet their needs. These men's job was not so much to take the corn, as to reconnoitre and get us information about the morale of the troops in the North-eastern Army and its plans. In this way we knew everything about the enemy, because they thought the villagers who brought them grain were well disposed towards them and they trusted them. These men also took leaflets with them into the town and distributed them.

In September that year I had been chosen to be the one responsible for military work in our hsien, the commander for our military district. But after the arrival of the North-eastern Army at Yenan, we had to retreat some distance from the immediate neighbourhood of the town. Mau Ke-yeh was at Seven-mile Village, where he had an illegal party headquarters. It was a sort of depot for guerrillas and party workers.

Then the Twenty-fifth army came here to the Yenan area, as did our Twenty-sixth Army that had been in Hongshan. The two joined up in Yungping and from there we marched on Laoshan and attacked Kanshoan. But this was just a cunning stratagem. We wanted to lure the enemy out from Yenan; and they did as we expected and tried to relieve Kanshoan, and we lay in ambush for them. It was a bloody fight. We wiped out one enemy division. After that we went on to Yulinchi and Taotsenpo, where we destroyed the enemy's regiment. After that we were able to surround Yenan again and restore the blockade. We now set up a government in Fusze hsien, the thirty li round Yenan. I was elected president of Fusze hsien in November 1935.

We had four garrison detachments, one in each valley round Yenan, and now began really harassing the enemy. We let nothing through to them, and at night we went up on to the hillside and shot at the town. We did not do that to harm them, but to keep them awake and make them waste their ammunition. It was usually enough to light a few fires on the hills and throw firework bangers into the town. Sometimes we shot someone too. The enemy was nervous and had to be in a continual state of readiness and used to shoot blindly into the dark. The morale of the North-eastern Army grew worse and worse. In the end they had neither food nor ammunition, having fired it all off unnecessarily. Then the enemy tried to supply his troops by air, but the planes flew too high. The pilots were Americans hired by Chiang Kai-shek and they didn't want to die, they were just flying for the money. So they dropped pancakes over Kanchuan where the enemy was starving, but the wind caught them and they drifted over to us and we ate them. They were still warm and we laughed loudly at the idea of our starving enemies watching us eat their pancakes. The enemy also dropped ammunition by parachute over Yenan, but it landed on the ice and exploded. In the end the enemy stopped trying to help his troops by air. It was proving too expensive, especially as we got most of it; but even so we were badly off for arms. We were always short of arms.

In September, for example, Ma Ming-fan, chairman of northern Shensi's soviet government, came to us. I told him that we had no arms and he wrote out a piece of paper authorizing me to collect 100 new rifles; but I didn't know much about administration then, so I never asked for ammunition as well. Thus, the paper just said: '100 rifles for Comrade Pai Yu-teh, military commander Fusze hsien.' Then we got five donkeys and went to Taotsenpo where our troops had just destroyed a regiment of the enemy and taken a lot of booty. Well, I got my 100 rifles, unloaded, but the comrades there refused to let me have any ammunition. 'There's nothing about ammunition on your requisition, Comrade!' they said. 'We have no right to hand out ammunition to anyone who just comes and asks for it.' And I had to be content with that, and we set off home with our five pack-donkeys laden with empty rifles. As we were passing Chang-hsin-chuan, we were stopped by the people there. They were having a great meeting. They said to me: 'You usually come here with only one rifle. Now you have many. The enemy's coming today to plunder the village. They are going to take our corn from us, because we have just got the harvest in. They want us to starve to death. So now you must stay and defend us. We won't let you go until you have defeated the enemy and protected us.'

What were we to do? After all, we had no ammunition. I could not let the enemy get hold of our rifles. But on the other hand I couldn't abandon the villagers. In the end I sent off two men with the five laden donkeys and kept eight men with unloaded rifles. Then I got hold of the chairman of the Poor Peasants' Association in the village. He was called Chuen Tien-ying and was a clever chap. We went off into a corner and I said to him: 'I have something I must tell you; but it is a secret and you mustn't let it out to anyone. We have no ammunition. None at all. I'll gladly let you have one rifle if you like, but we have no ammunition.' Then Chuen Tien-ying replied: 'I have some cartridges, left over from when we captured a K.M.T. plunderer.' After that we sent the women and children up on to the hill. The village Red Guard was placed at the foot of the hill, and I and my other soldiers took up position in front of the temple. Then the enemy came. There was a detachment of soldiers and a group of grain requisitioners. It was a whole regiment. At that time the K.M.T. would not venture out of the town unless there was at least a regiment of them. The soldiers surrounded the village and the grain requisitioners came towards the temple. Then I gave my order: 'Don't shoot into the brown. Choose one definite one. Shoot one at a time. See that each bullet hits an enemy!' Then the corn requisitioners arrived. First we shot and killed one. The women and children on the hill shouted our slogan: 'The triumphant Red Army has come!' Then we shot and killed another. And then another. Everyone was now shouting. When five of the enemy had fallen, the enemy fled. We still had five cartridges left. When the enemy fled, we held a great feast. People had more confidence in us than ever. They said: 'This is the real Red Army. Eight men defeat so many of the enemy.' When we got back home after this battle, our garrison certainly had one hundred rifles, but we still had no bullets.

To solve this problem, we sold some of the expropriated landowners' possessions and sent some men to Lochuan, which was occupied by the enemy, and there they bribed the commander and bought some ammunition from him. But he had been cunning and when we tried to shoot with the cartridges, they exploded and made the rifles burst in the faces of those trying them out. There was not much we could do about it. We could not accuse our comrades in Lochuan, but the enemy had outwitted us and taken our silver and given us ammunition that was no good. So then we took the cartridges and emptied out the powder. We moulded our own bullets and made powder from the heads of matches. That worked, and so gradually we acquired both rifles and ammunition for the garrison.

In October 1935 the First Route Army came here at the end of the 'Long March'. It was led by the Central Committee of the Party and Chairman Mao. Thus three armies joined forces: the First Route Army, the Twenty-fifth Army and the Twenty-sixth Army. Mao now led our forces against Fusze and wiped out two enemy regiments in Chilo. The Central Soviet Government was set up in Wayapo. The Central Committee came to us with this message: 'Go north to fight the Japanese! Resist Japan! Form a united front! Chinese do not fight Chinese! Let all unite against the Japanese invaders!' In November our soviet power was set up officially at all levels. It was then that I was elected soviet chairman for Fusze hsien. Till then we had had only a provisional revolutionary government committee. After that, order was restored everywhere.

Chairman Mao came to us and spoke of the necessity for forming a united front. The Central Committee now stopped our activities against the landowners. They insisted that we had been guilty of departing from the correct revolutionary way, so we re-investigated the true class circumstances of every family. We had been far too strict, we were told. We were now to fight shoulder-to-shoulder even with landlords.

In January 1936 the three armies were reorganized into the Fifteenth Unity Army and Chairman Mao led this army to the east to fight the Japanese. That left only the Twenty-eighth Recruit Army in Wayapo; but in Shansi there was Yen Hsi-shan. He was the war-lord in Shansi. We sent a message to him saying that we did not want to fight his troops, but wanted to fight with him against Japan to save our country. But then Chiang Kai-shek sent ten divisions to fight us and stop us from fighting against Japan. Liu Chih-tan had been given orders to lead his forces across the Yellow River. He was killed in the fighting at Linshien in March 1936. He was a great hero, our greatest hero of northern Shensi. We had to retreat from Shansi without having made contact with the Japanese. But even so this expedition proved of decisive importance. It opened everyone's eyes. They saw that we wanted to end the civil war and fight Japan.

During this time my job was to see that the blockade of Yenan was maintained effectively. We stayed in occupation of the hills and when the enemy came out to get corn we fell upon him from our ambush. During the daytime we used to assemble up in the hills round Yenan and curse the enemy. We continued organizing the masses and strengthening the power of the soviet.

In February 1936 I was transferred to the United Front that had just been formed. In March I was made responsible for it, and when our troops began marching east, we local party workers were given the job of taking the North-eastern Army in hand and forming a united front against the Japanese; the thing being that the North-eastern Army came from the areas captured by the Japanese and they did not like the idea of having to fight us, while the Japanese occupied their home territories, and they didn't like Chiang Kai-shek not letting them help fight the Japanese in order to recover their homes. So now we began secretly working on them. Their fighting morale was poor, of course; they had no food, they were hungry and cold, and lost all the engagements they were in with us, for they were fighting far from their homes in a war they did not understand.

The first conferences between us and the North-eastern Army took place in Tungchwankou, about twenty li from Yenan. Wu Liang-ping, who was then in charge of the propaganda department, represented the Central Committee of the party; the soviet government of northern Shensi was represented by Li Chi-lin, and I and Liu Ping-win represented Fusze hsien. An officer called Chao came from the North-eastern Army. I don't remember his rank, but he was a regimental officer. Then we began our discussion. We sat in a stone cave and had a friendly discussion. That was the first step in our collaboration that finally led to Chiang Kai-shek being taken prisoner in Sian and compelled to go to war with Japan. In that very first meeting we arrived at complete agreement as to the basic principles of our collaboration. These were:

(1) A non-intervention agreement.

(2) We marked out the areas that were occupied by armed forces and those that were to be neutralized. To enter these neutralized areas you had to have permission both from us and them. United Front Offices were to be set up to deal with matters of our collaboration. They were to be set up by us in their territory and by them in ours.

(3) Two markets were to be set up: one by us in the Date Garden. This was to be manned by our people and theirs in conjunction, and there we would sell corn, vegetables and fuel to them, and they would sell arms and ammunition and other war material to us. Only unarmed personnel was to enter these markets.

Our agreement also laid it down that the arrangement was in agreement with the Central Committee's statement that Chinese did not fight Chinese, but stood together to drive out the Japanese aggressors. These were the fundamental principles for our working together and we were in entire agreement about them. We also arranged— and that was made part of our agreement—that we were to stop all hostile acts against each other.

This agreement was, of course, strictly secret. Chiang Kai-shek suspected that something was brewing in the north-west, but he could not prove anything. The difficulty was that we could not include the Ming Tuan, the landowners' 'Peace-conserving Brigade', in the discussions. They were not reliable. We, of course, tried to make propaganda among them, and, of course, they had all been driven out of the countryside and into the town, but they were there and a continual source of disturbance. Militarily, they were under the command of the North-eastern Army, but as they thought this altogether too ineffectual in fighting the communists, they acted on their own. The only way of keeping them in check was for the North-eastern Army to delay issuing them ammunition.

The United Front was hard work. We sold corn to the army at the markets; but the class hatred of the landowners' troops was unquenchable. One night in May 1936 the Peace-conserving Brigade came to our United Front Bureau in the Date Garden. They were under the command of Li Han-hua and in breach of the agreement they were armed. I wasn't in the office at the time, but they took four others prisoner: Li San-chi, Ma Chan-piao, Liu Chung-piao and a comrade called Han, but I have forgotten the rest of his name. These four were responsible for the work of the United Front in the Date Garden open market. But they were irresponsibly credulous and not sufficiently prepared for the class hatred of the landowners, so they were all captured together and had their heads cut off that same night.

The difficult thing here was that the pact between the North-eastern Army and us was secret. We discussed the matter with the North-eastern Army and it was all hushed up. Of course we would have liked to avenge our comrades, but for political reasons we had to pretend that nothing had happened. The important thing was to preserve the United Front. That sort of thing happened quite frequently. I cannot remember that event ever being taken up afterwards, and no plaque was ever put up in their memory. It's like that in all revolutions. Many have to be sacrificed.

It wasn't easy work. The North-eastern Army came by day, but the Peace-conserving Brigade came at night, plundering and murdering. We did not want to shoot and kill them, but persisted in our work for the United Front. But the Peace-conserving Brigade went out into the villages and plundered the farmers' stores of grain and beheaded our ganbus. We refused to let ourselves be provoked and our iron party discipline prevented our own people from hitting back.

We also opened youth clubs in the open markets. We had a variety of printed matter in them, brochures and leaflets with wording like: 'Drive back the invaders and recapture our country.' We held a big market every fifth day and soldiers from the North-eastern Army came to those youth clubs to hear news from home and read our leaflets. I myself was engaged at this time in working on the officers. Later, when the Young Marshal, Chang Hsueh-liang, flew up to Yenan, Chou En-lai went and conferred with him. That was how we distributed our work.

Chou En-lai and Chang Hsueh-liang now reached a general agreement. Our relations with the North-eastern Army were so good that one could say they were friendly. But Chiang Kai-shek had become more and more suspicious. He did not send winter uniforms for the North-eastern Army and he would not pay them either. Not only that, but he had ordered the North-western Army under Yang Hu-chen to go to Sian in order to prevent Chang Hsueh-liang going over to us. Chiang Kai-shek also repeated his orders that the communist bandits, which was what he always called us, were to be wiped out.

Chou En-lai and Chang Hsueh-liang had long discussions about this situation. Something had to be done. We cooked up a plan between us that would solve all our problems; this was that the North-eastern Army should attack us, win a great victory and take lots of booty and make great propaganda out of it. When everything had been worked out, the North-eastern Army attacked Wayapo, where we had our government, as we had arranged. The government and the Central Committee and everyone else had withdrawn to Chitan hsien in good time, and, as we had arranged to fire only into the air, no one was even wounded. We had arranged with the North-eastern Army that we would leave all our unserviceable arms behind in Wayapo together with others the North-eastern Army had lent us for the purpose of being captured. After that Chang Hsueh-liang was able to telegraph to Chiang Kai-shek that he had dealt the communists a shattering blow, that Chairman Mao had fled or been killed in the fighting, his headquarters taken and much booty captured. This report was printed in the newspapers all over the world. Chiang Kai-shek was very happy and at once let the troops have all their back pay. After this, Chiang Kai-shek's confidence in the North-eastern Army was restored and he gave them all the material they needed. We asked the North-eastern Army to organize artillery for us, because we had none, and Chang Hsueh-liang telegraphed to Chiang Kai-shek for guns, saying that he needed modern ones for the final destruction of the power of the soviet. He got the guns and handed them over to us, so that we could together fight the Japanese.

Our relations with the North-eastern Army were now so friendly that we could even deal with the Peace-conserving Brigade; so, when they went out raiding the villages, we shot at them to kill. The Peace-conserving Brigade complained to the North-eastern Army and asked

59

for protection, and, since our agreement was secret, this could not be refused. The North-eastern Army got in touch with us and told us where they were going to attack the following day, promising to withdraw after a brief exchange of shots and tell the Peace-conserving Brigade that our numerical superiority had been too great, but they insisted that we must shoot too. I thought this difficult, because we did not have enough ammunition to be able to waste any shooting into the air. In the end, it was arranged that the day before they attacked anywhere, they would provide us with ammunition so that we had some to use. That is what was done, and thus the Peace-conserving Brigade got no help from the North-eastern Army. When we encountered each other, we and the North-eastern Army both fired, shooting up into the air, and then the North-eastern Army withdrew, and the Peace-conserving Brigade had to retreat as well, because we were shooting at them to kill. As it was difficult for the Peace-conserving Brigade to buy anything in our markets and they were kept from plundering the villages, their men became thinner and thinner. They were always hungry and so gradually they became unsettled and dissatisfied.

In July 1936, the North-western Army arrived and that altered the situation. They had the same slogan as the North-eastern Army: 'Exterminate all communist bands in northern Shensi.' We were not looking for a fight, so we let them occupy all our towns except Chitan, where the Central Committee and the soviet government were, and Wuchin, where we had a big concentration of troops; but the countryside was still ours. We tried to make contact with the men of the North-western Army and made intensive propaganda; but it was far more difficult with them because, coming from a part of the country that was not threatened by the Japanese, they were not so aware of the Japanese menace. Thus we had no success with the rank and file or the N.C.O.s. Our relations with the North-western Army only improved after Chang Hsueh-liang had got in contact with Yang Hu-chen and they had agreed together that, for the sake of their country, they would work with us against the Japanese.

While this was going on, the class struggle in the villages and countryside had had to take second place and we had stopped our attacks on the landowners. Certain of the landowners now took advantage of the situation to return to their villages and settle accounts with their tenants; but on these occasions our guerrillas hit back. We were not going to attack ourselves, but we certainly did not intend to let them attack our people. Shi Chung-je was one who returned thus to his village, Huchua. He was a pig-headed fellow. I went to see him and had a talk with him about forming a United Front with us to fight the Japanese together, but he would not co-operate. He had his own army. It was not big, but even a score of armed men can be dangerous, especially when they have a fortified camp. They treated the villagers very harshly. We decided to break them. We knew where they had their spies and we sent some men to walk along that road saying aloud how worried and anxious they were because they were so few and how they hoped Shi Chung-je's men would not be lying in ambush for them. The spies heard this and hurried to tell Shi Chung-je, who ordered his men to attack the few Red Army men. They made an ambush for our men; but we knew this and were prepared; so that, when they attacked, we took them in the rear. We killed one and took nineteen prisoners. That frightened Shi Chung-je and he wrote to me: 'I was wrong to be less than willing to co-operate. I had not thought the Red Army was so powerful. If you will just order my nineteen men to be let free, I promise to do as the Red Army wants and fight against Japan.' We re-educated our nineteen prisoners. That took us a fortnight. Then we released them. That landowner never dared do anything more. At the time of the happenings in Sian, when all the troops of the North-eastern and North-western Armies withdrew on 13 December 1936, he fled with them and went to Ichian. Later, in 1937, when the Communist Party and K.M.T. were working together, he returned to his house. We looked after him well, and when he died it was of disease.

The Sian happenings were the final result of our long negotiations with the North-eastern Army. On 12 December 1936, when Chang Hsueh-liang and Yang Hu-chen took Chiang Kai-shek prisoner, a plane was sent to Yenan to fetch Chou En-lai for discussions in Sian. These discussions later led to the collaboration between K.M.T. and us in the war against Japan. This was a great defeat for all un-national forces. Both Chang Hsueh-liang and Yang Hu-chen were patriots and Chiang Kai-shek never forgave them. Yang Hu-chen afterwards was murdered in one of the K.M.T.'s concentration camps and Chang Hsueh-liang, as far as I know, is still Chiang Kai-shek's private prisoner in Formosa.

While this was going on in Sian, Li Han-hua, commander of the

Peace-conserving Brigade, had become anxious and afraid of what might happen, and when he saw the plane coming in from the south to land in Yenan, he rushed to the airfield. He thought the plane was coming to help him. But the officers in the plane asked him: 'Who are you?' Li Han-hua answered: 'I am from the big government here in our hsien.' Then the officers said: 'Go away. We don't want to have anything more to do with you.' At that moment Chou En-lai rode on to the airfield. Seeing Li Han-hua and the Peace-conserving Brigade, he said to them: 'Don't worry. The soviet government and the K.M.T. are going to work together now in the struggle against Japan. We are going to set up a great national united front. I shall come back soon, and then I promise to see personally that all your problems are solved.' He said this in a friendly tone and he meant it to be friendly, because he saw that Li Han-hua was dismayed. But Li Han-hua and the Peace-conserving Brigade had no confidence in our promise and fled instead from Yenan that same night and went to Michi. Two detachments of the brigade did stay in Yenan and came over to us. The others ought to have trusted us and mended their ways in time. That's how it was with Li Han-hua.

Li Han-hua was a rich man, a moneylender and landowner, hard and vengeful and bloodthirsty. He had become leader of the Peace-conserving Brigade and he shrank from nothing. He murdered many villagers in the district that year. We spoke to him and gave him a chance to reform and join the United Front against Japan, but he chose to continue to fight the people. Eventually he took himself off to Yulin, where he remarried under a false name. When Yulin was liberated in 1948, he withdrew to a village, but we were on his track and in 1950 we caught him and brought him to Yenan, where he had been the cause of so many people's deaths. Many came to accuse and bear witness to his crimes, and after a proper trial he was condemned to death and we executed him.

His first wife died in 1960, and his second remarried. His sister and her children live in Liu Ling. There are a number of his relatives round here.

After this, I was sent to Hongchuan as party secretary. Then, in 1937, I was sent to the party central school in Yenan, took my exam in 1938 and was sent to the Southern District outside Yenan as party secretary. In February 1941 I became political commissar in the consumers' co-operative in our hsien. In December 1943 I was chosen to be in charge of the production department in Yenan hsien. In April 1949 I resumed my function as political commissar in the consumers' co-operative, which had to be built up again after Hu Tsuang-nan's occupation. In 1951 I was sent to Licha as regional party secretary and, in 1954, I was sent to the regional party school. In March I took my exam and was put in charge of dam construction in Yenan Water Regulation Board. In 1958 I became director of the board. That is all.

Mau Ke-yeh, cave-builder, farmer—revolutionary, aged 59

OF course, I can always tell you what I remember. But I've never been to school and can neither read nor write, so perhaps I'll get a date or something wrong now and again. One forgets, doesn't one? In the old society things were hard; life was harsh then. Taxation was heavy and we were not paid much for our corn. In 1926 and 1927 all we got was two silver dollars for 300 jin, and we had to pay two silver dollars a month in family tax. We had an ox then and two or three able-bodied people in the family. We got 5,000 jin in, but more than half went in taxes. We had no mats on the kang and our bedcover was twenty inches wide. We never ate our fill and we never had any cash. It was difficult to manage and things just got worse and worse every year.

My father was a mason. It was he who taught me to build stone caves. We lived in Yulin, but in 1917 we moved to Yenan district. People said it was better there. It was usual for people to move round in those days. One went from one village to the other, from one landowner to the other, trying to find a place with a lower rent. If you were in debt you could not move. You had to pay your debt first. We were five in our family and we had a small roll of bedding and a mirror. When we came down here, we rented sixty mu from a landowner called Chang. That was eighty li from here. The rental was 900 jin. We ploughed with the landowner's oxen and he took 1,800 jin for that. That autumn we harvested 9,000 jin of corn. Father did it all. I was only half-manpower then. I had a younger sister and a younger brother. Our landowner was not too hard, but he smoked opium and by 1924 he had ruined himself and became poor, so that year we moved to the village of Niuchang twenty li from here.

There, things were a bit better. We had an ox of our own and I was able to do a full day's work. We paid 600 jin rental for sixty mu. We used to get in 5,000–6,000 jin of corn and, when we had paid our taxes and the rent, there was just enough left to enable us to survive. Then came the great famine year of 1928. We starved in 1929 too. We plucked leaves and ate them; and we mixed chaff and elm-bark and made bread of it. The fact that we went so hungry in 1929 was not so much because of the harvest. Taxes and rental had taken their due, of course. But our harvest wasn't so bad. What happened was that I got married that year. That wasn't cheap. I had to pay 120 silver dollars for my wife. The following year I had a wife, I know, but the whole family had to go hungry, of course. We went on living with my parents. I had got a loan from a landowner and government official called Chia to help me pay the price for my wife. Chia lived in Yenan, where he was departmental chief in the K.M.T. administration. The interest on the loan was only two per cent a month, but even so I was never able to pay back the capital. I could not manage more than the interest. In 1935, when we made our revolution, the loan was written off. But Chia was already dead then. He smoked so much opium that he died of it. But I went on paying his widow till we had made our revolution.

In 1930 I moved to Matan Village. Up there in the hills, I could be my own master. It was, of course, common land there and we who broke new ground had to pay only one jin per mu a year. We had to pay taxes too, of course: two silver dollars a month. And we had to pay cash. It was hard work.

In 1935 an army calling itself the Red Army arrived. It was in the countryside. The K.M.T. was in the towns. This Red Army made propaganda and told us: 'The Red Army is good and we are going to divide up all the land and you won't have to pay taxes or rent to anyone any longer.' It was in the month of February 1935 that I met communists for the first time. These were Li Wen-yuan and Wang Hsiao-kang. They were both in their thirties. I met them again in later years, but whether they are alive or dead now, I don't know. They came to us one night and told us: 'We are propaganda-makers for the Red Army and now you are to make a revolution.' We replied: 'All right, we will.' But we didn't think they had any real power; they did not look as though they had and what could we poor farmers do? So we did nothing.

But in March that same year, they came back again. They called us all together for a meeting outdoors and told us to form a poor farmers' association and elect a leader. Then the others pointed to me and said: 'He's a calm and sensible chap and never does things hastily.' So I became leader. And Li Wen-yuan and Wang Hsiao-kang made us speeches and said: 'Why do you pay taxes to the K.M.T.?' Then we replied that we were afraid and that the K.M.T. had plenty of soldiers. But they said: 'Just stop paying taxes and don't be afraid, because the Red Army has its own methods of dealing with the K.M.T.'

They had their government in Lochuan then and the Red Army was commanded by Liu Chih-tan. To begin with, people were afraid of them and said that communists were murderers, but when they came here they were ordinary people and they always said: 'Divide up the land and fight against landowners and despots.' They talked a lot and held lots of meetings, and at the meetings we used to stand up and shout 'Yes, yes!', but we did not really believe in them or that they had any real power.

But in April 1935 the Red Army defeated an armed counter-revolutionary landowners' corps ten li from here. They killed the leader of the Southern District, Mu Hsin-tsai, and took lots of booty. After that they came more often. They also killed other counter-revolutionaries. Then the people saw that the Red Army did have power, and so we stopped driving into the town with our taxes and goods. Instead, we organized ourselves into guerrilla bands. Eight to ten men to each.

We no longer went to the town and we no longer sold grain to the town and we paid no taxes, and those who were K.M.T. no longer dared live out in the country, but began to run away. The town was isolated. It became a dead town. When tax collectors came, we took them prisoner, and, if any were decent, we let them go; the others we killed. So the town became quite isolated. Sometimes we fought Ming Tuan forces that came out from the town. We had spears and home-made rifles. But as all the people in the villages were organized and as the villages helped each other, when a landowner force came out from the town, they could not do anything to us.

In June 1935 we divided up the land. Everything was divided according to the size of each family and the quality of the land. Everybody got a paper with a stamp on it saying he now owned his land. But to begin with there were many who were doubtful and said: 'This is somebody else's land. It will bring us misfortune.' We also divided up the landowners' animals, and those who had none got goats and pigs. Thus, in the year 1935 we put an end to rent and taxes and we wrote off all our debts. We all lived better. Soldiers came out from the town, but when they did that, we villagers went up into the hills. When the soldiers went away, we came back again. K.M.T. wanted to steal our grain, but we hid it and fled up into the hills and K.M.T. had to go back empty-handed, and everyone had lots to eat.

My father had died by this time and in June 1935—no, not June—in May 1935 I was elected platoon leader of our Self-defence Corps. After that, I was quite convinced that the revolution would succeed, though I had doubted sometimes. I had changed my mind like the autumn weather. I was now responsible for a hundred families. We had spears with red tassels; we had knives and twenty homemade rifles. When necessary, all the men in the village assembled and off we marched with our spears, and as we marched along we were joined by the units from all the other villages round about.

The first big action I took part in was in May 1935. We had a message that we were to assemble to do in a landowner who would not surrender voluntarily. We came walking along all the paths with red flags on our spears. The landowner's name was Ma Sho-yen and he was all-powerful in Tsen-sanyan village. He had now barricaded himself in his house and had twenty armed men round him to defend his property. These were his own tenants, and it was their duty to defend him.

We had only twenty Red Army men, but the Self-defence Corps from all the villages had come too. The landowner's house was now surrounded by hundreds of men. We set up red flags on all the hills round about, and there were lots of them, so the horizon was quite red all round Ma Sho-yen. Then we all called to the landowner and held up our spears and said: 'If you don't give us your land and if you don't give us your rifles, you won't survive. You will die tonight.' After a while he came out. He was a big man in his fifties with a moustache, and he said: 'As long as I can keep my life, the land and rifles don't matter.' When we had got the rifles, we let him go off and he ran away to Kanchuan, where he had relatives. No one was even wounded in that action. And as soon as the landowner had fled, the villagers emerged; you see, they had been forced to stay with the landowner because they were afraid he would report them as 'bandits' or 'Red Army-men' and he had told them that if he did that, the

K.M.T. would cut off their heads. They were glad now and we held a big meeting and divided the land up and all the landowner's possessions.

I joined the party in 1935. I had become quite convinced by then and gave myself up body and soul to the revolution. In August 1935 I was elected leader of the district committee. At that time, we had our own revolutionary government in our hsien, and the district—which has now long since had its boundaries changed—consisted of these valleys here. I was responsible for agrarian reform, dividing up the land, fighting the landowners and for the employment of the labour forces. It was hard work, but there were ten of us together in the government then.

Here, in the village of Liu Ling, the landowner was Li Yu-tse. He owned several thousand mu of land. His family was one of the four that ruled Yenan and the area round Yenan. He owned half the valley here. Up as far as Ten-mile Village. But he had fled into the town and we never got hold of him. Then he fell ill and died. Li Hsiu-tang, who lives here in the village, is his son. He was so young at the time that he was given as much land as the rest. His children go to the school like all the others.

This Li Yu-tse had a relation who was a moneylender and a landowner. His name was Li Fa-fu and he lived in Fusichuan, thirty li from here. Li Han-hua, leader of the landowners' armed forces, was his son. He used to come with his men to the villages by night in order to strangle communists. Later, when the K.M.T. troops left Yenan, he fled to Sian. He never ventured here again, but took himself off to Yulin, where he worked for a war-lord called Kao Shua-chen. When Kao Shua-chen died, some time in the 1940s, Li Han-hua hid in a village beyond Yulin and disguised himself as a farmer. But then someone from here happened to go there and recognized him, and in the early '50s we caught Li Han-hua and brought him to Yenan, and there he was brought before the court and condemned and executed.

From April 1935 Yenan was blockaded by us farmers. We did not sell any corn to the town, nor any vegetables, nor fuel. This went on for seventeen months, then Yenan was liberated, the K.M.T. fled and the Red Army marched in. That was the time when the Central Committee and Chairman Mao came up to us in northern Shensi. They stayed here for ten years. The K.M.T. were only 200 li away. But those ten years were a good time. The farmers in the twenty

69

or thirty hsien we controlled had cattle and food and new clothes. Our army was not in the towns; it lay up in the hills. There, the army broke new ground and grew corn. They grew more than they needed for themselves. It was an army that did not live by exploiting the farmer; instead, it helped the farmer. Those years, there was corn in profusion.

In 1938 I went to another type of work. I began in the consumers' co-operative. I became manager of Liu Ling's co-operative shop. Then I handed my land in Matan over to my young brother, took my family and moved here to Liu Ling. There were twelve or thirteen households in the village then. As manager of the shop, I had to buy what the farmers produced and re-sell it. I also had to get hold of consumer goods and sell them to the village. This was quite a new field of activity for me. This was trading, of course, and I had never traded before. But it went all right.

We began collecting capital to make a start. In order to be a member, one did not need to contribute more than thirty or forty cents. Irrespective of the size of one's contribution, one had only one vote. Members could take out their share whenever they wanted. Though we made propaganda for them to stay in. They could take out the yearly dividend or they could leave it standing. After a time, everyone thought that co-operation was a good thing, because it made goods cheaper than they had been, and besides it was the members themselves who gained on all trading.

To begin with, many of the farmers in the district were doubtful of it. They said: 'This is just a trick to lure money out of us.' But then others said to them: 'Even if they cheat us, we shan't lose so much and one can always have a try.' We also made a lot of propaganda for co-operation. The most important argument was that the contribution was so low.

After a couple of years everyone could see that co-operation was a proper way. Because, when they noticed that our goods were always cheaper, and when they saw that they got a big dividend on their shares and also were at liberty to take out their shares when they wanted, everyone was agreed and gradually they began putting in more money. If anyone had no money, he could invest a donkey. If that was done, we valued the donkey and the amount was regarded as share capital. We ended up with 600 donkeys. We increased the dividend too. Before Hu Tsung-nan's attack on us in 1947 the dividend was up at 100 per cent per annum, and we had 300 employees. We had seven shops and were a big undertaking. I was still manager of the shop in Liu Ling.

In those ten years things got better and better in Liu Ling. Our prosperity just increased. New caves, new land brought into cultivation. More and more families moved here. Newcomers were able to borrow money and buy tools from our loans department. But we did not charge interest. We weren't usurers. In this way we increased production the whole time. After harvest the new ground clearers paid back what they had borrowed, then they joined the co-operative society and invested more money with us, so that we could lend more to other newcomers. So we went on building up for ten years.

Those were good years, you see, our Eighth Route Army had put such a lot of land under cultivation for itself, and when it went off to the war, it handed all this land over to the farmers. It gave it to them for nothing. We saw them march off against the Japanese. They had almost no uniforms and very few weapons, and we wondered if such an army would be able to defeat Japan. But then came reports of victories. There were only a few soldiers left in Yenan. Those years we all had big pigs, cattle and corn. Everybody had enough to eat and there was food over. But then came General Hu Tsung-nan.

It was at the turn of 1946-7 that we learned that Hu Tsung-nan and his troops were coming. We had lots of goods then and a big capital. It took a whole month for us to remove our store of goods. Then we buried what was left and fled into the hills. At that time, the co-operative association in the Southern District owned more than eighty room-units, where the school now stands. But that was all destroyed. There was nothing left of the shops and either Hu Tsung-nan's troops found what we had buried, or else people dug it up themselves, when they began getting hungry. Hu Tsung-nan's troops ate up everything there was in the district. The rest they destroyed. People said: 'What are we to do? We have nothing to live for any longer.' So, when I came down from the hills during the occupation and saw that everything had been destroyed and that there were Hu Tsung-nan's troops everywhere, there was no working in the co-operative association any longer for me, for there was no such thing. Instead, I began working politically. I became a guerrilla.

We organized ourselves in Liu Ling. The Nan valley is an important thoroughfare, after all. The big highway to Yulin runs through it.

There were five of us and we had two rifles. One night in April of the year 1947, we made our way across the river and up into the eastern hills. After a month there were forty-eight of us and we had twenty-eight rifles. I was elected leader. The enemy had occupied the valleys and the roads and the towns, and we kept to the hills. We slept by day and operated in the villages by night. We took our arms from the K.M.T. What we did was that, if we saw a small K.M.T. force, we surrounded them and told them to surrender. They soon learned to be afraid of us and surrender. In the first month we took thirty rifles from them. The villagers gave us food and kept us informed of what the K.M.T. was doing. Every time a big K.M.T. formation came, we fled; and every time they split into little groups of eight or ten, we destroyed them. In this way the K.M.T. could not employ small groups, but always had to go about in force and that made things difficult for them.

Actually, the K.M.T. soldiers didn't want to fight at all. If they came to any village by themselves, we took them prisoner and gave them food and spirits and talked with them. If they wanted to go home and get out of the war, we gave them journey money and helped them to get away. In this area round Yenan, we got about twenty K.M.T. men a day to desert. We treated the privates well. When we captured them, they usually said: 'We are farmers too. We too have parents and children and we don't like war, but want to go home to our villages.'

Here, round Yenan, there were three K.M.T. regiments and 2,000 Red guerrillas. K.M.T. tried to organize the population, but they did not succeed. After all, there were only children and old people left in the villages. K.M.T. arranged meetings and appointed section leaders, but these mostly maintained contact with us and told us everything, partly because they didn't like the K.M.T. and partly because they thought it safest to do that.

In our village there is no one who was with the K.M.T. the whole time of the occupation, right to the end. That happened in other villages, but here they withdrew after a time. It was the landowner element and those like Li Hsiu-tang who brought Hu Tsung-nan's troops to Yenan and then bore arms for the K.M.T. and worked for the K.M.T. People were pressed into the K.M.T. army. Tung Yang-chen was one; he was made to be a K.M.T. soldier for several months, before he succeeded in deserting. Tuan Fu-yin stayed here in the village and worked for the K.M.T. There were many among those who had fled into the hills who became anxious about their farms and so went down to the village again. Many of them were captured by the K.M.T. and forced to carry sacks of grain on carrying-poles in Hu Tsung-nan's baggage-train. Ma Hai-hsiu and others had to do this, but they deserted the moment they were left unguarded.

The K.M.T. frightened people. They forced old men to carry two heavy sacks apiece, and, when they could go no farther, the K.M.T. soldiers beat them. Our own army never asked anyone to carry anything and our soldiers were trained always to be courteous and always to say 'thank you', so people said: 'How well behaved and pleasant our own army is! It really is a people's army.' But the K.M.T. used to catch villagers and when they did, two soldiers would hold them and a third question them: 'Have you got the old Eighth here?' They always said that, when they were asking about the Eighth Route Army. Then the one they had caught would say: 'That's difficult to say. They come and they go.' But the soldiers asked: 'Where are they now?' If the villager would not answer that or couldn't, he was beaten. After a time everyone hated the K.M.T. But we in the guerrillas never beat people and never spoke harshly to them, and we operated by night and were far away again by the morning. By day, the K.M.T. organized its sections, but at night the section-leaders fled to us, and so the following day the K.M.T. had to begin all over again.

We in the guerrillas had good sources of information. Every time the K.M.T. asked for guides, they got in touch with us and then we made an ambush and the K.M.T. had a bad time of it. In the end, the K.M.T. thought that we were everywhere and that there were too many of us to count. But that was not so. There were never more than 2,000 of us. But we knew more than they did. If a lot of K.M.T. soldiers came, we hid; but if we knew that there was not many of them, we fought them. The more we fought, the more we won. The villagers also collected arms and ammunition for us, while the K.M.T. were asleep.

There were many fights that year. And the K.M.T. never knew whether they were fighting our army or guerrillas. We demoralized the K.M.T. in every way. We used to fire at their cantonments at night, so that they had to stand by. In that way we prevented them sleeping. We needed only to detail one man to keep a whole K.M.T. cantonment awake night after night. In the end, the K.M.T. began to become tired and irritable. They never got to grips with us.

After that, we saw to it that the privates were not frightened of us. When they came to us, we were friendly to them and talked sense with them and gave them journey money, so that they could get away out of the war. But we, of course, knew what would happen to us if we were captured. They did catch a communist in one of the neighbouring villages, and he was sent to Sian for interrogation, and there they drowned him in the river. So we preferred to die fighting to being taken prisoner. We could always move about in little groups of two or three, but there always had to be a lot of the K.M.T., so that they could guard each other. The officers there beat their own men, too. And the K.M.T. also tortured its prisoners. People did not like that. So the K.M.T. was never able to get the people on its side, despite its occupying the area for thirteen months. They themselves only became more and more demoralized the whole time. The K.M.T. captured several communists hereabouts. But the party managed to rescue most of them.

Well, after that the K.M.T. was forced to flee and we came back. I left political work and went back to the co-operative. We handed in our rifles and were going to start building the shop again. Everything had been destroyed. The K.M.T. had even cut down the trees and there was nothing left of our buildings and our stores. The villagers did not have anything either. Everything had been destroyed. We had certain resources even so. We had outstanding debts of about 1,000 yuan, so we were able to open one shop again. But it could never be as big as it had been. And most of our 300 employees went to other provinces to get trading started there. We were being victorious all over the country then and everybody was needed.

The K.M.T.'s section-leader in Seven-mile Village was called Sze; he fled, but the deputy section-leader was called Yü and he stayed. So, eventually, he was brought before a court. People accused him of having knocked them about and of stealing cows. He was given three years' imprisonment. He came back here afterwards. He died of some illness about a year ago. Li Hsiu-tang was condemned to three or three and a half years' imprisonment and loss of civic rights. He had been responsible for the K.M.T. agents here. He was employed in their espionage department. But his family lived here in Seven-mile Village and he had not escaped with the K.M.T. He hadn't murdered anyone either. If he had, his punishment would have been more severe. He came back some time at the beginning of the 'fifties. He looked after his fifty mu of land single-handed and in the end he was let into the

East Shines Red Higher Agricultural Co-operative as one of the last. That was in 1955. He has no right to vote and no civic rights, but his economic rights are the same as everyone else's. He is still under surveillance. You see, he is the only real counter-revolutionary we have here in the village. If he should ever show that he works hard and has become a new person, then he will get his civic rights back. But he hasn't shown any signs of that yet. Of course, his father owned many thousand mu here.

I myself worked with the co-operative shop until the year 1953. Then I was pensioned and returned to the labour group for mutual help as an agricultural worker. In 1954 I joined Liu Ling Farmers' Co-operative. There I was elected chairman of the supervisory committee. That doesn't carry a salary, of course. And I've stayed that all the time. Both when the East Shines Red Improved Agricultural Co-operative was formed, and when we set up Liu Ling People's Commune. Then, I'm on the board of the party organization in Liu Ling too. I'm still quite fit, but I am beginning to get old and I only count as semi-able-bodied. Now, in the people's commune, I work mostly in the vegetable plot. I'm in the labour group for vegetable cultivation. I have a lot of work for the supervisory committee of Liu Ling Labour Brigade. Our job is to see that the different functionaries really do their jobs and that money is not wasted. We haven't had any embezzlement, but there has been occasional negligence, and now and again one or other of the labour leaders has behaved improperly.

Looking back on my life, I can only say that everyone ought to take part in the revolution. It won't be a proper revolution if everyone does not accept his share of responsibility and look after it. Revolution is not a thing you can let others do for you. Even when you are as old as I, you must go on working in the revolution, for there is no pausing in revolution, even if it has different stages.

Chang Shi-ming, aged 58

It's raining again today, so we haven't gone out to the fields, so it doesn't matter, my sitting here chatting. It's good it's raining. If the rain had come a few days later it would have been bad. Though it would have been best if it had come ten days ago in the middle of August. But it's good that the rain comes at all.

We come from Hengshan hsien. We have always been farmers. But we did not have our own land. We rented it. For three generations we rented the same land. There were 120 mu. The landlord's name was Wang Ting-tung. When I was a child, I worked at home. When I was fourteen, I went out to work as herd-boy for Wang Ting-tung. There were ninety sheep in the flock, and it was herded by one shepherd and a boy. I was not given any wages, but I got my food. Three meals a day, millet gruel and 'sticky millet' bread. The shepherd had a lame leg. The landlord lived in the town, he had several houses and stone caves. We had an ordinary earth cave.

Landlords did not eat as we others did. They never used their bodies, and they ate meat and vegetables every day. There were seven or eight persons in Wang Ting-tung's family. He was an incredibly mean person. He made you give back the tiniest coin due to him. He was hard. If people could not pay, he punished them. He did not hit you, but he threatened and swore and took your land and possessions away.

When I was eighteen, I began working with Father in our fields. People hated the landlords, but there was no way of getting round them. 'As long as we have our daily food, we must be satisfied,' people said. 'We must do what our masters say. They own the land and the oxen.' Wang was called 'Wang the Bloodsucker'. In our dialect the two names sounded almost the same: Wang Peng-ton and Wang Ting-tung. Everybody owed him money. And as long as you owed him money, you could not get permission to leave the village in order to look for another landlord, who perhaps gave better terms.

Every year he put up our rental. In 1928—which with us was a normal year without any great crop failure—the rent was 15 jin per mu. In 1929 it was 15 jin per mu. In 1930 18 jin per mu. In 1931 21 jin per mu and that year we could not pay it all. We owed him 600 jin. It was a normal year without crop failure, but there were so many mouths to feed in our family and the rent was so high, that we could not manage to pay it. Then Wang Ting-tung said: 'You must pay your debt before you can have permission to move.'

If one reckoned up all that Grandfather, Father and I paid the landlord for these 120 mu that we rented during three generations, it would make an incalculable number of jin. The landlords ate up people's work. They ate and we worked. I myself have always worked for as far back as I can remember. When I was small, I helped Mother pluck grass for our animals. I have toiled ever since my earliest childhood. We had to give up our land, but we weren't able to move from there, because we owed 600 jin.

After the harvest in 1931, when we did not know what to do, my brother's father-in-law came on a visit. It was winter, and he had come up from Yenan to see his daughter. He was called Tsao San-tung. He told us things were better in Yenan district. There was more land there. He advised us to come down to Yenan and offered to relieve us from our debt to Wang Ting-tung. After a family discussion we decided to move to Yenan. In January 1932 we set off for Yenan. There were nine of us in the family then, Mother and four of us brothers and three wives and a younger sister.

Tsao San-tung lived about thirty li from here. At first we stayed with him, but the water was not so good there and we tried to find out where it was better. Tsao San-tung helped us. I also knew Tsao You-fan. He spoke with the landlord about me and I was given a promise that I could rent land in Liu Ling, here. The landlord's name was Li Yu-tse. He was Li Hsiu-tang's father. Being the eldest of us brothers, I then had to go to Yenan to see him. He lived in a big house in the town. I was shown into his office. He sat and I stood. He wore a Chinese woollen coat and a Western hat. He said: 'You may cultivate my land, but you must pay 600 jin for two ox-lands.' Then he waved me away. In his eyes I was just a beast. That was in the late winter of 1932.

An ox-land was about eighty mu. I had one piece of valley land roughly where the big latrine is now, another piece on the other side of the river, and the rest was hill land. Then I had to hire oxen. I did that from another landlord. He, too, lived in Yenan, and his name was Li Han-hua. He was Li Fa-fu's son and a brother of Li Hsiu-tang's wife. I hired two oxen. I had to pay 300 jin of corn a year for each. In January 1933 I had to borrow 300 jin of corn from Li Yu-tse. When I paid back the loan after the harvest, I paid 420 jin. I had to pay a household tax of two silver dollars every month. That meant that I had to sell 300 jin of corn each time to get the cash. We were poor and there were only two in the family able to work. There was tax on everything, even on killing your pig. We got in 9,000 jin and half went as rent and taxes.

The landlords, of course, Li Fa-fu, Li Han-hua and Li Yu-tse, had thousands of goats, donkeys and oxen, and they just gathered in their rent. They bought and sold grain and they always made money on everything. In the autumn, when we had to sell grain to get the cash to pay our taxes, the price of corn was low; and in the spring, when we had to borrow or buy corn, the price of corn was high. We starved and toiled, but they lived in luxury and profusion and never worked. They ate pork every day; they had steamed wheaten bread and noodles.

In February 1934 people began whispering about the Red Army and how it was saying: 'The poor will not have to pay taxes. The poor will not have to pay rent. Poor people's children shall go to school, and landlords will disappear.' Then the landlords said: 'Don't listen to rumours. The communists are bandits. They want to kill you and take your wives.' The only time I had heard about communists before was some years earlier, before we moved to Yenan. Some communist books had been found in the school at Yulin and people were saying: 'There are communists in Yulin. Track them down and kill them.' It was almost only landowners' children who went to school; and we in the villages only heard of communism when they brought their children home away from school, so that they should not be infected with communism. At that time I had heard someone say something about Sun Yat-sen's ideas, but I did not know what they were. We ordinary farmers did not know anything about politics. That was no concern of ours. Various armies were fighting each other, bringing misfortune over the land. The landlords and K.M.T. plundered and hit and swore and took people for forced labour, and one army was worse than the next; that was all we farmers knew. But now people were whispering about a new and quite different army, which was going to put an end to all injustice.

Then, in March 1934, the first propagandist came to the village of Liu Ling. This was Wang Shen-hai. He was about 30 then and, the last I heard of him, he was in Sian. He is working there now. He came to the village disguised as a donkey driver. He stayed in the village and sought out the poorest and most oppressed. But he also made inquiries as to whether they were respected. Then he took us to some hidden-away place and said: 'In northern Shensi Li Chih-tan and Hsei Tse-chiang are fighting now. They are the commanders of the Red Army. We are making revolution now and getting rid of all landlords and all taxes and oppression. You must make propaganda in all the villages here. But it must be done in secret. Rely only on yourself. Only on the poorest. Do not reveal who I am. In other people's eyes I am just an ordinary donkey driver.' Wang Shen-hai said this to those he trusted. He had a good eye for people, and he was never betrayed to the land-lords, though he lived right in their villages. He tried to select those who were honest and upright and strong and respected, and to win them for the cause of the revolution.

To begin with, we did not have much faith in him. There was, too, an intense propaganda battle in the villages. The landlords sent out agents, who went round the villages saying: 'At first the communists talk very friendlily, but if they come they will plunder you.' Gradually, we became more convinced. We organized the Poor Farmers' Associa-tion. Ma Hai-hsiu was elected president of it. Then we set up a Self-defence Corps and I was elected its platoon leader. Obviously, all this sort of thing was unpaid. That was in April, and then all the landlords began running away to Yenan.

In the daytime, the landlords sent out their armed corps, Ming Tuan, to plunder our corn. But there was the Self-defence Corps then and that co-operated with the guerrillas. We gave the guerrillas infor-mation about the enemy and they helped us protect our corn and hide it.

In October 1934 we organized a committee to divide up the land in the village of Liu Ling. There were seven members on the committee. Tung Chi-hwei was chairman. He was Tung Yang-chen's father and the landlords cut his head off. That happened in 1936, as far as I remem-ber. Li Yu-tse was the one who wanted to have him killed and Li Han-hua was the commander of the brigade that captured him and executed him. He was taken to Yenan and kept there imprisoned for a while, before his head was cut off. The other members of the land distribution committee were Ma Hai-hsiu, Li Fung-hua, who died last year and was Li Hai-kuei's father, Tsao Yiu-fa, who is a herdsman now and Tsao Chen-kuei's father, Ai Ke-liang, who is a herdsman too now, and Ho Chan-yu. This last died of some disease in 1953 or 1954. He had no relatives in the village here and his widow remarried to another village. Besides them, I, too, was a member of the committee.

There were about ten families in the village here, and everyone got land. We also allotted land to the landowner's family. The land was divided up according to the size of the families and the landowner's family got exactly the amount due to it according to the number of persons in it. None of them was living here, but in 1936 Li Hsiu-tang moved out here. He hired day labourers to work his land. His father, Li Yu-tse, was still alive then. He did not die till 1937 or 1938, in the time of the United Front.

Most families were happy to have been given land, but some of them were worried. They did not believe that we could keep power.

'When the landlords come back, we shan't be able to carry away the land we have been allotted,' they said. But, then, gradually they became calmer, as they saw that the power of the landlords was beginning to be broken.

There were nine of us in our family, and we got 100 mu. Those years, life was better than it had been before. Now, after this land reform, I was more politically minded than I had been, and, in August 1935, I joined the party. Then came the period of the United Front during the war with Japan, and up to 1947 there was no hard class struggle out in the countryside, but we helped each other. I was leader of the Self-defence Corps in Liu Ling village all this time. In 1947, when Hu Tsung-nan was approaching Yenan, I was commander of the People's militia in Liu Ling. Our task was, in the event of war, to send food, information and drinking water to the guerrillas. We were the guerrillas' base. In peacetime we were to maintain order in the village, and be responsible for security and on our watch against spies and saboteurs.

One month before Hu Tsung-nan came, a big conference was held in Yenan. All the different local commanders of the people's militia attended. General Chu Teh talked to us, describing the country's military and political situation. He told us that Mao Tse-tung had said: 'Keep Yenan, lose Yenan. Give up Yenan, win Yenan.' To begin with, we did not understand that. How could we keep Yenan by surrendering Yenan? There was a long discussion, and we got up and said that we thought this was wrong. The right thing would be to defend Yenan. But, in the course of the discussion, Chu Teh told us not to be anxious. It was not a question of giving up Yenan for good, but only of making a temporary withdrawal in order to entice Hu Tsung-nan into a trap. 'We are coming back. I promise that,' he said. We had a long discussion and gradually we agreed. 'Hu Tsung-nan is going to be our transport company,' Chu Teh said. 'He is bringing up modern weapons for us.' Then we made a detailed survey of the situation and decided on proper operational plans for our coming work under the occupation. After that, meetings were held with the military representatives in the hsien administration. There we received our orders. This meeting was held ten days before Hu Tsung-nan moved into Yenan. Different ones of us were given different duties. Each one of us was made responsible for his part of the fight.

We had to explain all this to the people, when we got back to Liu Ling. It was not easy. Most people were apprehensive, but we explained the position and quoted what Chu Teh had told us that Mao Tse-tung had said. We tried to explain to them the necessity of surrendering Yenan. It took a long time and some were never entirely convinced. But, in the end, when they saw our troops retreating through the village, they dug pits and buried their corn.

When the K.M.T. marched into the village, the villagers had all fled up into the hills. I myself returned to Liu Ling on 1 May. All the caves were destroyed; that is to say, the doors and window walls had been removed, the timber taken as firewood, so that the caves were little better than dens. As more and more of us came back, we crowded together in the actual village of Liu Ling on Naopanshan. No one dared live on his own, but we lived three or five families to a cave. The K.M.T. soldiers plundered and raped. Here, Chang Chen-pong's wife was raped. She died. He moved to Seven-mile Village. Jen Teh-wan's wife had a girl, her cousin's wife, living with her and she too was raped. It was safest to live together. Before Hu Tsung-nan came, when we were still working to explain to people what the soldiers were really like, many of the villagers had thought they must be quite ordinary people and that it would be all right to live under K.M.T. rule as well. But when the troops did come, they were just as brutal as we had said, and they were guilty of just the violent deeds we had said they would do, and everybody united and spontaneously sought contact with the guerrillas. People were beginning to hate the K.M.T., as they had not done before they had seen them.

When I saw the K.M.T. troops, I thought that there were so incredibly many of them, and sometimes I wondered if we really were going to be able to crush them. People compared them with our own army. No soldier in our Red Army had ever hit people, and none of our soldiers had ever sworn at people. One compared the two armies, and we heard about the first victories.

Li Hsiu-tang stayed on in Liu Ling when we were told Hu Tsung-nan was coming. He went to welcome the K.M.T. troops with boiling water. Then he went to the town. He worked in Yenan for their intelligence service, as a secret agent. He was in the police troops. Well, he was Li Yu-tse's son.

Tuan Fu-yin also stayed on in the village. When he saw Hu Tsung-nan's troops, he thought that the Red Army was finished and that the K.M.T. was victorious and would stay for ever. Tuan Fu-yin worked for the K.M.T. He was appointed K.M.T. leader for Liu Ling village. He gave information to Hu Tsung-nan's police about who were communists and who were not. He informed against the political commissar in our hsiang, Kao She-chi, who lived in Hsiao-chiayuantsa, ten li from here. The K.M.T. arrested him on Tuan Fu-yin's information and tied him to a tree and began flogging him. Then people said: 'He is not from the Eighth Route Army. He isn't a communist. Why are you flogging him? He is just an ordinary farmer.' Everybody said they would go guarantee for him. At first, the K.M.T. wanted to hang him and kill him straight away, but people swore that Kao She-chi had not been a Red; so then they decided to investigate further and took him to a cave, where he was to be kept till their superior officers came. But in the twilight he managed to get loose and went off into the hills. The K.M.T. security police were sitting in another cave. They had thought he was securely tied. He got up into the hills, but having been flogged had made him sickly and he died in August 1947. I used to know him well. We were good friends. He was a farmer from the district here and was the political manager for our hsiang.

Well, after a time, even the K.M.T. had had enough of Tuan Fu-yin. He had always been a liar and now he had lied to ingratiate himself with the K.M.T. In the end, they chucked him out, and he had to go back to being a vegetable hawker. He has always been a weak, lying wretch. When the K.M.T. withdrew, he fled with them, but we found him in Lochuan, when we liberated the town, and condemned him to three years. That was in April 1948. His wife went on living in Liu Ling. When he was released in 1950, he stayed on in Lochuan. His wife used to go down there to see him. He came back here in the end, in 1960, and since then the social care has had to look after him. He can't really work any more, you see. Well, his family had fled to the hills when the K.M.T. came and his cave was as well plundered as all the others; but he thought that the K.M.T. had won, that was all. He has always been stupid and short-sighted and tried to lie his way out of difficulties. When he was young, he was a street-seller in Yenan. That's what he has always been happiest at. Both his sons are working. One is a blacksmith and the other works with textiles.

During the occupation we in the people's militia fought the K.M.T. We called it 'the sparrow-war'. We worked in small groups, and whenever we came across an enemy soldier on his own, we killed him or took him prisoner. Here, we captured ten K.M.T. soldiers. Most were security agents. We knew them. When one of them came to the village, we smiled friendlily and invited him into a cave. They were always ready to eat and drink. We then gave him lots to eat and lots of spirits to drink. We kept pouring out more for him and laughed at everything he said, because then he enjoyed himself and joked a lot. Then, all at once, we held a spear to his back, tied him up and sent him up to the guerrillas. They did the interrogation and then sent the prisoner on to our safe area, where prisoners were kept for three or five months to be re-educated. Some of them then joined us and some were sent back to their villages. Every time we were asked about one of these security police who had disappeared, we replied that we had not seen him in our village; that he must have got somewhere else. They couldn't do anything.

(Chang Shi-ming was tired and breathless. He seemed feverish. Because of the state of his health, I did not want to press him and the rest of the interview was got through in a couple of minutes. J.M.)

In 1955 I joined Liu Ling Farmers' Co-operative. In 1956 we formed the East Shines Red Higher Agricultural Co-operative. In 1958 we formed Liu Ling People's Commune. In 1959 I began working in the grain office in Yenan hsien. I was to help with grain purchases. Had my work in one office. I was pensioned from that one year ago. There was no special reason for that. Now I'm working in the labour group for vegetable cultivation.

People say of Chang Shi-ming: He is greatly respected. He works hard. His health is bad and the chairman of the labour group for vegetable cultivation, Ching Chung-ying, has told him to take it easy and to stop working. But Chang Shi-ming just says: 'Work does no harm.'

His wife says that he has tuberculosis. 'He wasn't allowed to go on working in the grain bureau because of his tuberculosis. They wanted him to stay at home, lying down resting. But he won't.'

Part III
Liu Ling Village Labour Group

Tung Yang-chen, the martyr's son, K.M.T. deserter, aged 35

I was born in the village of Liu Ling. I don't remember much about my childhood. I was told that my father was taken by the white bandits and beheaded, and I used to think that when I was big I would exact vengeance. But I don't know if anyone really ever got hold of those who killed Father. That's all so long ago now. I don't know much about him. Most of those who knew him are dead.

I grew up during the time of the Shensi-Kansu-Ningsia Frontier Region. The land had all been divided up and we had twenty mu down in the valley. It was good land. We had land up on the hillside as well. Our family consisted of my grandmother, stepfather, mother and I. As a child, I herded the cattle. When I was fifteen, I began working in the fields. We had two donkeys and four oxen. We had just enough to give us food and clothes for our bodies. Right up to 1947, each year was filled with hard work. As I said, our work gave us exactly enough so that we could manage. I used to go into Yenan now and again to shop and see opera. They had just started the song-and-dance troupes then. They sang and danced and had short sketches about different things. But I didn't like them, I don't remember any sketch I saw that I liked. The old people say the same. We never go to see the song-and-dance pieces. We go to the opera or to the cinema. Then someone came and told us that General Hu Tsung-nan was coming. 'It's not true,' Stepfather said. But they replied: 'Yes, it is true. Now, Hu Tsung-nan's troops are coming.'

I was sent to Wayapo with our two donkeys. That was in February. There I was captured by K.M.T. soldiers. I was going along the high road, when four soldiers came along. They took hold of me and two of them hit me and said: 'You are an old Eighter'—a communist from the Eighth Route Army. Then they put a muzzle on me. Someone said that they ought to kill me, but they didn't, but made me be their porter. They disappeared with the donkeys. I don't know what they did with them. That was how I became a porter for Hu Tsung-nan's troops. I had to carry seventy-five jin of wheaten flour and an overcoat. At times I had to go from seventy to eighty li a day. Many of us farmers and villagers were caught and became porters. Guards with rifles walked behind us. There were seven guards. I was hungry the whole time, didn't get food and wanted to run away. But I saw what happened to those who tried to run away.

I had a friend from Wayapo, who was called Liu Ying-kwei and was twenty-two years old. He was taken the same day as I, and we worked together. When we got to Lochuan he thought he had had enough of being a porter and he did a bunk. He was caught the next day, and then we porters were assembled. There were twelve of us. The officer said: 'Liu Ying-kwei ran away from us. Now we are going to shoot him.' Then they shot him. Afterwards, the officer said: 'Does anybody else want to run away?' We were all very afraid and answered: 'No, no!' After that I stopped thinking of running away.

In April, all eleven of us were made soldiers. That was in Pinglian and we were in cantonments there for two months. We were given uniforms and rifles. We ought to have been paid for being porters, but we never saw the money. The officers took all the money. Our platoon commander was called Liu. He was a bad-tempered man; he hit people when he was angry. I was often beaten. Sometimes he hit me with a stick, and sometimes he took my rifle and hit me with that. I was hit the most of us eleven new ones. Then we began to march. We marched and marched and everywhere we ate up all the villagers' pigs and poultry. After all, we were hungry too. Then we heard that the Eighth Route Army had taken Yulin. We fought against the Eighth Route Army in Sachiatien. We lost many men. Now we had to recruit new soldiers, and we became veterans. Now we were no longer watched so much; it was we who guarded the new ones. Then we marched on Yenan and we ate up all the goats on the way. We reached Yenan on 13 August. We spent the night in a village just north of Yenan. The one where the pottery is. We thought we were going to be allowed to rest there. But in the night between 14 and 15 August we got orders to break up and march on.

As we marched off, I said that I had to shit and walked out into the kaoliang field with my rifle and squatted. That was in the middle of the night and it was dark. When I had finished and stood up again, they had all marched off and I was alone. So I deserted and went up into the hills. I knew all the paths round here from my childhood. I got back to Liu Ling village that night. When Mother caught sight of me, she laughed and then she cried and then she laughed again. She got my old clothes out, and I changed. After that I made a bundle of my rifle and uniform and went up into the hills. I had told my mother: 'Don't say anything to anyone in the village about my coming back.'

I buried my rifle and uniform, because I didn't want Mother to have them in her cave. Someone could have come and seen them and then the K.M.T. would have shot her. After that I stayed hidden up in the hills the whole time. They used to come up with food for me from the family now and again. Then Hu Tsung-nan withdrew and I came back to Liu Ling and began working in the fields again.

That was a difficult spring and a lot had been destroyed during the occupation. But the work went on as usual. We did at least have seed to sow. Hu Tsung-nan had not found all our grain. The harvest that year was not all that good. But we managed. Then I too joined the labour exchange group. We exchanged one person's work for another's. That was done on a private basis. I hadn't an elected function there. Then we

89

discussed the formation of a labour group for mutual help. I joined. We were all of us agreed. It wasn't a farmers' co-operative, but each one kept his land. We got bigger harvests than before. The problem, of course, was whose land should be tilled first. We decided to take turns. But that did not always work.

Then we began discussing a farmers' co-operative. Most agreed to turn the labour group for mutual help into a farmers' co-operative; but I thought that as I had both animals and land, I ought to be able to manage on my own, and that if I was in want of labour, I could perfectly well hire people. So I said that I had no use for any sort of farmers' co-operative. I kept my independence and worked for myself on my own land.

Then, little by little, people came to me and talked to me. They said: 'Your father had his head cut off by the K.M.T. and you were taken by the K.M.T. and you were made to carry sacks of flour for Hu Tsung-nan's army and were put into their army. When you were a child, you said that you wanted to take vengeance because of your father, but now you want to employ people and become an exploiter yourself. What's the meaning of this?' Then they talked about the advantages of the farmers' co-operative. It was mostly the Old Secretary, Li Yiu-hua, and Ma Juei-ching who talked with me. For a long time I thought about what they had said, and in the end I did see that it was probably best for me to join the farmers' co-operative.

My income increased too, once I did join, because, when I farmed on my own, I had had to hire people and that was difficult and expensive, and when at the end of the year I reckoned it all up, I found that my income was greater now as a member of the farmers' co-operative than in the days when I worked on my own.

Then they began discussing the formation of a higher agricultural co-operative. To begin with I was not at all convinced. I was thinking of the land. We had had good land. In the co-operative we had still had a certain return from our land; but in these discussions it was being said that each should be paid in accordance with the work he did. Not for anything else. Again it was the Old Secretary, Li Yiu-hua, and Ma Juei-ching, Ching Chung-ying and Tsao Chen-kuei who did most of the agitation for this reorganization. I listened to them and thought about it a lot. Then I heard that the party wanted us to form a higher agricultural co-operative and in the end I did apply for membership. But I wasn't elected to anything there either. My income in the

East Shines Red Higher Agricultural Co-operative that first year was 200 jin of corn more than it had been in the first farmers' co-operative. That was a big income.

In 1958 there was a new thing. People were talking then about a people's commune. I decided then, at the very beginning, that I would first hear what the party said and follow it and not argue. Because the party had always been right before. So I just voted yes for the people's commune and left it at that. In the autumn of 1961 I was elected deputy labour leader for Liu Ling Village Labour Group. I was very moved that people had confidence in me. I wanted to work better and show more enthusiasm, and if I planned my work properly and worked hard myself, it would mean that everyone achieved prosperity and happiness.

My task now is being responsible for agricultural production within the labour group. It isn't an easy job. As labour leader one has to have patience. Some of the members are pleasant, others aren't. Some are apathetic and have to be persuaded to work. The work, of course, has to be uniform. As labour leader I have much more to do than when I was an ordinary worker member. I have to organize all the work, get the people out to the fields every day, see that the ploughing and weeding is done properly. In the afternoons I plan the next day's work. I do that while I am working. I think as I go along. Before the others go home for the day, I tell them what has to be done the next day. In that way, they all know what they are to do. Sometimes they have different ideas and suggest that the work be done in a different way; sometimes they think I'm wrong. If so, they point this out to me, but they don't protest against my instructions. After all, I was elected labour leader and it is I who bear the responsibility. Being labour leader is an honorary position of trust.

Most of the members are decent people. Not all, but most. They say: 'Of course, we'll manage to get that field ploughed.' That helps me. Any big questions are always discussed at our meetings. The difficult thing, where I am concerned, is that I can neither read nor write. I have taken part in literacy courses and I did learn a few characters, but I forget them again at once. It's not easy to learn anything once you're grown-up.

The days pass in work. If you look at how the last few days have been for me, you'll know what almost all our weeks are like. The only things that alter are the seasons and the jobs we do.

Sunday, 26 August 1962

04.30 Alarm bell rings. My wife and I get up. I smoke a pipe of home-grown tobacco. We don't have anything to eat. I don't even have a glass of warm water in the morning. Then I go out and see that people get off to their work. Ten of them are to plough the wheatfields up on Loushan. Fifteen are to weed. I myself go with the ploughers.

08.00 The food-fetcher brings our breakfasts. This is our first meal of the day. One man in the team is detailed to collect all our breakfast dishes. He goes from household to household. We take it in turn to do this. The one who is doing it, of course, begins work later. He gets his work points for fetching our food. It isn't so easy carrying breakfast dishes with food for ten people.

12.00 We stop our morning's work. We drive the oxen down. They are tired now and need rest. Then we ourselves go home to eat and rest. My wife has food ready. After eating, I sleep for half an hour.

14.00 In the afternoon the ploughers get up potatoes. The others go on weeding.

19.30 When work is over for the day, we go home. I fetch four buckets of water from the well. Then I eat. Then we all go to bed.

Monday, 27 August 1962

04.30 Get up, smoke, ten for ploughing, fifteen for weeding.

08.00 Breakfast.

12.00 Bring oxen down, have dinner, half an hour's sleep.

14.00 All getting up potatoes.

19.20 Potatoes all up. Leader of the labour group, Li Hung-fu, returns from a meeting of the committee of Liu Ling's labour brigade. We hold a labour group meeting in the fields.

Li Hung-fu reports on the committee meeting. We had had our labour group's committee meeting a couple of days earlier, on the 23rd I think. After a short discussion, we agree to the suggestions of the brigade committee. Then we divide up the potato harvest. It is a clear starry night and we don't have to fetch paraffin lamps. After this, everyone goes home taking his potatoes, has supper and goes straight to bed.

Tuesday, 28 August 1962

04.30 Get up, smoke, ten on ploughing, fifteen on weeding.

08.00 Breakfast.

12.00 Dinner. Rest.

14.00 All twenty-five on weeding.
19.00 Home, fetch water, have supper, sleep.

Wednesday, 29 August 1962
04.30 Get up, smoke, ten on ploughing, fifteen on weeding.
08.00 Breakfast.
12.00 Dinner, rest.
14.00 Everybody on weeding.
16.30 Rain, can't work, sit in lee of a mound and wait for it to clear.
Rain does not stop, just gets harder.
17.00 Go home, work stops, raining too much. Stay in cave. Sit on
kang, resting.
19.30 Supper. Sleep.

Thursday, 30 August 1962
04.30 Get up, smoke, ten on ploughing, fifteen on weeding.
08.00 Breakfast.
12.00 Dinner, rest.
14.00 Everybody on weeding.
19.00 Home, fetch water, have supper, sleep.

Friday, 31 August 1962
This is my free day this week. I can do what I like.
04.30 Get up, smoke, fetch four buckets of water, sweep the yard in
front of the cave, go down and see to my private plot of land.
08.00 Home to the cave for breakfast.
09.00 Down to my private plot. Weeding, till it becomes too dark to
work.
19.00 Home, have supper, sleep.

There are no mornings when we sleep in. We don't do that in this
part of the country. In the busiest time, harvest-time, we don't take
our days off. We save them up till later in the year. No, I don't normally go and visit our neighbours in the village. After all, I see them
out in the fields every day, so I don't need to visit them in the evenings
as well.

It's in the winter that we rest. We collect fuel then. Either sticks
and dry wood that we find, or we hack up a little coal. Actually the
children are supposed to sweep in front of the cave, but they do it badly
and skimp if they can, and when I see that, I do it myself. We bought a
bicycle in 1960, and we bought a two-wheeled cart with rubber tyres

in 1961. I had been thinking of buying a bicycle for a long time. It is easier to get into the town if you have a bicycle. I ride the bicycle. My wife could not bicycle when we bought it. I have tried to teach her, but she still can't get on without help. I keep the bicycle up in the cave. I get it out when we want to go in to Yenan, then I take her, if she's coming too.

I bicycle into Yenan twice a month. Then I go to the opera. If there's a good opera in Yenan, we stop work at half past five. Perhaps we decide that the whole team will go to the opera. We ride in on seven or eight bicycles, each of us taking a passenger. I usually ride in with the other chaps, but now and again I take my wife and the children. Mostly she does not want to come. She wants to stay with our youngest. She won't take it to the opera. It's such a business. The older children like films best. None of us like song-and-dance. But when there's a film in the village, even Granny goes to it.

The years pass; they are all like one another. We begin with the spring ploughing and continue with it for a month. Then we sow millet, then kaoliang and maize. We plough for the two different kinds of 'sticky millet', that takes ten days, then we sow. We turn the soil for buckwheat and sow buckwheat. Then we begin weeding the fields, and we keep on with that the whole time till we harvest, one field after the other, and then we begin again with the first field. We harvest the wheat and bring it down off the hillside. We begin threshing the wheat and ploughing up the wheatfields. We sow wheat and harvest buckwheat and then the two kinds of 'sticky millet', millet, maize and beans. We bring our harvest down off the hillside. We use carrying-poles to carry it. We thresh, and finish threshing towards the end of the year. Then in January we have winter and then we rest and gather fuel and that sort of thing, unless there's some water-regulating work or something else on the go, and after that we begin the year with ploughing again.

In October we begin preparing the production plan for the next year. That's about all. Now and again we help on water regulation. Harder some years, not so hard others. During the winter twenty men are on repairing and maintaining the terraces we built before. We aren't making anything new this year; and we didn't make anything new last year either. We are just trying to keep it all in good order.

Life goes on. I have four children now. One girl goes to school; she's ten. I have a boy who's eight and a girl who is a hundred days. I also have a daughter of twelve; she went to school for one year, but the teachers sent her home. They said she was too stupid to go to school. That's all.

People say of Tung Yang-chen: Theirs is the biggest and finest cave in Liu Ling. It belonged to Li Hsiu-tang's father, Li Yu-tse. Tung Yang-chen's family was given it, because Tung Chi-hwei, Tung Chang-chen's father, was a hero and a martyr. Everybody loved Tung Chi-hwei. He did so much. He was one of the poor people's leaders and because he was beheaded, when the Red Army came back and was victorious, the biggest cave in the village was allotted to his family. His widow then married Chang Shi-ming.

The Tung Yang-chens aren't so well liked. They had the best land in the valley after it was divided up. They had the biggest caves, three big caves. Well, people don't dislike Tung Yang-chen, but his grandmother, Li Fong-lan, who is The Old Secretary, Li Yiu-hua's, older sister, is very obstinate. She has had the say in that family. She didn't like handing over their land to a collective.

Tung Yang-chen works hard. He always has. He is a good worker. His wife, Kao Kuei-fang, also works very hard. She can carry 100 jin on a carrying-pole. She isn't liked either. Her tongue is so sharp. The women won't talk with her. What she says is so hard and her voice so shrill. Tung Yang-chen's second daughter, Tung Er-wa, doesn't go to school, but is at home looking after the house, because her grandmother is too old now.

Chang Chung-liang, book-keeper, aged 33

WE come from Yulin. I went to school during one winter. That was when I was nine. Mother says that my father was a day-labourer. I myself don't remember him. When I was twelve, Mother got married again to a coalminer. Mother has told me that Father had once borrowed money. He could not pay the interest in time, so just before New Year the moneylender came and took our iron cooking-pot. Mother wept and we were unable to cook anything. Mother told me that herself. I don't remember anything from that time.

My stepfather was a coalminer. He had to sweat hard, and his wage was small. We lived on millet porridge. My uncle told me about the war against Japan. He was a pedlar. I myself saw Japanese bombers fly over our house, when they were on their way to Yenan to bomb it. They flew in a line, like birds. People looked at them and said: 'The Chinese people cannot be subdued by the Japanese.' It was said that the Japanese killed people as one slaughters animals. I wondered why the Japanese hated us Chinese so much. The way they behaved wasn't human. We had never done them any harm.

People said: 'The Eighth Route Army is strong. It will stand up to the Japanese.' I wondered if the Japanese were going to come and occupy us. I wondered, too, whether I shouldn't try to go to Yenan and become a soldier. I was young. When I was nineteen, and the war against Japan was over and the new war against the K.M.T. was going on and Hu Tsung-nan had had to get out of Yenan, we moved here. We had nothing left up in Yulin then. Hu Tsung-nan's troops had marched past that way and had taken our donkey and 300 jin of corn. They had slaughtered and eaten our pig and our goat. My uncle was living in Yenan, and as we had nothing left in Yulin any more, and Yenan had been freed, we walked to Yenan to search for my uncle.

He was living in Shachiakou. We got there after walking for ten days. I went into the cave first. Grandmother saw me and said: 'Has your mother come?' 'Yes,' I said. Then they all laughed and were glad, and Grandmother wept. They fetched Mother into the cave and seated her on the kang. She was very tired after walking from Yulin. Her feet were sore and her legs ached, she said.

That autumn of 1945, we stayed two months with my uncle. After that he found us an abandoned cave which we put in order, and, in January 1949, we began gathering firewood for him. He helped us a lot. In the summer of 1949, we were given land and an ox, and that gave us a lot of grain to eat. The family then consisted of Mother, Stepfather, me and my wife and my small brother and my little sister. We had got our land from Uncle. Another uncle had died the year before, and now we were given twenty-five mu to cultivate. Uncle gave us this without payment, of course. There was no mention of buying the land from him. We had a good harvest and things began to look brighter.

In 1949 a labour exchange group was formed. I had an older cousin living in Liu Ling. He's dead now. He came over to us to ask about Yulin and hear what things were like up there. Then he said to me: 'There's a lot of land to be brought into cultivation at Liu Ling. You can break as much new land there as you like.' My stepfather, my mother and my little sister stayed on in Shachiakou, while I and my wife and my young brother went to Liu Ling.

Here, I began breaking new ground up on the hillside. I joined the labour exchange group. People thought it better to work together, that that made the work easier, and that evening came quicker, if several of you were working together, than if you were working quite alone. To begin with, the group was not organized on a permanent basis, but was a direct agreement between the members to exchange their labour. In 1951 we decided to reorganize the group and put it on a permanent basis as a labour group for mutual help. Ma Juei-ching was its leader. The work went well, but there were lots of quarrels about whose land should be taken first. It was difficult to solve all these problems. Some said: 'Why should his field be taken first? I've got a heavier crop. It ought to be my turn now.' Whatever we did, this went on; so then we began talking about forming a farmers' co-operative. There was Li Yiu-hua's Farmers' Co-operative on the other side of the valley. They were doing better and better. We discussed this. First, we decided to form our own farmers' co-operative, then we joined Li

Yiu-hua's Farmers' Co-operative, which then changed its name to Liu Ling Farmers' Co-operative.

In 1955 Hutoma Village and Wangchiakou Village were also incorporated. We then formed the East Shines Red Higher Agricultural Co-operative. Our incomes had been rising the whole time, so the others had confidence in us. But, of course, there were also some who were against this development. For example, Chen Hung-liang in Hutoma Village. He had a lot of animals, three oxen, two donkeys, and there were two working in the family and only four mouths to feed. He had good fertile land down in the valley. He did not want to join at all; but then people worked out for him in detail how much bigger his income would be in the higher agricultural co-operative, so that in the end he too applied for membership.

In 1954 we formed Liu Ling People's Commune. A people's commune is a coalition of economic organizations. It makes it possible to employ greater labour resources, where these are needed. By this, one can make greater efforts and employ all one's force on one given point, which is much more efficient. We were now able to carry out more jobs that required capital. Our consciousness also increased. The labour groups worked better and we were able to decide to take care of those families which were in need of help.

In December 1958 I was elected book-keeper for Liu Ling Village Labour Group. I had kept the work daybook and the record of people's labour points in the labour group for mutual help. I am now responsible for keeping both the cash book and the grain book. I have to render statements every month to the labour group. But I am only responsible for the books, not for the actual money or grain. The treasurer is in charge of the stores and the cash, and he keeps his own books of what he has in cash and in store. Our two sets of books have to agree. We often check them.

If payments have to be made, Li Hai-ching, who is the one responsible for our finances, signs the bill; I enter the amount in my books and the treasurer pays the amount from his cash and enters the amount in his own books. When in-payments are made, we have to inform Li Hai-ching as well.

This work of mine as book-keeper is, of course, an honorary job, but at the same time it is a lot of work. I am credited with one and a half days' work for it, that is fifteen work points, for the months when there is a lot of work, and ten work points for the months when there is less work. As far as I have been able to see, this is fair. It corresponds more or less to the time I put into keeping the books. I use the evenings and night-time for this work.

I never went to school for more than that one winter, when I was nine; but since then I have attended several reading courses. In addition, I have learned by doing the work. I was compelled to learn quite a bit, while I was keeping the work journal and the record of labour points for the labour group for mutual help. I have also had to learn a lot as book-keeper. I can now read the newspaper and write letters. I can also read simpler books of fiction. I stick most to serial stories in parts with lots of pictures and a few simple characters on each page. The pictures make it possible to understand the characters I don't know.

I am very fond of films. Opera and that sort of thing doesn't appeal to me so much. Opera is a bit old-fashioned. Films have much more variety, more themes, more reality and much more that is funny and makes you laugh. I usually go to the cinema or opera once every ten days. We often have films in Liu Ling; but mostly I take myself into the town. Sometimes I go in with my wife and my eight-year-old son, my other children are far too small to appreciate going to the cinema. But, sometimes, when we have finished work for the day, someone will say: 'Come on, let's ride into town and go to the cinema.' Then we jump on to our bicycles and ride off.

The management committee of the labour group consists of five people. They are elected at the annual meeting of the labour group's members. Usually, it is people who are known to be good workers and to be knowledgeable about farming, and who have the reputation of being fair and honest, who are elected. After the past year's work has been discussed, the committee for the coming year is elected. The labour group has a members' meeting once a month or so. At these, anything can be discussed. The annual meeting is really a number of meetings held together at the end of the year.

First, we have a meeting to elect our delegate to the Liu Ling Labour Brigade's representatives. At this meeting we discuss the opinions the labour group wants ventilated at the meeting of the representatives. A couple of days after the meeting of the representatives, the labour group summons its members for a further meeting. At this the delegate to the representatives reports what was discussed and what was decided at the meeting of the representatives. After this, the chairman of the management committee of the labour group reports on the year's production and on what has been accomplished during the year. Then I inform them of the year's balance and report in detail on the economic situation. Then the member from our labour group who sits on Liu Ling Labour Brigade's supervisory committee reports on how the auditors found our books and our cash and stores. He reports if the auditors have had occasion to criticize anything or if they have had to take action over anything. After that we have a long discussion. This is the longest meeting of the year. At it, everything has to be talked over. Last year, it went on for three days running. My mother was ill, so I had got permission to visit her, but the meeting was held just the same, and when I got back to Liu Ling the discussions were still going on and I attended the last bit of the meeting. There wasn't anything special; there usually isn't. There doesn't need to be any special question for discussion, but everything that has happened has to be gone through and all that has been done during the year.

At the end of the discussion, when the members have approved the committee's work—or made their criticisms—a new committee is elected. The way this is done is that, first, the chairman is elected, the one who will be labour leader, then the deputy leader is chosen and he also becomes deputy labour leader; then we elect the one who is to be financially responsible and supervise the economy and counter-sign everything, and, finally, the treasurer is elected. The committee is elected. The committee is never elected in a body. Each one is discussed thoroughly before he is elected. When the new committee is elected, the annual meeting is at an end. The committee then meets and discusses the production plan and the labour group's budget for the coming year. When this has been worked out, a new members' meeting is called, and the committee presents its proposals for the coming year's budget and work. The members' meeting discusses these proposals, perhaps changes something in them and thereafter the proposals are handed over to the committee of the labour brigade for approval.

If the committee of the labour brigade has no objections to make, the committee of the labour group again puts forward the year's budget and work plan at a further members' meeting and has them finally approved. If the labour brigade committee should not have approved the budget and work plan, they are referred back to a further members' meeting for discussion and then again laid before the committee of the labour brigade, and so on, until everyone is agreed. The members' meeting of the labour group does thus have the final word.

But this complication does not occur. We keep the labour brigade's committee informed; after all we have representatives on it and we are in continual contact with each other. This is just the way things would have to go in theory, if there should ever be a dispute between the labour group and the committee of the labour brigade. A lot of meetings are held at the turn of the year. There is not much work to do on the land, of course, and the members have time to discuss all questions thoroughly. Everyone wants to say what he thinks.

My wife is a member of the League of Youth, but I myself am neither in the party nor the League of Youth. I have never asked to join.

My cave is next to the office of Wang Kwang-yung, the treasurer of Liu Ling Labour Brigade. On the night of 13 July I heard him and the labour brigade's book-keeper, Lo Han-hong, starting to go through their books. They were discussing why the two books, the book-keeper's and the treasurer's, did not agree. I did not like that. It did not sound nice at all. They were talking so loudly that I could hear it in my cave, so I went straight up to Li Hai-tsai, who is the representative of our labour group on the supervisory committee. I spoke to neither Lo Han-hong nor Wang Kwang-yung nor anyone else, before I spoke with him. Li Hai-tsai then went to Mau Ke-yeh, president of the supervisory committee of Liu Ling Labour Brigade, and they decided that Li Hai-tsai, who can read, should go through the books. They both went down to Wang Kwang-yung's office and took the books. I had gone to bed. Then they checked every account and finally found the mistake. It wasn't embezzlement. It was negligence. On 16 July they came to me and reported what they had done and what they had found. After that it was brought up at a members' meeting.

People say of Chang Chung-liang: He's nothing special. On the whole he's an honest fellow. He isn't very strong. He does not like talking with people. He is by nature uncommunicative and something of a recluse. But he is decent and honest. He has always had the reputation of being prudent and considerate. His wife, Chi Mei-ying, is a member of the League of Youth. She jokes a lot and chatters all day long. Some years ago she attended a course and learned the new scientific methods of delivering babies. Latterly, she has been midwife and attended most of the births in the village. Because of her, most children now survive. She is very liked. Theirs is a happy marriage.

Kao Pin-ying, the one who was strung up, aged 37

IF it doesn't rain worse than it is now, the animals can come down from the hills. Otherwise, they will have to stay up there on the stubble they are ploughing. This soil becomes smooth and slippery if it rains too much, and then they can easily break their legs. But if they can just be kept fat, there is no great risk of their catching a chill. One has to look after them. Anyway, the rain's good. We need rain now.

I'm from Yulin hsien. There were four of us in the family: my parents, myself and a young uncle of mine. We worked as day-labourers and farmhands and life wasn't easy. We heard that the communists here in Yenan were letting people have all the new ground they could break, and that they could keep their crops without deduction. In 1942, my parents died. Then Li San-soi had a talk with me. He had gone down to Yenan in 1941. He had come to Yulin to fetch his family. He said that things were better in Yenan. The Eighth Route Army was a good army. There was a government in Yenan that did not just oppress the farmers. Breakers of new ground didn't need to pay any taxes for the first three years. They could even get help from the government. Then I talked with my uncle; he stayed in Yulin and I went to Yenan with all I possessed in a bundle on my back. I wanted to be my own master and not have anyone over me any more.

I came to the village of Loutzekou, sixty li from here. My grandfather lived there. Grandfather took me to the authorities and I was shown where I could clear land. I became a breaker of new land. I worked on my land and, in 1943, I got an interest-free loan from the co-operative society to enable me to buy an ox. I paid the loan back in 1944. I was enthusiastic and happy and put in a lot of work. I had my own land, I had cleared twenty to thirty mu of hill land myself, and I harvested 3,000 jin and lived in an abandoned cave in the village of Loutzekou. It was hard work and I liked it.

In February 1947, Hu Tsung-nan came. I had hidden all my corn and all my possessions, had buried them and then made off into the hills. When I came down again, the K.M.T. was in the village, they had discovered my corn and stolen all that I had. They ordered me to carry it myself to their H.Q. Then they said that I was from the Eighth Route Army. They tied my hands behind my back and tied a rope round my wrists and strung me up in a tree. My arms were twisted. It hurt. I hung free above the ground and couldn't touch it even with the tips of my toes. Then they said that I was a communist. They whipped me for two hours. I wanted to die.

When you are strung up in this way, your head falls forward and hangs down. They put mud on the nape of my neck, big clods of it. I was young and strong and I didn't faint. But it hurt and I begged them to shoot me and have done with it. But they wouldn't. Instead, they whipped me again, and then they went back to the village and investigated. They discovered that I was just an ordinary breaker of new land and not someone from the Eighth Route Army, so they let me down and told me to get off home.

When the K.M.T. let me go, I went home to my village. I went to my cave and lay down. I was quite alone and I rested on my kang for twenty days. It took a long time before I was fit again. You can see that I still have scars from my flogging all over my body. There was nothing to eat. My neighbours gave me a little food. I just lay quiet. I thought a lot then. I had not been afraid of Hu Tsung-nan's troops before. I had gone off into the hills, just because I did not want to be in the war. But there had been nothing to eat in the hills, and so I had gone back down to the village. I had thought that perhaps Hu Tsung-nan's troops might hit me in the face or swear at me, but one can stand that. I was just an ordinary breaker of new land. I had never taken part in politics, nor been interested in them either. I didn't think they could do anything to me. Yes, I had, of course, been a stretcher-bearer and I had laid mines.

I lay there in my cave thinking about this, and it took me twenty days before I was well enough to get up again. Then one day some guerrillas came to Loutzekou. They were from Shansi and they were led by Liu Shi-hsiu. I went up to him and said: 'I want to join the guerrillas.' That was in April 1947. I was accepted. After two days we left the village. We operated in the surrounding hsiang. One day the villagers let us know that the enemy was going to send out a patrol to plunder. It was to steal corn from the villages. We lay in ambush and captured four rifles and took five prisoners. One of the prisoners was a cook. The others ran away and escaped. We schooled them and then let them go, so that they should be able to tell about the Eighth Route Army's policy towards prisoners-of-war.

One day, when we were in Laoshan, that was in July or August, we heard that the enemy was supposed to be coming along the highway. We laid an ambush and I was on guard. Then I saw a man whom I suspected of reconnoitring for the enemy. I captured him and he was armed. The unit that had strung me up in the tree was the same as the one that was coming. He was from it. I looked at my prisoner and wondered if I should kill him. He had helped to string me up. But I didn't kill him. We were not supposed to do that in spite of everything. I took him prisoner and led him to our headquarters.

There, we questioned him about the enemy. The enemy seemed to be far too strong for our ambush to be successful. We withdrew and sent a message for the regular army. The regulars came in the afternoon. They were commanded by Wang Chang. After that, we wiped out the enemy. We had a meeting after the fight. The regulars praised the guerrillas for their good work and gave us a machine-gun with ammunition, a mortar and several boxes of ammunition, twelve rifles with ammunition and the dead enemies' overcoats. We hadn't had any uniforms before that.

In that fight the enemy lost about 400 men. Of those thirty were killed. The prisoners were re-trained. Some joined us; the others went home to their villages to tell what it was we wanted and how we had treated them. We ourselves hadn't had any losses. The regular army lost a couple, though.

After that the Eighth Route Army marched on Lochuan and we went to my village. We rested there for five days. We were so happy. We had taken a lot of booty. We had a big feast the first evening. We sang in the northern Shensi way. We made up our own words to the song. It's called, 'Walk with the Wind' and you have to make up your own words for it. We had lots of arms now and we all had a big feast, guerrillas and villagers together. Our leader made a speech about the fight and praised various people for what they had done. Then he started the song. He sang: 'The cocks are crowing and the dogs are barking. Our brothers the guerrillas have come back.' Each of us sang a verse. I myself sang: 'There by the ditch the oxen are drinking water and red flags are flying over the hills. I take my guerrilla comrades to my home, the millet gruel is cooking and the steamed bread is hot.'

After these five days we left the village. We had many fights. They were almost all the same. We took part in a fight almost every day. Our task was to protect the population of a certain area, to support the regular army in its struggle, to demoralize the enemy and obtain information about the enemy. I was only wounded once and it wasn't anything serious. I and a comrade were to reconnoitre one of the enemy's forts. We were discovered. That was at Maping Hill, twenty li from here, at the beginning of September. I had a shot wound in the foot. My comrades carried me away and then I was transported on an ox and I lay hidden in Maping for a fortnight. It was often difficult for the wounded. We couldn't take them with us, you see. But I was with a neighbour who had known me since before the war. Four men were killed in our group. We knew each other as one does in a group. Their names were Ho, Chang, Chi and Liu. At the beginning we were fifty, but towards the end we were eighty.

Later I was given a medal: 'Liberation of the Great North-west'. We who were in the guerrillas often meet. Only yesterday I met our leader, Liu Shi-hsiu, in the town. He is head of a labour brigade in another people's commune. But I never have met my tormentors again since the war. But one day in 1960, when I was working in the fields down here, somebody called me. I went up to the road, where two men were standing. They said that they were from the public pros-ecutor's office and had some photographs they wanted me to look at. They wondered if I recognized any of them. I recognized one of the men in those photographs. It was the one who had given the orders for my hands to be tied behind my back and that I was to be strung up and flogged. I had had time to see my fill of him in 1947, and I shall never forget his face. I told them what I knew about him. They said that now they had caught him and that he had confessed how many people he had had strung up and flogged and executed, and that they were now busy checking his confession. He had caused many people's deaths. They took down my evidence and said that they would get in touch with me, if I was needed, but evidently I wasn't needed to get him condemned, because I never heard from them again. But I was so glad when they showed me his photograph, because I knew then that he had been captured. Now I shall be avenged, I thought. I remembered what had happened and felt hatred in my heart, because it's awful to be strung up as I was.

We did not take part in any fights after March 1948, when Hu Tsung-nan withdrew. We were stationed in the village of Linchen. There we had discussions and meetings, we analysed the fights and studied. Some of us were taken into the regular army; the others were demobilized and allowed to go home. I wanted to join the regular army. I wanted to stay on in the army. I liked the life and at this time we were going ahead all over the country and many people were needed for the army. But they didn't accept me. I was an only son. They accepted only those who had brothers, and they told me that they could not take me, because I was the last of my family and, if I was killed, my family would have died out. I tried to talk them round, but I couldn't. I was demobilized as well.

When I got back to Loutzekou, I found that my neighbours had begun tilling my land. That wasn't a thing I wanted to discuss with them. We don't take land back. You see, I had handed it over to them in order to go to the war, and there was more land to clear. In the guerrillas I had heard that Liu Ling was a good place and I had also met a girl from Liu Ling, so I moved there in October 1948 and married in April 1949.

1. Liu Ling village

2. (*Top*) The old doctor, Kao Chia-jen, in front of his clinic
3. (*Bottom*) Li Ying-teh, farmer, and the Old Secretary, Li Yiu-hua

4. Ma Hai-hsiu, farmer

5. Mau Ke-yeh, the cave-builder

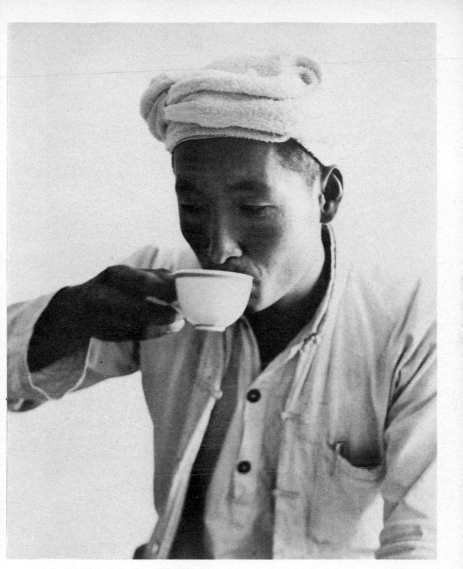

6. Li Hai-tsai, son of Li Yiu-hua

7. Ma Hung-tsai's wife

8. Li Hung-fu, battalion commander of the people's militia

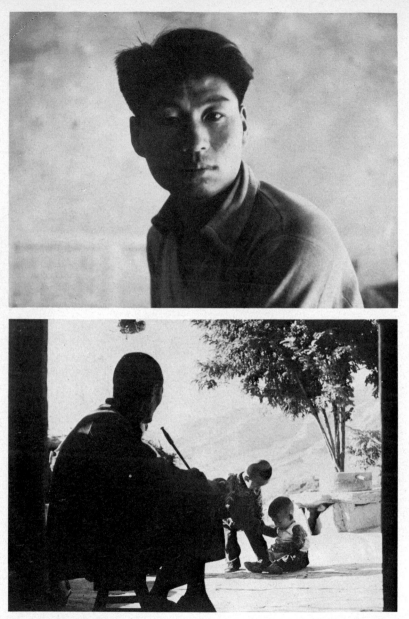

9. (*Top*) Han Ying-lin, the headmaster
10. (*Bottom*) Grandfather watching the grandchildren

11. Chang Shi-ming

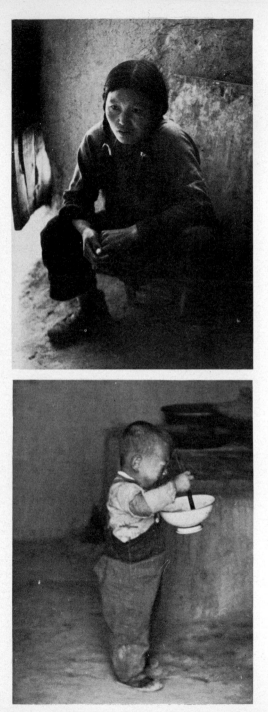

12. (*Top*) Tung Chi-fu
13. (*Bottom*) The little
Liu boy in Tu
Fang-lan's house

14. (*Top*) Autumn labour: ploughing for wheat
15. (*Bottom*) A plough

16. A street in the main part of Liu Ling

I began breaking new ground up on the hillside. I had to borrow a cave. It wasn't till 1955 that I had time to build one of my own. I joined the labour exchange group and the 1949 harvest was medium good. There were only two of us in my family, my wife and I, and I was the only one tilling the ground. That was hard. So I joined the labour group for mutual help. I did that in February 1950. Views were divided about the question in our labour exchange group. Four other families and I wanted to form a labour group for mutual help. None of us had land down in the valley and it was difficult for us to till the land alone and the labour exchange arrangements weren't enough. The other four were Jen Teh-wan, Ai Ke-kao and Chi Pei-fa, who all joined another labour group for mutual help, and Yang Yung-chien, who was Yang Kuei-ying's first husband and died a couple of years ago. He and I joined the same labour group for mutual help.

The others weren't so enthusiastic. Some were strongly against the whole thing. There's no need to mention names. Those are matters that don't need to be raked up now. It's all long ago and who they were is of no significance. They had better land and were afraid they would lose their land and preferred to be on their own. There were long discussions. People produced their reasons. I myself said: 'I cannot weed all the weeds in my fields by myself. It takes too long. Co-operation is better. Co-operation will make us strong.' Well, at all events we decided to form a labour group for mutual help in February 1950. There were fifteen families of us and we divided ourselves into two groups. I was leader of one group with seven families. They were Li Hung-fu, Li Hai-ching, Ma Hung-tsai, Li Hai-kuei, Yang Yung-chien and Li Hai-fu. Li Hai-fu and I ran the group. We discussed whose fields should be taken first. We took them in turn. The other group was led by Ma Juei-ching and Fu Hai-tsao. That year the harvest was good. We had no direct difficulties. I liked the work.

I joined Liu Ling's Farmers' Co-operative in 1954. There were long discussions about this for many days. At first I did not understand the point of a farmers' co-operative, but later I did see that it was right. I thought of how it had been when I was a day labourer, and I decided that now I ought not to think of working just for my own good, but that proper united action was needed now. Those most in favour of forming a farmers' co-operative were Li Hai-kuei, Li Hai-ching and Yang Yung-chien, all three of whom had fields on the hillside, and Ma Hung-tsai who had good land down in the valley.

Well, certain people did not want to be in on this, others were so enthusiastic that they raised both hands when we voted. Those in favour of the farmers' co-operative said that, in the old days, the owner of the land became rich and everyone else was poor, but now there was a new age, and now no one would be poor and no one would live on another's labour, but all would work and live well. Most of us, after all, had been farmhands, day labourers or poor tenant farmers, so we understood all that. But there were certain ones—the names are neither here nor there—who said: 'The more there are together, the worse it will just make things. Things have been all right as they are.' But, in the end, everyone was agreed and understood that with a farmers' co-operative there was no question of one gaining at the expense of another, but that all should achieve prosperity together.

At the first meeting, Ma Hai-hsiu was elected treasurer, but the next year, 1955, I was elected treasurer. My job was to be responsible for all cash, all grain and all stores. It is hard work, because you yourself are responsible for everything. One has to be very careful, especially careful as you are dealing with money and corn and tools and instruments, which are not even your own. I thought then that, as people were trusting me, I must be even more careful of their property than I had been of my own. For my work as treasurer I was credited with one day's work a month. All treasurers get the same. Labour leaders, however, get nothing extra.

In 1955 we talked of forming a higher agricultural co-operative. Most were for this. It was only a small minority that was against it. Li Hai-kuei talked with them; he explained to them why they ought to vote for the higher agricultural co-operative. Those who were against it did not like it that the higher agricultural co-operative would do away with the dividend on land. I don't remember how much it was. At any rate it was of no significance to me. Ten jin per mu per year or something like that, I believe it was. But, in the end, Li Hai-kuei persuaded them. I myself was for the higher agricultural co-operative from the very beginning. When I was a farmhand, I got only fifteen old dollars for a whole year's work, so I considered that the principle 'To each according to his work' was the only right one. Of course, it was one's own work that decided everything. Afterwards, we founded the East Shines Red Higher Agricultural Co-operative.

There was no mistrust of the people's commune among us. We considered it the only possibility. We had to develop our joint effort.

And that confirmed the principle 'To each according to his work'. That principle has never been changed with us. Before, the masters had cave after cave of corn, while the people went hungry. The people's commune was better, because it gave possibilities for better water-regulation works and terracing of the hillsides, more order in planting out trees, more cultivation of vegetables and more odd jobs. We in Liu Ling Labour Brigade have managed to carry out big water-regulation works and terracing thanks to the people's commune. My work as treasurer was not at all affected by the people's commune reform. It has been exactly the same all these eight years.

You see, I was never able to go to school as a child. So, one winter when there was not so much agricultural work, I decided to go to a literacy course. Now I can read the newspaper. I read *The Yenan Daily*. But I don't read it every day. I haven't time for that. The labour group subscribes to one copy of *The Yenan Daily*. We read certain articles aloud for the members who can't read, and then the paper goes the round of those who can read.

People say of Kao Pin-ying: He is good-looking, he is a cautious man and has a calm temperament. He was elected treasurer because he works hard and is very scrupulous. He often works cleaning out the shop and stores. He takes his job as treasurer very seriously and looks after the members' possessions in the best possible way. He dries the grain in the sun and actually puts considerably more work into his job than the day's work a month which he is credited with. He spends every free moment on it.

The women often joke with him because he is so cautious. He never hurries: 'Not even if the heavens fell would Kao Pin-ying lengthen his stride.' He is never nervous or anxious. He always thinks a long time and carefully.

His wife Liu Kuei-ying is tall and has bound feet, although she isn't more than thirty-eight. She is from the district. Before, she used to live with her mother, but her mother moved away. In 1959 she kept the labour diary for the women. She did that because the women's leader could not write at that time. She was very mistrustful. She had to write down the women's hours of effective work every day, and they came to her in the evenings to have their hours of work entered. But as the women often go to work in the morning a couple of hours late, she used to ask at what time they had really begun that morning. Then some replied: 'I began at sunrise.' But others said: 'No, she didn't. You see, Liu Kuei-ying was so mistrustful and scrupulous that the women liked making fun of her and getting her to write down, then have to cross it out and re-do it, and then cross that out and write it all over again. In the end, it reached such a pitch that Liu Kuei-ying no longer believed anyone. 'I went an hour later,' one woman might say. 'Have you any proper witnesses for that?' Liu Kuei-ying would ask. She is honest and she is strict and she is careful. There's nothing actually wrong with her. It's just that she doesn't like talking; she is taciturn and doesn't understand a joke.

Kao Pin-ying is henpecked. He is sat on by his wife. He is a kind man, but she is hard. He just smiles kindly at her, but she is like a storm. She was barren for a long time. They had no children. When she finally did have one some years ago, it was a daughter and then she had no milk. The child got goat's milk. But as Liu Kuei-ying didn't suckle it, she ought to have had another child long ago. She hopes to be able to give birth to a son, but it doesn't look as if anything is coming of it.

Actually, the women don't like her so much. She doesn't talk and she never jokes. 'She is one of those who does everything alone.' She isn't such a good worker either. She does her best, but that isn't so much. Besides she's far too finical.

Li Hai-yuan, the one who left the co-operative, aged 48

I AM from Hengshan. We were poor when I was growing up. Father worked on the land, and I helped at home till I was twelve. I never went to school. They didn't want people like us to learn to read and write. I can read a little now, but I learned that after my fortieth birthday. Before, I didn't know even one character. But at my age it isn't so easy to learn. I mean, it is easy to learn to recognize the characters, but it is difficult to remember how to write them and then one forgets easily. I'm always forgetting them.

At all events, I began earning as a farmhand, when I was twelve. I had my board and three silver dollars a year. It was a medium-sized landowner I worked for. I've forgotten his name, but it doesn't matter, landowners are all alike. I wasn't fully grown then, of course, so I wasn't good for a full day's work.

When I was eighteen, I began working for a landowner called Ma Tsu-chuan. I worked as a day labourer for him and at the same time I rented twenty mu from him. The rental was twenty-four jin a mu. I lived with my father then. I then took over my father's debt to Ma Tsu-chuan. It was fifty taels of silver. I don't know how much my father had borrowed to begin with, but my first memory of the debt as a child was that it was ten taels of silver. The interest was fifty per cent a year and with interest on interest and bad harvests we could never pay it back. Although we were paying and paying all the time, the debt grew bigger and bigger. We had too little land for it to pay to have an ox. It was bad land up there in Hengshan.

The taxes were heavy. We had to pay in cash twelve silver dollars a year. In 1931 we weren't able to pay. We just couldn't. Then soldiers came and took me. They put me in prison. Father had to go round to friends and relations and neighbours and beg money. In the end he got twelve silver dollars together. Then I was let out of prison. I early became responsible for the family. I had, of course, taken over Father's debt. But he did not die till 1954.

Then my brothers and my parents moved. The family split up. I took over the debt and the cave and 600 jin of grain, and the others were free of debt. After that they all moved to Yenan. I had Father's debt, so I was compelled to stay behind in Hengshan. I married and we had children—we worked hard. We had eleven children. Ten of them died. [He weeps.] Our eldest daughter died when she was eight. The others when they were seven, four, five and three. They all died. We were poor and we couldn't afford to have the doctor. Doctors weren't for people like us. The only one to survive the illness was my son, Li Te-chua. But it made him deaf and dull-witted. He went to school for four years. Now he's fifteen. He mostly gathers firewood. He's the only one of my family left now. Things were difficult for poor people. Hard work and big debts and nothing but hunger and illness all the time.

In 1945, I had a letter from my aunt, Li Fong-lan; she is Tung Yang-chen's grandmother. In that letter my aunt wrote: 'If life is hard for you, you should know that things are better here. If you come here, the communists will help you. There's land here. I'll help you and the communists won't let anyone who is willing to work starve.' But, of course, I had these fifty taels of silver to pay back, so I couldn't do anything. Ma Tsu-chuan had died, but his family was still there. Debts did not vanish so easily.

In the end, my aunt sent me an ox from Yenan. Oxen fetched high prices then. In that way she paid my debt and I became free. In the month of March according to the moon calendar of the year 1948 I went down to Yenan. When I got there I had a talk with my aunt. She said: 'I'll see you have a cave and food.' I was given some abandoned land and a pig. That was a very difficult year. Ma Hai-hsiu was leader of Liu Ling village then, and it was he who arranged that I got twenty mu of hill land. I didn't have to pay anything. I myself owned the land. In July that year my wife and son came here. They walked. All that we possessed then and had brought with us from Hengshan was an old quilt. We had had to sell the rest because of the debt.

Later, in the year 1949, everything was settled about my land in Liu Ling. I was given a stamped certificate and everything. But it had

been clear from the start that it was to be my own land. It was just that the formalities took time. Originally, Li Hsiu-tang's father had owned the land we took over. It was the first land we had owned. No one had cultivated it before. We were very happy. Before that we had never even dreamed of having our own land. Why should we? We didn't dream of anything. And if we didn't have quilts enough to keep out the winter's cold, we couldn't long for land of our own. That's how it was. But now that we had got land of our own, Father came to me and said: 'You should be grateful to the communists. Without them you would never have got this land. Before, things were just as hard winter and summer, and we worked and worked, but could never pay the land-owner. The debt just grew. Ten of your eleven children died. So be grateful to the communists.'

In 1948, I had begun with the spring work as soon as I came to Liu Ling, but I didn't have time to plough it all and that year my harvest was only 600 jin. But Aunt lent us corn, so that we were able to manage. In 1949, I got 1,200 jin and I didn't have to pay any taxes or other deductions, because breakers of new ground did not have to pay corn tax the first few years.

Then Li Yiu-hua spoke with me about joining his labour group for mutual help. 'You haven't enough corn,' he said. 'You cannot manage alone. It is only when there are several that one can do anything.' When, as I now did, I joined the labour group for mutual help, there were three members in my family. My parents were living with my elder brother, Li Hai-fu. My parents, my elder brother and my younger brother, Li Hai-ching, had all moved here in 1938 leaving me with the debt up there in Hengshan. To be honest, it was difficult for me to keep my family alive in Liu Ling too. We still had only one quilt. The land was not enough. I had been thinking of going out to work as a day labourer again, when Li Yiu-hua spoke with me and said: 'Now, you are to join my labour group for mutual help instead.' Well, I thought, that sounds all right.

My father, of course, was Li Yiu-hua's older brother. Now, Li Yiu-hua told us how we were going to work and how we were to share the income. I had less land and worse land than the other men, but Li Yiu-hua said that after the grain tax had been paid we were all to share the harvest alike. In that way, no one would lose anything, but all would gain. I thought that sounded all right.

That year was very slightly better. I had clothes to put on and enough corn to be able to eat the whole year. The following year we bought a new quilt. The third year, Li Yiu-hua's labour group for mutual help had four cattle and two donkeys. I was labour leader. We worked quite well together. I was the poorest of the four families in the labour group. Things went really well for us.

We worked harder than the others who had land down in the valley. We got up earlier and we rested less and went to bed later. Li Yiu-hua could work very hard and we were all prepared to work. We carried manure up to the fields on the hill. All of us, men and women, worked. We planted trees and we went to a lot of trouble. What was hard was that I had to be awake at night thinking how the work ought to be planned. A lot depended on everything being planned correctly. Hard work and sweat aren't enough by themselves; you also have to think what you are doing.

The fourth year, I had 2,400 jin of corn in store. And then our labour group was to be expanded. Then I thought that I could manage on my own. And if I left the labour group, I had the right to take my share of the common property, which would be two oxen, but if I stayed in the new farmers' co-operative, I should perhaps have more responsibility and have to rack my brains all night.

Li Hai-chun kept the accounts and I talked with him. After that I talked with Li Yiu-hua and the others and I said: 'If the whole village is going to come in, then I'm going out. The more people there are, the more of a burden it will be. More work for me. I shall wear myself out being labour leader. Besides it's not practical taking in all these villagers. Most of them can't work properly. So, if you decide to take the others in, I'm going to leave and take two oxen, and then I shall be able to manage without your help.'

My wife wanted this too. She had said to me: 'We have worked for so many years for landowners and got nothing; you've been a day labourer and possessed nothing. But we have land and two quilts and we have two oxen and it will be better if we manage on our own.' But Father and my brothers did not like me going out. Father talked to me and said: 'You ought not to go out, now that you've benefited from the communists. You came here a pauper and they helped you and you have worked together and you have been well off. It's not right that just you should leave.' But I said: 'I want to manage on my own, whatever you others say.'

Naturally, there was a lot of talk in Li Yiu-hua's Agricultural

Co-operative, as it was called before it changed its name to Liu Ling Agricultural Co-operative, when I left. Li Hai-chen said: 'If you don't like being labour leader, someone else can take on the responsibility, the main thing is that you don't let us down.' But I did not care what they said; the main thing for me was to get those two oxen and be on my own. In the end, the others had to agree to it, of course. The collective's voluntary, after all.

Well, after that I was on my own. My wife looked after the animals and I worked in the fields. I toiled away, scarcely ever sleeping. I worked even harder than before. After a time I began to regret what I had done, but I didn't say so. I wasn't going to give them that pleasure.

For two years I stayed on my own. It was difficult. You couldn't hire farmhands or day labourers any longer. I had to see to everything myself. I sweated my guts out. None of my brothers would help me. Not that I asked them, for that matter. I saw that Liu Ling Agricultural Co-operative was flourishing and I began to think that I was stupid to have left it. But then I thought of how the others would say: 'There! What did we say?' And when I thought of that, I worked harder still because, whatever happened, I did not intend to take the first step. Then in the third year I did not manage to finish my ploughing. I had two mu left. I wasn't going to manage it in time. Then the farmers' co-operative people came along: they stopped and watched me and then, without a word, they began ploughing those two mu for me. There were seventeen of them, and they did the work in less than an hour. I myself would have needed two days. Then I thought: 'It's good to be many.' But we didn't say anything to each other. I said nothing and they said nothing.

Later, when I was weeding a field of maize that I was behind with, they came once again to help me. I didn't really like that. I told them that I would pay them for their work. I didn't like people working without payment. But they replied: 'You are in difficulties and you can't manage this. We are strong and we are many, and we can help you as a brother.' After that they sent Tsao Chen-kuei to help me. But I hadn't asked for any help. I hadn't spoken to anyone. They had just seen for themselves how things were with me and come of their own accord. That was just before I joined the agricultural co-operative.

Liu Ling Farmers' Co-operative had then been re-organized into the East Shines Red Improved Agricultural Co-operative. They had bigger fields than before. The millet fields were very big and I looked at them and they were so beautiful. Just after that they came to me from the East Shines Red Improved Agricultural Co-operative and talked with me. They were polite and asked me to do them the service of joining. They said: 'Do you see how rich we've become? We'ye pooled all our land now. It's hard farming on your own. Come to us.' I thought they were right and, as they had come to me themselves and been courteous, and I hadn't had to ask them for anything, I said that I would agree to become a member of the East Shines Red Improved Agricultural Co-operative. That was 1955—I was the last in the whole district to join the farmers' collectives.

Then it was suggested that I should be labour leader for a labour group. I accepted this. I was that for two years. I thought it onerous. There was all too much headwork and all too much responsibility. But, however it was, I was better off than when I had been on my own. In 1955, my last harvest on my own, I had got 1,800 jin. In 1956 in the East Shines Red Agricultural Co-operative, I got 2,000 jin and also 60 Y in cash. And, despite having the extra responsibility as labour leader, I had not needed to work so hard.

After being labour leader for two years, I got up at the annual meeting and said: 'I don't want to be labour leader any longer. I don't want to have responsibility for others. I don't like being the one who has the responsibility.' But they just said: 'You work so hard. You organize the work of production so well. We can't do without you, because you are so clever at the work.' After that they elected me again, even though I protested. I didn't like that. That next year I didn't work all that well. It was the first time in my life that I had stopped working hard. After that harvest, the others agreed without discussion to elect a new labour leader.

I thought it so nice being an ordinary farm worker again and not having to be labour leader. You see, if you are labour leader, you have to plan everything, and then you have to urge people on and keep at them, and they get grumpy if you keep at them. They think you are persecuting them, because most people are so lazy and don't really know what work means. I thought it would be so nice only to have to do my work and not have to worry about what others were doing or not doing. It was lovely only having to do farm work and not having to plan. It's not that you have to work less in the fields if you're a labour leader; on the contrary, you can't get a labour group to do anything, if you don't go in front yourself and show them how the work should be done.

Now, as an ordinary worker, my income's increasing all the time. I don't remember properly how much corn I got the second year, but it was a lot. And also I got more than 300 Y in cash. I'm working now on the autumn ploughing. I plough in the mornings and in the afternoons I weed. I plough one mu every morning. I have a one-yoke plough and use the same ox every day. That's the best way. It is a good ox and I am responsible for it and the plough, and I know it well and can get the most out of it.

I really intend to be an ordinary farm worker all my life now. I don't intend ever to let myself be elected to anything, either to be labour leader or anything else that means having responsibility for others. But I have learned enough characters to be able to keep books, if I want. I let the book-keepers and ganbus teach me: the different characters for a work-day and wheat and millet and that sort of thing.

People say of Li Hai-yuan: He is an industrious, tenacious, hard-working man. He is known as a responsible person. No one mentions his leaving the collective. He himself doesn't talk about it either. 'He is a good man and a hard worker. But one must talk about propitious things and good events. One shouldn't mention unpleasantnesses unnecessarily because, whatever else he is, he is a good fellow.'

His wife, Chia Fu-lan, is from a very poor family. Her feet are badly misshapen, because they used to be bound. She is Chia Ying-lan's sister and they say she came to Li Hai-yuan as a child-bride. Their great grief in life is that their son, the only surviving one of their children, became deaf and dull-witted after an illness. Actually Li Te-chua is backward. His parents have built him a cave. They hope that he will marry. But he has no girl. The women think it will be difficult to get him a bride. Chia Fu-lan usually says to the women: 'I have to work harder than other mothers. I have had to see that he got a silk quilt and a fine big cave for himself and lots of things so that he can get married. The girl's parents must be able to see that it is a rich home she is going to, otherwise her mother won't allow the marriage, although they ought to have been transformed in the new society and not think of such things.' But even so the women don't think his parents are going to be able to find a bride for Li Te-chua. But they don't say that to his mother. They are sorry for her.

They have no other children alive. Chia Fu-lan hoped for a long time to be able to have another child, but now the last year she has said: 'Perhaps I look pregnant, but I'm not. I'd like to be and we've tried and tried, but now I'm too old to bear fruit.'

Li Hai-yuan does not talk about this. He does not mention it, but he grieves. He has gone to the party people and spoken to the ganbus who come from the town and said to them: 'Can't you find some specialist in Sian who can make my son well?' The ganbus have tried to help him, but the doctors say there is nothing to be done. After hearing that, he hasn't spoken with anyone about it again. His wife, Chia Fu-lan, however, still hopes that her son will get all right and often speaks with the women about it.

Tables

Management Committee

Li Hung-fu — Chairman, labour leader
Tung Yang-chen — Deputy labour leader
Chang Chung-liang — Book-keeper
Kao Pin-ying — Treasurer
Li Hai-ching — Responsible for economy

Grain Production

	Area 1961 mu	Crop 1961 jin	Area 1962 mu
Wheat	182	20,042	182
Millet	217	37,760	235
'Sticky millet'	156	25,485	145
Maize	133	28,987	120
Beans	86·7	12,552	83
Buckwheat	17	2,300	24
Kaoliang	17	2,677	21
	808·7	129,803	810

Sales of Animal Products

			1961		1962 (1 Jan.–1 Sept.)
Goats		9	63 Y	7	42 Y
Wool	jin	62	49·60	36	28·80
Sheepskins		18	36	8	16
Leather, goat	jin	51	96·90	48	91·20
			245·50		198

Family Incomes, 1961

Head of Household	Days' work	Grain, jin	Cash, Y
Kao Pin-ying	439	2,722	746·36
Chang Chung-liang	321	1,990	545·70
Li Hai-ching	353	2,189	600·10
Tu Yi-chen	173	1,073	294·10
Ai Ke-kao	349	2,164	593·30
He Huang-ho	269	1,668	457·30
Wang Fung-li	572	3,546	972·40
Li Hai-yuan	465	2,883	790·50
Hu Shen-chu	297	1,841	504·90
Jen Teh-wan	173	1,073	294·10
Liu Chen-yung	367	2,275	623·80
Chang Chung-wen	272	1,686	462·40
Liang He-yiu	410	2,542	697·00
Tung Chi-lian	90	558	153·00
Li Hung-fu	348	2,158	585·60
Li Yü-hsin	267	1,655	453·90
Fung Yü-lan	115	713	195·50
Tung Yang-chen	449	2,784	763·30
Ai Ke-liang	203	1,259	345·10
Li Hai-kuei	345	2,139	586·50
Kao Chin-lan	50	310	85·00
Chang Chu-liang	29	179	49·30
Ma Hung-tsai	335	2,077	569·50
Chi Pei-fa	395	2,449	671·50
Li Yiu-hua	1,059	6,516	1,800·30
Li Kuei-ying	73	453	124·10
Jen Huai-ying	59	366	100·30
Li Hai-fu	322	1,996	547·40
Chen Chung-yuan	338	2,096	574·60

Family Incomes, 1961 (continued)

Head of Household	Days' Work	Grain, jin	Cash, Y
Li Hsin-chen	186	1,153	316·20
Li Sha-chang	479	2,970	814·30
Wang (not in Liu Ling Village)	255	1,581	433·50

Social Subsidy from the Labour Group's Assistance Fund, 1961
Only grain

Name	Jin	Reason
Tuan Fong-ying	560	Husband works in Yenan. Parents-in-law old. Shortage of labour.
Tung Chi-lian	220	Alone at home. Son at school. Bound feet.
Li Yü-hsin	300	Widow with three children. Only one person working in the family.
Fung Yü-lan	200	Husband works in Seven-mile Village. Two children, no parents. Works at home.
He Huang-ho	50	Only person working in the family.
Kao Chin-lan	200	Husband works in Yenan. New member. A lot to do at home.
Chang Chu-liang	200	Husband works in Lochuan. On her own.
Li Kuei-ying	300	Husband away working. On her own.

Rewards to Merit Workers, 1961

Tung Yang-chen	Mattock
Kao Pin-ying	Mattock
Li Hung-fu	Mattock
Chang Chung-liang	Mattock
Li Tsuai-ying	Mattock
Li Kuei-ying	Mattock
Kao Kuei-fang	One handkerchief, one pair of stockings
Ai Lan-ying	One handkerchief, one pair of stockings
Li Hai-yuan	Felt mat

Part IV

The Labour Group for Vegetable Cultivation

Ching Chung-ying, leader of the vegetable group, aged 54

I AM from Hengshan. My family has always lived there, but for several generations we have not had the land to make a living from. We had ten mu and Father worked as a day labourer for various landowners. Ours was not good land; it lay high up the hillside. We were five brothers. Life was hard for us and when I was twelve I had to go out and earn.

It was in January 1920 that I began working for a landowner called Wang Kou-ho. I was to get 'two strings of cash' for the year; that is to say from January to October according to the moon calendar. The landowner woke me when the cock crowed. I had to carry the water and shit. I had to do everything. One summer day, when the melons had ripened, I dropped one on the ground and it split open. It was a sheer accident, but Wang Kou-ho was furious and took his mattock and hit me on the head. You can still see the scar. I was unconscious, and it was late afternoon when I came round; I was soaked in blood and he had just left me lying where I fell. [Weeps.] No one knows how the poor people suffered. I was twelve and had no trousers, and the landowner struck me without cause. He often struck me. Everything was my fault. I often got five or six beatings a day. He was a big landowner. He had 600 mu. It was both valley land and hill land.

One day Wang Kou-ho took me with him when he went out to the sheep. That was in the summer and it was hot. We went eight li from the village. At dinner-time I was sent back to fetch his food. First he took off my cloth shoes and pissed in them, then he said: 'You must be back with my food before my piss has dried.' It was a hot summer and I had to run barefoot across sand and I could not stop and rest on the way. I ran as fast as I could, but when I got back the landowner's piss had already dried, because the sun was strong, and Wang Kou-ho beat me after he had eaten. [Weeps.] I was only twelve.

Next year, when I was thirteen, I worked for a landowner called Chou Kuan-yü. I was his herd-boy. It was better there. I had only four beatings the whole year. Though I did get my ears boxed now and again. The following year, I moved to a landowner called Li Teh-chen. He was a decent man and I herded sheep for him and worked one day in the fields. I was getting bigger now. But his son was different. The son was about twenty-five and, when his father wasn't looking, he used to hit me. He thought it fun. He got hold of me and beat me up six times that year. But I tried to keep clear of him and stay within sight of Li Teh-chen. Because as long as he was looking, I wasn't thrashed. That was the last year I had a thrashing.

When I was fifteen years old, I went as farmhand to work in the fields of a landowner called Mau Ko-jen. The following year I moved over to Shou Huei-chen. Now I was reckoned as fully able-bodied. I worked hard. One does.

When I was twenty, the great famine came. That was 1928. One of my brothers died. After that, Father and I and my three other brothers went to Shansi. It was better there. We sold my two youngest brothers. We were forced to do that in order to survive. We got twenty-eight silver dollars for one and twenty silver dollars for the other. I don't know where they went. I have never heard of them since. After that it was only Father and I and my younger brother, Ching Chung-wan. He lives in Liu Ling too now. I fell ill. But I survived and two years later we came back to Hengshan again.

There, I worked as a day labourer. Then gradually we heard about the Red Army. It was supposed to be rather good. They took their land, cattle and corn from the rich and distributed it to the poor people. But I never met a communist till long afterwards. But I remember that Father and I talked about them one night, when I was twenty-six. That was in 1934 and there was revolution in northern Shensi. 'Why should one be a farmhand for others all one's life?' we said. But the Red Army didn't come.

It was only in 1938 that I met a communist. He was called Wu Shen-tsai. He was middle-aged, thirty or thereabouts. He had come up from Yenan to make propaganda. He talked with me in Hengshan. He said: 'You toil all year round for a landowner, but your life is wretched. You gather riches for others, while you go hungry yourself.' Then he talked to me about Yenan. That was in February 1938. After that I talked with Father, and we decided that I should go down to Yenan and see if it were true, as was said, that there people were given land, and that the government there was good. One night I set off for Yenan. When I reached the town, I didn't know where to go, so I asked a woman ganbu. She was polite to me. That surprised me. Then I saw that this was a good place. It was true what people said.

In March, I went back up to Hengshan. Father was ill. I was to fetch Father and the family. When I got there Father was dead. I got there about noon and he had died that morning. After the funeral, we went down to Yenan. That was Mother and I and my younger brother, Ching Chung-wan. The only thing we possessed was an iron pot. We took that with us.

I was given land in Liu Ling, and, since I came here, I have never worked as farmhand for others. I worked hard, but I did not have to toil as I had done when I was a farmhand. And every year life became better. At the beginning of 1947, we had six cattle, three big pigs, two donkeys and 21,000 jin of corn. After that Hu Tsung-nan came. His troops plundered. They stole everything we had. They destroyed everything. They took the seed in the fields to feed their horses. Everything was destroyed. In 1947 we had another famine. After thirteen months' occupation Hu Tsung-nan left us in March 1948. We then had nothing to eat and no seed. There was seed-corn in Lochuan. We got that from the government. That spring I went between Lochuan and Liu Ling with seed. I walked hundreds of li and carried two sacks on a carrying-pole on each trip. At night, I slept on the sacks by the roadside. Then we began building Liu Ling up again.

First we organized a labour exchange group. On the other side of the valley the Old Secretary, Li Yiu-hua, and some others were building up their farmers' co-operative. We watched them. Their working together there seemed to bring them luck. More people meant more strength and more manpower. They did the ploughing better than we and they manured more thoroughly. They had nice harvests. We discussed whether we shouldn't form our own labour group for mutual help. That was in February 1952.

Some of us were for this. I thought it would be good. Mau Ke-yeh and Ma Juei-ching also worked for the proposal. Others were against the idea. Fu Hai-tsao, for example. Their family had more manpower. Both he and his father worked. Also they had good land in the valley. They said: 'We two can manage our fields ourselves. We don't really like the idea of others looking after our land.' Then I went over and talked to them: 'If the others on the other side of the valley can do their job properly, why shouldn't we be able to do so?' I said. Three weeks later, Fu Hai-tsao came to me and said that he had thought it over and that he would join. I was chosen labour leader for Liu Ling Labour Group for Mutual Help and Ma Juei-ching became deputy leader.

The discussions took four evening meetings. Two were held in my cave and two in Mau Ke-yeh's. Then we began working. We got up early in the morning and worked hard. By the autumn of 1953, the Old Secretary's farmers' co-operative, Li Yiu-hua's Farmers' Co-operative, had become very prosperous. They had increased the number of their oxen to seven and they had 120 goats. Although we too had worked hard and had increased the number of our cattle and donkeys, things had gone better for them. We talked about joining his co-operative.

But many were against it. Those who were most against it were Fu Hai-tsao, Li Chiao, Tung Yang-chen and Li Yang-pei (he is dead now). They said: 'Over there they have no valley land, but we have. If they can manage with their poor land, we can do even better without them.' We held many meetings. We kept on at it evening after evening. There was great discussion. 'We have good land,' they said. 'We shall lose on the deal.' That was their only reason and their only argument.

At the first meeting, it had been four for and four against. But in January 1954, when we had the last meeting, I said: 'There are quite a lot of us. We shall have the right to vote. It isn't certain that we shall lose by going over. We shall be in the majority in this farmers' co-operative, so you don't need to be afraid. It will be all right, if we stick together.' Then Fu Hai-tsao said: 'All right. In that case we can join. If it is as you say, then I vote for joining. But we must stick together afterwards.' That gave us a majority for joining Li Yiu-hua's Farmers' Co-operative. When the three others realized this, they gave in. They said: 'All right. Then we'll join too, so that we can stick together.' After that we joined. In this way the whole of Liu Ling's Labour Group for Mutual Help joined Li Yiu-Hua's Agricultural Co-operative.

There were eight of us joined: Fu Hai-tsao, Li Yang-pei, Li Chiao, Li Hung-fu, Mau Ke-yeh, Tung Yang-chen, Ma Juei-ching and I. Later other households joined individually: Li Hai-kuei, Tsao Chen-kuei, Li Yü-hsin and Li Hai-ching. There were four members in Li Yiu-hua's Farmers' Co-operative: Li Yiu-hua, Li Hai-chen, Li Hai-chun and Li Hai-yuan. In the discussions that now began, Li Hai-yuan left the farmers' co-operative and farmed on his own.

In January 1954 we had a long meeting to lay down the rules for the farmers' co-operative. There were eight meetings in a row. We changed the name from Li Yiu-hua's Agricultural Co-operative to Liu Ling Agricultural Co-operative; we chose a leader and various labour leaders. We changed the name to Liu Ling Agricultural Co-operative because people got up at the meetings and said: 'We don't belong to Li Yiu-hua. If we belong to anyone, it's the village of Liu Ling.' Li Yiu-hua was elected leader; Ma Hai-hsiu became deputy leader; Li Hai-chun, Kao Yü-kuei's husband who now works in the offices of the people's commune, became book-keeper, and I became treasurer. Ma Juei-ching became labour leader and Li Hai-kuei deputy labour leader. One year later, in 1955, we comprised thirty-two households.

We held a meeting every time we were to buy anything. We decided what we were going to buy and who should buy it. They said that I was the best one to buy a horse and a mule. We were to have those for the carts. We had already bought a two-wheeled horse-cart with motor-car wheels. It had been a year of good progress. I went to the town and bought a mule that cost 115 Y and a horse that cost 45 Y. People were pleased with my purchases. Especially pleased that I had managed to get the horse so cheap.

Now the others could see that things were going well for us. They saw all the things we bought. They said: 'Things are going well for you. We are just as we were.' Then we told them that they could join; but most of them replied that they didn't want to do that. They had good land down in the valley, of course; they had good donkeys and they had no desire to go in with us. For them it was the good land they had which was the main thing.

For us, the work went better. Of course, at first, people saw to their own fields most and thought the others did things badly, but there was no great antagonism and little by little it was overcome. I myself had not really properly believed in it all, although I had been for the idea and had worked for it. But I saw that it was doing all right. On the other hand, I now thought seriously that I was far too old to be treasurer. At every meeting I got up and said: 'Let the young people look after the cash. I am old and I cannot read and I can't keep books and, if there's a mistake and there's money missing, it would be difficult for me to find out what has happened. Let me get out of doing this.' But the meeting just answered: 'You do the work well and you are honest and there has never been any money missing, and you are painstaking and thorough and you got that horse so cheap. You're the right person to be treasurer.' We had that discussion in March 1955. And when the other sixteen families joined, it just meant more work for me.

I had talked to them and told them to join. I said to Li Yü-teh, Wang Fung-li's father-in-law: 'Although you have a good ox and good land, you have no security as long as you are an individualist and farm by yourself. Do you remember what happened with Kau Yü-hua down in Seven-mile Village? His ox died and the whole family wept for several days, because then he had lost everything. If he had been a member of an agricultural co-operative, he would have been saved.

Then Li Yü-teh said: 'That is true. You are right there. At times it can be a good thing if there are several of you. It can be more secure.' I replied: 'Think about it. If, when you have thought about it, you reach the conclusion that you ought to join, you can speak to our book-keeper, Li Hai-chun.' A week later, Li Yü-teh came and said: 'I have thought now. I shall apply.' He was the last. Then, thirty-two house-holds had joined Liu Ling Agricultural Co-operative. After that, we elected Wang Fung-li, Li Yü-teh's son-in-law, to be labour leader. He was young and energetic, and was known to be a good farmer.

But there were still some who were reluctant. Tung Yang-chen worried for a long time about his land in the valley. He could not let it go; he thought about it the whole time and in the end the others talked to him about it and said: 'Don't be so anxious.' Then he calmed down. In the co-operative, we had one labour team and that was divided into two groups. Each group cultivated an area, but the two groups helped each other.

In February 1956 we formed the East Shines Red Higher Agricul-tural Co-operative. Then we incorporated Wangchiakou and Hutoma villages. We had spent a fortnight making propaganda. In this we had to drive home the socialist principle, 'To each according to his work', all the way. People were agreed about that. That was the right prin-ciple. Wangchiakou was with us about that, but Hutoma Village was not so easy. People there said that Hutoma would lose by it all. They thought that it would be an amalgamation at their expense. Liu Ling had more people and greater power and Hutoma would just be el-bowed aside. It was Mu Ju-tsai, who is now leader of Hutoma Village Labour Group, who was most against this amalgamation. He was not against the socialist principle, he told us; he thought that Hutoma Village could accept that. But he said at several meetings that Hutoma did not want to join up with Liu Ling.

Tung Yang-chen, for his part, did not like losing his land. Because now we were all pooling our land properly and were going to stop paying dividends on land; from then on we were just going to give dividends on actual work. Tung Yang-chen said: 'I have such good land in the valley. Why should I have to lose it? If I too had been one of those who only have poor hill land, then I would have been entirely for this principle, but I happen to have my land in the valley.' Anyway, gradually they were all talked over and we formed the East Shines Red Higher Agricultural Co-operative.

I continued as treasurer for it until April 1956. Then I had a very serious talk with the Old Secretary, Li Yiu-hua, and told him that it really could not go on any longer. Everything had now become so much bigger; it was all too complicated for me. It had not been onerous when it was just a question of looking after the money and stores for a small union of a few households, where everyone knew each other. It had become hard when it was a whole farmers' co-operative with over thirty households, but now that it was an improved agricultural co-operative comprising many villages, I simply could not manage the work any longer. So, a new treasurer for the improved agricultural co-operative was elected at the meeting in April and I moved to the labour group for vegetable cultivation. There I was elected leader in April 1956.

The income from the labour group for vegetable cultivation was large. In 1956 it was roughly 8,000 Y; after that it rose every year by about 1,000 Y. I was responsible for the labour group, but now I had the possibility of having my own treasurer, and I chose Chang Cheng-pong and got him elected. He has moved to Seven-mile Village, but he really is from Liu Ling and has worked as treasurer for the labour group for vegetable cultivation since he was elected in 1956.

In 1958 we became a people's commune, but there was no discussion to speak of and I don't remember anything special happening or anything being changed. The labour group for vegetable cultivation has worked in the same way right from 1956. We decide at our members' meetings how much we are going to cultivate and what we shall grow, we consult with the committee of the labour brigade about our plans and then we take our decisions at the members' meetings. It has been the same every year. There has never been any change at any time in any way after the introduction of the people's commune. All binding decisions have to be taken at our members' meetings. 1956 as 1958 and 1958 as 1962. Sometimes we hold a members' meeting every week, depending on the season and the work. Just now, during the harvest, there has been a short pause of a few weeks, but we shall be holding one in a few days' time immediately after the brigade committee meeting.

Now the green-vegetable season is almost over, and we are on onions now. Every day two of our members drive into Yenan to sell the vegetables. That is an easy and a pleasant job, so we take it in turns. We sell to the vegetable company and what's left we sell in the market. This has been so since 1951. The vegetable company pays twenty per cent less than the market price. But we are bound to go to them first, before we are allowed to sell in the market. We get the best prices in the morning; towards afternoon the market price drops all the time. There are no fixed prices. It's been market price for vegetables all the time since 1956. The vegetable company pays cash when it buys. If we have a lot to do, we can fetch the money later, if we like.

In 1961, the labour group for vegetable cultivation earned roughly 14,000 Y. But this money is not divided directly among the members of the group. We, of course, are part of Liu Ling Labour Brigade and we are the group that brings in the most cash. So, the money is handed over to Liu Ling Labour Brigade in the same way as the other labour groups hand their income over. Then the whole income from the entire labour brigade is divided among the members according to their amount of work. Incidentally, the labour group for vegetable cultivation also grows corn. The deputy labour leader, Fu Hai-tsao, is responsible for corn cultivation.

Three times a day we fetch a load of human excrement from the town. It's thanks to this manure that we can produce so many vegetables. We tip the shit into the big dung-pit on the other side of the road, from which we get the manure for growing our vegetables. Every load we fetch from the town is about 1,000 jin. That makes 3,000 jin a day. We have made an arrangement with the sanitary department of Yenan town administration, allowing us to empty twenty-one latrines a day. We take seven latrines at a time. The sanitary department has allocated all the latrines in Yenan town in this way, and the various labour groups empty them.

The excrement of the people in Liu Ling and the dung from their private pigs goes to their private plots. But if any family has any over, the labour group for vegetable cultivation will pay 0·40 Y cash for two buckets amounting to 100 jin together.

Last year we got electricity here. It reached this side, but not over to Shiaoyuanchihou. We have 220-volt A.C. and it costs 0·25–0·26 Y a kilowatt. Our costs of installation were roughly 10,000 Y. We borrowed part of this. Then the question of a pump cropped up. We are, of course, forced to water our vegetables a lot. We dug the well at the vegetable fields in 1957; that's the best water in the whole district, considerably better than the water here in the village. Vegetables need a lot of water, especially during the dry season. But we had to employ two donkeys and one man every day pumping up the water: one donkey in the morning and one in the evening. Altogether that cost ten yuan a day. Seeing that it was so expensive, we discussed buying an electric pump. In February 1961, the labour brigade decided that we should have an electric pump. That pump pays for itself. The cost of electricity for the pump from 1 January 1962 to 30 July 1962 was thirty-four yuan. We haven't had a bill for the autumn yet.

Things are going very well for us. There are two of us working in the family: my stepson, Liu Ching-tsei, and myself. We work. I am not a party member. I have never been interested in politics. Before, we were oppressed. The poor had no rights. We owned nothing. When I came here I had just an iron pot. Now I should need several ox-carts to move all my things. I have a bicycle and a hand-cart with rubber-tyred wheels. Now, if one works hard, one can live really well.

Fu Hai-tsao, the one who wanted to be a singer, aged 39

WE came to Yenan from Hengshan when I was five. That was during the great famine of 1928. We had been thrown out. My father brought the family with him here. Father starved to death the next year. We went about begging in 1929. We had nothing to eat. Father went to Chaochuan to gather firewood and beg food, but he didn't get any. He was carrying elm leaves and firewood when he fell by the roadside. We waited for him all night. In the morning, when he hadn't come, Mother said: 'Now let's go and see what's happened to him.' Then Mother and Uncle and I walked along the road towards Chaochuan. I was the one who saw him first. He was lying on his face and was dead. The elm leaves and firewood were still there beside him. No one had touched a thing. The elm leaves were for us to eat. He wasn't ill; he had just starved to death. Mother says that he used to be big and strong and had been a good worker, thoughtful and kind to the family and open-handed if anyone was ill. That is my earliest memory: of always being hungry, and of Father lying there dead in the road.

After that, we went into Yenan and lived by begging. Mother begged for us. She did not eat much. Six months later she married Tsao Shen-yung. That's why I am called Fu after my father and Tsao after Stepfather. He was poor. He also had debts of 300 silver dollars. He had an ox and brought in firewood for the town. But it was not easy for him to feed so many people and at the same time pay his debts. He had had to borrow the money from a merchant who had the shop, Yushenkwei, in Yenan town. He charged big interest on his money. Stepfather had bought the ox to enable him to till his land properly. We were living then in Suchianan, fifteen li from here. But he wasn't able to manage his debt, so we had to leave the land and in 1932 we came to Liu Ling. Here Stepfather rented ten mu from Li Hsiu-tang's father. But we worked most fetching firewood from the common lands and transporting it to the town.

I began working with Stepfather when I was eight. We cut firewood up on the hillside. We had to protect the ox from the authorities as well as we could, because the yamen in Yenan, that is the authorities there, used to requisition animals for their transports. Because of that, we had built a special cave for our ox up on the hillside. We drove into the town with the firewood early in the morning, then back to Liu Ling and up on to the hill to cut more wood. The most important thing was that the authorities should not get their eye on us and take our ox from us. In those days, the rentals were thirty jin per mu for hill land and forty-five jin per mu for valley land. We had to pay taxes besides. But we cut the firewood on the common lands. We were poor and I was always hungry. What I remember best of my childhood is that I was never able to eat my fill, but was always hungry. We were oppressed. One day, when I was eleven, Stepfather said to me: 'Child, the sufferings of the poor are going to end now. People are saying that there is a Red Army, which is setting up soviets everywhere and dividing everything up equally among the people. They are even dividing up heaven and earth and giving them to the poor, and if a poor person hasn't any food, they give him something to eat and they give land to those who haven't any and animals to those without.' Stepfather told me about this when we were working up on the common lands. That was before the Red Army came here.

In 1935, the whole of this region became red. The merchant stopped coming to demand his interest. There were eight households in Liu Ling then, and we made a distribution of the land. Many people were worried and anxious. They wondered if the communists would be able to stay in power. 'If we take the land and later the Red Army is beaten, we shall have to bear the blame,' they said. They didn't think the Red Army looked strong enough. One old man called Ai Shen-you said: 'I won't touch anyone's land. I have always been a day labourer and farmhand and I intend to go on being one. That's the safest.' An old woman called Hsiu said: 'I don't want to take any land. I have only one grandson left. He is the last of my family. If I take any of the land, the landowner will kill him when he comes back. And if they cut my grandson's head off, my family will be dead.' Stepfather and Mother discussed the question a great deal. Stepfather thought that we ought not

to take part in dividing up the land; that that would be dangerous and that it was unnecessary to run such a risk. The landowners were strong and they always used to win in the long run. But Mother said: 'There are only three of us in our family. If we don't take any land, we shall die just the same, because we shall starve to death. If the landowner comes back, he can't do more than kill us. So that we might just as well take the land from the beginning and hope for the best.' The communists had people making propaganda here, and they talked with people and in the end persuaded them. They said: 'We are strong enough to deal with the landowners. If we hadn't been strong enough, we should not have begun the revolution. You are all poor and how are you going to be able to live if you don't have any land?' So everyone joined forces and went and divided up Li Yü-tse's land.

I now worked with Stepfather in the fields, and every year he and I discussed what we should grow on our land. We lived very happy lives then. Ganbus often came and held meetings about the three mountains the Chinese people was in the process of casting off itself. I joined the Young Pioneers. There we had classes about which districts were red and liberated and which were held by the Whites or the Japanese. The twelve-year-olds joined the Red Guard. That was usual. After all, we had to learn to defend our land.

The leader of the people in our village was Tung Chi-hwei. He was Tung Yang-chen's father. He was the one who forced the distribution of land through. All the landowners hated him. He was a big strong man with a round face and laughed a lot. Whenever the enemy was on the way from the town making for the village, he sent a message to the soviet area, for we were on the very fringe of it. He organized the Red Guard in the village and scared off the enemy. He put up posters on the telegraph poles and talked with everyone about how we must root out the landowners and their gang.

Tung Chi-hwei had a brother and two children, a son, Tung Yang-chen, and a daughter. His brother took to the hills and became a guerrilla. Nobody knows what happened to him after that. He was probably killed somewhere. Everyone had confidence in Tung Chi-hwei and people asked his advice about everything. Once, when I was listening, he said: 'Things are difficult now, but a time's coming when our difficulties will be overcome and all our enemies crushed, and then everyone will be able to eat their fill and everyone will have clothes and plenty.' He comforted people, when the difficulties came. Everyone had faith in him. But one day the enemy came and caught him. It was Li Hsiu-tang's father who wanted to have him killed, and it was Li Han-hua who took him prisoner. Li Han-hua was Li Hsiu-tang's brother-in-law.

But the people loved Tung Chi-hwei, and they had a letter written and sent to the town saying that they would stand guarantee for him, but that did not help. Li Han-hua had his head cut off. And they did not even hand over the body, and his widow kept weeping loudly for a long time afterwards. But Li Yü-teh had a relative who lived in the town, and he was able to get hold of the body and smuggle it out of the town and hide it under some stones to stop the street-dogs from eating it. He had said: 'After all, it's one of our villagers they have beheaded!' He hid himself at the place of execution and, when the executioners had gone, he took the body and brought it to safety. Later, the body was brought to Liu Ling and buried here. But Tung Chi-hwei really came from Hengshan, so his uncle had him moved up there. But I've heard that the family is now planning to bring him back home to Liu Ling.

In the Young Pioneers, I was trained in bayonet fighting and learned how to use a spear. There, too, we had political talks about the war with Japan. More and more families moved here. There were more and more cattle and donkeys. We had got a lot of land in the land distribution. We had twenty-five mu of fertile land down in the valley and 105 mu up on the hillside. Stepfather and I worked in the fields; we had cattle and lived well.

They had begun teaching me to read and write in the Young Pioneers. I didn't like that. I preferred being outdoors working with Stepfather. But in the end they managed to persuade me to start going to school. I went for three days, then I ran away. Perhaps it was short-sighted, but I had starved when I was young and I never wanted to starve in my life again. We had land now and, if I worked hard in the fields, we would have more to eat. Now, of course, I see that that was a childish way to reason, because if I had really learned to read and write, I would have been of much more use to the village and the people and our country. Now I can hardly read at all.

Then Yenan was bombed by the Japs and everything was destroyed and the people there were evacuated. Then the Red Guard was re-organized and made a people's militia and I joined it. That was about 1945, I think. We were to look after the public safety. We were organized like the army, in platoons and so on. At night we kept guard against saboteurs and enemy agents.

The countryside was the most important, because the land and the harvest is the basis of everything, and so Chairman Mao asked us to till twice as much. In that way we should have enough and more than enough. We worked hard. When Hu Tsang-nan came, almost everyone left Liu Ling. We went up into the hills. I was in the people's militia then. We had buried all our possessions and all our corn. Hu Tsung-nan destroyed everything, and his troops ate and ate. They discovered our grain stores, and they stole our cattle. The guerrillas fought against Hu Tsung-nan's troops. They knew their hills, and we in the militia helped them.

At that time I was in Hsuchiachien. There were no K.M.T. soldiers in that village. If any came, we fled. When they left, we came back. We did not work. It was only a few who went out to the fields. We slept by day and at night we fought the K.M.T. We were in a different place every day. We went back to Liu Ling as soon as Hu Tsung-nan fled. At home, everything had been destroyed. They had even broken the mill-stones. It was like building a new farm. We dug up the corn the K.M.T. had not found. It was not much, but more than most people had. We managed. That year we sowed only the valley fields. Our own authorities came back and the people too.

We formed a labour exchange group, so as to be able to get the work done. We worked for each other in turn. Later, in 1952, we re-organized this into a labour group for mutual help. Strictly speaking, it was just the same thing, only better organized. We had now decided to work according to a plan every day and not just as things came along. Ma Juei-ching was made labour leader for the group, and I was elected deputy labour leader. There were eight households in the group. We drew up a timetable, and one day we worked for one household and the next day for another. The one we worked for had to provide food for the whole group. But it was not easy to make a timetable like that. There were many squabbles. Li Chung-ying was the worst; he always wanted to be first. Because it was often important to be the one who got ploughed first or his seed in first. In the end, we agreed to take it in turn. But he was never properly satisfied and then he married a girl from the town and, when his father-in-law died, he left the village and went to live in the house he had inherited.

Being leader of the labour group for mutual help was a thankless task. Every day there was someone who said: 'You are unfair.' Sometimes, for example, a person would say: 'Turn about, turn about! Can't you see that I have many more weeds in my field than he has? Weeds don't bother to grow in turn. If you don't weed my field today, I shall suffer for it.' In the end we chose a small group that had to deal with all such questions. If any was altogether too difficult to resolve, we had to have a democratic discussion. But, as I said, it wasn't easy and I think that these difficulties made certain persons more inclined to form a farmers' co-operative than they otherwise would have been. In 1953, we formed a farmers' co-operative, in which the land was to be employed alike. But then I didn't want to be a member any longer. We had a lot of land and good land, of course; we had cattle and were a small family with four grown-ups and two children and several able to work. I didn't think it looked as though there would be any such freedom in the farmers' co-operative. We knew how to run our own fields, we didn't need anyone to tell us now what we should do. So Stepfather and I agreed not to bother about it, but to manage on our own. Besides, I felt it had been onerous being labour leader. There was nothing but surliness and squabbling. People were never satisfied, and one was always being accused of being unfair and showing favouritism. In the mornings, when I had to fetch people for work, I was often told: 'What are you standing there nagging for?' Well, we discussed all that in the family and decided to farm on our own.

But things went well for the farmers' co-operative, better than for us. People from the village came and talked with us, wanting us to join. Stepfather let himself be persuaded. He talked with me and said: 'We eight neighbour families have worked together so long, we are neighbours and good friends and the others are in the farmers' co-operative and they have bigger incomes.' But I didn't want to. It took time, but in the end Stepfather talked so much about it that I applied to be a member. But I wasn't going to be labour leader.

I was one of the last families to join the co-operative. At the meeting people said: 'You work so hard. You should be elected group leader.' But then I got up and said: 'The group leader has to do as much work in the fields as anyone. But he has to get up earlier in the morning and he has to go to bed later in the evening and all the time he has to be thinking everything out and planning the work. He can only have time for that at night. But he isn't paid anything extra for this, but is just accused of being unfair. I remember what it was like when I was labour leader in the labour group for mutual help. But that was still possible. Because the labour group for mutual help was such that, there, each one owned his own land; but now in this farmers' co-operative, it is socialism, and that means that each is to work according to his ability and be paid according to his work, and that is a principle that I don't yet know; and, as I haven't any experience of it and anyway don't want to, I don't want to be made group leader.' But they elected me even so. And afterwards they came up to me and said: 'We are going to obey you and follow your instructions; we did that before and we shall do so now and we shan't grumble.' But I was still mistrustful and had no wish to do it, so ganbus from the party came to me and said: 'You are a hard worker. There's a lot you can do. One has to serve. And because you work well and can do a lot, you must also serve the people. Having to get up a little earlier in the morning surely isn't anything to complain about. You must serve the cause of the people.' So then I thought over what they had all said and changed my mind and agreed to let myself be elected group leader, and I have worked as that all these years since. In 1955 Liu Ling Farmers' Co-operative was re-organized as the East Shines Red Higher Agricultural Co-operative. I was beginning to have experience of the work and things were going easier. Everyone was to be paid according to the work he performed. The work had to be planned in the best possible way. One had to avoid any form of waste. If the labour group committee meetings are conducted in the right way and the labour leaders are reliable, the work should go smoothly and no unpleasantness arise.

Now we have more households than ever and that means even greater responsibility. There aren't the same households in the group as before. You see, in 1955, we re-organized the labour group. That year we set up the labour group for vegetable cultivation. After that we took the old people into our group. After he's fifty, no one is able to do a full day's work, but he can at least work with vegetables. We increased our production of vegetables. Since 1955, life has improved steadily. There haven't been any sensational changes, but it has become slowly better year by year. Two things have happened since the formation of the people's commune in 1958: we have got an electric water pump, that was decided at the brigade meeting, and last year we increased the vegetable area from twenty-four to fifty-two mu. We decide for ourselves how we are to work and what we shall grow. We have collective management, because everybody discusses everything until we are agreed.

One of the difficulties of working a farmers' collective is the necessity for keeping books. It is difficult to find people who can do this work. As long as we were just a labour group for mutual help, we managed without keeping proper books. Then we just had a simple work daybook. That was kept by Jen Huai-wan, who has now left the village and become party secretary in the pottery at Yenan.

I joined the party in 1955. Before that I was in the armed militia; now that I am older, I am an ordinary militia man. No, we have not introduced any extra remuneration for the labour leader. We aren't thinking of doing so either. It would not be good for production morale. One should be paid for physical work, not for the other. The other must be voluntary and unpaid.

The people who really persuaded me to join the co-operative and made me join the party were the Old Secretary, Li Yiu-hua, and my best friend, Li Hai-chen. I am a couple of years older than he, but he talked seriously with me: 'Now that I have joined, you must join,' he said.

I have always liked singing. No, my mother never sang; she had suffered too much to be bothered with that sort of thing. But under the occupation 1947-8 and the following year, I was a lot together with an old man, who was called Chou. He liked playing and singing. He taught me all I know. He used to say that he was the one who knew most songs in northern Shensi. He got many of us to sing. We used to sing when we went out to work in the mornings, and the older people said: 'Listen to the idiots.' Then old Chou died. But I went on singing. I sing mostly love songs, old songs, you know what I mean. I sing while we are working. It seems to go easier that way. When people are tired and the work is slow, they usually ask me to sing. We sing a lot in the village here now. We make up our own words and create quite new songs. We sing about the things we are thinking of. We sing mostly about love.

One day a man from Peking came. He was called Ching and he worked for some organization. I don't remember what it was called, but it had something to do with music. He travelled about writing down what people sang. When he came to Yenan, he went to Yenan's Art Ensemble and there he was told that I sang a lot and had taught them lots of songs. I had had three singers from that troupe out here for some days and taught them singing. They were called Li and Niu and Chou. They came out to me and sang with me here. Now they told Ching to come and see me. He came to Liu Ling and visited me and asked me to sing. As I sang, he sat beside me and wrote it all down in a little book, just as you are doing. Then he said to me: 'Come with me to Peking! You must study and become a singer. In Peking they will teach you everything. You will do your country great service as a singer. You will travel all over the world.' But Mother said: 'You are my only son. I gave you birth and I have worked and starved for you. Your father and stepfather and all their fathers before them worked on the land. If you go away from us, there is no one else to look after us. There will be no one to bury me.' Then she began to weep. Then I wept too. My wife did not weep. She said nothing at all. She just walked out. Then Ching said that I could at least promise to come to the big festival of folk music in Sian. He promised that I should be able to come home again, if I wanted. 'If you don't want to go to Peking, no one can force you,' he said. 'But you can at all events come to Sian. You must see a big city once in your life. You must know what it is you are missing if you don't come with me to Peking. If you come to Peking, the government will look after you. You and your family will never need to go hungry, even though you aren't working on the land. Your parents won't suffer any hardship.' When he said that, I could not refuse any longer, but decided to go with him to Sian and see what it was like.

But Mother wept and said: 'I shall die and you will never see me again. This is all the thanks I get for starving for you. You just leave us.' You see, of course, I was the only Fu and also the only Tsao left. My wife didn't say anything to me. My stepfather came with me into Yenan, whence I was to take the bus for Sian. We walked in together. He hadn't said anything about my trip, but just before the bus started, he said: 'It would be good, of course, if you did come back.'

I stayed twenty days in Sian. It was a big and beautiful city. We had a music festival the whole time, and when I was free and not singing myself, I went to the opera and recitals and shadow-plays. In the end, I was thinking: 'It is fun singing. I would like to sing all my life. I would like to go to Peking all right.' But Mother had said that she would die if I left the village, and the more I remembered that and the more I thought of Mother, the more I realized that it was impossible for me to go to Peking. After twenty days I said to Ching: 'I must go home now.' He just replied: 'That is a pity.' He gave me a ticket for the bus to Yenan, and I have never seen him since, nor heard of him. And so I returned to Liu Ling. When I came to the cave, Mother said: 'I thought you had gone for ever.'

People say of Fu Hai-tsao: He is a very nice chap. He and Lin Hu-fu are the best-looking men in the village. The women talk a lot about how good-looking he is. He sings very well. His wife is tall and slim. She has a savage temper. She talks aloud and is far from being the gentle wife. He is really rather henpecked at home. There's a standing joke about her: 'If she had married a man with the same temper as she has, their marriage would not have lasted a single day. But she has been lucky.' But she is the best worker among the women in the village. She is as strong as a big man. She can carry a hundred jin and think nothing of it, when other women can scarcely manage fifty. So one can also say that Fu Hai-tsao is a fortunate man to have got such a hard-working and industrious wife. She contributes a lot to the family's economy.

Actually, it is a pity that he did not go to Peking to study. He sings so well. But his mother has a very strong will, and he is her only son. So she wouldn't let go of him. He is very respectful to his stepfather. The older people in the village consider him an example to all the others, because he is the most faithful son in the village. He scolds his wife occasionally despite her temper and his being so nice, but only because she does not show enough respect to his parents.

He is well known for getting up early and going to bed late. He is considered one of the hardest workers in the village. He was elected labour leader, because he is good at organizing the work and does so much himself. Every evening he tells what has to be done the next day.

He speaks rather softly, but he likes a joke. He loves fun. The women like talking with him. He does not always reply, but he has such a good smile. They aren't irritated by his not replying, because he gives them such beautiful smiles. He is always calm and friendly. He is never agitated. He never swears. He never rushes about and he never flies out at you. His is a placid temperament. Perhaps he's a bit slow and it does take him some time to make up his mind; but whatever happens, he is always the same. He never lets himself be upset or ruffled.

He really wanted to go to Peking. In his heart of hearts he badly wanted to be able to sing. But he gave way to his family. The older people praise him for that. They say it shows that he is a good son. The young people, on the other hand, think he did wrong, that he ought to have gone.

Ma Chen-hai, aged 65

I GREW up in the village of Fengchiatsah in Suiteh hsien. It was a small village. My family had always been farmers. We owned fifteen mu and we rented thirty mu from Ma, the landlord. We had to pay thirty-four jin per mu in rent. The landlord, Ma, had a moneylending concern called Tsunteh. We did not borrow money from him, but we were not able to pay our rent. He took interest on it and interest on the interest. It was a high rent. The years were not bad ones and the crops were middling good, but we were six mouths to feed in the family, and in the end our debt had increased to 1,200 jin of grain, so then he took our fifteen mu of land from us. I was twelve or thirteen years old then. There was no way we could get out of it. We could not get out of his clutches. The next year we rented the fields that before had been our own, and had to pay thirty jin per mu rental for them. Father said: 'What can we do? The landowner is hard. He takes our land from us. But they have the money and the power, and there's no way out for us. We must bow to it.' Father had no hope any longer. He did not dare talk with the others in the village. If he had, he would have been suspected of stirring up mischief. Mother just wept. Having four children, it was hard for her to have lost those fifteen mu. She kept saying: 'Life is much worse now.'

I gathered fuel and plucked grass. I looked after our goat and the landowner's donkey. We were to feed it and, if it foaled, the landlord and we were to share equally. During the winter the landlord took the donkey back and rode round gathering his rents. My older brother went to Chitan hsien and started work there as a day labourer. My second brother worked in our fields and I was now fourteen, so I went out as herd-boy. I got five strings of cash a year and three meals a day. I worked for a relation, an uncle. The landlord, Ma, lived forty li away, so we did not see him often. But his agent, the manager of Tsunteh, his moneylending business, had a round, bearded face. He was called Ma Shou-chen. He collected rents and ran the moneylending. He was not a nice person. He was always stiff and dignified. He never smiled. He never showed either anger or pleasure. He was just suave and as hard as stone. We never saw a government official and I have no idea when the dynasty went. At all events, we never noticed anything in our village of those revolutions. Everything stayed the same, and the farmers suffered just as much all the time.

When I was twenty, I began work as a day labourer. I worked now here, now there, and at the same time in Father's fields. I used to earn ten cents and my food for a day's work. I did that for ten years. During those ten years Mother died and I got married. Father had become crippled with rheumatism and unable to work in the fields any longer and so had become doorkeeper for the moneylending business, Tsunteh, and all we brothers had set up households of our own. All our land was now out of the family's hands, and we all rented land from the landowner and did odd work as day labourers as well. We brothers took fifteen mu each of the forty-five mu that father used to rent. The total rental remained the same. It was not a good life. It was even a bit worse than when I was a child.

When I was thirty, I had three children. That made five mouths to feed. The heaviest harvest I ever had was 2,100 jin; 450 jin went to the landlord, leaving 1,650 for seed and the family's food. And that was our best year. On the average we got about 900 jin, and of this the landlord took 450 and we got 450. That wasn't enough and we could not live on it, so I went on going out as a day labourer. We ate wild herbs and made bread out of chaff. We mixed pumpkin and potato with our food. We did not pay taxes. No one in our village did.

I worked by the day for the landlord as well as other people. If one worked hard, they were pleased, and if one didn't work well, they said 'We don't want to see you again.' I was known as a good worker. They often came to me to ask for my help. There was no valley land in my village. All our fields were on the slopes. I cultivated the fifteen mu I rented.

In 1928, there was a famine. There was a bad drought. The whole crop from all the fifteen mu I rented was only 100 jin that year. We could not pay our rent. After the harvest, we were eating grass. Then we walked the fifty li down to the Yellow River. There, we got ourselves, the children and I, across to Shansi. In Shansi I worked as a porter. I carried rice. Then, with the money I earned, I bought and sold corn. In that way, I was able to get enough corn to survive. But we were starving the whole time. I sold all our possessions. That is all long ago now. I was young and strong then, and could bear a lot.

The following year, 1929, was even worse. There was no rain in the first half of the year and the drought was awful. We were starving. We bought chaff from the landowner. It was expensive. We had to pay three silver dollars for a measure, each measure containing thirteen or fourteen jin. I was working as a day labourer. It was not difficult for me to get work then. Many people had moved away from the village, some had died, and there was a shortage of decent labour. I got thirty cents a day. But I could no longer get a jin of corn with a day's work. Though my wage was so much higher, I only got a jin of chaff for a day's work. Rain fell in the second half of the year and there was a harvest of sorts. We got in 400 jin and the landlord took 200 of it.

But 1930 was better. We got 900 jin then. But the landowner claimed 700 jin, saying: 'You paid nothing in 1928 and you owe 250 jin from 1929. But I shall be generous, because times were bad, and not charge interest or interest on interest.' Later, we repaid the debt with between thirty and sixty jin a year.

No, we never heard the K.M.T. mentioned and no one ever said anything about Sun Yat-sen. Or, if anyone did, or about the revolution, I must have forgotten it. We are just uneducated farmers and we forget so easily. Life went on as before. Everything was as usual. But in 1932–3 I heard people talking of the Red Army. 'Now there's a Red Army. When it comes, it will kill all the landowners and landlords,' they said. At this time, officials and officers from the K.M.T. went to other villages, but we never saw any in ours. But the landowner was said to have had dinner with them. So, it was all sudden my discovering that the K.M.T. and the Red Army existed and hearing about the revolution.

Ma Shou-chen, who managed the moneylending business, Tsunteh, and was the landowner's agent, spoke to us about the K.M.T. and the communists. He said: 'The K.M.T. wants what is best for you. The K.M.T. is good. The communists, on the other hand, want to steal your possessions and take your wives from you. The communists will share your wives with each other. The K.M.T. will protect you from that.' No, in our village no one was ever beaten or put in prison by the landowner. That wasn't necessary. Because, if you could not pay the rent, the landowner took the land you owned, and if you did not own land, you had to work to pay off the rent in the future.

I remember the day the Red Guard reached the village. That was in November 1934. People were saying: 'There are Red Guard men in the village.' We were very afraid. I scarcely dared go out. If I did go out and met one of my neighbours, we spoke softly together. One of the neighbours I met on the road said to me in a whisper: 'They're saying we shan't be oppressed any more.' It was only propagandists from the Red Guard that had come to the village, not the armed men of the army, and there was a K.M.T. band in the neighbourhood, so we were cautious. The propagandist who came then was called Kao Wen-shen. He was a man with a swarthy, sunburned face. He was a poor farmer from a neighbouring village, and I knew him. No, I don't know how he got into the Red Army or how he became a propagandist. But now I heard that he was in our village and was talking about the revolution. He stayed one night with us, and then went on somewhere else. Some days later, we heard that he had been executed by the K.M.T. He had come to another village and one of the poor farmers with whom he talked had informed his landlord about him, and the landlord had sent for the K.M.T. and they had come in the night and shot him on the spot. We told each other in whispers what he had said about the revolution and what had happened to him.

The first propagandist with whom I ever talked properly was Ma Chien-hsiang. I knew him well. He was a poor farmer who lived three li from here. He was chosen propagandist after the Red Guard took his village. Afterwards, he became a guerrilla commander. I believe he's still alive. He came to my home one evening and said: 'We ought not to listen to the K.M.T.'s rumours. We are not going to be oppressed by them any longer. We communists are going to destroy all the land-owners and all the war lords and generals and officials and share out the land as equals and then never pay any more taxes or rent to anyone.' I thought that sounded very nice, but I wondered whether poor people really would be able to overthrow the powerful. I could scarcely believe it. It was the winter of 1934-5 that we had these discussions.

But all the same, it was only propagandists who came to us, and the K.M.T. was still there. Everything had to be secret. Kao had been shot. Then, suddenly, all these propagandists vanished. The Red Guard never came and the K.M.T. was still there and everything was the same as before.

Some time later, people again began talking about the communists. They talked about Yenan and what things were like there. It was my younger brother, Ma Cheng-pong, who talked most to me about this. He had a donkey which he used for transport work and was in Yenan several times a year. He said: 'In Yenan there's a Chairman Mao, who has a government there. Life is not bad in Yenan now. The land has been divided up and the poor get enough to eat. and can have clothes and fuel and are not oppressed by landowners.' Lots of people talked about this, but it's my brother I remember best. He was my brother, of course, and I had faith in what he told me. There were many people in my district who had started making for Yenan.

In March 1938, I had a talk with my wife about what we should do. I had given the land I had been renting back to its owner and was released from the rental, and we discussed what we ought to do now. 'Seeing it is hard for us here,' she said, 'couldn't you take the boy with you and go down to Yenan? If things really are so good there as people say, you can have a letter written to us or yourself come up and fetch us.' So then I sold all that I owned except my mattock. Then I gave all the money and all our corn to my wife and my two daughters and told them to wait for me. So then, I took my mattock, and I and the boy walked to Yenan. No one bothered to stop us. We were just poor refugees and nobody bothered his head about us. The K.M.T. knew where we were off to all right, but that made no difference, because we were poor.

We got to Yenan in May 1938. We searched out a relation, who had a little tea stall outside the town and there we lived. My relation said: 'There's a boy needed in Liu Ling to herd the beasts.' My boy was twelve years old then, and he went to Liu Ling. I myself began working in the mill at Peichuan. Yenan really was as good as people had said it was. Poor people were building themselves big caves. Everywhere were people moving in. After one year's work one could have corn, money, jute and much, much besides.

I worked at the mill for a month. Then I went over to Liu Ling to see how the boy was getting on. That was in the busiest month and they were weeding the fields. I helped them that day and then I went to Tsao Yu-fao and said: 'I would like to settle here.' 'That will be all right,' he said. So then I searched and found an abandoned cave, and I was told that I could start clearing new ground. I cultivated land up on the hillside, and I was able to borrow seed and tools from the communists. These loans were interest-free. In August 1938, I wrote to my wife, and, later, my brother, Ma Cheng-pong, sent her and my two daughters down to me in Liu Ling. After that, life became better and better every year. Then Hu Tsung-nan came. He stole 240 jin of millet from me. He slaughtered and ate my two pigs and he smashed everything of mine that could be smashed.

We had fled into the hills when Hu Tsung-nan was coming. We had tried to hide our corn first and we took our two pigs with us. We kept them hidden in a ravine. But one day, when I went down into the ravine to feed the pigs, the K.M.T. was there. They boxed my ears, hit me in the face and butchered the pigs on the spot. They swore at me and cursed me. The only payment I received for my pigs was a box on the ears. I did not dare protest or say anything. After that, they took me and my son with them to the town. When we got there, they let me go, but kept my son. When I got back to the village, there were only a few people there. Ten days later my son came back. He had been made to carry sacks of flour for them, but had managed to escape from them one night.

We wanted to be rid of Hu Tsung-nan. Whenever K.M.T. soldiers came to the village, we ran up into the hills. When they left the village, we came down again. The fields up on the hillsides could not be cultivated then. Nothing was grown then. When the corn began to grow up in the valley, Hu Tsung-nan put his horses to graze in the fields. They destroyed it all. Then they were driven out, and we began to work once more. Again life became slowly better and better.

We set up a labour group for mutual help. That is better than working on your own. The young people work together and chatter and sing, and that makes the work easier and go quicker than when they are all working on their own. If one falls ill, then the others look after one's fields in the meantime, and later on one can repay their day's work with one's own work. But there was a lot of squabbling in our labour group for mutual help and quarrelling about who was to be ploughed first. Earlier ploughing often means better crops.

People began talking about a farmers' co-operative. With one we would be able to get over those difficulties, they said, plough up the march lands, pool our oxen and get better crops. I agreed with the idea from the beginning. The harvest was good in the farmers' co-operative. But certain persons who had had more land or better land in the valley, or who had had more beasts, had not worked half as hard as I, because they were wretched workers, yet they got more corn and more money than I. That I thought was unfair and so, when the discussion about the improved agricultural co-operative began, I was from the very beginning all for us introducing the socialist principle. But now I am getting very old, and my son has had to take on responsibility for the family's affairs. But I talk a lot with him.

Life is good now. I do the household work, and at times I go down to our private plot and do a little work there. Mine is a peaceful old age. My two daughters are married and have children. My son is married and has children. I believe I have thirteen grandchildren now, and my eldest granddaughter is twenty and married and has children of her own. I have a calm and peaceful time of it. I spend the daytime with my grandchildren. But I don't see well. My eyes are almost finished and my teeth ache all the time. It is difficult for me to chew. I have toothache the whole time, especially in my left lower jaw.

Some years ago I went to my old village on a visit, but all my relatives were aged or dead, and the young did not know me. I shall have myself buried here in Liu Ling. I've decided that. I have my coffin all ready. It's made of proper thick wood. It's a very fine coffin.

People say of Ma Chen-hai: He is respected. He's an old man and respected.

His son, Ma Juei-ching, works very hard and is a capable person. He is responsible for one of the draught animals. His wife, Fan Yu-lien, died of heart disease last year. Ma Juei-ching married again in July 1962. He has a new wife.

Tables

Management Committee

Ching Chung-ying — Chairman, labour leader
Fu Hai-tsao — Deputy labour leader
Li Hai-fa — Book-keeper
Chang Chen-pong — Treasurer

Family Incomes, 1961

Head of household	Days' Work	Grain, jin	Cash, Y
From Seven-mile Village			
Chang Chen-an	307	1,535	644·70
Chang Chen-pong	279	1,395	585·90
Chang Hu-chen	285	1,425	598·50
Chao Huai-teh	187	935	392·90
From Hutoma Village			
Shueh Shen-huei	163	815	342·30

154

From Liu Ling Village

Ching Chung-ying	546	2,730	1,148·60
Tien Kuei-hua	119	595	249·90
Ma Juei-ching	266	1,330	558·60
Chang Shi-ming	164	820	344·40
Fu Hai-tsao	578	2,890	1,213·80
Mau Ke-yeh	159	795	333·90
Tsao Chen-yung	447	2,235	938·70
Tsao Chen-kuei	583	2,915	1,224·30
Ching Chung-wan	346	1,730	726·60
Tuan Fu-yin	163	815	343·30
Ma Hai-hsiu	97	485	203·70
Yang Kuei-ying	73	365	153·30
Yang Fu-lien	45	225	94·50
Kao Yü-kuei	36	180	75·60
Shi Yü-chieh	60	300	126·00

Social Subsidies from the Labour Groups' Assistance Fund, 1961:

Name	Jin	Reason
Tuan Fu-yin	200	Only one of five family members working.
Kao Yü-kuei	200	Husband working in Yenan.
Shi Yü-chieh	85	No able-bodied person in family. Recipient occupied mostly on his private plot.
Yang Kuei-ying	160	Husband working in Yenan.
Yang Fu-lien	120	Husband working in Yenan.

Resident in Seven-mile Village

Shu Hsiu-chu	60	Husband studying in Peking.
Chang Chen-pong	300	Only one of the eight members of the family is working.

Resident in Hutoma Village

Shueh Shen-huei	320	Only one person of the seven in family working.

Rewards to Merit Workers, 1961

Resident in Liu Ling Village

Fu Hai-tsao	Mattock
Ma Juei-ching	Mattock

Resident in Seven-mile Village

Chang Chen-an	Mattock
Chang Chen-ping	Scarf

Vegetable Production

	Area 1961 mu	Crop 1961 (round figs)	Area 1962 mu	Crop to 1 Sept. 1962
Chinese cabbage	8	48,000 jin	8	
Potatoes	9	27,000 jin	12	
Yellow carrots	2	6,000 jin	2	
Carrots	1	2,500 jin	1	
Lettuce	2	10,000	2	10,100
Turnips	3	10,500 jin	3	
Cucumber	2	2,000 jin	3	
Egg-fruit	4	12,000 jin	4	13,280 jin
Chilis	3	1,950 jin	3·5	
Leeks	1·5	1,350 jin	1·5	1,350 jin
Onion	2	13,000 bundles of 50	2	
Garlic	2	600 jin	2	618 jin
Tomatoes	3	7,840 jin	4	
Cabbage	5	15,000 jin	7	

Area 1961: 47·5 mu
Value of sales, 1961: 14,998 Y

Area 1962: 54 mu
Value of sales to 1 Sept. 1962: 8,885 Y

Grain Production
No figures for 1961
No figures for 1962

Part V
Liu Ling Labour Brigade

Feng Chang-yeh, leader of the brigade, aged 38

MY grandfather and my father and all my ancestors have been farmers. I myself began at the age of seven, herding for others, and at twelve I began working in Father's fields. We had seventy-eight mu in Heng-shan hsien. In the month of January 1948, my wife and my son and I moved to Ten-mile Village. That was during the occupation. My son died later, and since then we have had a daughter. The first year I broke new ground up on the hillside. I was a breaker of new ground. I worked on my own like that for two years. In 1950 I was able to buy an ox, and things were easier then. The following year, 1951, I bought a donkey. In the first six months of 1952 we organized a labour exchange group, and I was elected its leader. There we helped each other with our work. But one never knew if people would turn up or not; it was just as it might be. So, during the next six months, we turned the labour exchange group into a labour group for mutual help. That was more organized. In that labour group, we decided at the start that we were going to turn up at definite times and do the work properly.

In 1953, we had got most of the farmers in the village to join the group. There were proper discussions and divided opinions about doing this. You see, in the labour exchange group, you could choose the best workers to exchange labour with; but in the labour group for mutual help each worker had a certain point rating. His day's work was rated at between one and ten points. At first, those who were good workers wouldn't hear of a permanently organized labour group for mutual help. 'If we exchange labour with a bad worker, we shall only lose by doing so,' they said. Then we discussed matters with them and explained that everyone's work was to be given a point rating in the democratic way, so that no one would suffer by exchanging labour, nor would anyone gain by being lazy or having a poor physique. 'Those who work properly shall have many points, those who work badly shall have few,' we told them. I myself saw from the beginning that this transformation was necessary. If people help one another, everyone can be better off, I thought. But it had to be done properly and properly thought out.

Between December 1953 and January 1954, we discussed turning our labour group into an agricultural co-operative. In general, one can say that those whose land was not good were for the idea; and that those who had good land down in the valley and a lot of manpower were against it. My neighbour, Chao Teh-pa, for example, got up during the discussion and said: 'I don't want to go up the hill and toil on the hill fields. I have good, fertile land down here in the valley, and this agricultural co-operative won't pay me. I can manage by myself.' Well, we reckoned out properly how many days' work he would get in an agricultural co-operative and how much his fields in the valley gave him as it was. We proved to him that large-scale farming and joint effort was much more rational, and that, in actual fact, he would gain by joining the agricultural co-operative. 'I'll hire people,' he replied. We told him that would become rather difficult. There would be no day labourers or farmhands to be had, once we had formed our collective. They would prefer to work for themselves in an agricultural co-operative than for anyone farming on his own. In the end we proved to him that he would get much more corn and more cash for his work if he joined the agricultural co-operative.

'That isn't of any significance,' he replied. 'It may well be that I should earn more. But if I am to choose between earning more and having to climb up the hill and toil there, or earn less and only have to cultivate my own fields down in the valley, then I prefer to earn less and not have to clamber about up on the hill.' After that, we had a serious talk with him. 'You want to hire people to work for you. That's exploitation. Why do you want to become rich on other people's work? Why should only you become rich? You are not going to get anyone to exploit. Choose how you want things to be. Do you want to be rich alone, or do you want us all to be well-off together? Do you want to be a decent person or not? Think about it.' He thought about it and joined.

I was elected leader of Wanchiakou Agricultural Co-operative. After the harvest of 1954, I reckoned that what we had said really was true. We had all got more corn than we had had before. There were two reasons for this. First, we had been able to plan to use our labour more rationally; and, secondly, we had manured better. We had been able to manure better, because we had bought a flock of goats, and because now, as a co-operative, we had detailed two men, who every day drove in to Yenan town and fetched a load of human excrement. This was new and we would not have been able to get it without being organized. We had made an arrangement with the town that we got the shit in return for emptying the latrines. That was a fair exchange. The townspeople were rid of it and we got manure.

There still were people who farmed on their own here and there. We had ten of them. That year we helped them as well. In that way they too had better harvests. We helped them weed, if we had finished weeding our fields and theirs were still unweeded; we also helped them with their harvest. We did not take payment for this. We just let them feed us on the days we worked for them. They wanted to pay all right, but we would not accept anything. We did it to help them, to increase the output for the district and to give them practical proof of the power of collaboration.

The next winter, 1955–6, all the households in our area had joined Wangchiakou Agricultural Co-operative, and then we discussed transforming ourselves into a higher agricultural co-operative. At that time there was our agricultural co-operative, Wangchiakou Agricultural

Co-operative and also Liu Ling Agricultural Co-operative, and, in Hutoma, there was a labour group for mutual help. Well, to begin with, there were a lot who did not want to agree to the change. Again, it was a question of those who had the better land and those with many animals being afraid of losing by it. They did not want their animals to become collective property. 'We don't want to lose our animals,' they said. We proved to them that they would not lose anything economically. The animals would be bought from them by the co-operative, and they would be paid for them in instalments over several years. Now we were going to be more efficient and look after our resources in quite a different way. We were doing all that so that everybody would be able to live better. The discussions went on till late at night. Kou Chen-you, who has a stiff leg and a knee that hurts, said: 'The economic side's all very well, but I am a cripple and I have a horse and I need that for getting into the town and doing my business and I need it when I go to see my relations. So I shall keep my horse and not go in with you again.' So then we all sat down with him and made proper calculations with him. We demonstrated for him that many of his errands to the town would no longer be necessary, when there was a higher agricultural co-operative, because all visits to the town could be organized in a more rational way. As far as visiting relations went, that would be easy to arrange. Everybody knew that he had a bad leg and needed a horse to get about. There would be no difficulty about his borrowing a horse whenever he wanted to visit his relatives. Before, he had not travelled about visiting people in the busiest time of the year, when a horse could not be spared; so there would be no inconvenience or difficulty for him, quite the reverse. Gradually, he became convinced that we were right.

Now, I was elected leader of the East Shines Red Higher Agricultural Co-operative. We comprised four villages: Wangchiakou, Hutoma, Liu Ling and Erchuankou. We had more manpower and were able to do more. Our incomes increased. I have had the job for eight years now. It is a heavy responsibility. The responsibility gets heavier every year. At the same time, the work becomes easier every day, because people's consciousness increases every day.

The whole time, the work has meant having the personal responsibility for everything that happens, all that is done in tilling, looking after the animals, forestry, subsidiary occupations and so on. The leaders of the labour groups are responsible for the day-to-day work, but my task is to co-ordinate all the work and see that all goes smoothly and that we stick to our plans and that we don't distort production. When we went into Liu Ling People's Commune in 1958, I became leader of Liu Ling Labour Brigade. My job and my responsibility remained the same: planning, supervising, training, solving problems, finding out the members' views and listening to them.

The discussion about forming a people's commune was short. Some people thought it an unnecessary measure. Lo Wen-ming and Li Shen-yung in Wangchiakou said: 'Why should we change everything again now? Things are going well as they are. It's just unnecessary trouble and complication and doesn't serve any purpose.' But we discussed and made propaganda. The central committee of the party, of course, had said that we ought to form people's communes. People's communes were supposed to be a more effective employment of manpower, to give greater possibilities for capital investment; with one we should be maintaining the principle of everyone being paid according to the work he did and be able to give more help to those who got into difficulties. We said other things too. After this propaganda work, we joined Liu Ling People's Commune and, instead of the East Shines Red Higher Agricultural Co-operative, we became Liu Ling Labour Brigade.

We had heard about that business of free food. But we didn't think it would be suitable here with us. We simply did not believe in it. We were afraid that it would undermine our members' trust in the principle of the day's work as the unit. It would make consumption independent of the work contributed, and we did not think that would work well. So we discussed this among ourselves quite briefly. After that we decided not to allow any discussion of it outside, among the members. If any such discussion was to start, we would check it. But no one took the idea up.

But the organization of a people's commune also involved changes in our social care. From the beginning we had had no direct social care. Of course, from the very first days of the people's government a state public assistance fund had been set up, and that still exists. Grants are made from it every quarter. These go to certain individual cases: it can be a case of an accident or there can be other specific grounds for giving assistance. We of the labour brigade's committee deal with this and send our suggestions into the people's commune, which passes them on to the administration of the hsien. People can apply for grants from the fund. As a member of the committee, I am responsible for drawing up the proposals. But, of course, this is not social care in the proper sense. But, even when we first formed the East Shines Red Higher Agricultural Co-operative, we started giving social help to the families that needed it. But then we could only help those who were directly incapable of working, cripples and invalids who had been left on their own. The labour group decided what share of the harvest was to go to social help, and the committee of the higher agricultural co-operative saw to the distribution of the labour brigade's grants.

After the introduction of the people's commune, we were able to increase these grants considerably. After that, we were able to give grants not only to those who were actually ill, but also to families which had got into difficulties for one reason or another. It could be a family with many members in it, but few of them able-bodied; or it could be a dwelling-grant for new arrivals or for young people setting up their own home. But the principle remained the same as before. The labour groups decide what portion of the harvest is to go towards this, and then the committee of the labour brigade takes the proposals for grants made by the labour groups and decides what actual amounts each family is to receive. There is thus no difference in the sources, from which we get our resources, to those of social care. But that, of course, is obvious. There is no other source. Work is the only basis. You can't get social care out of the sky. Those who work must themselves agree what proportion of their work they are prepared to hand over to their neighbours, for whom things are difficult. That is a question of social responsibility and solidarity. You can't solve that question by taking the possibility of deciding this from the workers. That would reduce their social consciousness and be the end of solidarity. In the same way, there is no difference in who is entitled to decide; the decision still rests with the members of the labour groups and is taken in general meeting. This, too, is essential in a democratic society. The workers must themselves assume the responsibility. The difference consists in the fact that with the introduction of the people's commune and the big propaganda campaigns we had during that time, the members' consciousness increased and their sense of responsibility was strengthened so greatly that it became possible to introduce rational social care. This is also one of the main points in our propaganda: the mutual responsibility of members.

At the same time, we have to see that the social grants don't become so big that social help is greater than the workers' incomes. One must not undermine the value of work. But one has to see that everyone, even those who for various reasons have got into difficulties, have the possibility to live decent lives. You will understand that better if you will take a look at the figures.

The year before the formation of Liu Ling People's Commune, 1957, we in the East Shines Red Higher Agricultural Co-operative handed over as social help 3,360 jin of corn and 6,000 jin of fuel. During 1958, when Liu Ling People's Commune was formed, these figures rose to 13,900 and 14,000 respectively, and, in 1959, the first whole year with the commune, when we had stabilized the position, 13,300 and 16,000; and last year, 1961, we had got up to 16,300 and 18,000.

There you have the development. I consider this one of the most important changes of recent years. Illness, death and accident are no longer catastrophes. Citizens now have security.

Even if the whole labour brigade should be hit by some natural catastrophe, it would still be possible to apply for help from the hsien administration through the people's commune. The people's commune is the citizen's guarantee of security. It is this requirement of security that has largely been responsible for getting the people's commune accepted. Even the higher agricultural co-operatives were too small to be able to provide a real guarantee.

The labour brigade can also borrow money. If we need to make an investment for which we do not have the means available, we make an application, which is then considered by the management of Liu Ling People's Commune and, if it recommends it—which it always does, because we never make an application unless we have had preparatory discussions with the various persons responsible—it is sent up to the hsien administration for final approval, and the loan is then made by the Yenan branch of the Chinese People's State Bank. The rate of interest can vary, for long-term loans it is usually about 2½ per cent per annum. At the present we have a loan of 4,000 Y for installing electricity.

Then, the people's commune has a loan department, which makes various private loans. Members have to apply to us on the committee of the labour brigade, and we recommend the loan department of the people's commune to make the loan.

Between September 1958 and February 1959, we experimented producing iron by our local method. We have, of course, both coal and iron-ore up in the hills. We built a blast furnace and I was responsible for organizing the work. There were seventy of us working on this. We were given work points for all other work. But this was a non-recurrent phenomenon. I can't remember the exact figures now, but, as far as I can remember, it didn't pay. You had best ask at the people's commune's office; it's some years ago now, but they have the books there. But it wasn't just a question of profitability. We learned the technique, and it's a good thing to be able to do it, if the need should ever arise.

Then, in February 1959, I joined the party. I had been thinking about it for a long time. When I came here in 1948, I had joined the people's militia, as you know. That was when the K.M.T. controlled the area and we were fighting them. Then, gradually, I became more and more conscious; I was given responsible posts and I thought a long time about joining the party. I did so finally in February 1957. When I was a child, I attended school for three winters. Those were the winters when I was eight, nine and sixteen. But I have forgotten most of what I learned there. When I came here, I began trying to learn to read and write. Mostly teaching myself. I learned to read, and the first things I set about reading were the newspaper articles about the collectivization of farming. That was what I was most interested to read about.

I am head of Liu Ling Labour Brigade, of course. I was elected that, and I shall try to explain its structure for you. First, you have the labour groups. They forgather and hold meetings, quite often. All members take part in the meetings. They elect delegates to the Liu Ling Labour Brigade's representation. Each labour group has a certain number of delegates in the representation. The number is calculated according to the number of members in the population. There is one delegate for every thirteen to seventeen individuals in the schedule of population. Infants and old people count as individuals here. But it is only the working members of the labour groups over sixteen who are entitled to vote and who can be elected. The delegates to the representation are elected at the meetings of the labour group.

The representation of the labour brigade holds four ordinary meetings a year: in winter, spring, summer and autumn. The representation is the highest enacting organ in the labour brigade. At the annual meeting, the committee and the supervisory committee report to the representation, their reports are then discussed and accepted, after which a new management committee and supervisory committee are elected, and also the delegates to the Liu Ling People's Commune's representation. These delegates represent about 170 individuals a piece. We have four delegates in the representation of the people's commune. This meets three or four times a year. Our delegates report to the management committee of the labour brigade what decisions have been taken at the meetings of the representation of the people's commune.

A chairman and deputy chairman are elected for the committee of the labour brigade. Then the members of the committee are elected. Then, we of the committee allot the various duties among ourselves. There has to be a representative of every labour group in the brigade on the brigade management committee. If a labour group is large, it ought to have both a male and a female representative. It is not stated anywhere that the leaders of the labour groups should be members of the committee of the labour brigade. But that is customary.

After the representation of the labour brigade has held its annual meeting, the labour groups hold theirs. At these they elect their leaders and committees. All are elected for one year, and have to be re-elected in the proper way every year. You cannot just stay on. The members have the right to dismiss anyone who behaves improperly or who does not represent the members' interests in the right way. This has never happened in our brigade. But last year it did with one of the delegates to the representation of Liu Ling People's Commune. The man's name was Yang, and he was from Yuanchuan Labour Brigade. He had a hot temper. He behaved improperly, swearing at people and being thoroughly unpleasant; but it's not much to talk about. Having been given a post it had gone to his head. At all events the members got together and demanded that he should be dismissed and chose another in his place.

The internal functions of the committee are divided in a number of ways. Partly, there is common responsibility, but then, too, I, as chairman, am directly responsible for, and supervise, all production, except agricultural production. Tsao Chen-kuei, who is deputy chairman, is directly responsible for agricultural production. Then there is also a committee member responsible for each labour group: I am responsible for Wangchiakou village labour group, Lo Han-hong is responsible for Hutoma Village Labour Group. The Old Secretary, Li Yua-hua, is responsible for Liu Ling Village Labour Group, and Ching Chung-ying is responsible for the labour group for vegetable cultivation. Besides, each of us is responsible for certain specific tasks. The division of work within the committee can be seen from the list we drew up this morning. Perhaps you ought to add to that, that this division of duties is made by the committee itself. For example, it is usual that the committee member responsible for public safety is also battalion commander of the people's militia, as he is with us. But it isn't stated anywhere that this has to be so.

The committee of the labour brigade meets every ten days or fortnight. This depends on how urgent the work is and what matters have to be settled. But, of course, we are in continual contact with each other. we have no sub-committees. The supervisory committee is quite separate. No one can be on the supervisory committee and at the same time be one whose work has to be scrutinized. That would be impossible. And it is also laid down in the regulations.

The labour groups have to keep up the small country roads within their areas. They maintain them and are responsible for them. On the other hand, the labour brigade is responsible for the upkeep of that section of the highway which crosses its area, from Seven-mile Village past Ten-mile Village and as far as our boundary with Chaochuan Labour Brigade. In our committee, it is Jen Yü-chen from Hutoma who has the job of seeing to this. He maintains contact with the Department for Highways Construction in Yenan hsien. This calls meetings of the various representatives of the labour brigades concerned and at their meetings they discuss the question of roads and what ought to be done during the year. These meetings then take the requisite decisions about roadworks. The decisions are subsequently implemented by the labour brigades. In principle, every able-bodied member of a labour brigade gives two days' work per annum to the upkeep of the highway. This applies to minor repairs and ordinary maintenance. When it is a case of really big roadworks, such as are of provincial importance, that will be discussed higher up. But we are in this way responsible for the road being kept open.

The postmen are no concern of ours. The post finances itself out of postage receipts. But we are to a certain extent responsible for the school. There are two types of school. Some are schools established by the labour brigades, and with these the labour brigades pay fifty per cent of the school expenses and the state fifty per cent. Some are schools wholly financed by the state, that is to say, the hsien administration. The school we have here, Liu Ling Basic School, is of the latter type and wholly financed by Yenan hsien.

We have a parents' representation for the school and a school committee. This committee, however, has no responsibility for the school's budget: if the school had been of the other type, then this school committee would also have been responsible for the budget, for the salaries and for engaging the teachers. As it is, our responsibility is limited. We discuss the work in the school and correct faults; we discuss the results obtained by the teachers and the behaviour of the pupils. If necessary, we report to those responsible for schools in the hsien administration and ask them to take steps. This school has pupils from three labour brigades and also from Seven-mile Village. Usually, the labour brigades appoint the member on their committee who is responsible for culture and educational matters to serve on the school committee. In our labour group it is Jen Yü-chen who is responsible for culture, but even so I have been appointed as our representative on the school committee. There are seven members of the committee: the head of the school, two teachers elected by the teachers themselves, one representative from Seven-mile Village and one from each of the labour brigades.

Here, in this district, there are a lot of meetings and conferences every year about various matters. They may be concerned with care of cattle, propaganda, forestry, work among women, grain production, the use of artificial manures and so on. Meetings are often held about different matters. In most cases, the committee member responsible for the thing in question is sent to the meeting. In certain cases another member, who is specially interested in the matter, may be sent. If a meeting or conference is called by the administration of the hsien and is held by day, delegates are given an allowance by the hsien of 1·20 Y a day, if they are not given food as well; or of 0·70 Y, if they are provided with food. If the meeting is of such a character that we consider it to deal with a production matter of direct interest to the labour brigade, the representative attending from the labour brigade is credited with one day's work. In this case, he does not receive the hsien administration's allowance. Last year the number of days' work credited in this way by the labour brigade exceeded 250. Ask the book-keeper for the exact figure. If a meeting is held in the evening or in the night, those taking part are not credited with a day's work. It will then take place in their spare time and is an honorary task.

People say of Feng Chang-yeh: He has a brain like an abacus. At first he appears cold and haughty, but he is easy to get into contact with. It is only on the surface that he appears to be distrait. Actually he is listening to everything, though it may not look like it. Then, gradually, you notice that he remembers it all and is thinking of it all. He is always smiling, but he often seems to be looking right through one at something far away. He can calculate anything and work anything out, and when he takes up a problem, it's as though he had an abacus in his head. That is why he was elected chairman. You get accustomed to him, and then gradually you come to like him. He is greatly liked and respected now.

Tsao Chen-kuei, 'The Little Author', aged 28

FATHER moved here from Hengshan in 1927. I myself was born in 1934. I was born here, of course, and have no knowledge from my own experience of what it was like up there, but Father says that his landlord was hard, and that they were not able to manage. When Father heard that there was more land in the area round Yenan, the family moved here. It consisted of Grandfather and Grandmother, Father and Father's younger brother. At that time, there were still landowners in Liu Ling. But in the distribution of land in 1935 we got forty mu of valley land and sixty mu of poor hill land. This had all belonged to Li Hsiu-tang's family. The valley land lay down there and the hill fields were up there on the far side of the valley.

In 1946 I started at the basic school here in Liu Ling. The school was run by the government of the Shensi-Kansu-Ningsia Frontier Region. That was our Red government up here. By that year, 1946, life had become quite good. We had a horse, but no ox. We exchanged days' work with others when we needed to borrow an ox. One ox-day was equivalent to 2½ days' work. With three years' work, we harvested enough for four years' consumption. That means that life was quite good, and that everything was going ahead nicely. We were worse off where clothes were concerned. We were, of course, blockaded by the K.M.T. and had to wear homespun that wasn't always of such wonderful quality. In 1947, Hu Tsung-nan came. The school stopped, and I fled with my parents to the village of Louta up in the hills.

Before this, Father had been up at the front helping our army dig trenches. We ourselves had buried all our corn in response to the government's appeal. We had 2,400 jin in store then. I hadn't been digging, for I was young, of course, and only able to carry light things. During the night of 10 and 11 March 1957, Father came back from the front and said that now the enemy was coming at any moment and that we were to fly, because our army was in full retreat. That night we did all our packing and the next morning we fled into the hills. On the 13th Hu Tsung-nan's troops marched in, but we were then no longer here.

K.M.T. troops also came to the village of Louta. But we did not stay in the village during the day; we just slept there at night. We kept up on the hill. One day, the soldiers came and succeeded in getting our horse and the things we had in our cave. They even took our sieve. Then the soldiers began coming up on to the slopes. We saw them coming up through the bushes. Before that, I had seen only the Eighth Route Army soldiers; but these, who were coming then, had proper uniforms and steel helmets. They shouted and fired into the air, and we were so frightened that we could not even bring ourselves to run away. I know now that we would have been able to run away, but when we saw those soldiers in their uniforms and steel helmets and with rifles, we were quite paralysed. They took us back to the village. They took Father away with them. We were not allowed to go with him.

Everything in our cave in Liu Ling had been destroyed. It had all been smashed or stolen. Only a few people had come back to the village. There was Tung Yang-chen and his grandmother, Li Hai-kuei's and Fu Hai-tsao's mother, and ourselves. They were the only ones on this side. Li Hsiu-tang and his family were on the other side, of course. We had no contact with him and his family. People said that Li Hsiu-tang had joined the K.M.T. then, others say that he fled to the hills and came down after a while and was captured by the K.M.T., and others again say that he had secretly been waiting and longing for the K.M.T. for years and years and had always worked for them. I don't know. People talk such a lot. At all events we had no contact with his family.

All of us who had come back now lived together in the same cave. It was Tu Yi-chen's cave, it had been standing empty and was a double cave with several exits. We all lived in it together. In that way we could help each other.

Father came home little more than a week after we had been taken back to the village. They had flogged him, he told us. He had been kept a prisoner in the village of Koumen. They had accused him of being a communist and of doing transport work for the Eighth Route Army. He couldn't tell them anything about the Eighth Army's transports, not having taken part in them; he had just dug trenches for them and given them food. Father said to the K.M.T. soldiers: 'I am a farmer from the district here. I can prove that.' They kept him locked up, and he talked to the guards and said: 'If any of the older people come back down to the village from the hill, they can confirm that I am just an old farmer from Liu Ling.' Father was kept shut up in a potato cellar. But then Ma Chien-kai, Fen Tse-wen and Liu Tsung-yuan came. All three were old farmers in the village of Koumen. They guaranteed to the K.M.T. that Father really was what he made himself out to be, an ordinary local farmer. After that they let him go. Father still talks about them today and says that they were his true benefactors.

We fetched corn from our buried stores; but someone had discovered them and most of it had been stolen. We don't know whether it was the K.M.T. or someone from the village. Then, in June, we again lost a lot of corn. One night I had dug up thirty jin of the millet we had in one of our hiding places up on the hillside, which had not been plundered. But the very next day a K.M.T. patrol came. We had hidden the millet by spreading it on our kang and putting a blanket over it and then sitting on the blanket. But the K.M.T. soldiers just went straight to the kang, shoved us off on to the floor, lifted the blanket and took all our millet. So then we had nothing to eat. After that Mother and I gathered different herbs during the day, and, at night, I crept up cautiously to one of our hiding places and dug up a little corn. But I only took enough to last for the following day. In that way, if the K.M.T. soldiers came, they were not able to take so much from us. And they did come.

Once again they took our millet. Mother began to weep and

pleaded with them: 'Let us keep our millet! We are starving!' But the soldiers kicked her over and threatened her with their rifles. They said that she had insulted the K.M.T., and that they would stick their bayonets through her in various ways. I was so afraid that I didn't know what to do. The entire family fell on their knees and begged for mercy for Mother. Tung Yang-chen's grandmother, who is my grandmother too, also begged for mercy for Mother. Then the soldiers said: 'We pardon you. But you have forfeited your millet.' So then they took the millet and went.

One night, we heard the sound of many men and horses in the village. There were thunderous crashes. We were so afraid that we stayed right at the back of the cave. Not till the morning did we see what had happened. The Southern District Co-operative Society had had seventy or eighty rooms in the village here, where the school now stands. They had had two-storied houses and a big warehouse and everything. That night the K.M.T. had pulled it all down, and the troops had gone off with all the timber. There were only ruins left. Before, there used to be quantities of big willows here, down by the river. A whole wood it had been. The K.M.T. cut almost the whole lot down.

A couple of days before Hu Tsung-nan's troops withdrew, they had big manœuvres up in the hills. They shot and called and talked loudly and marched about everywhere. No one knew what they were doing, or why they were doing it. People did not dare come out of their caves. The soldiers were shooting all over the place, though there were neither guerrillas nor Eighth Route Army anywhere near. I was living then with Hu Chan-yü; he's dead now. A couple of nights later the enemy nearly took Father again. There were great explosions and crashes everywhere. There were sounds of troops up on the hillside. Nobody dared sleep. We were all sitting on the kang and had not lit any lights. Nobody dared look out through the door to see what was happening. Suddenly some K.M.T. soldiers walked into the cave. They shone pocket torches on us and then they took Ai Shen-tang away with them; he was from Hengshan, but was hiding in Liu Ling. He was to act as guide for them. Then a solitary K.M.T. soldier came back. He fetched Father. Father was to be their guide too. But when they got outside into the dark, Father managed to tear himself free and get away. He ran up on to the hill and remained hidden there till the K.M.T. had marched away.

Then we had to start building it all up from the beginning again. We had nothing to eat; we had neither door nor windows to our caves. We collected bushes and made a protection of sorts with them, and in that way we were able to use our cave again. The government now organized the people. They got seed-corn for us. Those families with people able to work were given the job of going to fetch the corn. It was a hard spring. But things began to brighten a bit when the maize was harvested that autumn. In 1948, we got 1,200 jin of grain. Then I went back to school, and in the spring of 1949 I joined the League of Youth. In 1949, the harvest was better, and towards the end of 1950 I left school. In our family Father was the only one who worked in the fields, but ever since Hu Tsung-nan's soldiers had flogged him, he had pains in his back and trouble with his legs. He was no longer able to deal with our land alone, so I gave up school in order to help the family.

I was young then and had not worked properly before and did not know so very much. In 1951, we joined Li Hai-kuei's Labour Group for Mutual Help. We managed better there. I had the job of keeping the work daybook and entering the work points. That was because I had some schooling. But the cultivation of the land was still done on an individual basis. The yield per mu had not increased, nor had the number of cattle. In December 1952 I joined the party. During the winter of 1953–4 we discussed the situation. You see, Li Yiu-hua had organized his farmers' co-operative then, and ganbus from the party apparatus and the state administration in our hsien had come out to study what had been done and draw conclusions. Li Yiu-hua's Agricultural Co-operative now had seven oxen and a few donkeys, and their harvests had been better than ours. Their yield per mu was greater, too. The party then told us that we ought to organize ourselves, so we studied the agricultural co-operative. We members of the labour group for mutual help saw with our own eyes that the agricultural co-operative was superior. After that winter's discussions, we applied to join the agricultural co-operative in the spring of 1954.

I myself realized that Liu Ling Agricultural Co-operative was only a semi-socialistic structure, and that it was necessary to reform it and make it socialistic, a higher agricultural co-operative. This was no problem where I was concerned, but Father was reluctant to start with. This was because he did not want to give up his land. In Liu Ling Agricultural Co-operative he still got a dividend on the land he had; while in the higher agricultural co-operative the land was to become collective property and he would be paid according to the socialistic principle 'To each according to his work'. Father was afraid that we would lose by this. He said that in the agricultural co-operative we got twenty jin of corn per mu of valley land and seven to eight jin of corn per mu of hill land, and he didn't want to lose this.

I now explained the whole thing to Father, as his son and as a communist. I pointed out that we had never been able to manure our hill fields. Our own manure was only enough for the valley land. This meant that we were not exploiting our land rationally or effectively. In the collective, on the other hand, we could work effectively. This meant that all the land had to be cultivated in the way that provided the greatest yield. We would be paid for our work and we would earn many work points, since there were now two of us in the family working. Since I was his son, he listened to me, though he had refused to listen to the others, and after I had had two or three talks with him, he agreed to join.

Our ox was old and not worth much. Together, our animals were valued at thirty yuan. We invested this in the East Shines Red Higher Agricultural Co-operative. It was paid back in five years.

I had only been to school for a few years. In the country, most people cannot read or write. Now I read at night and in the wintertime. I wanted to learn things. To understand what life was like. I was a communist and I was dying to convince people like Tung Yang-chen, who was reluctant in the beginning. In 1956, when the East Shines Red Higher Agricultural Co-operative was formed, I was appointed deputy chairman. That was my first public job. Before that, I had been responsible for propaganda work in our hsiang; that is, the administrative unit there was at that time and which corresponds roughly to our people's commune. After the people's commune was set up, I became deputy chairman of Liu Ling Labour Brigade. That's the same thing.

In the East Shines Red Higher Agricultural Co-operative I was from the start responsible for cultural questions, education and health. This work was later taken over by Jen Yü-chen from Hutoma and I became responsible for the agricultural work. This did not involve any change in organization; it was just a question of persons. I had studied the technique of farming and was transferred to that work, because it was thought to suit me better. Besides that, I work in the labour group for vegetable cultivation.

In the winter, the labour groups put forward their production plans for the coming year. I go through these and collate them into a general plan, which is then discussed by the labour brigade's management committee. I am responsible for the agricultural work. This means that I make regular inspections to see that the work progresses in accordance with our plans. If any problems arise, I have to tackle them. This work, of course, is carried out in the closest collaboration with the responsible persons in the labour groups.

I have, of course, tried to educate myself further. In 1952, I took a course that used a quick method of learning to write the new characters. In that way, I improved my ability to write. Later, I attended evening classes. Besides, I sat up at night and studied on my own. In the League of Youth, between 1949 and 1952, I studied the league's basic course, theory of agriculture and the party's general plan for the socialistic reform of China's agriculture, and read about our bright future under socialism. When I joined the party, I studied the party's programme, the rights and duties of party members, the party's policy, and writings by Chairman Mao. Besides this, I read various things on my own: the history of the party and the selected writings of Chairman Mao.

After that I began on literature. I read novels and collections of short stories. Not so much classic literature. I have read only three of the Chinese classics: *The Eastern Expedition, The Western Expedition* and *The March North*. All three are about war under the Tang dynasty. The modern Chinese authors I like best are Feng Te-yin, Liu Ching and Tu Peng-cheng. Lately, I have been reading Tu Peng-cheng's *Defend Yenan!* This is about how northern Shensi fought Hu Tsung-nan. Then I have read *The Song of Youth* by Yang Mo. This is about the student movement many years ago. It has been made into a film, too. I thought the film was quite good but that the book was much better. No, I have never read any foreign authors. I read in my spare time, and I read when I am resting and I read at nights. I do not need to sleep as much as other people. I like reading and I want to know what things were like in the old days, and I want to learn the technique of writing. When I read, I am always thinking of how what I am reading is constructed, and how one could have expressed it better.

Actually, I am trying to learn to write. I have been thinking of becoming a writer ever since 1954. First, I sent in various things to the local newspapers here in Yenan. Then, after 1958, I began wondering how one could ever describe all that had been happening. I know, of course, that such a lot has happened in the country in the last few years.

But it is very difficult to describe it. I would like to write about how I have experienced it. After all, I am a farmer's son and a farmer myself. I have also published some short stories. Three altogether. They were included in *The Yen River Magazine*. This is a literary periodical printed in Sian. It is published by the Sian branch of the Writers' Association.

I had my first short story published in January 1959. It was called 'We long for our beloved'. It is about how people here in the district have a bumper harvest and how they go into the fields and think about Chairman Mao. That was my first short story. It was a bit fumbly. Then, in 1960, I had my next short story published. It was called 'Visiting Aunt'. I tried to show by describing a visit to an aunt how life had become better and better. How this woman who had been oppressed in the old society had now become a merit worker in a people's commune.

In the summer of 1961 I had my third short story published: 'Two Men Called Hsiu.' In this I tried to describe how the new man who is now beginning to take shape in the countryside loves our collective property. I began by describing two men, who were both called Hsiu. In their brigade there were two oxen which were ill. The oxen were thin and not fit to work. People were talking about them and saying that they ought to be sold for butchering. But these two Hsiu men had a sentiment for collective property, and proposed keeping the oxen. They promised at the meeting to look after them and make them well. Then I go on to relate how they looked after the oxen, and how they thought up every possible way of curing them and so on. And in the end both oxen get well and strong again and are able to work in the fields. The story ends with all the members of the labour brigade honouring the two old men called Hsiu by making them merit workers.

I have not written anything this year. This year I have mostly gone about thinking. I have been thinking of a story, but it won't come right. I haven't been able to get started on it. Perhaps it's not a good idea.

Most people in the village back me up, but they often make fun of me and call me 'the little author'. But they like the idea of me writing. It's as though they liked my writing about them and people's being able to read it. Before I send anything in, I read it out to my close friends. I want to hear their opinion of what I have written. But I don't read out my things publicly, so to speak. One can't call a meeting just so that the deputy chairman of the labour brigade can read out a short story.

What I have written are only just exercises. They aren't master-pieces. But I wanted to see how what one writes looks in print. I am trying to learn the technique of writing. Those in the village who can read have read my short stories. They haven't said much about them. When I have asked them, they have said: 'They are all right as they are.'

The authors in Sian have helped me. They have elected me to the Sian branch of the Authors' Society. They have sent me different study material. I haven't written much. Actually, I am ashamed to be sitting here talking about it. But I have wanted to write for a long time. In April 1960, I also attended a course in Sian itself. It was a study course for amateur writers. We were all workers or farmers. First, we read theory. Then we swotted Chairman Mao's speech about art and literature that he made in Yenan in 1942. Then various well-known authors came and told us about their technique and the methods used in literary work. Then we analysed various short stories. We chose the best stories written by those taking part in the course. None of mine was chosen. We then talked about these stories and tried to arrive at what was good in them and what was bad. At the end of the course, I thought that I knew a bit more about literary theory; I think, too, that it has helped me to describe characteristic people. Since then, I have written very little.

Actually, I would like to write a big novel. It would be like no novel I have ever read. A novel about what actually has happened to us here. I mean a novel about my own life. So far, I have just been practising using words, trying to get a story to hang together and tell something. I have a plan that I have been working on for a long time. I would like to describe everything that has happened here. That would make a long, long novel, a broad description of this region, its people and their destinies. Not an 'I' novel. Not that I am against 'I' novels, but because I am far too young and would like to describe much more than what I myself have been able to witness. To go a long way back in time. The whole revolution, everything that has happened in the country. A big novel.

I don't know when I first thought of it. I think probably I have always been thinking of it in one way or another. But, consciously, I have been thinking about it ever since I met Han Chi-hsiang. He is a blind story-teller and singer. I saw him in Yenan and listened to him. He is engaged on a description of his own life, and I thought that if a blind man can write a novel about his own life, I ought to be able to write one too, having a good pair of eyes. I had read things by him already in 1956, but it wasn't till 1958 that I was able to meet him. He made a profound impression on me. He told me that he was now writing a fat book about his own life. I thought then that perhaps . . . I have met him several times since. He has been out here in Liu Ling telling stories for us.

Chou Chia-fu lives in Yenan, too. He writes about the Red Guard. But he has not made anything like the same impression on me that Han Chi-hsiang did. This is the first time I have spoken about my novel to anyone. Of course, these are things that you can talk about with your friends, and things that you daren't discuss with anyone else but yourself. But now I have said it. Some day I am going to write my big novel. I think about it all the time; and I am usually thinking it over while I am working.

But I have talked about my short stories with Lo Han-hong. I usually start by having a talk with Lo Han-hong about what I am thinking of writing. I talk to him about it, because he is very fond of literature, he reads a lot and himself writes for the newspapers and such. He writes articles mostly and other things. He isn't working on any book, as far as I know.

There is a library here in Liu Ling Labour Brigade. But there isn't much fiction in it. I usually go in to Yenan every now and again and go to the bookshop and buy books. And then we borrow from each other. There are four or five of us in the labour brigade here who read books. Many read the newspapers, but there are only a few who love reading books.

People in the village here laugh at me a lot, as I have told you. But not so much because I write. They like my writing about the village and the country, and they read what I have written. They laugh at me because I sit up at night instead of sleeping. They say that I write in my sleep. You see, everyone else in the village here goes to bed early and falls asleep at once.

I like the cinema and opera. When I was small, I preferred the opera. The music and the costumes and all that interested me. But now that I'm older, I prefer films. I have occupied myself and experimented with play writing a bit. Han-hong and I wrote a play together, or rather a collection of small sketches that were performed by amateurs at the spring festival. It was about what had happened in the brigade. That was a sort of exercise, too. But people liked it. A real opera is something quite different.

My wife cannot read, so she isn't against my writing. But she does not help me either. She does not say anything about it. I never read her what I have written. She has never heard anything that I have written. I only read it for those who can understand what I mean and who can criticize it. She has three children to see to, and if I were to start reading to her, the children would come and disturb us. My parents have no objections to my writing either. But when I sit up late at night, my mother says: 'You'll make yourself tired. It's bad for you to be awake at night. You have to get up early.' But when they heard that my things had been printed and when they saw them in print and could hold them in their hands, she stopped saying anything. Now she is just proud that I, who am only a farmer's son, have had something printed in a real periodical.

I had, of course, begun writing for the local press up here. I didn't, then, even know that there was a magazine called *The Yen River Magazine*. Then a man called Ho Hung-chi came up to Yenan from Sian. He heard about me from the editorial offices in Yenan and came out here to meet me. I told him about my plans. Not about them all, of course, but I told him a lot. Then I showed him what I had written and he criticized it for me. He helped me to work over what I had written. I did not need to change much. Just polish the language and correct mistakes. He also changed the plot in my first short story, the one where they get a bumper harvest and go about yearning for Chairman Mao. After those corrections, he took the manuscript to Yenan and there it was printed. That's how I made my début.

I have also tried writing poetry, but that hasn't been very successful.

At present, I am thinking out my big novel. But I'm not intending to tell anyone about that or discuss it with anyone. Not until it's quite ready.

People say of Tsao Chen-kuei: He is a fortunate person. He thinks clearly and is quick-witted. He is very knowledgeable. Although he is still so young, he is very respected. He is a great enthusiast. People in the village don't say much about what he has written. 'He has been to Liu Ling Basic School for only a couple of years, and yet he publishes things in a proper magazine.' He writes a lot of articles. People are proud that the village possesses its own author. His mother especially is proud of him and says: 'Even though he was just a short time at school, he is learned and has studied. He sits up every night reading. He sits up at night even during harvest and it never makes any difference to his work.' People call out: 'There goes Chen-kuei, our little author.' When Tsao Chen-kuei hears that, he doesn't say anything, but he blushes.

He is an open person, good, and has an even temper. He has a good wife, who has a placid temperament. She is rather silent and a bit uncommunicative, but he talks enough for two. Theirs is a happy marriage. Their children are well brought up and well looked after. His mother loves her grandchildren, sits with them on her lap all day long. The whole family is happy.

It is characteristic of Tsao Chen-kuei that people's moods always change when he comes. Everyone becomes glad and laughs. He is never hard or violent. But even though he's so open, he is a very cautious man. 'You may think him vague and easy-going, but that is just appearance; actually he is very particular and very methodical.'

Lo Han-hong, the book-keeper, aged 28

FATHER'S name is Lo Wen-ming and he comes from Hengshan. I myself was born up there. Things were difficult for us and Father came here to Yenan district when I was five years old. A year later Father came up to us and took my mother, myself and my little sister back with him. I remember almost nothing of that. Father rented land here in Wangchiakou from a landlord called Tsao. This was already a Red area, but it was during the unity period, so Father had to be a tenant. Three or four years after we moved down here, however, the land was divided up, and we were given a small hill for our own. Then there were seven or eight years before Hu Tsung-nan came. During those years Father worked a lot and harvested a lot of corn, 6,000 to 7,000 jin a year. We built three caves, had lots of space and a lot of food and lots of clothes. Life was good. I was thirteen when Hu Tsung-nan came, in 1947. We had an ox then, a donkey and twenty mu of land. We had both valley land and hill land. The K.M.T. destroyed everything and the troops ate our ox. All the animals in the area vanished.

When Hu Tsung-nan came, Father went to the guerrillas. We went into the hills. But at harvest-time 1947 Father came back from the guerrillas and we went down to the village. We could maintain contact with the guerrillas from the village. We had nothing to eat, because the enemy had discovered the place where we had hidden our corn. We had nowhere to live. Most people in the village worked for the guerrillas. The people now hated Hu Tsung-nan. One day some other children and I were out playing. There were eight of us. We were discovered by K.M.T. soldiers and started to run when they shouted to us to halt. They chased us. Then all the soldiers began shooting. Then other K.M.T. soldiers on the hill fired. They were trying to capture us. But they shot at each other instead and killed one of their own men. We children thought that funny. We escaped, but that same night the K.M.T. soldiers came to the village and plundered it. Later that night, some of the older youths went into the hills to join the guerrillas.

Hu Tsung-nan opened a school in Liu Ling and tried to compel us to go to it. But that didn't do him any good, because his troops had plundered so much. There were seven or eight children in our class. Our teacher was called Lei. We didn't try to learn, we just behaved badly, because we knew that the teachers were from Hu Tsung-nan. There were also secret agents going round in ordinary farmers' clothes. But they weren't so dangerous, because in their heart of hearts they were really on the side of the guerrillas. The teachers in the school, however, were real agents. They made propaganda for the K.M.T. They said: 'The K.M.T. is for the people.' But we had seen quite a lot and, being quite big, we said: 'If the K.M.T. is for the people and the K.M.T. is so good, why did they steal our ox?' After that we were beaten. The teachers drank themselves intoxicated in the evenings. We children discussed the different armies: the Red Army and Hu Tsung-nan's army. The teachers heard us and hit us with their steel rulers. The next day I played truant, because I was tired of the school; so then they came and fetched me. But I just sat there pretending to be studying. I wasn't doing anything. Things at school got so bad, and the teachers were so hated by all the children and parents, that the villagers got in contact with the guerrillas and told them that something had to be done. One night the guerrillas came. We had told the K.M.T. agents in the village to go to bed and sleep heavily that night. All the teachers were taken prisoner except Lei, who managed to escape and got away to Seven-mile Village. That night was the end of the village school.

More and more were working for us and, now, the enemy became frightened and fled to the town and no longer dared work out in the countryside. The K.M.T. was short of goods now and their food was bad, and when they came out to the villages to steal food, they were attacked by the guerrillas and things went badly for the K.M.T. in their fights, we were told. In the spring of 1948 the K.M.T. withdrew from northern Shensi.

Then we began building up our home again. The three caves we had built had fallen in and we built new ones. In the autumn of 1948 I began school in Liu Ling. At that time it comprised only the first few classes. It was a lower basic school then. I began in the higher basic school in Yenan in 1953. I went there for eighteen months. In March 1954 my mother died. After that Father wanted me to stop school and come back. I didn't want to stop school at all; I wanted to go on studying. But Father insisted. The family needed me, and I had no choice. I had to go back home to the village at the end of the spring term of 1954. Father was afraid that, if I was able to go on studying, I would start working outside the family. I was the only son, and Father wanted to keep me there in the family. I was very sorry, but I thought of my sister and my father and went back to Wangchiakou village.

The farmers' co-operative had also written to me that they needed someone who could keep books. There were thirty-seven households and not a single person in them who could write. Father had been keeping the books, but he had only been to school for two winters as a child and he was the only one in the village who could read a little. Father found it difficult and the collective was not satisfied. I came back in the month of July 1954, and then our labour group for mutual help was turned into a farmers' co-operative. I was elected book-keeper at the first meeting in which I took part. I was given a big red paper flower as a welcoming present. Although I had been studying for a number of years now, I did not know anything about book-keeping. The party school sent out notices to the villages that it was starting a course for book-keeping and the farmers' co-operative sent me to it. I attended that course from August to December 1954. After that course I did know something about book-keeping and had learned to count with an abacus.

Life was so different in the village. At school, everything had been done at a fixed time and had followed the timetable laid down. Now, in the village, where I was supposed to enter people's work points, it was made difficult, because none of the members of the farmers' co-operative keep any proper hours. I could not get any order in their work and nobody bothered about what I said, because I was so young. I was so agitated I used to weep at nights. I could not get all the households to come every day. When we were to have a settling, there would suddenly be no one there. I thought that life in a farmers' co-operative was intolerable compared with life as a student. I wanted to go back to school.

Then Feng Chang-yeh had a talk with me. He was very serious and upright and talked logically with me. He said: 'You must understand that things are like that in the country. That's obvious. We have all farmed on our own and are accustomed to being our own masters and we can't yet be as disciplined as workers or people studying. You have a big future ahead of you if you stay here in the country. We need young people who are gifted and knowledgeable here. We need intellectuals of our own kind. Gradually you will learn to work with the villagers, and they will end by keeping to hours and realize that order is necessary. The villagers here rely on you. They have elected you. They have big ideas for your future, and they have great hopes of you. You must remember that they have paid for your studies and that they used their own money to send you to a book-keeping course.' I was very moved when he said that. I remembered how kind everybody had been to me, and I thought how there were thirty-seven households there and no one in them who could read or write properly, and no one able to keep books. So then I decided not to go back to school, but to stay in my village and work.

In the spring of 1955, several of my schoolmates returned. There was Liang Hsing-chen, Li Kwei-ling, Liu Fu-min and Chang Kwei-lin. I was glad to meet them again. We decided to organize a study group, in which we would first make sure of what we had learned in school and then study further on our own. Feng Chang-yeh agreed to this, and we began to study. First, we revised our school lessons, then we collected money enough to subscribe to two newspapers. We read the newspapers out loud to the other members of the farmers' co-operative, and in the evenings we studied and had discussions.

After some time other young people came and asked if they might join our study group. We told them that we had been hoping from the beginning that our group would grow. Feng Chang-yeh encouraged us to start a reading class. 'Now you should become a teacher,' he said. We used various methods to make more people able to read. We wrote the characters for the different agricultural tools on the tools themselves, so that people would see the character as they used the tool. We had eighteen young pupils. Later, they asked to be allowed to study in books. We could not find any suitable reader for them, so we wrote a book which gave 500 characters specially suited to Wangchiakou village. We had help from various people in the village, who told us what they would think interesting to read. Later our reader was used also in Liu Ling. We, who were teachers, wrote out six copies of it each. There were twenty pages in each copy and this gave us an opportunity to practise our skill in calligraphy.

That year everyone was very enthusiastic. Even the older people wanted to join us. Tung Shen-ming, who was fifty-two and the shepherd, came to us and said: 'Will you also take an old man as a pupil?' We did and he learned to read. In 1956 we had read through this reader and by then all nineteen were able to read. Even the old man. They knew 500 characters; they could write their names, they could read the co-operative's books and no one could any longer diddle them over work points or cheat them over money.

Tung Shen-ming said: 'Before, I was always being diddled. Once, when I went to the market in Yenan to sell corn, I was to have had 2·50 Y for three jin of corn, for that was the market price then; I sold my twelve jin, but got only 2 Y; the buyer reckoned it all out in front of me, but I could neither read nor write and just knew that I was being cheated, but could not prove it. That's what always happened to us farmers in those days. The townspeople cheated us and we couldn't read. I always thought it was my parents' fault for not sending me to school for a winter. But now I can read and no one can cheat me any more.'

That year we formed an amateur group. We sang songs, we wrote short sketches, we made up our own songs, we read newspapers aloud. The members of the co-operative wanted to hear what was in the newspapers. Especially they wanted to hear what was written about farming. They listened to all the farming articles. They were interested in that, and afterwards they discussed the articles.

Then I wrote a small play that I called 'Old Kou joins the farmers'

187

co-operative'. We put this on, and it was a success. Then, one day, I discovered that the young people used to have fights with millet out at the threshing floor. They threw the millet at each other. So, I wrote a little piece I called 'A ridiculous young man took fresh golden rice to fight with. That is good food and it is a silly thing to do.' I posted this up on the wall-newspaper, and people read it and, after my criticizing them, the young people mended their ways.

In 1956 we reformed ourselves into the East Shines Red Higher Agricultural Co-operative. These three groups, the self-study group, the amateur group and the reading group, put a lot of propaganda work into this. I myself kept on being elected book-keeper for Wangchiakou Labour Group, as we were now called. I saw that production was developed at the same pace as that of the bigger collectives. Wangchiakou Agricultural Co-operative had borrowed money and was in debt to the state when we joined the improved farmers' co-operative. But the East Shines Red Higher Agricultural Co-operative paid this loan off in 1957.

In July 1957, I was sent to the School for Agricultural Ganbus in Yenan. We were to learn new methods of farming, and in December I came back. I was very enthusiastic then. I had learned a lot about varieties, fruit growing, manuring, how to fight insect pests, economic sizes of fields, new crops to sow, organization of farmwork, new implements, new types of plough and much more. Besides, I had been able to study politics.

In January 1958, with the support of the Old Secretary, Li Yiu-hua, I formed an experimental group. The young people in this group did not have to do other work. We were given a field in which we could experiment. I was leader of the group, and we experimented with different kinds of seed. We arrived at three good varieties of millet, two of maize and three of wheat. In the autumn of 1958, I had taught them all that I had learned, and the other young people went back to their labour groups. The Old Secretary, Li Yiu-hua, said that we had done a good job and that we in our turn should learn from the old experienced farmers. He said to me: 'They have eaten more salt than you have eaten corn.' At that time, too, there was a party slogan: 'Combine knowledge with experience.'

When Liu Ling People's Commune was set up, I first worked in the loan department of the people's commune. I worked there for two months, and then the book-keeper of Liu Ling Labour Brigade died.

He was old. Then I was chosen book-keeper for Liu Ling Labour Brigade, and I have been re-elected every year since. That was in 1959.

I had joined the League of Youth in 1952, when I was going to school. In 1956 I was elected secretary of the East Shines Red Higher Agricultural Co-operative's branch of the League of Youth. I have been re-elected to this post every year since. In 1960, I was elected deputy secretary of the committee of the Liu Ling People's Commune's branch of the League of Youth. The League of Youth has twenty-four members in the labour brigade. In the two labour groups with which you are concerned, the league has ten members. The main task of China's Communist League of Youth is to act as auxiliaries for the party. We are to help production under the party's guidance. We have one or two branch meetings a month. The groups meet once a week. They discuss their studies, and they discuss production work. Before the meetings, reports are submitted about what has been done during the week. In the League of Youth we study four subjects: (1) The league's programme. This is explained and we have a thorough discussion of each point. (2) Day-to-day politics. We read the newspaper. We discuss the important articles carefully. (3) The works of Chairman Mao. We concentrate on the following works: (a) On practice; (b) On contradiction; (c) Reforming our studies; (d) Presenting a farmers' co-operative. (4) The history of China's Communist Party.

Besides that we read literary works. We read stories about merit workers and the heroes of the revolution. Our study circle meets once a week. We study one thing at a time, and we study it very thoroughly. Just now we are studying a little brochure produced locally up here in northern Shensi: 'How to be a good young communist.' It is a collection of articles. We have been studying this since the winter and we shall continue doing so throughout the year. It will take at least fifty-two meetings. I am not a party member.

People live better than they used to, and they are beginning to have new needs. This began immediately after the East Shines Red Higher Agricultural Co-operative was formed, by people starting to whitewash the caves and get decorations for them. What's happening now is that people are providing themselves with means of transport. Almost every household has already got itself a two-wheeled cart on rubber wheels. These can either be pulled by hand or harnessed to a bicycle. Some have also begun getting bicycles. There are more and more bicycles all the time. And those who have carts and bicycles are now wanting to have radios and alarm clocks. There is no limit to their needs. The better life is, the greater become one's requirements.

The new agricultural implements make farmwork easier. We are hoping for tractors. If you come back in ten years' time, we shall be working all the land down here in the valley by tractor. The same thing will happen with manuring. At the moment, we have carts for manure and that itself is a step forward. That is to say, we have carts for the manure we fetch from the town and the manure we use on the fields down in the valley. The rest still has to be carried. But in ten years' time we shall have manure trucks. In as little as five years we anticipate that our fruit trees will be showing a real profit and bearing plenty of fruit. We are going to electrify more. When we have more power, we shall be able to water our fields more as they should be watered. We are going to drive our mill-stones with electricity instead of by hand or donkey. Life will be much better then. We reckoned that for New Year 1962 one in every three or four households had slaughtered a pig. But for New Year 1963 we reckon that every family in Liu Ling Labour Brigade will be slaughtering a pig. Now every family, or nearly every family, has a goat. Besides them, the number of collective goats is growing the whole time. Things are progressing.

Members are accounted fully able-bodied between the ages of sixteen and fifty. After fifty, members are put along with the sickly and most of the women in the reserve force. Social grants are made by the labour groups first submitting to the brigade committee a list of those in need of social care and of the extent of their need. The brigade committee discusses this and the matter is then referred back to the labour group. If the production plan is exceeded, that is to say, if a certain labour group produces more than anticipated in the plan, the surplus is not divided among all the members of the labour brigade. Once the labour brigade committee has deducted one per cent of the surplus for distribution to merit workers, the whole surplus is divided among the actual members of the labour group in question. The labour brigade does not make any contribution to the people's commune. All that we hand over is the corn tax to the state. This amounts to about ten jin per mu. As corn tax, the state will accept any form of grain, and beans also count as grain. We send roughly twenty-five per cent wheat and seventy-five per cent millet. Oil-yielding plants are counted separately. Last year we planted 130 mu of jute and sold 550 jin of jute-seed. We paid no tax on that. There is also a bit of tax on goats. Last year we had 537 goats and paid 322·20 Y in cattle tax. That means that we pay 0·60 Y in tax on each goat. There is no tax on private goats, private pigs, draught animals and fruit trees, etc. In 1960 the tax was reduced, as the harvest had been so bad. We paid less than ten jin per mu then.

The main aim of our budget is that not more than thirty-five per cent of the total revenue should go to accumulation, welfare funds, taxation, production costs, etc. In reality these items do not amount to more than thirty per cent of our budget. The rest is distributed among the members in accordance with the socialist principle, 'To each according to his work'.

Since the East Shines Red Higher Agricultural Co-operative was formed, we have saved and invested more than 130,000 Y. We have used this to buy donkeys and cattle and goats and instruments, to build caves and to install electric light and to buy an electric water pump for the vegetable group. In the budget we are just working out now for 1963, we shall perhaps increase somewhat the percentage of grain delivered to the state and reduce that of investment, that is to say, purchases. Other items will not be changed and these changes in percentages will presumably be very small. We reckon on a grain harvest of about 320,000 jin and a cash income of about 40,000 Y.

When we sell our corn, we take the actual grain to the grain office of the people's commune. There, a receipt is made out in triplicate. One copy goes to the bank, one copy is retained in the grain office, and the labour brigade has the third copy. Then, when we need money, we go to the bank.

When we got electricity here, we installed an electric pump. The Old Secretary, Li Yiu-hua, came back from a conference he had been attending. He had seen there that other labour brigades had electric water pumps and electric mills. That had made a profound impression on him. When we got back, he said: 'We could have an electric water pump down by the vegetable fields.' At the meeting of the representatives on 29 and 30 August 1961 we discussed this idea. We had calculated that the method we were then using to draw water, by donkey, was costing us 240 Y a year for the donkey power and the person in charge of the donkey, and that the actual drawing cost 200 days' work a year. That meant that the total cost of watering was considerably more than 400 Y a year. We had also talked with people from the electricity works in Yenan and they had told us: 'If you buy an electric pump, this will involve a big outlay the first year, because the motor is expensive, but after that it will pay you.'

We calculated what it would cost to use an electric pump. Purchase price and running costs. We discovered that we should get our money back after little more than a year. If we added to this the fact that we should also have an extra donkey and man to use in the fields, we arrived at the result that it would really involve a gain of almost 400 Y the very first year. Everyone in the brigade committee had been agreed that this was the best and cheapest solution.

The representatives went into the matter very thoroughly. Two of them were strongly against the idea. There were Liu Tsung-hai and Li Wong-shen, both from the village of Wangchiakou. They said: 'Who knows if this electricity really works. It sounds all right, but what happens if we're cut off? If it shouldn't work after we've spent so much money on it, we'll burn up with mortification.' Wangchiakou hasn't electricity. There are plans to electrify the village in 1965. This has been discussed with people from the electricity works. They have approved the electrification plan. When these two from Wangchiakou had spoken like that against the idea, many others, who before had thought a pump a good idea, also began to hesitate. The representatives were on the point of voting that it shouldn't be bought; but then Fu Hai-tsao said: 'I have visited another labour brigade. There they had big vegetable plots and everything was done with electricity. It really is both cheap and efficient.' Then Li Yiu-hua told what he had seen and the discussion continued. In the end, the opponents of the electric pump said: 'If it is true that it functions, that's all right. We only want to be quite sure before we decide. But if you say that it really is so that it is more efficient and cheaper and sure, we are only pleased. In that case we'll vote for it.' After that everyone was agreed, and the proposal was accepted and all the representatives were happy. At the end of the meeting we all forgathered and ate wheat noodles. They bring luck and it was propitious to eat them after making that decision. The noodles were paid for by the welfare fund. This decision that we should eat at the welfare fund's expense was taken last thing at the representatives' meeting.

We have a big library in the brigade here. I have been elected the person responsible for the library, and we now have 2,468 volumes; of these 824 are agricultural textbooks, 681 political literature, 418 belles-lettres and 545 scientific literature. The library was started in 1956. There were a lot of people in the reading class and they thought that there ought to be books in the East Shines Red Higher Agricultural Co-operative. I put the suggestion forward at a committee meeting and was told: 'If people want to read books, we suppose we can vote money for that.' Then I and Tsao Chen-kuei and Kao Liu-chiang from Wangchiakou were given the job of buying books. We went round the villages asking what people wanted, and then one day we went in to Yenan to the bookshop and bought more than 400 books of different kinds. Later that autumn we made another trip to Yenan and bought another 200 books. That was one of the nicest things I have ever had to do. In 1960, we did not buy any books ourselves, but we managed to get an allocation of 400 volumes from the cultural department of Yenan hsien. In 1961, the brigade committee voted twenty yuan to buy brochures containing Chairman Mao's articles. That same year we also got the party school in Yenan to give us 600 volumes. Yenan Intermediate School also gave us books. In 1962 we have not had any money for books voted. We have just got the committee to agree to have the newspapers in the reading-room here.

The reading-room is open two evenings a week during the dead season, and one evening a week during the busy season. I have a book in which people have to register when they borrow a book. They can have one book a week, then they have to re-register. Up to the first of September this year, I have registered 300 borrowers. But that doesn't tell you anything about how many books have been borrowed, because among the borrowers you will find the book members of the labour groups. Each labour group has chosen a book member. In Liu Ling Village Labour Group it is the book-keeper, Chang Chung-liang, and in the labour group for vegetable cultivation, the book-keeper, Li Hai-fa. It does not need to be the book-keeper, but it is easy that way. These book members are chosen by the members at the meeting of the labour groups. They are responsible and usually fetch thirty or forty books a time.

There are several of us young people in the labour brigade who read a lot. We read till late in the evening. At the moment I am reading a Soviet book. It is called *Youth* and is written by a Soviet author with a difficult name. He's called Aleksander Boytchenko (Kiev 1955, Peking 1958).

Actually, I like Chinese books better. Reading foreign authors is difficult, because the characters in their books have such long and complicated names which are difficult to remember, so that it is easy to muddle them up. This book is good. The heroes are very well described and they are all so courageous. They want to defend their country and are prepared to sacrifice their own lives for it. Reading such a book helps me to raise my ideals. This book makes me realize that we in China are poor and backward, but if we work hard we can change our lives as in this book. At the beginning, with the October Revolution, the Soviet people had great difficulties. They had economic difficulties and many other difficulties. But they contended with all these difficulties, and now they have everything and live in affluence. If we work hard, we shall be yet able to have it as good ourselves.

But mostly I read Chinese books. Not just because of the names, but also because the language in Chinese books is so much more comprehensible and alive. Translations always seem so dead in their language, and a translated book is often just the skeleton of a book. I am sure this is not because the foreign authors are like that, but is due to the translation. It is as though our translators only managed to get across the mere idea of the book. The book itself isn't there. I don't know; I don't know foreign languages and don't understand this business of translating. It takes me a month to read a book like this. I have only time to read in the evenings, before I go to sleep.

I try to write little things too. Short reportage and that sort of thing. I write about what has happened in the valley here. I am correspondent for the newspaper in Yenan. I describe what is happening in our sector of the agricultural production front. I know so few characters that it is difficult for me to write. I can now manage 2,000 characters. That is enough for me to be able to write something. I am trying to increase the number of characters I know. I hope soon to know 3,000, and I try to write as much as possible. You see, I didn't go right through the basic school, but even so I read books and newspapers. I write myself, too, but I still come across far too many characters I don't know in the newspapers and books.

I want to work well and be one of the builders of my country. I hope to be able sometime to write something literary, but I don't know if I shall succeed in that field. I want to be a good farmer. If I could write, I would describe the farmer's life. This is an important subject. To be able to describe it, one must oneself both be a good farmer and also have inherited the experience and knowledge that the old people have. I still have a lot to learn from my father.

People say of Lo Han-hong: He is gifted. He is actually very gifted. He has only been a few years in school, but he does his job as book-keeper well. He writes a lot of reports for the newspapers; he often contributes to *The Yenan Daily* and he sometimes even writes in *Shensi's Daily*. He describes what goes on in Wangchiakou Village Labour Group. He has just written a long article about how Wangchiakou Village Labour Group, despite having poorer land and a smaller labour force than Liu Ling Labour Group, has achieved much better results, thanks to better organization and better labour discipline. You could call him Wangchiakou's author. And actually he knows more than 2,000 characters. He is just being modest. He knows quite a lot more. But perhaps he means that he can write 2,000 characters nicely and without thinking about them. He can certainly read twice as many.

He is very fond of reading novels. He is both reader and writer. He is engaged to Li Chin-wa, who is Li Hsiu-tang's daughter. She left the basic school last year. People say that, in Lo Han-hong's opinion, Li Hsiu-tang has not had any bad influence on his daughter. Of course, Li Hsiu-tang was never a landlord himself, he says. They fell in love last year. But he is secretary of the League of Youth and one does not pass comments on him. People are pleased with his work.

Tables

Liu Ling Labour Brigade

Liu Ling Village Labour Group
The Labour Group for Vegetable Cultivation
Wangchiakou Village Labour Group
Hutoma Village Labour Group
Erchuankou Village Labour Group

122 households
2,368 mu of cultivated land (of which 630 mu is valley land)
72 head of cattle, including oxen
40 donkeys
7 horses
4 mules
630 goats
183 pigs, privately owned
640 head of poultry, privately owned

Management Committee

Feng Chang-yeh	Chairman.
Tsao Chen-kuei	Deputy chairman, chiefly responsible for agricultural work.
Lo Han-hong	Book-keeper, youth work.
(Wang Kwang-yung	Treasurer, not a member of the committee.)
Li Yiu-hua	Secretary of Liu Ling Party Association, China's Communist Party, attends meetings *ex officio*.
Ching Chung-ying	Responsible for production.
Fu Hai-tsao	Responsible for production.
Wong Hsin-ying	Responsible for production.
Liu Tsung-hai	Responsible for production.
Liu Ching-tsei	Forestry, cattle.
Li Hung-fu	General security, armed forces.
Jen Yü-chen	Culture, health, communications.
Li Kuei-ying	Women's affairs.

Representatives of Liu Ling Labour Brigade to Liu Ling People's Commune

Li Yiu-hua
Li Kuei-ying
Feng Chang-yeh
Chao Shen-chen

Representatives to Liu Ling Labour Brigade

Ching Chung-ying
She Shiu-ying
Li Hai-fa
Chang Chung-liang
Li Yiu-hua
Tung Yang-chen
Tsao Chen-kuei
Chang Chen-pong
Liu Ching-tsei
Mu Ju-tsai
Wang Hsiu-ying
Kiang Chuen-liang
Liu Ching-hai
Wang Ting-ching
Liang Hsiu-chen
Wang Hung-yün
Chao Shen-chen

Ma Juei-ching
Fu Hai-tsao
Li Hung-fu
Li Hai-ching
Li Hai-kuei
Tsao Chen-hua
Chang Chen-an
Jen Yü-chen
Lo Han-hong
Kao Hsiu-chen
Yang Shu-chih
Chao Chang-ching
Chang Yao-lung
Feng Chang-yeh
Fung Chin-fu
Kiang Hao-wu
Liu Ho-chang

Social grants from the state assistance fund made in 1961 via the management committee of Liu Ling Labour Brigade

Name	Y	Reason
Shi Yü-chieh	26	No fully able-bodied member
Chen Chung-yuan	22	One able-bodied and five in family
Tung Yang-chen	25	Son of a martyr
Li Hai-kuei	34	Father had died
Hseh Shen-kuei	38	One able-bodied and seven in family

Grain production (including bean crops) 1961

Planned production of grain for year 1961	269,985 jin
Actual production	326,784 jin
Planned production exceeded by	56,799 jin

Distribution of 1961 grain harvest

State grain tax	23,680 jin
Sold to state	22,060 jin
Seed	15,980 jin
Fodder	32,700 jin
Social care grant	16,300 jin
Distributed among members of the brigade in accordance with work points	159,265 jin

Distribution of excess grain

Rewards to 20 merit workers	568 jin
To those labour groups which exceeded the plan, for distribution among members according to their work points	56,232 jin

Budget, 1961

Income	Y
Agricultural produce, grain, tobacco, melons, etc.	45,588
Forestry, fruit-growing	1,200
Cattle, slaughtered or sold	8,450
Joinery, repairs, transport work	10,528
Sale of vegetables	14,998
Work performed for other brigades	7,249
Sundries	2,383
Total	90,396

Expenditure   Y
   Production costs: seed, fodder, manure, insecticide, repairs, etc.   13,400
   Investments: purchase of oxen, larger repairs   5,360
   Welfare fund, social assistance, grant to day nursery and collective dining-hall, rewards for merit workers, etc.   1,675
   Administrative costs, purchase of paper, account books, table for book-keeper, etc.   670
   Taxation:
      (a) Grain tax   1,998·13
      (b) Tax on goats   322·20
      (c) Registration fees for bicycles, and horse-drawn vehicles   24·67
   Distributed among members of labour brigade   66,946·00

                                      Total 90,396·00

Assets at 1 Jan. 1961
   Stores in hand   8,447·90
   Cash   5,126·50

                                      Total 13,574·40

Debts at 1 Jan. 1961
   Bank loan   4,000·00

Assets at 1 Jan. 1962
   Stores in hand   17,170·68
   Cash   6,265·32

                                      Total 23,436·00

Debts at 1 Jan. 1962
   Bank Loan   4,000·00

Plant, machinery, implements, pump, etc., are not included among the 'assets', nor are any animals. Because of the system used for distribution, neither the real cost of social care nor that of administration can be ascertained from the budget. As each day's work (10 work points) in 1961 corresponded to 2·10 Y and at the same time 144 days' work were credited to members of the brigade injured at work, the true expenditure on social care was 1,977·40 Y.

Four persons are credited annually with 84 days' work each for their work in administering the brigade. These are the chairman, the deputy chairman, the book-keeper and the party secretary. This amounts to 336 days' work. In addition, the brigade has credited those attending various conferences and meetings with a total of 212 days' work. This makes altogether 648 days' work, equivalent to 1,360·80 Y. This makes the total cost of administration 2,030·80 Y.

In addition, there are the days' work the labour groups credit their book-keepers and treasurers. The cost of this amounts to roughly 63 Y per labour group per year.

Five members of the labour brigade work on service duties for the whole brigade. They are paid direct by the labour brigade and do not come under the labour groups. These are two joiners, one repairer, one herdsman and one driver. Each of these receives 280 days' work annually for his work. This amounts to a cost to the brigade of the equivalent of 1,400 days' work, i.e. 2,940 Y.

Budget for 1962

Income	Y
Agricultural production	46,000
Forestry	1,500
Cattle	8,200
Incidentals	14,000
Sale of vegetables	15,000
Work done for other brigades	2,040
Sundries	6,102
Total	92,842

Expenditure	
Production costs	14,400
Purchases	5,460
Welfare fund	2,385
Administration	680
Taxation	1,500
Distributed among members	68,417
Total	92,842

Part VI
Women

Chia Ying-lan, the one who was sold, aged 53

I AM from Hengshan hsien. Li Hai-yuan's wife, Chia Fu-lan, is my sister. Ours was a poor family, and when I was sixteen I was married off to a pedlar and tinker, who took me with him to Hopeh. He began smoking opium and stopped working his land and so he lost it. He began going round the villages mending cooking vessels. He was often away for long times at a stretch.

I looked after our house in Wuan hsien. I don't know what he paid for his opium, but I got less and less from him and in the end I was getting nothing at all. As I did not want myself and our daughter to starve to death, I took a place with a farmer called Sung. He was a medium-sized farmer with his own land. I worked there for four months. I had no pay, but food for myself and my daughter.

When I was twenty-two I was sold. [Weeps.] He came one day and fetched me and my daughter and took us to a slave dealer called Yang. [Weeps.] My husband sold us so as to get money for opium. I never saw him after that. Some years ago I was told that he was dead. When I had been two days with Yang, the slave dealer, he sold me. He sold me and my daughter for 220 silver dollars to a farmer called He Nung-kung.

I was very unhappy. Mr He was an old man. He was twenty-three years older than I was. We did not love each other. But he was kind. I wasn't ill-treated there, neither by him nor by his family. Actually, he was a nice old man. [Weeps.] He had his own household and did not live with his family. I bore him a son, so everyone was kind to me.

Then he fell ill and died. I was thirty-five then. I had a daughter and a son. One child by either marriage. [Weeps.] He Nung-kung died on 29 April according to the moon calendar. That was during the war. It was 1944. [Weeps.] In January the following year, I gave birth to a daughter. She died when she was seven. [Weeps.] I was pregnant when Mr He died, so they had not been able to marry me off again immediately.

I was, of course, a widow and a burden on the village. The landlord wanted to marry me off. My husband's relatives, that is Mr He's relatives, wanted to marry me off, too, in order to get the house and my children. There was a man in the village who was willing to buy me. I don't know how they arranged it, and I don't know who he was. But I didn't want to any longer. I just wanted to be with my children. [Weeps.] In order to get out of this new marriage, I lied and said that I was already forty-one. Then he thought that I would not be fertile any more and wouldn't have me. That was what I had reckoned on. After that I was left in peace.

Some years after that, we were liberated, and the new government protected us widows and the fatherless. In 1958 I began longing for my sister. She, of course, was still living up here in northern Shensi, and my son and I travelled up to visit her. Then she said that we might as well stay here. That's why we are living here now.

My son is working and life is good. But I want him to marry. I have lived in bitterness all my life [weeps] and now I want him to marry so that I may see a grandson before I die.

All in all, the new society is a good one. But my life has been so bitter. I was sold for opium [weeps] and I have never even told my son all this. [Weeps.]

People say of Chia Ying-lan: She has had a hard life. But she can be happy in having a son. If she did not have him, she would be quite alone. She can read and she has taught her son to read. Her son, He Huang-ho, is strong and healthy and works well.

Chia Ying-lan gets very upset because her son hasn't married. He is twenty-five already and he's still without a wife. But in this village there are only one or two girls who are eighteen or nineteen and free. Most of the girls are far too young. It's going to be difficult for him to find a bride. Their neighbours have tried to get someone for him, but they have not been able to find anyone who will have him. He is strong and fit and a good worker, and there's really nothing wrong with him, but the girls won't have him. Probably this is because he speaks Hopeh dialect and has Hopeh ways. People say: 'It's an ugly language he speaks. The intonation is repulsive and one can't understand what he says. People speak so uglily in Hopeh.'

In all probability he will remain unmarried and that worries Chia Ying-lan greatly, because then the family will die out.

Tu Fang-lan, 'Don't hang us, Father!', aged 56

I GREW up in Hengshan hsien. There were six of us children, three sons and three daughters. Mother is still alive. She is seventy-two. Father was drowned. I send Mother money. In 1961 I gave her twenty yuan. All six children send her the same amount and this means that she has proper pocket money. She lives alone up in Hengshan, but her daughters-in-law go and cook for her. She still hears well and still makes quilted jackets for the family.

But life was hard when we were children. [Weeps.] Father was so hopeless. He gambled and drank. We children had to go out and gather edible plants and roots. When I was digging them up, people asked me: 'Has your father been losing again?' It was some game with dice he always played. I don't know it. I would never touch it.

When he lost, he came home and beat Mother. He was angry then and we were all afraid. We children tried to hide. Once he said: 'I'm utterly useless. I can't support them.' Then he took a rope and was going to hang me. Then we all cried out: 'Don't hang us, Father! We can work and help to support the family.' He drank a lot and when he came home he was dangerous. But if he had drunk too much, he just fell over and was so ridiculous that everyone laughed at him. When he became older, even his grandchildren laughed at him.

But sometimes it was better. Father was a good worker. He could work very hard. He was nice then, and then he did support the family and all was well. But then he would meet some friends and they would take him with them and it was as if he couldn't say no, but went with them and drank and gambled and lost and came home and was furious and beat us and didn't work any more. We girls were more afraid of him than our brothers were, but they feared him too.

When I was very young, my feet were bound. Later my mother said: 'This girl has big ugly feet even though we bound her young.' It hurt a lot having your feet bound. It was like someone pinching very hard all the time. But one had to walk on one's feet. I am old now, but I'm still strong; I have good eyes and I no longer feel anything in my feet, even though they were so tightly bound that they are small, like this.

Mother took a long strip of cloth and bound my feet as tight as she could. It was always Mother who did this. Big feet must be soft and lovely to walk on. But you get accustomed to small feet too. When I became older and heard that girls could have big feet, I thought that it must be lovely for them. My youngest sister, who is forty now, has big feet and short hair. When she was small, this business of big feet had been accepted. I remember my mother saying: 'It is good not to have to bind her feet. This sister has been lucky.' She is much younger than I and therefore she has had a better life.

When I was sixteen, I was married off to an even poorer family. It was Mother decided that. I had to marry the person Mother decided on. Father had no say in the matter. He just said: 'Get her married!' I now moved into a different family. Life now became more bitter. [Weeps.] We had to live on potatoes and melons and my stomach was upset. It was bitter being a daughter-in-law. To begin with I used to cry at every meal. I had to sample every suffering. Gradually, however, my parents-in-law became nice to me. But if we had food, my father-in-law and mother-in-law had to eat first, and I had to eat last of all.

Now we were day labourers for a landlord, and some years we were given to eat what the animals had. We even had grass to eat. I was with child eight times in that marriage. Four died. The first three were boys. They survived. The fourth and fifth were boys too. They fell ill when they were four and died. My husband wept and grieved a lot after the fifth child's death. He burst into tears each time it was mentioned. But then I gave birth to a sixth child and that too was a boy and that made him happy. The sixth child survived. The seventh and eighth were miscarriages. The two miscarriages perhaps were daughters. I had wanted to have at least one daughter. But after those miscarriages there were no more.

A daughter is much closer to her mother than a daughter-in-law. But I never had a daughter. Now it is too late.

My parents-in-law died in 1929. Later, we went to Paoan to take service with a landlord. But my husband died five days after we got there. Our eldest son was then thirteen and our second eight. We had of course nowhere to go, so we stayed there in Paoan, and the two elder boys began working as herdsmen in order to help support the family. I worked in the fields, and life was very hard for us. The rich had all the food they wanted. They ate their fill of wheat. But we had nothing. We were poor. I went hungry to such an extent that my hair fell out in great tufts if I pulled at it. That time in Paoan was the worst I experienced. I made shoes for the boys and had to do this at night by the light of the fire in the hearth. It was bitter then. [Weeps.] If second brother had not helped me with a little rice, we would have starved to death.

Then, in 1939, we came here to Yenan. There were communists here and the boys began working as herdsmen. For that they were given corn. There was land here too. I worked harvesting jute-seed and pressing oil. We lived in the town of Yenan then. When the town was bombed, we hid, but I was wounded in the arm by a piece of flying steel. I still have a scar. Then, during the war, the boys all married, one after the other. They joined the guerrillas, but came back alive.

When Hu Tsang-nan came, he stole our pig and four hens. We had moved out to Thirty-mile Village then, and there we had twenty mu of land. They ate up our little ox and all our corn and destroyed everything we had, and because of that, my grandson, who was three years old, died.

I moved to Liu Ling in 1955. I began making shoes for people. In 1961, I married Ching Chung-wan. You see, my relations in Yulin wanted me to go back up there, but I liked the maize here in Liu Ling; here the millet is good too and so are the potatoes. The labour brigade did not want me to work in the fields, but I told them that I had always worked and intended to go on working till I died. 'Everything that a young girl can do, I can do. And I'll do it better,' I said to them. They had to give in, and in the end they even gave me a diploma as a merit worker.

People say of Tu Fang-lan: She has had a hard life. She was badly treated by her mother-in-law and she weeps a lot. She comes from a poor family. Up in Hengshan hsien she did not eat all that well. Her mother-in-law ate millet and she had to make do with grass. She was not entitled to eat with her parents-in-law, of course; she was just the daughter-in-law. She became ill up there; the bad food gave her stomach disease, and her stomach is still delicate. She has a lot of pain, especially in the winter, and the women in Liu Ling are sorry for her. But sometimes she gets a bit muddle-headed and all at once she will start talking nonsense, and if you ask her about a thing, she will answer about something quite different.

She works well. She does more work than the young women. That comes out when the income from the harvest is distributed. If the young women get nine yuan, she will get twelve yuan. She was obliged to marry Ching Chung-wan. It's the custom for people to marry. Women marry, even if they are over forty. They can even be fifty when they marry. After all, a woman can't live alone. If a middle-aged woman wants to marry, people will have no objection. Tu Fang-lan was known to be wanting to marry. She wanted to get hold of a man. She needed a man.

She married Ching Chung-wan. He is eight years younger than she is. He is the younger brother of Ching Chung-ying, leader of the labour group for vegetable cultivation. As I said, people remarry a lot here in Liu Ling. As soon as the husband or wife has died, the survivor tries to remarry. 'People should not live alone, and if a woman can remarry, she should do so. Who is going to carry water for her otherwise?'

But the Ching family has a great sorrow. It is on the point of dying out. There is no young generation in the Ching family. Ching Chung-ying married a woman who already had children. He himself had no children. So he expected his younger brother Ching Chung-wan to have children. They particularly expected a son who could continue the family. But Ching Chung-wan had no children by his first marriage, and when his wife died he was so old that no young woman would have him. The young women all refused to marry him and, in the end, he had to marry Tu Fang-lan.

But that marriage hasn't been a happy one. He's thinking all the time that he is childless, and that he is going to die without an heir. Tu Fang-lan, of course, is already too old to have children. Their mutual relations therefore are not good. He couldn't find anyone else, of course, but had to make do with her. He had lived alone for many years without being able to get hold of a woman, so in the end he married Tu Fang-lan, because he had to have a woman. After all, someone had to cook for him. Now he nags at her and says: 'I want to have a son.' But she just replies: 'I can't help you there. I am too old. You should have married a younger woman. But the younger women wouldn't have you, would they?' He ought not to nag at her, because he knew this before they married. And it isn't her fault either that she is too old. She has had sons too. He isn't a particularly good worker. He is a mediocre fellow. But she works well, and she's to be pitied.

Ma Hung-tsai's wife, aged 25

My husband's father is Ma Hai-hsiu. My husband's mother is dead. She was Tuan Fu-yin's younger sister. Li Hung-fu is my husband's eldest stepbrother. They had the same mother. My own mother lives in Koumen Village twenty li from here. I moved here when we married. I have two children, a boy of seven and a girl, who is three. My husband's grandmother, old Mrs Tuan, looks after the children while I am out working. Today, I have my monthly trouble and am not feeling too well, so I am at home today.

My husband goes out to the fields at daybreak. When he has gone, I make breakfast for myself and the children and for him. A special food carrier from his group fetches him breakfast. He is ploughing today. There is a lot to do now, but in the winter he usually stays at home till he has had breakfast, about seven o'clock.

I myself usually go out to work at about seven or eight o'clock. I get home to the cave about twelve and make dinner. My husband rests while I am preparing the food, then we eat and he has a little sleep. Sometimes he helps me. He looks after the children then. We do help each other at times. We are a young couple, of course. At two in the afternoon, we go out to work again, and we usually get home about eight in the evening. Then we have supper and go to bed.

I feed the pig, the hens and the goats before I go to work in the morning. I also see to the animals in the evenings. That's my responsibility. Sometimes my husband helps me clean up, sometimes I do it by myself. The men have four free days a month; women have six free days. We can take our free days when we need them.

Our family has a private plot of $1\frac{1}{2}$ mu. We grow maize, potatoes and beans there. My husband does most of the work there on his free days, but I help him. Every year we discuss what we are going to grow there. In the older families, it is the husband alone who decides, but my husband and I discuss everything together, because we are a young couple. Sometimes he gives in and sometimes I give in. We have just re-whitewashed our cave. We do that ourselves. I want it to look neat and tidy here. We are going to slaughter the pig for the New Year.

Li Shang-wa, the young girl, aged 16

My mother died long ago. My father, Li Yü-hsin, is Li Yü-teh's older brother. I left school this spring.

Actually, I would have liked to go on studying, but as my mother is dead I had to start working in the household instead. We have a pig and two goats; I look after those. But we have no hens or chickens. I like cooking and I look after my small brothers and sisters. Although, really, I would have liked to go to Yenan Middle School. But then someone has to take care of the family, too. Just now I'm laying down turnips and lotus for the winter.

I haven't joined the League of Youth, and I'm too old for the pioneers now that I've left school. I like singing and usually sing to myself all the songs that my teacher, Kou, taught me. I go into Yenan to shop and to go to the cinema once a week. I like adventure films best and war films and films about heroes. I like reading and I read different children's books. Both where films and books are concerned, I prefer those books and films that improve my morale and enhance my quality.

I don't like opera. I don't understand about the operas. Everything in operas is all so peculiar. I like the song-and-dance shows. I often go to the school in order to be able to sing with my schoolmates.

I am proud of being able to work on the land. Agriculture is the foundation of society. No society could exist without agriculture. Or course, I would be happy with whatever work the party gave me to do. We who are young now have a bright future ahead of us. I hope to be able to make my contribution on the agricultural front and be a good 'swallow', as the teachers in school taught me. I'm not contemplating marriage. I shall marry late. I'm altogether too young to be able to think of love. I'm running the house for my father. Later, I am going to work on the land.

People say of Li Shang-wa: She is a sweet, nice girl. She is pleasant-looking and efficient. She and Li Hsiu-tang's daughter, Li Ai-liang, were the only ones from Liu Ling to finish school this spring. They had roughly the same marks. Li Ai-liang's were very slightly better. Li Shang-wa would have liked to go on to Yenan Middle School and she is the type for it; but her father did not want her to. It was Li Hsiu-tang's daughter who went on to do higher studies. People say that the party and the brigade committee talked with Li Yü-hsin to try to get him to let his daughter continue her studies, but when he wouldn't she had to stay at home. Li Yü-hsin thinks it's good to have her at home to run the house.

Li Kuei-ying, woman pioneer, aged 32

I HAVEN'T much to tell. I haven't many experiences. I was born into a farming family. I grew up in the country and have never been anything but just a country woman.

We moved to Yenan in 1950. I don't remember anything of our life in Hengshan. But my father, Li Yiu-hua, and my mother say that they worked for a landowner, and that, though they worked hard, they did not have enough to eat. There were six of us in the family when we moved: Father, Mother and four children. Father carried two worn quilts and a felt rug on his back. I walked and walked, and I was so tired that I cried. When we reached Yenan, we still had to work for a landowner. Father worked for Li Hsiu-tang's family. Then he broke new ground for himself up on the slopes. Mother looked after our pig, and I plucked grass.

I don't remember exactly what year that was, but we children worked too. We worked in Father's labour group. He had organized one. When Hu Tsung-nan was coming with his troops, Uncle took us children with him to Ansai. That was a week before the enemy occupied Liu Ling. Father and Mother went somewhere else. In Ansai, we lived with another of Mother's brothers. It was a small village of four or five households. When the K.M.T. troops finally came there, all the villagers were afraid. They hid all the young girls and women. They were put into abandoned caves and the entrances blocked up with bushes and branches. In that way they tried to protect them from the soldiers.

Now all we children were living in Ansai and we ate lots. The soldiers plundered Uncle, too, and he had difficulties. When the guerrillas came that way, he got out some corn and gave it to them; but when Hu Tsung-nan's troops came he didn't give them anything, but hid everything from them.

One day, when the troops came to the village, my little brother and I were ill. We had high temperatures with bleeding at the nose and mouth and diarrhoea. Uncle's only child was ill too. One of Uncle's female relations was staying with us in the cave to look after us and Uncle. The woman's husband was a stretcher-bearer for the guerrillas. She was living with Uncle, as she had been left alone in the village. Now she was to look after us children. That is why she was not hidden when the soldiers came. They stood outside the cave and told us to come out. We replied: 'All those who are well are away, it is only we ill ones left.' Then they asked what illness we had. 'It's catching.' At that they took two paces back. Then they said: 'Those who are not ill must come out, otherwise we shall shoot.' After that Uncle and the woman stepped outside. They did not bother with Uncle, but they took the woman away with them. Two hours later she came back. Her face was quite grey then, and she was quite silent. She just sat and sat and never said a word. That night her husband came. They sat side by side for a while, then they stood up and walked out, in the middle of the night. No one has heard of them since. No one knows where they went. They just walked out into the dark.

In July, we children went back to Liu Ling. Uncle had no more corn to give us and our parents had already returned. Father had moved across to this side of the village. The whole village was in great disorder. Many families had disappeared and their caves were abandoned.

Everything had been smashed, cooking stoves, windows, everything had been destroyed. Everyone was depressed and unhappy. We had breakfast, but no dinner. The corn had been growing in the fields, but the troops had cut the maize before it had had time to ripen and used it as fodder for their horses. Sometimes they had set fire to it. At night, the fields would burn. In the end people became quite indifferent. It was as if nothing mattered any longer. No one went out to the fields any more. Not even to the fields high up on the hillside. Nobody worked. People just lay on their backs and slept. It was as if people no longer wanted to live.

In the autumn, there was almost no harvest to get in. We had no hope for the future. That winter Mother and I did washing for the troops. In that way we survived. Father had no work and it was difficult for him. That was the first time in his life he hadn't worked, and he was so upset. He wasn't accustomed to not working.

In March or April 1948, Hu Tsung-nan withdrew. We then had no grain at all. Father went to Lochuan to fetch seed-corn. My two younger brothers were working in the fields although they were very young. Father went back to Lochuan to fetch more corn. This he sold. He carried the sacks on a carrying-pole. He kept on doing this right till the maize could be harvested. Then he stopped carrying grain from Lochuan. The harvest that year was not too bad. I don't remember exactly when it was, but I think it was the year after that that Father organized a labour group for mutual help. In this the families worked for each other and helped each other. Our family was very poor, and I used to go up on to the hill and pluck grass for our pig. I was also supposed to look after the goats and the group's cattle.

In 1951, we were told that the party school in Yenan was having a training course for female ganbus. It was said that as half the population consisted of women, trained women were needed as well. Our labour group for mutual help was now to be turned into a farmer's co-operative. It was Father who forced that through. It was the first of its kind and it was an experiment. The labour group for mutual help told the party school about me, and I was accepted and sent off to attend the course and study for six months. Ever since I had been small, I had dreamed of being able to learn to read and write. I had dreamed daydreams of becoming a student. Yet when they talked with me and told me that I had got permission to go to the party school, I became worried. Because what could a farm girl learn at school? I was worried about the housework too: the spring sowing was about to start and there was so much that ought to be seen to at home.

When I got to the school, I met a lot of women and men there. After a couple of weeks, I had got accustomed to being in school. The main object was for us to learn to read and write. To begin with, it was rather difficult for me to live a collective life, but afterwards it went quite all right. I decided to learn all that I could. Now that I had managed to get to a school I was not going to lose a minute. I thought of how things were in the new society and how they had been under Hu Tsung-nan's occupation and I promised myself that, when I was finished with the school, I would organize all the women in the village for this new life, and I read seriously.

At the school, I got up as early as in the village. First, we had a lesson of forty minutes, when our homework was corrected. Then, after a short break, we had another lesson, which was either arithmetic or Chinese. At eight o'clock we had breakfast. We usually got steam bread and vegetables. Then we had three lessons of arithmetic and Chinese. We had fifteen minutes' interval between each lesson. Then we had a rest period of one and a half hours. After that a further three lessons of arithmetic and Chinese. Then we had dinner. We used to get steamed millet and vegetables. Once a week we had a meat dish. This, of course, was better food than we were accustomed to at home, but we needed it, because we were working hard and had to learn everything at once. After dinner, we had ninety minutes' prep. After that we did different kinds of personal activities. We did not have any political studies. This was a course at which we were to learn to read. In the evenings we used to sing and discuss things. We learned lots of songs and talked a lot about our home villages and all the things that could be done. We all knew that we must learn to read as soon as possible. Six of us women shared a room. I still see a lot of two of them; they live near by; but I have lost touch with the others. We were free on Sundays. I used to go home to the village then and help in the fields. I was needed there too.

That time at the party school was the decisive time of my life. It was then I realized what I must do with my life. I came back to Liu Ling in July 1951. I could then read and write, and I took part in the autumn harvest and, in the winter, I began organizing the women to study. When I got back, the women said: 'We didn't think grown-ups could learn to read and write, but you have.' Because of that, the younger women now wanted to learn to read too, and I told them all how good it was to be able to read and write; that she who could read could see; and she who couldn't was blind.

That winter I taught ten women to read and write a hundred characters each. That isn't enough to be able to read a newspaper or such, but it is enough to be able to write simple accounts and receipts and to keep notes. They have gone on with it since, but it has been difficult for them. They can't read much more now after ten years, though I have been working with them the whole time.

I continued studying on my own. I got hold of old books of legends which I read. I swotted up more characters; I read newspapers and began reading simple new stories. In 1952, I married. That was in August and I was very happy. It was a marriage of free will. We had met at the party school and fallen in love with each other. He was attending a different course. When I told Mother that I was in love and wanted to get married, she said nothing at all, but Father said: 'If it's so that you really want to, then I don't intend to oppose it.'

There were three labour groups in the farmers' co-operative in 1953. Two of men and one of women. I was chosen leader of the women's group. At the meeting, the women said: 'She is young and hard-working and she can read.' So I thought that, if they had such faith in me, I must show that I was worthy of their opinion of me. That I must work much harder than before. I wanted to get the women as a group moving. I wanted to get them to break away from the past. I was thinking of the time when Hu Tsung-nan had occupied the area. There was a cavalry regiment quartered here in Liu Ling then. Its duties were to track down and capture deserters. They shot the deserters in our potato plot. Every day I used to stand by my cooking stove in the cave and see them shoot deserters down there. I thought then that that must never be allowed to happen again. That we women must all get together to see that it never happened again.

That winter I opened a winter school. We had lessons in the school and in the homes of Shi Yü-chieh and Li Hai-kuei, who had large caves. We helped the women to make shoes and clothes and to improve their agricultural tools. We gave them lessons in feeding poultry and in spinning. We had discussions after the lessons. We tried to get the women to tell us themselves what things had been like before, and how it was now, and how it ought to be in the future. For example, they said: 'My feet were bound so that I could not walk. In the old society, a woman was not supposed to go beyond the threshold of her home for the first three years of her marriage. We weren't allowed to eat on the kang, but had to sit on a stool when we ate, and if my parents had decided to marry me off with a cur, then I had to be content with a cur. But now you are allowed to see your husband before you marry, and you can refuse to marry him if you don't like the look of him. The old society was bad and the new is good.' We discussed whether women are men's equals or not, and most said: 'Within the family, man and woman are equal. We help the men when they work in the fields and they should help us in the house.' But many of the older women said: 'Women are born to attend to the household. A woman cannot work in the fields. That can't be helped. It is just that men and women are born different. A person is born either a man or a woman. To work in the fields or in the house.' We had long discussions. The young ones were all on the side of equality and freedom. It had now become quite usual with our generation for husband and wife to discuss the family's problems and decide about them together. Women now no longer work just in the house; they also work in the fields and earn their own money. But the men of the older generation still say: 'What does a woman know? Women know nothing! What's a woman worth? Women are worth nothing!' In such families the men decide everything and their wives say: 'We are just women. We are not allowed to say anything.'

The first time we women took part as a group in an open discussion was at the meeting about whether or not we should turn Liu Ling Farmers' Co-operative into the East Shines Red Higher Agricultural Co-operative. Officially, we had the same political and economic rights as the men. We were citizens too, so She Shiu-ying and Li Yang-ching asked to speak and stood up in the middle of the meeting and said: 'The old women still say that they don't understand things and are just women, and that it is the men's business to decide and that the women should do as the men decide. But we say that we do understand. We are women and we know what this discussion is about. Everything has to progress. We must increase production. It isn't fair to pay a dividend on land. That can mean that a person who works a lot can be paid less than one who works less well. That is not right. We must increase our investment instead, so that we can all increase production and be better off by doing more work. Therefore we must join forces and do away with land interest. That is progress and we stand for that.'

Li Ying-teh, who is an old man and Li Hsin-chen's father, then said: 'We should not listen to women when it is a question of serious business. They understand nothing. After all, they are only women and ought not to disturb our discussions. We do not need to concern ourselves with what they have said.' But my brother, Li Hai-tsai, replied to this: 'Why shouldn't we listen to the women? Every other Chinese is a woman. There is a lot of sense in what they've just said about investment and production and land interest and joint effort. I am entirely with them.'

We won. Gradually the others were voted down and persuaded and got to agree. I was elected a member of the committee of the East Shines Red Higher Agricultural Co-operative. Besides this, I had three children. We wanted to have three children, so I had a boy in 1953, a boy in 1957 and a girl in 1958.

I joined the party in 1955. There were women party members in the other villages. We often had meetings with them. Then Yang Fu-lien said: 'Why don't you join the party? The party needs women ganbus.' But I didn't want to join. I said: 'I can work just as well for the people without being in the party.' 'No,' Yang Fu-lien said, 'you can't. You will do better work if you are in the party.' I thought a lot about what she said. Then I went home to my parents and borrowed Father's copy of the party programme and read it through. I realized then that I would be able to work better and train myself better if I joined the party. So I sent in an application. Yang Fu-lien and Li Hai-kuei recommended me. This was in the middle of the discussion about the change to a higher agricultural co-operative. My husband had been a party member since 1948 and he had tried to talk me over several times, but I had not listened to him. It carried more weight when other comrades, who didn't belong to the family, talked to me about it.

After joining the party, I studied the party programme, the series of articles called 'How does a party member serve the people?' Comrade Liu Shao-chi's 'How to become a good communist', our party's history and different articles on topical questions. We studied together in the party association and after the studies held discussions. Besides this, we studied on our own. After this, I thought that everything had become more clear and easier to understand. I have become more assured in my work. After studying those questions, I could understand the whole implication of them. If I make mistakes, the others come and tell me and help me to put things right.

In 1958, we formed Liu Ling People's Commune. It was even bigger than the higher agricultural co-operative. It took in the whole of our hsiang. We had only a short discussion before we agreed to it. Most people were convinced from the start, but some, like Kao Kuei-fang, said: 'Why cause all this trouble? Why go on altering everything all the time? It's going well as it is. I think it's a mistake just altering and altering.' But Wang Yü-lan replied: 'What Kao Kuei-fang says is not correct. She is forgetting that production must go on increasing if we are to be better off. The people's commune will provide better possibilities for accumulation. We will be able to carry out more new building works that require capital, and we can have better-arranged social care. We must keep our objective in view the whole time. If we are on our way to Yenan, we can't stop in Seven-mile Village and settle there.' The discussion was very short. The introduction of the people's commune did not involve any great changes in our work. It was mostly that it made it possible for us to do without a number of salaried officials, who had previously been in the hsiang administration and who were no longer needed once we were doing the administration ourselves. Besides that, it gave us the ability to carry out works requiring capital, and we set up a proper system for exchanging labour between the brigades. We had heard it said that in different parts of the country they had food and other things free, but that did not sound right to us. At all events, it wouldn't suit us in northern Shensi. We decided not even to discuss the idea. It was never put on the agenda for any of our meetings.

We carried out great irrigation works in the winter of 1958-9. We built terraced fields and were able to do so because we had arranged for exchange of labour between brigades in the people's commune. There was a bad drought in 1959. We had to fight a hard battle with nature. But the 1959 harvest was not bad at all and that strengthened the members in their belief that the people's commune was the right form. We would not have got through that drought without a people's commune.

In the winter of 1959-60 we had a discussion about our work among the women. I sent a proposal in to the committee of the party association for setting up a special women's committee for our work among the women. I told them that, in my opinion, so far I had been the only one working on the women, and that we could not let so important a matter be dealt with like that. It mustn't be left to a few comrades to do the work more or less on their own. The party itself must be responsible, both politically and organizationally. We discussed the matter thoroughly, and in the end my proposal got a majority of votes and went through. The party association decided to set up a labour group for work with women. Ma Ping and I were elected Liu Ling's representatives in the group. This group now has regular meetings. It has representatives from the various villages, and we now plan our work among the women properly.

I was head of the women's organization in Liu Ling from 1955 to 1961. It wasn't a real organization. It automatically comprised all the women in the village. It was one way of activating the women in social work and getting them to develop and accept responsibility and get up at the different meetings and give their opinion. We abolished it in 1961, because it was no longer needed. We had quite enough women then who realized that women can be in the ordinary organizations and speak at their meetings. Instead, we formed a women's work group. I was chosen leader of this. We work directly in production.

But the party group for women's work still functions. It has five different tasks: (1) To organize women to take an active part in production; (2) To spread literacy among women and get them to study and take an interest in social questions; (3) To help them do their domestic work effectively and economically, to help them when any economic problem arises in their family; (4) To teach them personal and public hygiene; (5) To give help and advice over marriage or other personal problems of wedded life.

I have already told you about our work in teaching and production. Otherwise, there are no great problems. One gets those mostly with the older people. That goes for marriage: some of the older people do not believe in marriage of free will. 'How can a girl run off with the first chap she sees?' the older women ask. We have to talk to them and make propaganda for the new marriage. We have to remind them of how they felt when they were young and how they were made to suffer under the old system of marriage. It isn't so often it ever comes to a real conflict, but we did have a case in 1960.

That was when Tuan Fu-yin's eighteen-year-old daughter, Tuan Ai-chen, fell in love with a boy from Seven-mile Village. But her parents refused to let her marry. They said that the boy was poor and that they wanted to marry her to somebody better off. One evening Tuan Ai-chen came to me and wept and complained. I went with her to her cave and talked with her parents. I said to them: 'You have no right to prevent your daughter from marrying, you know that, don't you? Purchase marriage is not allowed in the new society. It is a crime to sell your daughter these days. Before, you could sell your daughter like a cow, but you can't do that any longer.' I told them about the things that used to happen in the old days, about girls drowning themselves in wells, of girls hanging themselves and that sort of thing, about all the unhappiness purchase marriage caused. At first, Tuan Fu-yin tried to stand up to me. He said: 'I had to pay dearly for my wife. Now I have been giving this girl food and clothes, I have brought her up and she just goes off. It isn't right. I just lose and lose all the time. I must get back something of all the money I have laid out on her. If she can't fall in love with a man who can pay back what she's cost, then it isn't right for her to marry.'

I talked a long time with them that evening, and in the end I said: 'You don't live badly in the new society. If you ever have difficulties, your daughter and son-in-law will help you. They are not rich, but they won't refuse to help you.' Then they replied: 'We must think about it.' The next time I went there, only the girl's mother was at home. She had thought about it and she now told me her own story. I hadn't known it, otherwise I would have made use of it on the first occasion. She said: 'I was sold to Tuan Fu-yin when I was a little girl. I was sold in the same way you sell a goat. But my parents got a lot for me. Tuan's father had to take out a loan. That made them nasty to me. I was forced to work hard so as to make the loan worth while. They were all nagging at me. I can remember how much I used to cry. Now that I think of that, I don't want my daughter to marry someone she can't like.' Then she wept. Tuan Fu-yin didn't say anything more. But such cases are rare. It is the only one I remember. Tuan Fu-yin's own sons had been allowed to marry in the new way, of course, because that meant that he did not need to pay anything for his daughters-in-law.

Another thing we have to deal with now and again is that the old women find it difficult to understand that nowadays women laugh and joke with men. They scold their daughters and daughters-in-law and granddaughters for not observing decent behaviour. When that happens, we have to speak with the old women about the equality of the sexes. We tell them that, now, a woman is the equal of a man in the family and in society. She does not just look after the home, she also works in the fields. She has to vote and she can be elected. It is obvious that she also talks with men and jokes with them as comrades. We remind the old people about their own bitter youth and keep telling them that as women now are equal, they also have the right to chat and joke. The old people say that they agree we are right. But in their heart of hearts they always feel uneasy and uncertain when they see girls joking with men. But we are patient with the old people. They can't help their attitude. Perhaps not all old women are like that, but most, I'm sure, think it indecent and immoral and shocking that young people talk with each other. The young people, of course, are all agreed. None of the young people think like the old ones on this question. So it will solve itself in time.

We have continued our work with hygiene and public health all the time, especially since 1958, when we formed the people's commune. The public health work was better organized after that. We go to see the women who are pregnant and talk with them about what to do in their pregnancy. We instruct them in the new delivery art and tell them how to look after their infants. Before, a woman had to be sitting straight up and down on her kang three days after having her baby. And you can understand how that must have felt. Now we say to them: 'That is all just stupidity and superstition. Lie down with the child beside you and rest. You're not to sit up at all.' We tell the women to let themselves be examined regularly and follow the doctor's advice. We instruct them in birth control and contraceptive methods. The women follow our advice because they have found that with the old methods many children died, but with our new scientific methods both mother and child survive.

Birth control is primarily a matter of propaganda. Firstly, many say: 'We want to have more children'; secondly, after all birth control is voluntary. We have discussed which contraceptives are best. Personally I find the condom to be the most reliable. They are rather inexpensive too: Thirty-three pieces for one yuan. But there are other methods, too, and certain of the families don't use any contraceptives at all but only simple techniques. A lot of women still believe that they can't become with child as long as they are suckling. And each time, they are as surprised as ever, when they find they are pregnant again. But we are working to enlighten them.

In certain families with lots of children, the women would like birth control, but their husbands won't. In those families the husbands say: 'There's not going to be any family planning here!' Then we women go to them and try to talk sense into them. We say: 'Look how many children you have. Your wife looks after the household and sees to all the children and she makes shoes and clothes for both you and the children, but you don't think of all she has to do or of her health, but just make her with child again and again. Wait now for three or four years. Then you can have more if you want.' Usually, they will eventually say: 'If it isn't going to go on all one's life, then all right. But if she's going to go on with birth control for ever, then I'm not having any.' In those cases, all goes well and usually they do not decide to have any more afterwards. But in other cases, the husband just says: 'No.' Then we women speak to him about it every day, till he agrees to birth control. No husband has yet managed to stand out for any length of time, when we are talking to him. Actually, of course, they know that we are right. They know, of course, that they are responsible. It's only their pride that stands in the way, and we have to tell them that such pride is false and not at all right. But there are, too, families, where both husband and wife are agreed that they want to have children all the time. We can't do anything there. The whole thing's voluntary. The chief thing is to have a healthy family, and that the mother feels all right.

Since 1958, we have also established a children's day nursery and a collective dining-hall. These are used in the busiest of the harvest season, when it is important that as many as possible work, and so the women have to be relieved of their domestic work for a time. It's the same at the ploughing. Li Hai-ching is in charge of the collective dining-hall, and Wang Yü-lan of the children's day nursery. They were elected by the representatives of the labour brigade. Those are positions of trust. During harvest and ploughing, the women who are pregnant and the old ones with small, crippled feet do the work in the day nursery and the collective dining-hall. All the others are out in the fields. It works very well. In that way the women earn money. They like that. Neither the day nursery, nor the collective dining-hall is free. But the labour brigade contributes a certain share of the cost. This, too, was discussed and decided at a meeting of the representatives. Every child that spends a month in the day nursery entails a cost of thirty work points, that is to say three days' work. Of this the child's family pays fifteen work points and the labour brigade fifteen. The collective dining-hall serves three meals a day. For these, those who eat there pay seven or eight work points a month and the labour brigade pays three.

That's how we women work in Liu Ling Labour Brigade. We are making progress all the time. Every year the labour brigade chooses a few merit workers. They are given various prizes as a token of appreciation. I have had a pair of socks, a fountain-pen, a hoe, some notebooks and some diplomas. In 1960, the women elected me their delegate to a conference of merit workers that was being held down in Sian. They did that because I had taught them to read and write. I was very touched by it. I could not help thinking how they were commending me, though really I had not done all that I ought to have done. I determined to work even better, seeing that the women believed in me. I want to solve all our women's problems here. You see, not all women by any means are aware that they are their husband's equals. Some still look up to their husbands as in the old days, before women became free. They suffer because of that, and that they must be freed from it.

People say of Li Kuei-ying: She is always clear and sensible. She speaks in a low voice, but she always knows what she wants, and when she says a thing, then it is so. She does not like loose talk and she is not much of a one for laughing or joking. One has no need to be shy with her. One can talk with her about everything and she understands everything. She likes children and children like her, but they have respect for her too. If children are making a noise and fighting and she comes along, they will stop fighting at once. She is like her father, she is unselfish and hard-working and straight and helpful and serious. But she does not condemn and, whatever one discusses with her, she will help over it. She is the sort of person you can discuss your gravest problems with. She helps the women to earn money. If anyone in a family is ill, she organizes the neighbours to help. She is liked and no woman has ever said anything nasty about her. Even the old women respect her. Besides this, she is a good housewife and a good cook.

She studied for six months at the party school, and her husband is a ganbu. All the women admire her, because she has always decided exactly when she is to have children or not have children. Chi Mei-ying said: 'I am not like Li Kuei-ying. We too, tried, to be clever and plan, but it went wrong and so I had my last child. Not everyone can be as decided as Li Kuei-ying.'

Li Yang-ching, housewife, aged 29

I AM married to Liu Chen-yung. Li Hsiu-tang is my uncle, he is my father's younger cousin. Li Yü-teh is my half-brother. We have different mothers. My mother is dead, my father is dead, my mother-in-law is dead, my father-in-law is dead. I look after the house and work in the fields when I have time. We have three children. My sister-in-law, old Mrs Li, looks after them when I am working. My oldest daughter is ten and goes to school.

I work in the fields, when it is possible for me to do so. I have to look after the cave, too, of course. My year is roughly like this, going by the moon calendar. I don't know the sun calendar.

January, February. I make clothes and shoes for the family.

March, April. I work in the fields, turning the earth in places they can't get at to plough with the oxen, and preparing the manure for spreading.

May, June. I weed the fields, beans, wheat, millet, potatoes.

July, August. We weed a second time, then we begin cutting the wheat.

September, October. We take up the potatoes, harvest the beans and jute, and plough the fields for wheat, manure them and sow the wheat. We have brought the harvest down from the fields up on the hillside to the threshing floor and we thresh it. Towards the end of October, the threshing will be almost finished.

November, December. There is less to do in the fields, and we women do not need to go out and work on the land. The men gather firewood and are busy with the manure. Then the year begins again.

We women who are working in the fields leave home around half past seven in the morning. We come home about twelve to prepare food for the family. Then we sleep for an hour. At about three o'clock, we go out again and get back home at seven or eight o'clock in the evening. My husband and I get up at the same time in the morning. That's before five o'clock. Then he goes to work at five, has breakfast out in the fields later; I get breakfast ready, clear away and do the cave, dress the children, feed the pig and see to the hen and her six chicks. After that, it is time for me to go to work. In the midday break, when I come home, I cook a meal, and, when I come home in the evening, the first thing is to feed the family; then I feed the pig, the hen and her six chicks, then I see to the children and when they're asleep, I do my sewing and make clothes and attend to such things, until about ten o'clock, when I am tired and fall asleep.

In the busiest time in the summer, when the days are longer, we get up before four and my husband goes to work at four. We then work on until it is so dark that we can't see to do any more. We have dinner in the middle of the day, but then we have it at the collective dining-hall so as not to lose time. But at such times I don't sit up at night making clothes. It isn't so hard; people have always done it.

In the dead season, we stay in bed a bit longer. We don't get up then till six o'clock, with the dawn. Then I make breakfast and my husband has it with us. After that I see to the animals and perhaps go down to the big donkey-driven collective mill to mill flour. That takes half a day and I do it now and then during the winter. Then I make quilted coats for the family, sew shoes and that sort of thing. At midday, my husband comes home and we eat. In the winter he does not need a midday rest after dinner. He has slept longer in the morning and it is cool outside. In the afternoons he works outdoors and I sit at home making shoes and clothes. He comes home at dusk and if there isn't anything special on, we go to bed immediately after supper.

He has one rest day a week. Being a woman, I have a little more. In the summer, we use these to work in our private plot. We grow maize and millet and 'sticky millet' of two kinds. We have both our own private plot of good land down in the village and the new land we cleared for ourselves last year. You are allowed to clear as much as you like up on the hill; it's just a question of what you can manage. Last year our private crops brought us in about 800 jin of grain. In the winter, he uses his rest day to cut wood or do other of the heavier household jobs.

We don't often go into Yenan. Once a month roughly, and then to shop and see the opera. I don't go regularly, but if a good, famous opera company comes, I'll go in more often, otherwise not so often.

We never go together. I go in the daytime and he in the evenings. That's because of the children. When one's working and has children, one can never go out together in the evenings. I like the Shansi opera best. Sometimes films come to the village. Then I see them. We have a film show every month or six weeks. But I don't like films all that much. Opera is much better. When we have a film show, it is in the collective dining-hall.

I go more often to Seven-mile Village. I go there every fortnight to buy salt and soya and that sort of thing. Every fortnight we in the family use roughly:

Salt (we salt down a lot)	2·5 jin
Soya	1·0 jin
Vinegar	1·0 jin
Cooking oil	1·0 jin
Biscuits	1·0 jin
Sugar	2·0 liang

That's the food we buy. The biscuits and sweet cakes are for the children. The whole thing usually costs about four or five yuan.

We women usually sit together by day, so that we can chat. That makes the work go easier. Sometimes there are two or three of us, sometimes five or six. The more we are, the more fun it is. In summer we haven't time to see each other, but in the winter our work is of such a kind that we can sit together. We who meet to chat and sew are all of the same age. We haven't much to chatter about with the older women.

You can also divide the year by the festivals. I'm still speaking of the moon year. We haven't anything to do with the sun year. We butcher our pig and goats for the New Year festival. Then we make millet cakes and 'Chinese bean pudding'. We eat dumplings filled with pork and lots of other things. Then we go visiting, and our neighbours come to see us, and, on New Year's Day, everyone eats until you can't squeeze another bit of food down. We drink home-made wine and spirits from the shop. We paste paper cut-outs on the paper windows of the cave. My sister does that. She is clever at that sort of thing. We fix up verses beside the door, but I can't read those, because I can't read.

Then comes the mid-spring festival. We go to our ancestors' graves then to make offerings. We take food and wine with us and offer a little at the graves, pouring out a little wine in front of them. I and my husband and the children all go together. Everyone in the whole village goes to their ancestors' graves on that day. No, there isn't anyone who neglects to do so. In the old days, people used to make pilgrimage to the pagoda in Yenan. Now they have a fair there, instead. There are plays and performances, story-tellers and lots of other things. The whole family goes for the fun of it. It doesn't cost much if you are careful; but if you don't look out, you can run through all your money.

Our next festival is on 5 May. I don't properly know why it is celebrated. Some old custom, I expect. The only thing we do then is to eat triangular cakes of 'sticky millet', filled with dates.

On 6 June summer has come, and we have a summer festival and eat cold buckwheat pudding; 15 July is the 'harvest's birthday' and we celebrate it by eating better food than usual and as much as we can; 15 August is the full moon and then we eat moon cakes with sweetmeats inside. On 9 September the buckwheat has just ripened and we celebrate that by making buckwheat noodles. They bring you good luck. On 1 October the millet has just been harvested and we have a millet festival with cakes of steamed 'sticky millet'.* Then we have a festival in November, when we eat golden millet bread and the second kind of 'sticky millet'. On 18 December we eat gruel made of 'sticky millet'.

On these feast days the men go to work as usual and the women stay at home in the caves to prepare the food. Otherwise, we eat the same things the whole year round. Millet is our main food; we cook it in various ways. Mostly, though, we eat it as porridge. We have meat at the New Year. We have a proper meat meal then; afterwards we salt down the rest of the pig and use a bit for each of the festivals when one eats meat. Sometimes, if we have guests, we will buy meat in the market and make something. This year we must have had meat three or four times in addition to the festivals. Vegetables we have according to the season. We don't grow tobacco. My husband does not smoke.

In October, I put down cabbage. This lasts then through the winter until into March, when fresh vegetables start. I boil up the water, put

---

* Not China's national day, 1 October, but the first day of the tenth month of the lunar calendar. According to the lunar calendar the year consists of 354 or 355 days divided into twelve months. To make the lunar year agree with nature's year, an intercalary month of 29 days is added every so often. Such years then have 383 or 384 days in them. Now, the Gregorian calendar is used in China.

the cabbage in, take it out again quickly and put it in cold water. Then I put it in a big earthenware jar in layers with lots of salt. One layer cabbage, one layer salt. Then I press it all together with a big, well-cleaned stone. This same month, too, I lay down turnips and radishes. I cut them into narrow strips and layer them with salt in a stoneware jar and press with a stone.

In the spring I dry vegetables. I cut mustard-root into pieces, steam it and then let it dry in the sun; the beans dry on their own, and maize and potatoes can be stored in a potato pit.

In December, I begin making my red wine. I leave some 'sticky millet' to soak overnight; then I pour off the water, grind the millet and steam it. It is then like thick gruel. Then I mix in some yeast and pour the mixture into a jar. I put the jar on the warm kang. It has to stand there fermenting for four or five days, then the wine will be ready. When you want to drink it, you take some of the gruel from the jar, mix it well with water, then sieve it so that the liquid is almost clear. Then you boil it up, and it is drunk hot. I give the mush to the pig. It loves it.

If this wine is made the right way, it will be sweet and weak. If you let it stand fermenting for a long time, it becomes sour and strong. I prefer sweet wine, but there are people who want it strong, so they leave the jar a long time on the kang, because the longer it stands, the stronger the wine will be. I only make this in wintertime, because in the summer it isn't so easy to ferment it. Besides that, we buy spirits in the shop. We usually buy two bottles every New Year. My husband isn't very fond of drinking, and I myself think spirits altogether too strong. After all, it's sixty per cent. This year I am putting by six jin of millet to make wine with.

This week, my husband hasn't had a free day. He took two free days the week before last. He has thus worked all week without one. Yes, our food is pretty monotonous. There's not much variety. Our menu this week has been:

Monday, 20 August 1962*

Breakfast. Millet porridge and maize bread and a vegetable dish of tomatoes, beans and potatoes, chopped up and fried in oil. We have fried chili with this and all our meals. The children don't like this, so we fry it separately and each mixes it in with the food as he likes along with vinegar. We don't drink water or tea with our food, but have

* Author's dating according to the solar calendar.

17. (*Top*) The melon fields near the temple
18. (*Bottom*) 'The Little Author' bringing in his vegetable crop

19. The threshing floor and new stables in Liu Ling

20. (*Top*) Women working at the manure-heaps
21. (*Bottom*) Latrines

22. (*Top*) The author interviewing Tsao Chen-kuei, 'The Little Author', with the aid of the interpreter Pei Kwang-li

23. (*Bottom*) Li Yiu-hua, the Old Secretary, in his cave with one of his grandchildren. Behind them are vessels for storing preserved vegetables

24. (*Top*) The Old Secretary's daughters-in-law, She Shiu-ying (the mark on her forehead is from a cupping-glass used in treating headache) and Chang Yü-ying

25. (*Bottom*) Li Shi-ping and Li Ai-ping eating noodles during a celebration

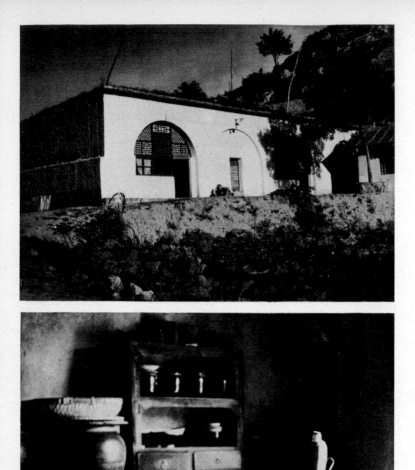

26. (*Top*) Stone caves. From left to right: the library, the
meeting-hall (where interviews took place), the granary, the
Old Secretary's office (where the author and his wife lived).
The field in the foreground is planted with melons
27. (*Bottom*) The stove in Shi Yü-chieh's kitchen

28. (*Top*) The kitchen in Shi Yü-chieh's cave. Note the table
    and chair. This is the only family to have such an
    arrangement for mealtimes
29. (*Bottom*) First-year pupils at recreation. The school's cook
    is on the left

30. A classroom

31. (*Top*) The school
32. (*Bottom*) The school's recreation area. Vegetables for winter
    are being dried on the platform in the foreground

33. The mill near Naopachan

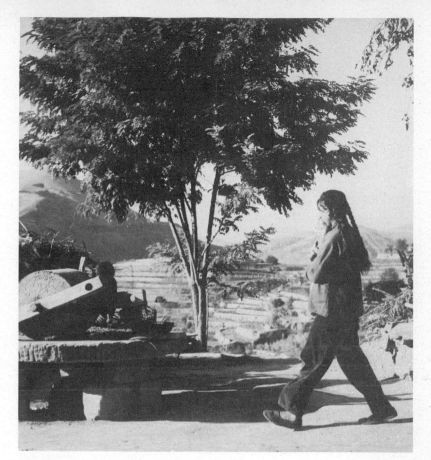

34. The mill beside the temple

35. Li Hai-yuan, the one who left the co-operative, at the
Naopachan mill

broth instead at every meal. At breakfast this consists of watere gruel.

Dinner. Steamed 'golden rice', that is millet, the same vegetables as in the morning and a broth of vegetable water.

Supper. Millet porridge.

Tuesday, 21 August 1962

Breakfast. Millet porridge with pumpkin. That makes a thick sweet gruel. Potato chips fried in oil.

Dinner. Noodles made of bean flour and wheat meal, fifty/fifty; tomatoes, beans and potatoes, chopped and fried in oil. With noodles we always have a strong sauce made of chives, strong pepper and salt. First, the chives are ground, then salted and peppered.

Supper. Millet porridge.

Wednesday, 22 August 1962

Breakfast. As Tuesday.

Dinner. Steamed 'golden rice' of millet, fried beans.

Supper. Millet porridge.

Thursday, 23 August 1962

Breakfast. Millet porridge, turnips, maize bread and fried vegetables.

Dinner. Thick maize porridge made with potatoes and fresh cabbage.

Supper. Millet porridge.

On this day we also ate a watermelon and three jin of small yellow melons.

Friday, 24 August 1962

Breakfast. As Thursday's.

Dinner. Wheat noodles with strong sauce and a vegetable dish of tomatoes and cabbage.

Supper. Millet porridge with maize cobs and steamed pumpkin. We have started to harvest our maize and so are eating a lot of maize cobs.

Saturday, 25 August 1962

Breakfast. As Tuesday's.

Dinner. Steamed cakes of finely chopped potato kneaded with wheat flour. With this we had fresh green beans, onion and garlic. We have onion and garlic with all meals, but that's obvious at this time of the year. It goes without saying.

Supper. Millet porridge. Maize cobs. Steamed pumpkin.

Sunday, 26 August 1962

Breakfast. Millet porridge and maize bread.

Dinner. Steamed wheaten bread with a vegetable dish of beans and tomatoes.

Supper. Millet porridge. Maize cobs. Steamed pumpkin.

We always cook our vegetables the same way: they are chopped finely and then cooked briefly in vegetable oil. Just now I am busy making ketchup, because there are plenty of tomatoes. I put the tomatoes in boiling water for a short time, take them out, peel them, take out the seeds and such, and then the tomato mush is boiled for a long time with salt and black pepper. We use this sauce for noodles.

I usually reckon on a good five jin of grain a day for the family. That does us. We are two adults and three children after all.

For the New Year I make salt patties of 'sticky millet'. I leave the 'sticky millet' soaking overnight, pound and steam it. Then I make a filling of potato and salt or grated carrots and salt; this filling is given a quick fry, stirring strongly. I roll out the dough and make it into patties with the salty mass as filling. Then I fry the patties in oil. If you want to make sweet patties, you do just the same, but fill them with pumpkin and sugar or beans and sugar. This filling is fried just the same as the salt filling, and the patties are made in the same way. Children like them. If you want to make 'sticky millet' cakes, the recipe is basically the same, but you don't use any filling and the dough is fried in oil as square cakes. They can be eaten with sugar or with gruel or how you like.

Bean curd is made for the New Year. I take some black beans and let them stand in water overnight. Then I peel them and grind them. I put the pulp in a piece of cloth and squeeze out the water. Then I boil them up in a pot, then I put in a little soda, which makes it like jelly. Then I put in a cloth again and press it till it becomes quite hard. Then I cut it into bits and fry or boil them and serve.

We got electric light in 1961. In the winter it costs us roughly 1·80 Y a month. In July we paid about 0·80 Y. Last month it had gone up to 1·47 Y. We haven't a dog or a cat, because our cave is new and there are no rats or mice here.

I make all the family's clothes. That is a lot of work, because the children are growing and wear things so. I either make a new, or re-make, a quilted coat, an unquilted coat, a pair of quilted trousers and a pair of unquilted trousers for everyone in the family each year. Last winter I bought twenty chi of cotton material; we had quite a lot left over from the year before; and I also bought five jin of cotton wadding. I mixed the new wadding with the old, which I had first cleaned, washed and carded. When I unpick an old garment, I use the old material as lining or for the children's clothes. But I wash it well first. No, I don't use a sewing-machine. There is only one person in the village who has a sewing-machine. That is Yang Fu-lien, who lives in Shiaoyuanchihou on the other side of the valley. That's a good way from Naopanshan, here. I make a whole new quilted coat for each member of the family every other year. In between, I unpick, wash and mend the old one.

I also make all the family's shoes. I make two pairs per person. Ten pairs each winter. The children have wadded shoes, but we grown-ups are hardened. No, I'm not cold in winter. The cave is warm. Each pair takes almost ten days to make. The winter's long and I work at the shoes whenever I get a free moment. First, I collect all the old worn-out cloth that can't even be used as lining any more. I wash it carefully, then I paste the pieces together, on top of each other, between layers of new cloth. When this has dried, I cut it out into soles. I make thicker soles for my husband and thinner soles for the children. Then I sew them with jute thread. That is the most laborious. You have to stitch very close and pull hard. The wear of the shoes depends in the first place on how the soles are sewn together. It is the jute you wear, not the cloth. I make the paste myself; I take roughly equal quantities of wheat and bean flour, mix it with water and boil it. I also make the jute thread myself. I cut the jute, remove the leaves, etc., then I put it in the stream. I dam this up with stones, so that the jute is quite covered with water. I put stones on the bundles of jute to keep them in place, and there they have to stay for a week, rotting. After that, I take the jute out, peel it and there the fibres are. I wind these into thread by rolling them on my thigh.

My husband knits. In this district, it is the husband's job to knit. He does this in the winter, when he's resting. Last winter, he knitted four pairs of stockings. One pair for himself and one for each of the children. I don't need any. I'm indoors most of the time, you see.

Yes, I'm from Liu Ling here. I learned how to run a cave from my mother and sister-in-law. I helped my sister-in-law when I was young and unmarried. I never went to school and I was never a pioneer. Instead, when I got a bit older, I looked after the family's children.

I was married when I was eighteen. I was betrothed when I was thirteen. My husband was then fourteen. It was our parents who decided it, but we were shown to each other and accepted it. I have never thought of anyone else. When we married, my parents-in-law were still alive and we lived with them. Life was much harder for me then, and I had much harder work than when I was a girl.

Talking of marriage and that, has anyone told you that Li Chin-wa, who is Li Hsiu-tang's daughter, has become engaged to the brigade book-keeper, Lo Han-hong, who is secretary of the League of Youth?

Well, life became more difficult for me when the children started coming. It isn't easy being a woman. My husband brings up four buckets of water a day from the well. I myself go down to the river to wash clothes once or twice a week. We often go down, a lot of us together. We do that when we have our day off. Or we do it during the midday rest, when our husbands are asleep. When we have our rest out in the field, we take out clothes to make or shoes to sew. The men either sleep then or walk about collecting fuel.

Women work much more than men. We have two jobs: we work both in the fields and in our caves. I know my husband helps me, we're a young family, of course, but he isn't as particular about housework as a woman is. Life is a lot of hard work. I don't take part in any kind of women's activities, political or otherwise. I just meet a few friends and chat with them.

I would, of course, like all my children to be able to study. I hope that they will work properly at school, so that they can be of some use here in the world and do something for people. The party and the school will have to decide what they are good for. But I am proud of my daughter. She is clever at school and helps me at home with the housework. She works hard. I hope that we shall be able to work and be healthy, so that we can live better and that our children will grow up into good people.

People say of Li Yang-ching: She loves a chat and jokes a lot. She is a gentle, well-brought-up woman and talks lovely Chinese with elegant phrases. She talks all the time when she's working in the fields, chattering and laughing. She talks a lot about the men in the village. She is very orderly and knowledgeable, though there isn't anyone of the older generation in her home. Everything in her cave is well looked after, and her children are well brought up and she works hard. She does more than other women. Most other women stop working in the fields when they have their first child, and don't find the day long enough even to look after the children; but she does work in the fields and sees to her home and the children, and has time to chat with her friends and run her home properly.

Her husband, Liu Chen-yung, is good. Most men here, or at least half of them, anyway, go straight to the kang and lie down and sleep when they get home from work; but he helps her and does things in the home. He is calm, quiet and doesn't speak much. They never quarrel; everyone considers them a happy family. He was anxious during her last pregnancy, in case she wasn't going to give birth to a son. She had had two girls before, you see. But she just told him not to worry, because she had decided to have a son. Then, when she did give birth to a son, all the women in the village were talking about her and envying her for being able to decide about such things herself. But, of course, she had been just as anxious in case it should be another girl.

Li Yang-ching is economical and thrifty. In 1961, they made a new cave, and the same year she went in to Yenan and bought a bicycle for her husband in the shop. She bought it with money she had earned herself. Liu Chen-yung is proud of his wife. She put a hundred days' work into that bicycle. He says: 'We haven't inherited what we have. We have worked for it.' They have also bought a two-wheeled cart with rubber wheels. That's a happy family.

Part VII
The People's Militia

The People's Militia

EVERY person *with civic rights*, only excepting invalids or the disabled, is a member of the people's militia: men between the ages of 16 and 45, women between 16 and 35. The people's militia is, however, a voluntary organization. It is at one and the same time a mass organization, with leaders elected at meetings of its members, and the ultimate backing of the power of the state: the people under arms acting as the organized violence in the defence of democracy and socialism.

There are three people in Liu Ling who do not belong to the people's militia: Tsao Chen-yung, because of an injured leg; Ai Ke-kao because of bad eyesight; and Li Hsiu-tang because he has been deprived of his civic rights. He is not regarded as a citizen.

Between the ages of 16 and 25 the members of the militia are in the armed militia, the crack unit of the people's militia. After that age, members are in the ordinary militia.

The duties of the people's militia are to ensure public safety; to see that order is maintained and that laws and regulations are complied with, to prevent and combat crime and track down any criminals there may be; to provide local defence in the event of war and, in the event of occupation, to act as guerrilla forces and local support forces.

Elected to the staff of Liu Ling Battalion

Battalion commander	Li Hung-fu
Political commissar	Li Hai-kuei
In charge of women	Li Kuei-ying
Battalion scribe	Lo Han-hong
Squadron leader*	Li Hai-ching
Group commander for the armed unit	Ma Hung-tsai
Group commander of the ordinary militia	Tung Yang-chen

* The squadron leaders for the other villages are not given.   J.M.

Li Hung-fu, battalion commander, aged 33

I HAVE worked on the land as long as I can remember. I cannot remember any time in my life when I wasn't doing that. I began when I was so small that I no longer remember anything of that time. I was never able to go to school. We were poor and rented eighteen mu of land from Li Hsiu-tang's family. We had to pay more than fifteen jin of corn per mu in rental. Later, when the K.M.T. fled and the Eighth Route Army came, the land was divided up and we got thirty mu of good land in the valley, as well as 100 mu of poor, dry land up on the hillside. After that, life was better. Having land and not needing to pay rent to anyone, there was enough for us to eat. We got ourselves an ox and a donkey. We weren't so well off for clothes, of course; ours were poor, but we could eat our fill.

After that Hu Tsung-nan came. We fled into the hills. We took the donkey with us, loading our baggage on it. It starved to death, because there was no fodder up there. We made our way to the village of Kelaikou, some fifty li from here. I had joined the Young Pioneers when I was twelve, and I entered the Self-defence Corps when I became sixteen. We were to help the guerrillas. We were to get them information about the enemy; we were to examine strangers and question them, find out which were enemies. Of course we knew all the people in the villages round about, but we had to check up on any strangers who came to the village. This was still my job when we moved to Kelaikou.

Hu Tsung-nan also organized something he called a 'Self-defence Corps'. Their agents came to the village. We captured two, tied them up with rope and sent them to the guerrillas higher up in the hills. I don't know what happened to them. We didn't ask. We had other things to think about.

One day I was keeping watch in the village, when one of Hu

245

Tsung-nan's soldiers came, quite on his own. I called the others and we hid, so that he could not see us. We let him come right into the village. He went into a cave. We caught him there, as in a trap. He had a grey uniform. Hu Tsung-nan's soldiers had both grey and yellow uniforms. People said that they had got the yellow ones from the U.S.A., but I don't know. It was in May this happened. When the man saw us, he dropped the corn he had managed to grab. He made an attempt to escape. One of the chaps caught hold of him and we two others had a rope ready and we wound him up in that, so that he could not move. Then we sent him up to the guerrillas. He looked very anxious when we carted him off. When he got to the guerrillas, he said to them: 'Don't kill me. I'm just a farm boy too. I don't like being a soldier at all. I was forced into the army.' The guerrillas replied: 'We shan't kill you. We communists don't kill our prisoners. We are going to convert you.' So then they gave him instruction and after that he was let go, so that he could go back to his own village, where he was to tell people what the Eighth Route Army was and what our aims were and how we treated prisoners.

Then we went back to Liu Ling. That was under the occupation. When we got back, we saw that Hu Tsung-nan had destroyed everything. We had had both a house and a cave. But the troops had torn down the house, they had used the window-wall of the cave for firewood, and they had smashed all our cooking-pots and jars and things. They had used a lot of force to smash our things. That's what they were like. They had eaten our ox and found and stolen our corn. We borrowed a cave from Chang Chen-pong. He lives in Seven-mile Village now. That year we were only able to till three or four mu.

By the spring of 1948, our corn was all at an end. After that we ate elm leaves and chaff. People were very hungry. When the Eighth Route Army came back, they gave people loans. I borrowed twenty dollars. Then I carted supplies for the Self-defence Corps for a time. After that we began tilling the land again.

I was living then with my stepfather, Ma Hai-hsiu. He joined the labour exchange group. This was later turned into the labour group for mutual help. There was no great discussion about it. My ox was a miserable one, and I found it difficult to manage. The labour group for mutual help was useful for us. I had been leader of the labour exchange group, but Ma Juei-ching became leader of the labour group for mutual help.

After that we discussed the idea of an agricultural co-operative. We said: 'Let us plough up the marches. They are just in the way.' Besides that, it had always been difficult to decide whose turn it was to have his fields ploughed or harvested, when we had the labour group for mutual help. That was a long discussion. On the first day twelve families applied to join the agricultural co-operative. I was one of them. On the second day, five more families applied. Li Hai-yuan, who had been one of the founders of the agricultural co-operative, then resigned from it, saying that he wanted to farm on his own again. But things did not go as well with him as he had thought they would. They went as we had told him they would; and in the end he had to apply to join again.

I now married and moved from Stepfather's, setting up my own household. That was in 1952. A lot of people were joining the League of Youth then. I saw that and wondered about it. I realized that I could serve the cause of the people better if I was organized. It was Jen Teh-wan's son, Jen Huai-wan, who recommended me for the League of Youth. But the person who really made me decide was Li Hai-chun, who is now in charge of the loan department of the people's commune. He was the sort of person I wanted to be. Everything he said and did was honest, moderate and restrained. He was always correct, always helping the people in the village, without favouring anyone. He was always calm and collected and always able to say the right thing to relieve a situation. I understood that this was because he was organized. Therefore, I considered that I ought to join an organization too. Being a member of an organization meant that you were trained and educated by the organization and your comrades. My first teacher, though, had been my stepfather, Ma Hai-hsiu. When I was a child, he had often talked to me about the fight for the people's cause, and how one must be honest and impartial and always serve the cause of the people. He was a communist, and he often talked to me about the future and the time when the people would be victorious in all countries. What he said and what he did had always been the same thing. He helped me a lot, and he brought me up to be a conscious being.

I was now working as group leader in Liu Ling Agricultural Co-operative and in the League of Youth. I joined the party in 1955. Then came the discussions about the higher agricultural co-operative. During these, Li Chung-ying said that he would not join. He had enough land to manage on his own, he said. He would hire a farmhand. Well, there were no farmhands to be had any more. We all told him that, in the new society, all that with farmhands and day labourers was over. He had to sweat in his fields by himself. And while he was sweating by himself and not getting much of a harvest, we were working together in the agricultural co-operative and singing as we worked. So, in the end, he applied to rejoin.

The three people who from the start were the most enthusiastic advocates of the higher agricultural co-operative were the Old Secretary, Li Yiu-hua, my stepfather, Ma Hai-hsiu, and Mau Ke-yeh.

In 1957, I became leader of the labour group. The following year, we formed Liu Ling People's Commune. That was better than the East Shines Red Higher Agricultural Co-operative. It was stronger and had a more comprehensive economy; it enabled us to terrace and that sort of thing. We had begun with big water-regulation works already in the spring of 1958, before the people's commune. We built a dam at Yuanchihkou. We began building it immediately after the spring sowing, and we finished some time in October or November. We borrowed people from the other brigades in the people's commune, because the people's commune was set up while we were in the middle of working on it. We ran the building work in the same way before and after the formation of the people's commune. We borrowed labour from other places and kept count of their days' work. That is to say, we paid them back either in days' work or in money. When we began, it was an exchange of work between higher agricultural co-operatives and, when we ended, between labour brigades. The people's commune did not really involve any change there.

Since that, we have done certain terracing jobs in Liu Ling Labour Brigade. We have done them within the frame of the people's commune, in the same way as we worked in 1958, and afterwards we helped other labour brigades with their terracing work. Since 1959, we have mostly been occupied keeping the big dam in good order. It keeps filling up with mud the whole time, of course. Besides that, we have made smaller irrigation dams and terrace fields. We did not begin any new project in the winter of 1961-2. And it will be the same in the coming winter. We shall be content to keep what we've already built in good repair. After harvest in 1959 we made some iron. But I hadn't anything to do with that. I stick to agricultural work. Feng Chang-yeh was the one responsible for that job.

With the years, life has got better. We are making progress all the time. In the old days, for example, we had few possessions. Now we have thermoses, galoshes, blankets, hand-carts with rubber wheels, bicycles. There's no comparison between what it was like before and what it is like now. We had been hoping for a long time to be able to buy a bicycle. We had planned to buy one. Eventually, in 1959, we had got enough together to buy one. We use it for transporting things, for bringing things home when we have been in the town shopping, and I usually take it to ride over to my relations in other villages. Sometimes I take my wife and children with me. I give them a lift then. It's a quick way of getting there. Women walk so slowly. I also take the bicycle when I am going into the town to go to the opera or the cinema. I like the opera and cinema; but on the other hand I am not particularly amused by the song-and-dance troupes. It's mostly operas that are already classics that I like. Of the films I remember, I can mention 'The Monkey King Conquers the White Bone Spirit Three Times', that is a filmed opera, and 'Hwa Mountain is Conquered'. I like films. My ten-year-old son can't get on with opera, but he likes films, he wants to see films like 'A Warrior of Steel'. He wants adventure and excitement and war and that sort of thing.

I am in charge of the people's militia within Liu Ling Labour Brigade. I have been a member of the militia for twenty years, ever since I was twelve years old. I was chosen battalion commander three years ago, since when I have been re-elected each year. The battalion includes the whole of Liu Ling Labour Brigade. It has 180 members who are capable of carrying arms. Here, in the village of Liu Ling—Liu Ling Village Labour Group and the Labour Group for Vegetable Cultivation—we have roughly eighty members. Small labour groups organize themselves as militia groups, and the larger labour groups as militia squadrons. The whole people's commune comprises a regiment. Up to battalion commander, we are elected by direct vote at general meetings. Beyond that, this would be too long-winded, so we battalion commanders elect the regimental commander and so on. I myself was never a squadron commander.

We are responsible for public order and security, and if there is war and the enemy dares to come here, we form guerrilla forces. There is no actual police as such. We provide our own police service. We have no badges of rank, by the way; we don't call ourselves lieutenants or colonels or suchlike. We are just elected leaders.

There are, of course, wholetime employees in the hsien administration who are concerned with police work. We can call on these if we need help. In the towns, too, there are traffic police and that sort of thing. But, in the country, we see to all that ourselves. We don't get any pay for it; nor are we credited with any days' work for taking part in manœuvres and that sort of thing, nor do we commanders get any sort of remuneration. The regimental commander in charge of the whole of the armed forces of Liu Ling People's Commune is at the same time one of the ten wholetime administrative ganbus employed in our people's commune. The people's commune, of course, constitutes a regiment, and this regiment is commanded by a regimental staff, which meets every three months. As battalion commander, I am a member of the regimental staff.

In this way we are, on the one hand, a mass organization with meetings and elections, and, on the other hand, a military organization which is responsible for security and which has military duties in time of war. For that reason, our order system is of a military kind. The commanders are elected at general meetings of the members, but their orders have to be obeyed while on duty. Our firearms are stored centrally by the hsien administration. The people's militia is an organization of the whole people. If the people have the political and economic power, it must also have the real power. In this way, we can be sure of not losing the democracy we fought to get.

But, of course, not everybody is in it. There are always some who are ill or lame or blind and thus unable to bear arms. Also, our counter-revolutionaries are not in it. We really don't want to give them weapons. It was difficult enough once to take their weapons from them. Nor can they be in it, because their civic rights have been taken from them by decision of the court. If they had reformed and if they really had been re-educated, they would get their civic rights back and thereby be able to be taken into the people's militia as members. But Li Hsiu-tang's children are in the people's militia. They are very efficient. They do a lot in the people's militia. They belong to the new age.

We have a ceremony at the annual meeting, when we take the new members in, those who have turned seventeen and can apply for admission. At the same time, we say thank you to those who have to leave the militia because of age.

In wintertime we hold manœuvres lasting one or two weeks. We chose the time so as not to interfere with production. We practise shooting then and have a programme of gymnastics and sports. We who have been elected commanders have more lectures than the ordinary members, but our training is the same. During training, people from outside come to help us. Also, we choose the best of us to lead the manœuvres. We get trainers and lecturers from the people's commune and the hsien administration. But we have never had an officer or trainer from the Chinese People's Liberation Army.

We have various courses and lectures and discussions among ourselves. We hold the larger meetings in the collective dining-hall, smaller gatherings are held in this cave, and the talks we have in the fields during the rests. Besides, we usually go into the town on 1 May and 1 October and listen to what is said at the big meetings, at which leading comrades speak. We also have a lot of material sent to us. We read this aloud to the members and then discuss it. We do this mostly out in the fields during rests. We usually hold all these meetings and lectures at some time that cannot be used in production. So it is mostly in the winter evenings. We study three subjects in the people's militia: military science, politics and agricultural theory.

In the old days, there was a lot of stealing and many unpleasant things happened. I remember that, when I was a child, we had our donkey stolen once. But since the Eighth Route Army came and our lives changed, things have been better. In the last ten years nothing has happened. Of course, our task is first and foremost to prevent crime and see that nothing disturbs peace and order. We are not a police organization that busies itself tracking people down; we are the might of the people itself which comprises the whole people and therefore prevents crime.

But we have had one case of theft which we discovered. That was in April 1960. There had been opera in the town and we were patrolling the highway in the evening. Then a man came along pulling a hand-cart. He was from a village farther on. We wondered why he was pulling a hand-cart in the middle of the night, and we asked him that. He could not give us a clear explanation and behaved so strangely that it looked as though he had a bad conscience. So we took him and the hand-cart to the office of Liu Ling's People's Commune in Seven-mile Village. It later transpired that he had been to the opera and, when he had left the town and was on his way back to his own village, he had seen the hand-cart standing outside a house and had just taken it with him. And the family from whom the hand-cart had been stolen got it back before they even discovered that they had been robbed. That's the only case there's been. Because, if the people itself is responsible for order, crimes are prevented before they are committed. In this village, there hasn't been anything at all. Nothing that I know of, at least.

In 1959, I was chosen, as a merit worker, to attend a conference of merit workers in our hsien. On 28 December 1961 I had a diploma conferred on me by Liu Ling People's Commune for 'Good work in production and good work in the people's militia'. That was given me in part for my agricultural work, and in part because there had been no accidents nor any crimes committed within the area for which I am responsible. In June this year I was given yet another diploma. The text was the same, but this time the citation was for 'Services in organizing the people's militia for agricultural work; meritorious leadership in agricultural work; exemplary style of working, hard work and simple way of life; good security work, no accidents, no crimes'.

My wife does not do any political work. She has never been elected to any post; she isn't a member of either the League of Youth or of the party. I have, of course, talked politics with her on occasion, but that hasn't been often. I myself was never able to go to school as a child. Since then, I have been working on other matters and have not been able to spare much time for learning to read and write. But I have attended various reading courses in my spare time in the winter, and I now know roughly a hundred characters.

But that also means that I do not know enough characters to be able to read a newspaper. But I can keep notes of a kind.

People say of Li Hung-fu: He is good-looking. He is an ordinary person. He is taciturn and never speaks unnecessarily. He is quite respected, but the women do not like joking with him. He does not understand joking, and laughing and that sort of thing. 'Though he doesn't like chatting and never jokes, and though he can go days at a stretch without opening his mouth or saying a word to anyone, there's a lot in his head.' He is a good organizer. He understands how to get people to work. He himself spares no effort and is always an example in any situation calling for energy and endurance. His manner of living is that which the party recommends: hard work and a simple way of life.

He has married again. His new wife is very young. She is not the least interested in politics. She talks a lot, sings and laughs and jokes, and they are utterly different. He often asks her to be quiet. She wants to sing, but he prefers to have quiet. She is an easy, pleasant person. Life is a game to her. She does not bother much about looking after the children; they have to manage on their own; and the house just has to get along too. But she is very young. She was scarcely eighteen when they married after his first wife's death. But she treats her stepson very well. She is just as fond of him as if he was her own. 'She is lazy and sings and laughs all day long, but she is nice to her stepson.' Her stepson is also very fond of her. Most children are.

The women say: 'Li Hung-fu is a stylish chap, but she is just a child. If she had married some young fellow, who was as fond as she of talking and laughing, they would have starved to death. It was lucky for her she married Li Hung-fu, who is always calm and sure and never fusses her, but just does his bit and gets on with his work.'

Part VIII

Liu Ling Labour Brigade's Supervisory Committee

Members of the Supervisory Committee:

Mau Ke-yeh, Chairman	Labour Group for Vegetable Cultivation
Li Kwang-yung	Wangchiakou Village Labour Group
Han Fu-chieh	Hutoma Village Labour Group
Li Hai-tsai	Liu Ling Village Labour Group
Chiang Hao-wu	Erchuankou Village Labour Group

Li Hai-tsai, member of the supervisory committee, aged 28

I AM the Old Secretary, Li Yiu-hua's second son, so I do not need to talk about my background and childhood. You know all that from the others. But I did go to school for three years. It was Liu Ling's basic school, and I was there from the time I was thirteen till I had turned sixteen. I began school immediately after Hu Tsung-nan had to buzz off, and I finished in the winter of 1950. My father was head of the farmers' co-operative then and labour was needed for it. That was a hard time for us, and we had to show that we got bigger harvests than either those farming on their own or the other labour groups for mutual help. And this in spite of our land not being so good. One of Father's difficulties was that there was no one in his farmers' co-operative able to read or write. There was no one who could even keep a work daybook.

Father told me then that I ought to come home. He asked me if I would not leave school and start work in the farmers' co-operative instead. It was a hard choice for me. I loved school and had hoped to be able to go on studying, but I thought that farmwork was glorious too. Besides, I saw how hard Father had to toil and what difficulties he was up against, so I told him that I would leave school and start working on the land instead. I have been working as a farmer ever since.

I have not joined any organization of any kind. I have been wondering for a long time about joining the party, and now, at last, I have sent in my application. The party is in the course of considering it just now. They are testing me to see if I am worthy. I have never been a member of the League of Youth. I am too old to join now, and when I was young I was too immature. When I matured, I found I was too old. When I was young, I was not very politically minded: I liked singing and acting and playing. I thought the League of Youth dull and boring;

I just wanted to laugh and sing in those days. I used to sing every morning on my way out to the fields. That irritated some people. Of course, there's no harm in singing, but somehow I and the League of Youth just did not fit in.

I arranged my own marriage. I am of the first generation of the new society, and nobody else arranged my marriage for me. You attend to that sort of thing yourself these days. I was on a visit to another village, had gone to see a relative we had there. And there I saw a girl. I liked her. After that I used to go often to visit that relative. And mostly I saw the girl. Then we got engaged. Her parents agreed to it without much opposition. Mine were just happy. That was 1956. She was nineteen and I was twenty-two then.

I was working on the land the whole time. From 1950 to 1958 I kept the work daybook and calculated people's days' work. After that, I was just an ordinary worker until December last year. We were due to have the annual meeting. At this we were to elect a new member for the supervisory committee, to replace Fu Hai-tsao. People said: 'You are just and you are known not to be easy-going or the sort of person to look through your fingers at other people's mistakes. So, at the annual meeting of the representatives we are going to elect you to the supervisory committee.' Fu Hai-tsao's place was to fall vacant because he was going to be elected deputy labour leader of the labour group for vegetable cultivation, and, besides, he had been proposed for election to the management of the labour brigade. So I was asked: 'Will you stand?' I said: 'I'll stand. But only if I really am going to be elected, and if the voting is unanimous. I don't want to have any discussion about it. Either people have confidence in me or they don't have confidence in me. If they have, then I shall be happy to have their trust and shall do my best to be of service.' Well, the meeting was held and I was elected, unanimously.

The supervisory committee has a whole lot of duties. Its members, of course, are unpaid. And we are not allowed to be on any other committee or board. We have to supervise how the ganbus work, see that they are doing their bit and organizing the work in the right way. We have to supervise the implementation of production plans. We have to keep an eye out for extravagance or irresponsibility. We have to supervise the book-keeping. Apart from the different quick checks we make, we have to do an annual audit of the books and the stores and everything. We meet once a month for ordinary meetings, but we can be called for an extra meeting whenever necessary. We have the right to call anyone we wish before us at these meetings. But, of course, no one can invite himself. No one can come and sit down with us and try to influence us.

We have full powers from the representatives and it is to them we are responsible. We are not to have respect for persons, nor be bound by ties of friendship in our work. No one can deny us the right to go through his books and investigate how he is doing his job. That is to say, we do not investigate private persons nor people's private lives; that is no concern of ours. We just investigate the various people who have been elected to positions of trust and how they are discharging their duties, dealing with the money and common property in their charge and so on.

We make our most important reports at the annual meeting. What happens is this: there is the annual meeting of the representatives. First, the chairman of the committee of the labour brigade makes his report. Next, the labour brigade's book-keeper makes his. After that, the chairman of the supervisory committee makes his report. He reports on what the supervisory committee has done during the year, and also on the results of the annual audit of the labour brigade's books, funds and stores. Only then does the general discussion begin. After that, the report is accepted, unless there is any reason to find fault with it, and after that there is the voting for the posts for the coming year.

But, of course, we submit reports at every meeting of the representatives during the year: what the position is and what action we have taken. We are duty-bound to report everything directly to the representatives. But the annual meeting is the most important. I can give you some examples of what we do:

A complaint against Tung Yang-chen, deputy labour leader of Liu Ling Village Labour Group, was made to us at our meeting on 15 August this year. It was made by the older farmers, and they wanted us to check his work. This was because, when they were ploughing for wheat, he had simplified the work and adopted a subjective attitude. He was a newly elected labour leader and did not have a great deal of experience. The old farmers had said: 'Remove all the weeds from the headlands.' But Tung Yang-chen had refused to listen to them and had said: 'We are short of labour. We are not going to waste time on the headlands. Just get on with the ploughing.' He decided simply to let the headlands go. All the others were against him, but he would not listen. He just gave the order.

The old farmers were thoroughly upset by this. They came to us and demanded that we take the matter up. The chairman of the supervisory committee, Mau Ke-yeh, was given the job of discussing the matter with the old experienced farmers. They all said: 'It is best to weed the headlands straight away, so that next year's harvest isn't a bad one.' Then we discussed the matter; and then we sent for Tung Yang-chen and had a serious talk with him. In the end, he admitted his mistake; the older and more experienced farmers were right, you see, and his conduct had not been what a labour leader's should have been: he had disregarded their advice and instead tried to give them orders. The headlands were then weeded. That is one sort of problem that we have to deal with.

Another kind of problem with which we have to deal is the book-keeping problem. In July, the book-keeper of Liu Ling Village Labour Group, Chang Chung-liang, came to me one night. Chang Chung-liang's cave is just next to Wang Kwang-yung's office. He is the treasurer of the labour brigade. Once a month he and the brigade book-keeper, Lo Han-hong, go through their books. The two books have to agree. But on this night, when Lo Han-hong and Wang Kwang-yung were sitting checking their books, Chang Chung-liang heard them say that there was a discrepancy of a hundred yuan or so. He came to me as soon as he heard that, since I am Liu Ling Labour Brigade's representative on the supervisory committee. Chang Chung-liang then left and went home to bed. I went to the chairman of the supervisory committee, Mau Ke-yeh, and we had a brief discussion about what ought to be done, and, as I had been to school and also had done a bit of book-keeping at the beginning of the 'fifties, we decided that I should go through the books.

So then we both went down to Wang Kwang-yung's cave and confiscated both his and Lo Han-hong's books, and made a quick check. They were taken by surprise. I worked all night going through the books and checking each item. In the end, by which time it was already noon the following day, I had found the error. One of the members, He Huang-ho, had handed in a certain cash sum to the treasurer, and the book-keeper had entered this in his books. But the treasurer, Wang Kwang-yung, had forgotten to enter the amount in his book. It was a sum of 100 Y. But when we went through the cash—

we had naturally confiscated that along with the books—we found the hundred yuan there. The cash in hand agreed with the book-keeper's books; but the treasurer's own books did not agree with his cash in hand. There was thus no question of misappropriation, but there was gross negligence. The treasurer, Wang Kwang-yung, was subjected to sharp criticism. We pointed out to him that this was irresponsibility. This he admitted. He promised for the future to endeavour to be more accurate.

We then reported to Chang Chung-liang what had been done and what the discrepancy had amounted to. It is our duty to do this. We have to report at once to whoever has informed us of any irregularity or proposed a check. This is very important. If the supervisory committee was not obliged to do this, it could happen that a soft member of the committee failed to act on an unpleasant report, out of friendship. As it is, we have to show that we really do do our jobs, otherwise the informant is entitled to demand our removal at the next meeting of the representatives. If we neglect our duties in any way—though I have never heard of anyone doing so really—the representatives can dismiss us, even in the middle of the year. Thus we reported the result to Chang Chung-liang, and he was satisfied. We did not summon any extra meeting of the supervisory committee, however. We did not think that was necessary, since there was an ordinary meeting due in two days' time. Later, the whole matter was put before a meeting of the representatives.

We have not had any more serious case. We have never discovered any embezzlement or that sort of thing. But we are constantly on the watch. It is a big responsibility to have to look after the people's money. That is why we check all books and stores very carefully. We go through every item. We do this as thoroughly as we can.

Every member of the supervisory committee has the right to make an on-the-spot investigation, if he suddenly comes across anything that seems not right. But he must get into touch with the chairman of the supervisory committee immediately afterwards and confer with him. There are five of us in the supervisory committee. Four members and a chairman. I am, naturally, proud of the fact that people have trust in me. Because it is a great proof of trust to be elected member of the supervisory committee. No one may be on the supervisory committee if he has relatives or friends in charge of funds. However honest he is, one can never know if he won't one day temper justice with mercy. He might, perhaps, shut his eyes to mistakes. But a member of the supervisory committee must never shut his eyes to any mistake, whoever has made it. Our chairman, Mau Ke-yeh, is an old and experienced party member, who has been in many positions of trust, and who knows a lot about organizations and economic associations. You ought to have someone like that as chairman of a supervisory committee. Someone one can rely on absolutely, and whom one knows not to have any personal ambition in his work, but who can stick to a fixed line of principle the whole time.

People say of Li Hai-tsai: He is never tired. He works hard and he talks the whole time. But his isn't exactly a mild or gentle nature. He often gets angry, and it does not take much to make him fly off the handle. His wife is just the same, and they have fearful quarrels. They can be heard all over the village. But no one interferes in their squabbles, because after a bit they will be laughing together again. They just like slanging-matches and say what they think, straight out.

He is incredibly frank. He will say anything to anyone. He is no respecter of persons. He has never seemed to be afraid of anything, but says exactly what he thinks. That is why we chose him for the supervisory committee: he is both honest and frank. And his temperament is such that no one could influence him and get him to do anything dishonourable.

But he jokes with his wife even when they are out among other people, and that is a bit peculiar. He does not care what people think, but will say to her: 'I'm not handsome, but that doesn't matter, you being as ugly as you are.' Then they both laugh. One doesn't say that sort of thing. Nor does one talk about one's own looks or joke about someone else's appearance. But Li Hai-tsai does. He'll joke with anyone, and never bothers what people think. But he is gay and friendly, too, and he isn't nasty or resentful. It's just that he's so incredibly outspoken.

Part IX
The Counter-Revolutionary

Li Hsiu-tang, aged 38

I AM of a landowning family. My father died when I was a child, and I do not remember so very much of my early childhood. But it was happy. We lived well, even after Father died. We had good food and life was pleasant. We ate pork every day, we had chicken and eggs and wheat noodles and stuffed wheaten bread. I practically never tasted millet as a child. That is grown a lot round here, but we didn't eat it. It was only the ordinary people who ate millet; we ate rice and wheat. We had a big house in Old Yenan. It does not exist any longer. The whole of the old town was wiped out during a bomb raid in the war. But I remember our house very well. There was a big hall in it, and it had lots of rooms. Our family consisted of over forty people. Father had four brothers, but I was his only son. Mother, though, was just a concubine. There were many relations and they were all nice to me. I remember Li Han-hua as one of my older uncles. I met him when I was ten. He was my bride's brother. Mine was a happy childhood.

When my father died, the inheritance was divided into five shares. The eldest of the cousins, Li Niu, became the head of the family, and he got the land. Another cousin took over the shops; he was responsible for the finances. A third cousin had all the cash. My mother and my elder sister and I got the property in the town. That brought in a lot in rentals. The youngest cousin got the animals, the oxen, sheep and goats. After that, we each moved into a house of our own. That was easily arranged, because we owned a lot of property, and we only had to give notice to a few tenants and move in.

Li Niu, who had got the land, moved to Liu Ling. I did not know much about what was going on out there. We didn't hear anything about Liu Ling. That was partly because I was so young, and partly because the land was in Li Niu's share. On the other hand, I knew a lot about our house property. Mother used to discuss the management of it with me. Though I did know that, later on, Li Niu's land was divided up. He was living then in the cave where Tung Yang-chen lives now. The cave was taken from him when everything was divided up, and given to Tung Yang-chen, because of what had happened to his father. At that time there were only seven or eight households in the village, and they were all able to have good land. We also had a plot. Later, Li Niu moved to another cave and, when he did, I took his over. But that comes later.

I went to Kao Hsiao's school in Yenan. It was a good school and I liked being there. We studied Chinese language and literature, mathematics and history and Sun Yat-sen's principles. Nothing serious happened in my life until the Red Guard entered the town. Mother had never spoken to me about the Red Guard. I knew, of course, that other people did not dare leave the town and were short of food, but my mother was a widow and had only been my father's concubine, so she always went outside the town to buy things and used to come back with lots of food. I know that there were people in Yenan who were starving and in difficulties during the blockade, but I myself noticed nothing. Our table was the same as ever. We had lots of courses.

Then the Red Army came. They summoned a mass meeting. It was to be held at the East Gate. There was a rumour that the communists were going to cut people's throats, and we wondered. I went to the meeting with my school class, because the schools had all been ordered to attend. The meeting was held in the middle of the day and was well attended. Everyone wondered what the communists would have to say. Three people made speeches. Liu Chih-tan was one of them, I remember. I had heard his name. He said: 'Be calm, don't worry, carry on with your ordinary work. There is no reason to run away.'

Mother had been worried before this and wondered if we should try to get away, but after this she decided to stay. Many of our tenants were tradesmen from Shansi. One of them, who was head of the town's chamber of commerce, came to see Mother. He said: 'There's no reason to be afraid. The Red Guard has spoken with me and promised to protect trade and safeguard the interests of the tradesmen. They asked me whose house I lived in, and I told them: '"A poor widow's house", so there's no cause for anxiety.' Then women ganbus from the Red Guard came and talked with us.

School was closed for ten days. Then it opened again. Now certain teachers had been replaced. We had the same timetable as before, but there was more talk of Sun Yat-sen's three principles and the teachers told us that we must fight against Japan. Till then, nobody had spoken to us about Japan. Then I joined the Young Pioneers. The main thing was that one helped the teachers see that everyone studied properly. Besides that, we sang songs. Then the school was incorporated in the Normal School and I left. I did not see the fun of going to school and, anyway, I was Mother's only son. She was afraid that I would abandon the family if I went on studying. I was to learn to be a tradesman instead.

I now began working in a shop. I had no difficulty in getting work, because most of our tenants were tradesmen and, in many cases, we owned half their shops. I began by keeping the yards clean and sweeping out the floor of the shop, but then gradually I was also allowed to serve in the shop. I liked that better than going to school. I had always dreamed of becoming a merchant. I still went to the Pioneer meetings once a week. There, we discussed abolishing gambling games and that sort of thing. We still lived as well as we had before. Actually, the arrival of the Red Army did not cause any change in our lives. We still ate pork and chicken and eggs. I did not need to eat millet. I liked my work and had great hopes for the future.

Then came the bombing. Most of our houses were demolished. The others were damaged and had to be pulled down. The whole town was destroyed. The bombing was a hard blow for us. Mother wept, because we had lost all we possessed. My mother's uncle came to help us. We moved to Liu Ling. There we had a mill and the land that we had got ourselves allotted, and we were hiring day labourers to look after it. We now had twenty mu of valley land and thirty mu of hill land. We did not work on the land ourselves. The day labourers did that. We were exploiters, as it's called.

We got on well with the people in Liu Ling right from the beginning. When we moved out there, everyone was kind to Mother. She was a woman and a concubine, and she had always been courteous and friendly to the people there when Father was alive. But when our second cousin wanted to come out there, too, people said no. So he never came to Liu Ling. But life had become worse than before. We no longer had any income from our houses, of course. All that we had to live on was the land, the mill and a little trading. We ate better than our neighbours, to be sure, that was obvious, but life wasn't what it had been.

I had married before we moved out from Yenan. That was in 1938. It had been arranged by my parents before I was born. After that we were four in the family: Mother, Mother's uncle, I and my wife. I now began working as a street trader. There was a big co-operative here down by the road, and I used to go there in the morning and sit down by the roadside with my wares. I sold cigarettes and melon seeds and walnuts and groundnuts and that sort of thing, and when the villagers from roundabout came to the co-operative to buy or sell, they stopped and talked with me and bought something. It was something of an event for them to go to the big shop, so it all fitted in well that I should be there and could sell them a few delicacies.

Mother's uncle was in charge of the land and the mill. The day labourers came from Yulin. We made quite a lot from the mill. Between twenty-eight and thirty jin of grain yielded roughly twenty-two jin of wheaten flour; for milling we charged two jin of flour and all the bran. My income from peddling was not large. It perhaps bought my food. I came and went as I liked; I was my own master, and I did not need to over-exert myself. I liked trading, I liked chatting with people and doing what I wished. That's the life that has always suited me best. I have always wanted to be a tradesman. And we lived much better then than we do now. Much better. We felt better and ate better.

Mother kept saying: 'If it hadn't been for the Japanese, we would still have been there in the town. We would have had our houses and not needed to live like this. But their bombs destroyed it all.' Then we heard that the Japanese had been beaten, but that there was a new war between the communists and the K.M.T. government. Now the situation hardened, and I gave up my street trading and ran the mill instead. I often used to think of what might happen. Actually, I wanted to live a more comfortable life. I had been accustomed to that since childhood. Though life was not as good as before, it was still better than most people's. The mill milled 300 jin a day. That brought in a good lot. There was a lot of talk about the war between the communists and the K.M.T., and I wondered what was going to happen. To be on the safe side, I joined the militia. You see, I had always been a Young Pioneer. Mother used to say: 'If we hadn't had the misfortune to live in Yenan, but had been in the K.M.T. area, what happy lives we should have led.' All the elder members of the family said that, and I thought the same.

Then we heard that the Eighth Route Army was to retreat and that General Hu Tsung-nan's troops were coming. A mass meeting was held in Yenan before it was evacuated. At this they quoted Chairman Mao, who was supposed to have said: 'Hold Yenan, lose Yenan. Surrender Yenan, keep Yenan.' But that just bewildered me and didn't know what to think. I was so worried. One did not know what was going to come of it all, and it was important to steer the right course. It's always like that in war. You can never be sure. We were anxious, and Mother kept saying: 'If only we had been in K.M.T. territory all the time. Now nobody knows what can happen.' Then Yenan was evacuated, and I saw the Eighth Route Army withdraw. After that, General Hu Tsung-nan's troops arrived, and I had never seen so many soldiers before. They had modern weapons and guns and everything, and I thought: 'Well, at all events the communists have had it.'

I remember the day the K.M.T. troops marched in. Our mill was on the other side of the river. We had tried to protect that. People had been told to evacuate their possessions and bury their grain. This had been done rather tardily. It was only in the last few days that people made any attempt to hide their grain. Now, I and Tuan Fu-yin and some others had taken ourselves up on to Naopanshan, just here beside us. We had several bottles of spirits with us and sat up there on the hillside, drinking and talking. Then we saw the troops arrive. It was ten o'clock. It was just as people were due to go out with the goats. General Hu Tsung-nan made his troops march on Yenan in two detachments. One came from Kanchuan and the other from Ichuan. This was the one from Ichuan arriving. As we sat there talking, one of us suddenly said: 'Now they're coming!' We stood up and watched them. The troops came marching along. First came the cavalry on big horses. Then the infantry. There were soldiers everywhere; they were spread over the whole landscape; they occupied all the eminences along the road, there seemed no end to the soldiers. Uniforms and weapons everywhere and the cavalry riding along on big fine horses. We stood there watching them, Tuan Fu-yin and a person from the co-operative shop, he has gone back to Shansi now, and another from Michi, he has gone back there too, a man called Yen Chu-tsai who is in Shansi now, and another called Yen something, and myself. Then we saw the police troops coming towards the village. Then Tuan Fu-yin called: 'Quick! Quick! Let us boil up water and bid these troops welcome. Let us not wait until it's too late.'

I thought: 'These K.M.T. troops are not going to do anything to me. But if I don't go down and meet them now, something might happen to my property.' Then we finished off the last of the spirits and ran down to the village to welcome the troops.

There we were taken prisoner. They told us to fetch water for them, and then we had to guide them the safest way into the town. We did this. Three days later the others were released and ordered to get back to their home villages as quickly as they could. But I was kept. They interrogated me. They did not trust me. You see, I did not dress as a farmer in those days. I wore European clothes and cut my hair the European way. I had trousers and a jacket with three pockets and wore a hat on my head. The officer took hold of me and said: 'Are you from the Eighth?' 'No, I am not,' I replied. He looked at me and said: 'You are not dressed like the farmers.' 'But I'm still not from the Eighth Army,' I said. He did not believe me, but said: 'You're an inveterate communist and now you're going to tell us about the communists' illegal organization and where the Eighth Army is and what plans the guerrillas have.' But I couldn't tell them anything, because I didn't know anything. 'I don't know any military secrets. After all, I'm just a mill-owner.' But the K.M.T. did not believe me, but took me to a cell. They locked me in. The prison was in the garrison. A judge called Kao interrogated me. Then they tortured me. They sat me on a chair and tied my knees down and stretched out my feet and put bricks under them. More and more bricks. But whatever they tried, I could not tell them anything, because I didn't know anything. Then they let me alone.

We prisoners were now divided into different groups. They called us prisoners-of-war. Each group was attached to a unit. One of the K.M.T.'s difficulties was that they had taken Yenan without getting any prisoners, and that there hadn't been a fight. The Eighth Route Army and the communists had evacuated in time and avoided fighting. But the K.M.T., you see, had to be able to show that it had won a victory. The officers needed prisoners to show off with. They were given prize money for every prisoner. They now brought visitors in to see us and said: 'These are our prisoners. They are from the Eighth Route Army.'

Then, we were to have more important visitors. We were given old worn uniforms. Foreign journalists were coming. I was to tell them that I was from the Eighth Route Army and belonged to the 358th Detachment. Several delegations of journalists came to look at us. Some of these foreigners had yellow hair and long noses. Others looked more normal. Some wore big boots with spurs, others tall boots with laces. Some of them had K.M.T. caps and others sheepskin caps. They spoke to us, and a K.M.T. officer stood in front of us and translated their questions, and we answered as we had been told to answer. Then they photographed us, and some had cameras like yours and others had film cameras. Then they took group pictures of us.

Then, in June, more peculiar things happened. We were ordered out to dig false graves up on the hillsides. I had to dig them up on Lokoushan beyond the vegetable plots. There were no corpses in the graves, but we were to say that this was where this or that communist officer was buried. People then came to see them and inspected the graves and interviewed us as witnesses. We told them how the communist officers had died and that we were local farmers. After that the

K.M.T. officers were given tens of dollars for each of the graves. But later that same month my period of being a prisoner ended.

Two officials came to Yenan. They were both from the town here. One, who was called Yuan, had served in Yenan earlier, and the other, Chu, was also from the district. Both used to come to my family's house. When they saw me, they said: 'But why in the world are you in prison?' I told them the truth, that I was suspected of being a communist, and that I had been tortured and had not been believed when I said that I was a mill-owner and a landowner's son. Then they saw to it that I was released at once.

I was now made a batman in the garrison headquarters. My officer was called Wong. He was from the General Staff and was responsible for prisoners-of-war. I had to tidy up and serve at meals and all that sort of thing. I worked for him like this for a month and he got to know me. Then all the so-called prisoners-of-war were to be transported down to Sian. Hundreds of people were to be sent off. Then Hsia, the General Staff officer responsible for army intelligence, sent for me and said: 'We need twelve men to work in the radio communications department and run the intelligence service in Yenan.' It was to be a secret organization, and therefore was to be called the 'northwestern News Bureau'. My officer Wong selected the men. Most were from Yenan. I was made leader of the group. I don't know how it happened that they chose me. It must have been pure chance. I hadn't done anything.

We were not paid. We were just given our food. One day a month, we put on uniform; that was the day the pay was supposed to be paid. But after that they took our uniforms away again, and the officers held on to our money. That was customary in the K.M.T. army. It was a common trick. There were always more men on the roll than there were in reality, and in that way the officers were able to get more money.

Our group was stationed behind the buildings that now house the offices of Yenan hsien. In the mornings we had to start up the motor that supplied the garrison with electricity, and then we were supposed to go out into the town and listen to what people were saying. We always wore civilian clothes. What the two officers, Wong and Hsia, wanted to hear about most was what people were saying about the Eighth Route Army and the guerrillas. We had strict orders not to say anything about our working for the intelligence service. But people knew it, of course, and it wasn't much we heard. We didn't get any money, because the officers took our pay, so we couldn't go in anywhere and eat and drink and listen to what people were saying, but had to walk about in the streets and try to listen. I heard that my mother had said that she was anxious about me and my work. I wasn't earning anything for the family, of course, and it wasn't work that had any advantages. My deputy and I had each been given a pistol with ten cartridges, but I was careful not to carry mine on me. I locked it up and never touched it and never fired a single shot, because there was no knowing what might not happen in the future.

We had orders not to go more than ten li from our garrison. Out there were the guerrillas, and they might capture us. I had been given the pistol to use against the guerrillas, but I preferred to keep it hidden and try to avoid getting in contact with the guerrillas. I was the one who gave the others in the group their orders, but I made them report direct to Hsia. I never interrogated any prisoners. We did duty in the radio communications section at night, between ten in the evening and four in the morning. During the first month, all went well and we liked our work, but then people became more and more reluctant to have anything to do with us and that made us feel uncomfortable.

At first, no one dared make a fuss, but then our wives and mothers came and cursed us for not earning anything, and those working in the group began to be discontented. People in the group began saying that they were working for the K.M.T. intelligence service, yet their families still had to starve. Besides, it did not look as if the communists were as thoroughly beaten as we had thought.

Then the garrison headquarters was to be moved and the Seventeenth Division transferred to Yenan. At first, the garrison wanted to take us with them, but we did not want to go on with this work and I went to see our official, Chu. The other official I knew, Yuan, had already left Yenan. I spoke frankly to Chu and told him the whole thing, and as he had known my father and wanted to do me a good turn, he said: 'You can go off if you like.' So then we handed in our pistols and cartridges, and, in September, I went home to Mother.

The family was then living in Seven-mile Village. They had moved there from Liu Ling. When Mother saw me, she said: 'I am afraid.' I was at home only one night. Mother had a talk with me. She had not been expecting me home so soon. She was worried that I had brought no money home. She did not like me working for the K.M.T. 'Don't get yourself mixed up with that sort of thing,' she told me. 'Take up trading instead.' I said: 'One has to say yes when those who hold the power ask one. If you want to get away from here, we must find a way.' You see, at the beginning we had thought that the K.M.T. would win for good, but now, that August and September, we all understood that the K.M.T. would soon have to get out again. The guerrillas were active all the time, and the K.M.T. troops and K.M.T. officers themselves no longer even believed that they had won. We talked a lot that night about what we were to do. Now everything had become rather dangerous for me. The guerrillas might come at any moment and capture me, and on the other hand the K.M.T. might decide to fetch me back for its intelligence service again, so we decided that I should go to Lochuan that very night.

I had a lot of friends in Lochuan. There, I borrowed 400 silver dollars from a friend and bought cloth in Fuping. It was good home-spun, and there was, of course, a shortage of goods up in Yenan. A month later, I was back in Seven-mile Village with my cloth. There, in October, I opened a shop. But I did not dare serve in it myself, because I might either be taken by the guerrillas or by the K.M.T., and I would have fared just as badly with either. So I was very cautious and went into partnership with a man called Pai Hsin-hwa. He was to serve in the shop, while I would be out in the countryside buying up more cloth. He is a book-keeper in Yenan now. For myself, I tried to make myself as unobtrusive as possible.

One evening, when I was at the opera in Yenan, I heard rumblings in the street outside. When the opera was over and I went out, I saw that General Hu Tsung-nan's troops were in the act of leaving. They were fleeing. They were so scared, they were quite ridiculous, yet there wasn't a single guerrilla soldier anywhere near, nor yet one man from the Eighth Route Army. They did not arrive until the following afternoon.

As I was going home that evening, I thought: 'Now I really have made a mess of things. The K.M.T. appeared to be so strong when it came, and now its troops are running away like dogs with their tails between their legs. This is going to be serious for me.' But we never thought of leaving Liu Ling and escaping along with the K.M.T. You see, we could not have taken our possessions with us. Our land must lie where it lay. If we lost that, we should have become beggars, and what future could we have looked forward to then? But I was afraid of the Eighth Route Army.

Yet when it came, nothing happened. The people in Liu Ling and Seven-mile Village were reasonably all right to us. I began driving a horse and cart, being carrier and transporter. I had gone into partnership over this and I was always on the road. We wound up the shop gradually and closed it in November 1946. We had also closed the mill. I drove my horse and cart for two years; then little by little I began tilling the land again, and rejoined the people's militia and began exchanging work with other people. Life was better than under the occupation, but far from as good as it had been before General Hu Tsung-nan's time. Then it happened.

It was the fifteenth or sixteenth of February 1950 or 1951, I don't remember exactly. I was working in the fields, when two men came. One was the district chief and the other, Liu Pao-ying, the battalion commander of the Self-defence Corps. They came up to me and said: 'Hsiu-tang, have you had dinner?' I replied that I hadn't. 'Then go and have it,' they said. I invited them to come home and eat with me, but they just said: 'We have eaten.' As I set off for home, they said: 'Eat quickly, because we want a word with you.'

I went home to eat. I realized that something was going to happen, but I didn't know exactly what. I had been anxious immediately after the Eighth Route Army had come back, but then, as time passed, I had begun to think that the authorities were letting bygones be bygones. I supposed that they were now going to have a talk with me. I had not much appetite and had soon finished. They were waiting for me when I came out. They showed me a paper and said: 'Now you are under arrest.' And I would never have believed that they would arrest me straight off like that.

Then I was taken to the Office of Public Security. There was I locked up for the night, and the next day I was taken to the court in Yenan. When I was brought before the court, they said to me: 'Li Hsiu-tang, do you know that there is a big campaign now to suppress counter-revolutionaries?' 'No, I didn't know that,' I replied. 'I haven't heard anything about that.' Then they told me about the big campaign and told me to tell the truth about what I had been guilty of doing. They said: 'The party and the state are lenient and forbearing and prepared to let bygones be bygones and carry on, if you are frank and honest and confess everything. But if you conceal the truth and try to get out of it, it won't be so nice for you. You should not be afraid of confessing. Your mistake in life has already been made and cannot be unmade. But what was done was done several years ago, and if you tell us, you have many years in front of you. You are still young, and your future lies in your own hands. But if you keep anything back, you will be suppressed. Now you are to go to your cell and think this over.'

I was prepared to confess everything straight away, but they wanted me to go back to my cell and have time to think. The next time I was brought before the court, I made a complete confession. I had nothing to hide, because I had not interrogated prisoners and I hadn't shot anyone or even carried my pistol, but kept it locked up. But they had a fair amount of evidence from other quarters too, and the third time I was taken before the court it was to be sentenced. There were only a few in the court that day. There was just the judge, his assistant, a guard and me. I was condemned to three years. Then I was taken back to my cell.

It was hard, of course, to be condemned to three years, but I was also relieved, because, though before I had thought that the authorities had forgotten me, while in the cell I had remembered that counter-revolutionaries usually had a pretty bad time of it. They told me that, if I worked and behaved well, I would return to society and be accepted back into it and the past would be forgotten for ever. I said that I accepted everything.

After that, I was twenty days in the cell. This was the time which I had to appeal in. I told them that I had no desire to appeal and didn't want to go before any higher court, but just to start serving my three years straight away. But they said that whether I wanted to appeal or not, I still had to stay in the cell and wait till the period for appealing was over; because such was the law.

When the twenty days were up, I was transferred to a reformatory farm called Hunsze, which was near Thirty-mile Village. We worked there to be reformed. We were given food, clothes, hand towels, soap, shoes and stockings, but no money. The food wasn't so bad: we had maize bread, millet, sometimes rice and even meat now and again. Once a week we had steamed wheaten bread. We were considered mild cases. That was a reform farm for little counter-revolutionaries. Our families often came to see us.

We had an eight-hour working-day, and the work was the same kind of thing as at home in the village. There were no guards, but sometimes prisoners who did not belong to our farm came to work with us in the fields, and they had armed guards with them. They were more serious cases. They were people who had been responsible for executions and that sort of thing. We had nothing to do with them and made no contact with them. I don't know exactly where their camp was, but it must have been somewhere in the neighbourhood. It was certainly a much stricter place, with locked cells and armed guards.

We had no guards, and we slept in ordinary rooms. There were two of us to a room, and the rooms were never locked. If we wanted them locked, we had to provide our own locks. We could ask for leave to go home and see our families. Every time I drove the horse and cart into Yenan to fetch things or deliver our products, I used to stay the night with the family. At this juncture, my cousin Li Niu died, and the family moved into his cave in Liu Ling.

I do not know the details of the administration of that reform farm. I never became anything more than a labourer in the fields at that farm; but there were thirty of us small counter-revolutionaries and one director. All the organization's work was done by the prisoners: the cooking, the selling, everything. There were no guards and, as far as I know, the director had no firearms.

We had a meeting and entertainment every Monday and Tuesday afternoon. We played cards and sang, and we had discussions. We were told that we were now having to be useful and repay society for all the harm we had done. We had to study the party's policies. Those who could not read or write had to learn to do so, and we others read the newspapers.

During the three years that I was there, there was only one case of a person running away, and he came back of his own accord after a time. He had found it difficult to manage. He hadn't, of course, been able to live in his own village, but had had to stay in hiding. Then he realized that he would be taken sooner or later, and that that would make it more difficult for him to be freed later. When he came back of his own accord, we held a meeting. We prisoners had a long talk with the authorities and we passed a resolution that, since he had himself thought better of it and come back of his own accord, he ought not to have his sentence increased, but that it should be enough to say that he had been guilty of a foolish action. The authorities agreed with us, and his sentence was not increased. Then, gradually, some of the prisoners were freed. One after the other they served their sentences. One or two preferred to stay on the farm, and so they were made fully paid farmhands. They had no families to go to and they did not think things would be so easy for them in their home villages any longer, so they preferred to stay among friends on the farm. There were, perhaps, some who had other ideas too. I don't know. People are so different, aren't they? But there weren't many. Most of us wanted to get back home as quickly as possible.

I think it was in December 1954 that I was released. I was glad when I was told that I could leave the reform farm. I hadn't kept a proper account of the months, which were very monotonous, and I was surprised when they told me that I had done my time. They said: 'You have done your time now. You can leave us. The authorities in your home village will look after you and see that you get a proper start.' People were nice to me when I got back to Liu Ling. Nobody mentioned my term of imprisonment or anything about it. They all pretended it had never been. For one year I farmed on my own. My mother's uncle, who had been looking after our land while I was away, moved back to his own home; Mother was happy, and I thought it was very pleasant to have got away from the reform school. Then I joined the East Shines Red Improved Farmers' Co-operative.

What happened to the others in my group, I do not know. Some were punished and others were so insignificant that they were just given a warning. There was no one else from Liu Ling in the group, and I haven't tried to get in touch with any of them since. Life is different now. There is a lot of work; there are many mouths to feed and not much manpower in the family. But we manage.

People say of Li Hsiu-tang: His is the only cave with flowers to grace it. The whole family is well looked after and well fed. He always has a big store of food. His children are the healthiest in the village. They are always the best dressed, the best washed and the best behaved. No one mentions his past any more. He never speaks of it himself. The younger people scarcely even know that he was ever an active counter-revolutionary. He and his wife have not yet been granted civic rights. They have never shown the least interest in regaining them.

He does not work hard and shows no signs of being reformed. His way of thinking hasn't altered. But he never says anything against socialism. He prefers to say nothing about public matters. He prefers easy work. If he is given a choice, he will always find an easy job that gives him a good return in the form of work points. He is clever at that.

But when he likes, he can really get down to it, though mostly he can't be bothered. 'Once a landlord, always a landlord.'

His manner is gentle and friendly and he gets on well with everyone, yet at the same time he does not worry about having friends. He is shrewd and cautious and is good with mechanical things. He likes doing repairs to bicycles and motors. As he avoids all really heavy work, he spends most of his time driving the shit-carts from the town. That lets him go about Yenan a bit, too.

The family is badly off for manpower, but his wife is very clever. She is one of the best housewives in the village. Her children are always the best looked after, her cave is the cleanest. But she has a very sharp tongue. He would never have been able to manage without her. Otherwise, he would perhaps have become like Tuan Fu-yin. People never mention her family, and the young ones don't even know that Li Han-hua was her brother. They have two children in Yenan Middle School. There are only four children from Liu Ling in the school altogether. One of their daughters has just become engaged to the secretary of the League of Youth, the Labour Brigade's book-keeper, Lo Han-hong. One laughs at this; but one does not comment.

Part X
Old Doctor Kao

Kao Chia-jen, aged 72

I WAS born under the Ching dynasty, in the seventeenth year of the government named Kuang Hsu, 'Brilliant Course'. I come from this valley here. Father was a farmer. He rented his land. When I was a child, the old people in Yenan used to tell about the Moslem rising in which many people lost their lives. The armies had marched through the land, plundering and pillaging. There was a big battle at Thirty-mile Village, where the Moslems fought the troops of the Ching dynasty. One general was killed and many fell. A little stone plaque has been set up on an eminence there.

The family wanted me to start school. Father sent me to the school in Yenan. At that time, there was still the old system of state examinations. The family, I suppose, would have liked me to become a hsiu tsai, but I was not so ambitious; Father also thought that the main thing was for me to learn to read and write. In those days there were very few of the ordinary people who could read and write. There were eleven of us poor children in the school. It was not too easy for us. And even if I had taken my examination, there were several more exams to be passed before you could hope to be a government official. And it wasn't so easy to become one, even if you had passed the necessary exams. You had to have influence and pay bribes as well.

At school I studied the four classics. Later, the whole of this system of examinations was abolished. My family was also too poor to keep me at school any longer; so, when I was fourteen, I left the school, after having studied for four years. I was not sorry to have to leave school; quite the reverse. The masters were old and they required you to know the texts by heart. If you faltered, you had to hold out your hands and the master hit you.

I now began working on the land. First, I was herd-boy in Louping village, fifty li from here. I worked for some rich people, and they gave

me food and I must have got a sort of wage too. When I was nineteen,
I got myself sheep and goats of my own, and two years after that we
heard that there was a revolution. I ran off to the hills. Then we were
told that now we were called the Republic of China, and that the Ching
dynasty was at an end. That was all. We were old country people, and
we seldom went into the town and never talked about such things as the

emperor or government. Nobody would have dared do that. And we never saw them either. The officials in the nearest yamen watched over us, and they were the same after the revolution as before it.

Ordinary people did not like going to see the officials. That was a thing one did only if compelled. If one met them, one had to kneel before them. It was exactly the same after the revolution. I could not see that there was any difference at all.

But at that time we did, at all events, hear it said that there were foreigners in China. I had known, of course, that there were barbarians beyond China, but now I heard about foreign countries and that there were foreigners in China. But we did not bother ourselves about that. We were farmers and it was not our business to worry about that. We lived in our village and everything else was very remote. When I was living in Louping, three or five years could pass between my visits to Yenan.

Then my father died, and I began farming. I rented twenty to thirty mu. This was freshly cultivated land quite close to the village. I rented it from a small landowner called Mr Pei. We called him Old Third Pei, because he was the third of three brothers Pei. He had only just become a landowner. After the Moslem revolt, there was a lot of abandoned land, and if you paid the authorities a small sum you were entitled to take possession of this land and keep it as long as you paid your taxes every year. Well, for that reason, the rental of this land I had from him was low too. I had to pay only fifteen jin for three mu. The rent was paid only once a year. Those were good years. The rent was low and the harvests good. It was then I began studying medicine.

When I was twenty-three or twenty-four, I had gone to the doctor with a stomach complaint. He treated me for two years, and I began to get interested in medicine. He was one of my neighbours. He was called Chang, and his father and all his ancestors before him had been doctors. But his own sons could neither read nor write; they were not interested in the art of healing and preferred working on the land. Chang had some mu of land and was both a doctor and a farmer. That was usual. When Dr Chang saw that I was interested, he said: 'You have talent. You could become a doctor.'

Chang had many old medical books. He lent them to me. 'Read them properly,' he said. 'Then I will help you to learn to be a doctor.' We were neighbours and he took no payment for this. But every year I used to send him a present of a little corn. After all he was my teacher and like a second father to me. He was over sixty then and used to explain the books to me. 'It's important to learn all this properly,' he said, 'because, when you become a doctor, you must be able to help people.'

To begin with, I was just his pupil and watched while he treated his patients. He explained to me what he was doing and let me feel the pulse and understand about it. Then, gradually, I was allowed to treat the less serious cases myself, under his supervision. When he considered me fully trained, he said: 'I am old now and cannot go on being a doctor any longer. You are to have my books and take over the work.' He then gave me his books. They were old books that had been handed down from father to son for many generations. Immediately after that, he died. Chang was both my teacher and my friend.

In this way, I worked as a farmer, studied medicine and practised as a doctor in Louping Village right up to 1923. By then life had begun to get more and more unsafe, and there were many bandits up in the hills. I no longer dared live on in Louping and, Chang being dead, there was no longer anything to keep me there, so I moved back to Yenan. I had my practice there and, at the same time, I rented land in Seven-mile Village. I rented it from a man called Hu. I rented twenty mu and was to hand over twenty per cent of the harvest to him. Now, I was worse off than before. Times were worse and taxation heavy.

I had a sign outside my house in Yenan saying that I was a doctor. In the beginning, I did not get many patients, one or two, perhaps three a day. I examined them and wrote out prescriptions for them, and they took the prescriptions to the chemist. Patients usually paid 200 cash for a consultation: 4,000 cash went to a silver dollar, so for a consultation fee I could buy roughly three jin of rice or two jin of wheat. Sometimes they paid for the next consultation, sometimes they didn't pay. I lived mainly by farming.

In 1928, we had a lot of refugees from the famine areas. They came from Hengshan and Yulin. The first time I was told about the communists was in 1933. I was told how awful they were and how they murdered and plundered. Then, eventually, the Red Army did come, but it was certainly not as bad as people had said.

The Red Army took Yenan, but that changed nothing for me. The years passed exactly as before. I still had to pay Hu the same as before for the land I rented from him. This stayed at twenty per cent of the crop from 1922, when I moved to Yenan, right till Hu Tsung-nan's troops came, in 1947. The only thing that happened during those years was that I began gradually to get more patients. I was older then and more experienced and better known. Besides that, the Japanese had bombed Yenan, so I had moved from the town and settled in Seven-mile Village. Otherwise, I could call that quarter of a century in Yenan uneventful.

In 1947, Hu Tsung-nan's troops came. I fled up into the hills and lived far away in a remote hill village. I stayed there hidden throughout the occupation. I came back when Hu Tsung-nan's troops had fled. By then I had lost everything: my books, my corn, even the doors of my dwelling. I was very sad and felt that I hated the K.M.T., because they had stolen or destroyed all my books. I had loved those books so much. I have bought new medical books since then, but they are not like my old books. Hu Tsung-nan ruined everything for me. As everything had been destroyed, I could not bring myself to take up farming again. I could no longer face starting all over again. Anyway, I was already an old man. So, in April 1948, I set out as itinerant doctor. I went from village to village in the neighbourhood, curing people. They knew me, of course.

My son and my daughter-in-law worked in the fields. I sent them a little corn now and again. I liked going round the villages. One met so many people. The other doctors had suggested my doing this. In this way we shared the burden of work. Later, when I was getting altogether too old and it had become more and more difficult to walk the roads, I was sent back to Seven-mile Village. I was told to take charge of the chemist's, but I did not like that. I found it difficult too; because there were a lot of Western medicaments in it and I did not know anything about Western medicine. I had never studied it.

Then, one day, the Old Secretary, Li Yiu-hua, had a talk with me. We had known each other for many years. We were, of course, neighbours. 'Why don't you come to our brigade?' he said. 'You will then be near Seven-mile Village, and we would be glad to have a doctor of our own, whom we know and who knows us.' I, of course, knew all the people in Liu Ling. I had treated almost all of them. In 1960, I moved to the village here. My family stayed on in Seven-mile Village. I now get thirty-eight yuan a month. I have my own little plot and grow maize and beans. I am content with that. I am having a peaceful life in my old age. I have money, I have food and clothes; people are friendly. I usually have eight or ten patients a day. These last few days, it has been more, because the weather has been changeable.

I gather herbs, and I buy herbs. I take roughly one yuan from each patient. The brigade has given me an assistant who sees to the book-keeping and finance and all that. This is Li Kuei-lien, the Old Secretary's daughter. I think this is a good way of spending one's old age. I don't know how the whole thing works out financially; I don't deal with that. But we are not altogether part of the labour brigade. We constitute an independent unit that pays for itself. Part comes from the brigade's welfare fund, and the brigade provides us with dwelling and that sort of thing.

I have spent all my life in this hsien. I have only once been outside it, and that was at the age of sixty-five, when I went to Sian. One of my patients was working there and had fallen ill and, having no confidence in any other doctor, he had sent for me. I took the bus down to Sian. He paid for the journey. Then I treated him and, when he was well again, I came home. Many things have happened during my lifetime. The thing which grieves me most is that my old medical books were destroyed by Hu Tsung-nan. Because books are like old friends: one knows them and one likes to associate with them. I have never bothered about reading other books, novels and that sort of thing. But now I am happy: all is peaceful and I have a grandson who is growing up healthy and strong.

People say of Kao Chia-jen: He is good for children's complaints and women's ailments. He is known for that. Therefore, we were all glad when he agreed to come and live in Liu Ling. Chiao Kuei-lan used to have bad pains in her womb every day, but now that she has had Dr Kao's help, she is much better; the pains have gone. Tung Kuei-ying, her mother-in-law, had a constant cough. Some people said that it was her lungs were finished; others said that it was tuberculosis. She went to many doctors, but never became any better. When Dr Kao moved to Liu Ling, she went to see him. He examined her and said: 'This is weakness of old age and inflammation of the bronchii.' In wintertime she had trouble with asthma and could scarcely breathe; but now that Dr Kao is treating her, she is much better. She scarcely coughs at all and she has been better and better every year. Chen Chung-yuan's youngest son, who is four, had continual diarrhoea and became very thin and weak. His mother took him to Dr Kao and he has been healthier since. His stomach is still not quite in order, but he is almost well now and Dr Kao says that in a year's time he will be quite all right.

Part XI
The School

Han Ying-lin, headmaster, aged 28

I AM the head of Liu Ling Basic School. I was born in 1934 in Lochuan. My mother is dead and my father is a farmer. He can neither read nor write. I went to school in Lochuan. By the time I was ten, I had been through the first section of the basic school, and I then went to Lochuan Normal School. In 1949, I joined the League of Youth. In 1953, I joined the party. That same year I began as a teacher. In 1958, I began as assistant to the head in Yenan Middle School. In 1960, I studied at Yenan University. In 1961, I was appointed headmaster of Liu Ling Basic School.

I was fourteen when Hu Tsung-nan's troops withdrew from the area. All my conscious life has been spent in the new society. I am a rural intellectual of the new type.

The school has ten teachers, one of whom is an assistant teacher who works in the whole of our district, helping school-teachers with their own education. Most of the teachers are new. Our experience is short. The most experienced of us has ten years' service. Three of the teachers are women. We all belong to the trade union. The school is, of course, mixed; 109 of our pupils are boys and 68 girls. We have six classes. The first four classes constitute the lower basic school and the two highest the higher basic school. The school was started in 1940 with 24 pupils. It closed down during the occupation, but reopened in 1949 with 8 pupils. The higher basic school was opened in 1956. Our pupils come from this and surrounding labour brigades, and also from Seven-mile Village.

Our school fulfils the task the party has given us. Teaching has to serve the policy of the proletariat, and teaching has to be combined with productive work. We are to inculcate the fundamentals of knowledge and basic techniques. The pupils study, but after lessons they have to contribute, as well as they can, in productive work in the school's vegetable garden. They have to know the honour of working, so that they don't look down on work. There are many good little workers among our pupils. I myself can remember that in my schooldays the pupils never cleaned out the latrines. If we met a farmworker carrying a couple of buckets of human excrement, we felt unclean and hid. But now, in our school, the pupils have such a feeling for the honour of work that they will crawl down into the latrines with enthusiasm and bring up the shit. This teaches them cleanliness and respect for work.

At the parents' meetings, people often say that, before, their children had not helped in the house, but that now they sweep the yard, carry the rubbish away and collect grass for the pig. But it is not just a question of production. It is also a matter of proletarian policy. Of knowing how. The teachers are young and enthusiastic and they work hard and prepare their lessons well. Before, the teachers never bothered about anything. Now they all study so much that I have to go round at night and myself see that they put their lights out and go to sleep.

The pupils have two kinds of preparatory work: that which they do in school during private study hours, and proper homework. We have rather a problem with this latter. It is often difficult for the pupils to study undisturbed at home in their caves. We have discussed this with the parents at the parents' meetings. The teachers are, besides, in touch with parents over various questions. If any problems arise with pupils, if their work is not satisfactory, or if there are difficulties at home, we discuss this at the parents' meetings and in the school management. Teachers will also go to a home and have a talk with a pupil's parents. They discuss how the pupil concerned is studying, how he lives, how he works at home. They assess his good and his bad sides. We try to foster his good side and correct his bad side. It may also happen that parents do not consider that their children should go to school. Perhaps the family is badly off for labour and want to have the child at home in order to put it to work. We then have a talk with the parents about the necessity for education. We try to get them to understand this and to agree. We had one of these problems some time ago. Tuan Fu-yin, whose son, Tuan Shao-tang, is one of the best pupils in the school, forbade him to go to school. This was during the spring term 1962. Tuan Fu-yin wanted to have his son at home, so that he could work and earn money. It took three visits before we could get this father to agree to his son's staying on at school.

All forms of physical punishment are forbidden. For a teacher to raise his hand against a pupil is a crime, no matter what the circumstances under which it is done. We discuss problems with the pupils, we discuss them with the parents. In extreme cases we can expel a pupil. But that is only on paper. We have never had to expel anyone. We have never come up against a case as grave as that. We also have different kinds of activities outside school hours. We organize the children's play, because children ought to learn as they play. Then we have the work in the vegetable garden I mentioned.

The methods we use are different from those of the old days. We have no learning off by heart. We try to stimulate the pupils' own interest in what is being studied. They must want to learn the thing. School education must be such that they of their own accord long to go to school and love their studies and understand why education is necessary. The new school must be attractive. Especially now, when education is still not compulsory, and it will certainly be some time before that can be introduced.

Before, school used to train bookworms who had no understanding of real life. One of my classmates had a father who was a farmer, too. When this father came to visit his son at his school in Lochuan, the boy used to run away and hide, because he was ashamed before the others of having a father who worked with his hands. Now, pupils are brought up to do work with their own hands and to love their parents and have respect for all who are elderly. Children no longer learn mere theory, but practice as well. In mathematics, for example, we teach them to work with an abacus. One of our pupils from Seven-mile Village is already doing all the family's book-keeping.

Because we explain to the children that the purpose of their studying is to make them fit to build up their country, our pupils now work with great enthusiasm. That was not the case in the old days. Then, one just learned things by heart. In general, the children do obey us. Their grades are not particularly good, but they themselves are good. We attach great weight to their moral education. We hold up various models and heroes as moral examples for them. We tell them what they should do, and what they should not do. We make it clear to them where the line runs between right and wrong. If something seems not clear or doubtful to them, we announce a class discussion, and, when this has been held, the teacher draws the conclusions from it for them, emphasizing right and wrong.

We instruct the children in hygiene and cleanliness. They do not know much about this when they first come to school. This is, of course, a backward, dirty part of the country. People here do not have good habits in hygiene. After our training, the children become better. We help their families to change their habits. We teach the children gradually to persuade their parents to change their habits, where hygiene is concerned. We certainly do not encourage them to argue stubbornly with their parents. On the contrary, we attach great importance to their respecting their elders. Our task is to collaborate with their parents. School and home must stand united. Our aim is to turn the children into healthy bearers of culture, willing to work with others and loving their socialist country.

We do not want any smooth, slippery personalities. But it is very necessary that they should have the feeling of being ready to work and be collective-minded. Children ought to be group-conscious. We teach the children to help each other. Not to compete with each other, but to help each other. Take, for example, the river-crossing down here. After rain it is not easy, and so the older children have to help the younger, and the boys the girls. The older ones carry the young ones across. We also train them to be honest. If they find anything on the road, they are to bring it to school. We have had two examples this month of our pupils' moral growth:

After the rain we had a few days ago, two boys in the older classes noticed an old woman with crippled feet standing down by the river.

The river was up, and she could not get across. The boys at once picked her up and carried her across and saw her home to Ten-mile Village. Later, that old woman came to me and said: 'The school does not just foster good pupils, but also respectful, good social beings.'

One boy found a pocketbook with a lot of money in it on the road. He brought it to me without opening it. Later, the owner thanked us.

Those who go through our school become good people. Some go on to higher studies, like Li Hsiu-tang's daughter, Li Ali-liang, who left us this spring and is now in Yenan Middle School. Others are doing their bit on the production front, like Lo Han-hong and others. We have former pupils who have become merit workers, and others in high administrative and other posts. But none of these has been from the village of Liu Ling. They came from other villages. Our pupils are hard-working and show great interest in their studies. In the spring term of 1962, there were fourteen pupils who had the highest grade in all subjects. But none of them was from Liu Ling.

Our timetable follows that generally laid down for schools. In the lower basic school the lessons are of forty minutes and the breaks of fifteen. The school day begins at 08.00 and goes on till 12.00. Afternoon work starts at 14.00 and goes on till 17.00 Between 08.00 and 08.20 and between 14.00 and 14.25 the classes join up for reading aloud without a teacher. This is to allow those who have a long way to come to get here. They are allowed to arrive later.

First Class
Mathematics, 6 periods a week:
    addition, subtraction and multiplication up to 100.
Chinese language, 14 periods a week, of which 3 are calligraphy:
    no fixed number of characters.
Drawing, 2 periods a week:
    the teacher presents a simple model which has to be copied. The
    principles of drawing.
Gymnastics and sport, 2 periods a week:
    games and exercises for small children (running, etc.).
Music, 2 periods a week:
    Various choral songs.
Private study, 16 periods a week:
    Going through preparatory work under supervision of a teacher.
Homework is reckoned to take one hour a day.

No garden work.
No form of handicraft.

Second Class
Mathematics, 6 periods a week:
>   multiplication and division with 2-figure numbers. Addition and
>   subtraction of larger numbers.

Chinese language, 14 periods a week, of which 3 are calligraphy:
>   studying characters. No definite number.

Drawing, 2 periods a week:
>   copying.

Music, 2 periods a week:
>   choral singing.

Gymnastics and sport, 2 periods a week:
>   games and exercises suitable for children.

Private study, 16 periods a week.
Homework is reckoned to take one hour a day.
No garden work.
No form of handicraft.

Third Class
Mathematics, 6 periods a week:
>   multiplication and division of big numbers.
>   Telling the time and the clock.
>   Solving practical problems.

Chinese language, 14 periods a week, of which 2 are periods of calligraphy and 2 periods of composition:
>   writing simpler essays. Describing a picture.
>   'My Family'. 'What does my mother do?'

Drawing, 1 period a week:
>   copying.

Music, 2 periods a week:
>   choral singing. Those who are musical now start singing solo.

Gymnastics and sport, 2 periods a week:
>   exercises and games. Simple sport. Football, running.

Private study, 17 periods a week:
>   pupils should now be keeping a diary.

Homework is reckoned to take one hour a day.
No form of handicraft; but the pupils are now allowed to weed in the
vegetable plot, sweep the floors and sweep the yard, if they wish.

Fourth Class

Mathematics, 5 periods a week:
  calculation of time. Calculation of area.
  Conversion from Chinese measure to metric scale. Practical use of
  the four rules of arithmetic.

Use of abacus, 2 periods a week:
  addition, subtraction, multiplication, division and decimal calculation on the abacus.

Chinese language, 14 periods a week, of which 2 are of calligraphy and
  2 of composition:
  understand all composite characters in the textbook. Simple descriptive compositions: 'What we did at the New Year'. Be able to
  read simple newspapers specially written for children.

Drawing, 1 period a week:
  copying, somewhat more difficult objects than before, but still just
  the principles of drawing. Still just black and white.

Gymnastics and sport, 2 periods a week:
  exercises and games. Simple sport.

Private study, 17 periods a week. A weekly diary is kept.
Homework is now reckoned to take one and a half hours a day.
Garden work, 80 minutes a week:
  voluntary, but organized.
No form of handicraft.

Fifth and sixth classes comprise the higher basic school.
Periods are 45 minutes and breaks 10 minutes.

Fifth Class

Mathematics, 6 periods a week:
  practical tasks. Use of abacus included, but not an independent
  subject. Calculation of cubic content.

Chinese language, 12 periods a week, of which 1 period for calligraphy
  and 2 periods for composition:
  compositions are no longer just descriptive, but should be in the
  form of essays. Pupils should understand all terms in the text read
  and be able to give an independent summary of a newspaper text
  that has been read out.

Nature study, 1 period a week:
  the air, soil, simple mechanical principles.

Geography, 1 period a week:
   China's geography, China's provinces, China's climate.
Agriculture, 2 hours a week:
   climate, fertilizers, cattle, poultry, grain.
   Only theory.
Drawing, 1 period a week:
   start water-colours. First colour work.
   First creative sketches. Theory.
Music, 1 period a week:
   choral singing. Simple theory.
Gymnastics and sport, 2 periods a week:
   ball games. Athletics.
Private study, 15 hours a week.
Garden work, 80 minutes a week after school hours:
   looking after the school garden.
Handicraft, in spare time after school, no fixed period:
   making stones for grinding colour for Indian ink. Simple wood-
   work.
Homework reckoned to take one and a half hours.

Sixth Class
Mathematics, 6 periods a week:
   decimal system, fractions, statistical tables, book-keeping. Use of
   abacus included.
Chinese language, 12 periods a week, of which 1 for calligraphy and 2
for composition:
   describe a person, a landscape. Acquire a fine style and a correct
   way of writing. Read aloud with the correct Peking pronunciation.
Nature study, 1 period a week:
   the air, soil, simple mechanical principles.
History, 2 periods a week:
   only Chinese history. From Peking man to the Big Leap Forward.
Agricultural theory, 1 period a week:
   climate, fertilizers, cattle, poultry, grain.
   Only theory.
Drawing, 1 period a week:
   more complicated sketches.
Gymnastics and sport, 2 periods a week:
   ball games. Athletics.

Music, 1 period a week:
  songs. Simple theory.
Care of garden, after school hours, 80 minutes a week. Handicraft, in
  free time after school hours, no fixed period:
  clay work, making colour-grinding stones for Indian ink. Simple
  woodwork.
Homework reckoned to take one and a half hours a day.

That is our timetable. Teachers stay with their classes from the
first to the sixth class. The school year begins on 1 August and ends on
20 June. The school works six days a week. Together, the year's holidays
amount to seventy-five days. The time of the winter holiday depends
on the weather. There are eight individual holidays: two at the
National Day in October, one on 1 May, one at the New Year, one on
International Children's Day and three at the spring festival, if this does
not coincide with the winter holiday.

The teachers are quite free during the holidays. They can go home
if they wish, they can go away somewhere, they can do further study
or anything else they like.

If a pupil fails in two basic subjects, like mathematics and Chinese
language, he cannot move up to the next class. If a pupil fails in one
basic subject, he has to be re-examined before the autumn term and can
move up if he passes. If a pupil fails in three other subjects, he cannot
move up. If he fails in two other subjects, he can move up. Last year,
we had seven who had not moved up. A pupil who has failed to move
up twice and then again gets such grades that he cannot be moved up
has to leave the school. Pupils can be absent owing to sickness or with
the special permission of the head.

The numbers in our classes are high, of course. Last year the
numbers in the different classes were:

First Class	42	Fourth Class	24
Second Class	31	Fifth Class	37
Third Class	28	Sixth Class	21

Certain children transfer to other schools or leave school altogether.
There are also children of school age who do not attend school. We
speak with their parents and often succeed in persuading them to send
their children to school. Though not always. Sometimes the children
themselves don't want to go to school. They manage to get their
grandmother to feel sorry for them, and some parents are unable to

stand up to their elders. Then, of course, there are also parents who want to exploit their children's labour.

We did, however, succeed in getting Hu Yen-ching back to school. Last year, when she was eight, she ran away and refused to live with her parents. She went to her grandmother, Ching Chung-ying's wife. Granny thought the poor child was made to work far too hard at school, and she even accused the teachers of having a grudge against her. She loved her granddaughter and let her stay with her. But now we have managed to persuade Hu Yen-ching to go back to her parents and to come to school again.

We have no real difficulties over discipline. The only difficulty is that certain children are late for school. Of course, we have this period both in the morning and afternoon with reading aloud to give them time to get to school, and we try to get the children to help each other keep to the hours. But some of the children have a long way to come, and it is difficult for them to keep to the hours. The farthest any of our children has to come is eight li. Seven of the children have so far to come that they do not go home for the midday rest. They bring food with them, and the cook heats it up in the staff kitchen, then they have their rest in the school. We have one room for the boys to sleep in and another for the girls.

Another difficulty is that certain children find it difficult to sit still and be quiet. Thus, in the first class there is not much discipline. There everything's more of a game. The children must think all the time that school is fun. Then gradually, as they become older, they see the necessity of work discipline, and then we require more of them.

There is a certain amount of fighting and quarrelling. We try to quell this and sort it all out with discussion and persuasion. As I've said, no teacher must ever try to settle anything by striking a child. We have to check disorder by other means. And it always succeeds. Before, in the old days, schoolmasters used to beat their pupils, but then the children had no real respect for their teachers. They were just afraid of them. That was why the teachers found it difficult to keep order. Now teachers and pupils love one another, and all goes well.

We take certain fees from the parents. There is an instruction fee of 1 Y per pupil per term. Then there are certain school costs which the pupils have to pay themselves: gymnastic apparatus, water for the children's tea and heating during the winter. The gymnastic costs are 0.50 Y per pupil per term; the boiled drinking water costs 1.50 Y per pupil per term; the cost of fuel for the winter works out at 1·50 Y per pupil for each autumn term. Parents also pay the cost of school material. In the first class this amounts to 0·30–0·40 Y per term for each pupil, and in the higher classes it rises to 0·50–0·70 Y.

The teachers' salaries are paid by the hsien authorities. This school in Liu Ling is, of course, wholly state-supported. With us the highest salary is 49·50 Y a month and the lowest 35 Y. Salaries are calculated according to education and length of service. On questions of salary, the teachers make suggestions, and the amount is fixed by the hsien authorities. Free dwelling quarters and a cook paid by the state are supplied in addition to the salary. We receive full pay during the school holidays. We are not expected to take other work. Teaching is an exacting task, and for a teacher to be able to give of his best, it is preferred that he both rest and continue his own studies. Then there is the staff garden. This is not the same as the school garden. We look after the staff garden ourselves. In it we grow vegetables and corn and keep chickens and pigs. This does not mean that we are anything like self-supporting as far as food is concerned. We eat communally, and we usually reckon on having to contribute five yuan a head each month to the catering fund for outside purchases.

Teachers are duty-bound to spend nine hours a week on private study over and above their teaching duties. The teachers' timetable is three hours for teaching subjects, four hours for pedagogy, and two hours for private study. Lu Huan-ping is in charge of this instruction and supervises it.

The school's budget is quite simple. In the spring term 1962 it was as follows, apart from wages to staff, headmaster, teachers and cook:

Income	Y
From Education Office in Yenan hsien	1,375·33
Fees from pupils	177·00
Total	1,552·33

Expenditure	
Installation of electric light	1,100·00
Two-wheeled hand-cart with rubber tyres	125·60
Indian ink, paper, chalk, sickles, mattocks	236·24
Total	1,461·84
Balance at the end of spring term, transferred to following year	90·49

Expenditure on gymnastic apparatus, water and heating have its own budget, since it is paid direct by the pupils:

Income, Spring Term 1962   Y

Gymnastics fees	88·50
Water fees	305·50
Fuel fee (not applicable in spring term)	
Fuel in hand, carried over from autumn 1961	69·72
Total	463·72

Expenditure, Spring Term 1962

Gymnastic apparatus	84·96
Boiled water	216·28
Fuel in hand consumed	69·72
	370·96

Balance at end of spring term, carried over to next school year   92·76

The staff garden comprises four mu. There we grow food for our own account. Any surplus we sell. In 1961, my share of the year's crops sold amounted to twenty yuan.

The children's garden, the school garden proper, in 1961 produced goods to a total value of 740 Y. Of this we sold produce to the value of 147·19 Y in the market and bought prizes for the pupils.

Each pupil got some sort of prize. Its size depended on his or her grading. These prizes consisted of such things as pens, books, notebooks and similar things. When we had put aside what was needed to increase the following year's production, we were left with produce to a value of roughly 300 Y. This the pupils ate.

The school garden, you see, is not run for income, but to teach the pupils to love agricultural work. That, too, is why we do not distribute the produce in accordance with the amount of work put into it by the pupils. We sell or exchange part of the produce in order to buy food-stuffs, and with these the school cook makes one or two 'feasts' every year. All the pupils come to these feasts, even those who have not done any garden work. We do this to induce a right attitude to work. It is part of the pupils' moral upbringing to grow their own food and eat it, sharing it and their labour with others.

The school is run by a headmaster's council. This consists of five people: the headmaster, convener and representative of the party; Li Juei-chen, deputy head; Chang Chang-li, in charge of administration; Chang Chung-fang, representative of the staff; and Lu Huan-ping. This headmaster's council is there to discuss the school's educational work and its internal administrative problems. Questions raised at the headmaster's council are taken up at the staff meeting, attended by every member of the staff in the school: the head, the nine teachers and the cook. There, they are discussed, decisions are reached and recommendations may be sent to the education office in Yenan hsien.

Another group which is of great significance is the school council. I am the chairman of this. On it are representatives from all the labour brigades from which we have pupils. The school council studies relations between the labour brigades and the council, between the pupils' homes and the school; it investigates any problems that may arise. Last year there was, for example, electrification: that was a question that had to be solved in collaboration with the labour brigades. The school council can, on the one hand, only recommend measures to the education office in Yenan hsien; but, on the other hand, it has the power of decision in certain questions, namely those concerning co-operation with the different labour brigades.

There is yet another school group, the parents' representation. In each village, the parents of our pupils choose one to represent them. There are seven of these representatives, and they come under the headmaster's council. I am their chairman by virtue of being head. Their duties are undefined; but one can say that the school council concerns itself with the practical problems, whereas the parents' representatives deal with the more personal problems. One can discuss the children's work with them and any faults there may be in the liaison between school and home. The parents' representatives have only advisory powers.

If, for example, you could imagine one of the children behaving so badly that it really became necessary to consider expulsion—but I must once again emphasize that this has never happened here—the matter would be discussed first at a meeting of the parents' representatives. If no solution of the problem was found, then the headmaster's council would have to discuss it and finally propose expulsion. After the school council had discussed this decision, it would have to be referred to the education office in Yenan hsien and approved by it before it could be put into effect.

All the teachers are members of the trade union. The trade union's duty is to help the teachers in their studies and to see to their social welfare. One per cent of the teacher's salary goes to the trade union's funds. The union receives an equal amount from its central office, and this is used to ensure the teachers' material welfare, to buy study material for them and for other similar purposes. I am the head of the trade union here in Liu Ling Basic School.

It is essential for the school to have good contacts with the people in the village. The pupils are expected to help teach at the reading classes in the winter; that is, of course, only the older pupils in the highest classes. The school has its own library, but here, too, we have established close co-operation with Liu Ling's Labour Brigade. We have over 300 volumes, and we have borrowed a further 300 from the labour brigade's library. These are mainly works of fiction suitable for children and pure children's books. The older children borrow them. In addition, each class has a class library. That of the sixth class comprises almost forty volumes.

The children elect a leader for each class. The leader's job is to help the teacher maintain order; and he also has to help organize the pupils when on excursions and that sort of thing. He also presides over the committee of three that the pupils of each class elect to manage the various jobs the class does jointly. The committee of three consists of the class leader, a study leader and one who is responsible for practical matters, such as keeping the classroom clean, work in the garden, etc.

Kou Chao-lan, schoolmistress, aged 25

I STARTED school when I was ten. Having gone through Yenan Middle School, I passed the entrance exam for Sian Normal School, and there I studied at the faculty of history for one year. After that I had to ask for sick leave. After I had been away from my studies for a year, I was still too ill to be able to resume them. Later, when I became fit for work again, I was partly too tired and too much of an invalid, and partly had fallen so far behind my classmates in Sian Normal School, that I decided not to continue with higher studies, but to start work instead.

I had dreamed of becoming a schoolmistress ever since I was in the first few classes of the middle school. So I was sent as schoolmistress to Liu Ling and began work here on 1 October 1961. I began by teaching mathematics and history in the sixth class and Chinese language in the second class, and I also taught all classes music and singing.

I am fond of my work, but I am inexperienced. The children are lively and I have always loved children, but when I came here, I did not know much about pedagogy and, naturally, I made a number of mistakes. I was too hasty-tempered and too easily became irritated with the children. The other teachers helped me. There are special ways of dealing with difficult children. You have to go about it in the right way. Now things are better. I am fond of children and I am fond of my work, and that is a prerequisite for being a pedagogue.

As we teachers go with the children from class to class, we get to know them. After six years of working together teacher and pupil know each other very well. I remember that from my own schooldays. This makes the school-teacher a better educator.

You see, we do not just help the children during lessons, but afterwards, too. We sit with the children during the private-study periods and help any who have problems. That is why we are there during these periods. I was put in charge of the second class when I came. The children there are about eight or nine. They are fond of playing and find it difficult to maintain order and to sit still. To a large extent, this is due to the fact that they have had no prior training. What upbringing they have had at home does not amount to much.

My children have now reached the third class. If I look at those who come from Liu Ling, they are all different.

Tuan Shao-tang, Tuan Fu-yin's son, is very gifted. He studies hard and his homework is always thoroughly done. He is good at mathematics and Chinese language. He is fond of singing and dancing and is one of the best in his class. But he is also a fidget and a chatterbox; he can never sit still and is never quiet. He always starts playing with something under the desk. He gets many admonitions and bad marks. Of course, he is the youngest son in his family and very spoiled by his mother. I have gone to his home to talk about this with Tuan Fu-yin, but he is seldom at home and does not bother much about what I say, either.

Li Shung-chen is Li Yu-hsin's youngest son. His mother is dead. He is quite gifted and high-spirited. He sings and dances with enthusiasm and loves to take part in physical work, if we allow him. He likes organizing the children in this and is responsible in his class for practical matters. But he is also inattentive and lacks interest in book learning. He is not persevering, and he is careless. The reason why his grades are so bad is that his mother is dead and his father works in the fields, so that it is only his older sister, Li Shang-wa, who looks after him, and he has to help with a lot of work in the home.

Tsao Shan-nü, daughter of Fu Hai-tsao, is not very gifted, but she is industrious and painstaking. She lives near the school and sometimes comes here in the evenings to sit in the school and read. Her results are average. Her family has given her a better upbringing at home than is usual. Her mother is strict and sees that she studies properly. Her mother is high-spirited, and the family background is better than with the two previous ones.

Liu Lan-shuan is Liu Chen-yung's daughter. She studies hard, but is rather dull-witted. Her way of studying is not a good one. She won't study alone; she likes collective studies best. She is always wanting the teachers to gather everyone together and have singing and dancing. Her mother is strict and the girl is almost too docile.

Tung Er-wa is Tung Yang-chen's daughter. She is very hard-working. If she isn't told not to, she will come back to the school every evening. She says that she likes being here so much. She is a little slow in grasping things, but she is fearfully particular about hygiene and cleanliness. She loves school and is always bringing different things from home to give to the school. In a country school like this there is always so much that is needed.

Li Yu-shen is Li Hai-kuei's son. He is one who has failed to move up, and I don't know him so well. Everything goes so desperately slowly with him. But this year he really is trying to work. But even though he makes great efforts to read, he finds it difficult to understand. He is older than the others in the class and likes to try and be their leader.

I am fond of my children, and, when I consider them, it seems to me they have a bright future ahead of them. Some will study and follow that path; others will leave school to work in agriculture or some other field of activity. They are going to make good builders of their country; they are calm and steady. I have a very strong sense of this. I often wonder what this one or that will make of life. One does, when one is a teacher. But it's still too early to say anything.

They don't even know themselves yet. They are so young. If they have seen a film about the Chinese People's Liberation Army, they all want to be soldiers; and, if they have seen a film about tractor drivers, they all want to be tractor drivers. Some time ago, I gave them a composition to write: 'What are you going to be when you grow up?' Some said they were going to join the Chinese People's Liberation Army. A couple wanted to be airmen, in order, as they said, to 'defend China's wide frontiers'. One girl wanted to be a schoolmistress. 'There have to be some who educate those who later are going to build up communism in China,' she said. Several wanted to be tractor drivers. Many of these were girls: 'We must harvest more grain, and one does that with machines.' A couple just said that they wanted to become merit workers in agriculture. One wanted to be a navvy.

We tell the children that, now, women can have any post in society, so it's natural that some girls also want to be soldiers or air-women. All their ideals are the same, both the girls' and the boys'. They read things in the newspapers and see things at the cinema, and then talk among themselves about what they want to be. But, in general, you can say that the girls in my class are more obedient and quieter and work harder than the boys. But there are more boys who are gifted.

Of course, at this age, all children are still very naïve and touching. When the 26th World Table Tennis Championship was held in Peking, most of the pupils told me in confidence that they thought they would be world champions at table tennis when they grew up.

Chi Chung-chou, in charge of the Young Pioneers, aged 24

I AM from the country too. My parents and my ancestors were all farmers. I was eleven when I began school in Lichiachi Basic School, thirty li from here. By the time I was seventeen, I had left the basic school and begun in Yenan Middle School. After three years there I took my exam and was sent here to Liu Ling as schoolmaster in 1961.

I had decided to become a schoolmaster when I was still only in the first class of the basic school. We had a very good master there, an old man called Ma Sze-chao. When I was a child, I thought that he knew everything and could answer everything. He had educated so many children, who had then grown up and yet still respected him. It was glorious to be a teacher. Wherever you went, you would meet your pupils. That's what I thought when I was a child. Later, in middle school, I still wanted to be a schoolmaster. I thought that was a profession that would suit me. The teachers in the middle school agreed with me. My parents had no special views about this, and my father just said: 'I suppose you must do as you like.'

When I came here, I was put in charge of the fifth class. That's the sixth class this year. I now teach Chinese language in the sixth class, nature study in the fifth class and drawing in the fourth, fifth and sixth classes. Before Kou Chao-lan came here, I also had music and singing in the fifth and sixth classes. Besides that, I am responsible for the school work with the Young Pioneers.

Of the school's 177 pupils, 103 are members of the Young Pioneers. Most of the seventy-four who are not members are too young to join. The age for being a Young Pioneer is from nine to sixteen. But there are also cases like Li Shung-chen. He dreams of being a Pioneer, but he hasn't been allowed to join. He is far too undisciplined, and he does not

311

work at his studies. So he has not been accepted as a member. It's not his dull-wittedness that is the obstacle—he can't help that—but the fact that he neglects his work. Li Shuei-ming is definitely subnormal where ability is concerned, but nevertheless he is a pioneer. Li Shung-chen longs so much to join, but now we have had a serious talk with him and told him that, if he is good, he may join. He has promised to improve. Now he is trying to do his best. At least, he is doing so for the time being; one will have to see how long it lasts.

I have two pupils from Liu Ling in my class, the sixth class:

Tsao Ming-wa, Fu Hai-tsao's son, who is continuing the name of his father's stepfather, Tsao Shen-yung. He is fifteen and very fond of books. He reads everything he can lay hands on. He is very quick at grasping things and is serious about his work. He does his homework most excellently. But he is pig-headed and stubborn, and also hasty-tempered and impetuous. He has to be coaxed along. If one wants to get him to do anything, one has to be very careful to speak to him about it in the right way. We praise him for his good work, but criticize him for his behaviour in other respects. He ought to go on to Yenan Middle School. He is not the dreamy type. He reads a lot, but I don't think he has any special daydreams. He writes a composition once a week, and these show that he has read a lot outside the school curriculum, but he cannot express himself on paper all that well. He himself wants to study. He wants to become an engineer. He draws well; he has a dashing way of drawing with wide sweeps.

Tsao Shi-lien is Tsao Chen-kuei's sister. She is older than Tsao Ming-wa. She is seventeen and very sensitive. She is honest and sturdy, and she makes great efforts to study well. Her family background is not bad, but she is a little slow and dull-witted. She has difficulty in understanding. She struggles hugely to overcome her difficulties. She does work hard. Her homework is well done. If she makes the least mistake in writing, she prefers to start again from the beginning. No one had asked her to do that. She does it on her own. But she makes a lot of mistakes and has to work hard, and it all takes her such a long time. She is always particular about being clean and neat. When she draws, she is very accurate and carefully draws in every little detail. She cannot draw a flower without drawing both pistil and stamen. She has just entered puberty. In general, pupils manage to get through basic school before that happens. She wants to be a tractor driver.

Most of the pupils in my class will go on to the middle school. They say: 'Our studies are of value to the party and country, too.' But they will joyfully take up agricultural work, even so, if necessary. Most of their career dreams are connected with agriculture. They want to be tractor drivers, book-keepers, merit workers in agriculture and so on. Those who think they will be able to study further want to be engineers.

We have certain difficulties in our work. The greatest is that we teachers are so young and inexperienced. For that reason our results are not so satisfactory. You can see for yourself what grades the children have. That is our fault. Another difficulty is that, when they come to school, the children have had no previous training. Farmers don't really bring their children up at all. They simply do not have time to attend to their children. So, when the children do go to the school, they are quite undisciplined. They are also quite unaccustomed to keeping fixed hours. At home, you see, they have been allowed to come and go as they like.

Hygiene and cleanliness is another difficulty. Before they come to school, some of the children are used to drinking unboiled water. If they become thirsty and are by the river, they just bend down and drink. We make them boil their water. We tell them about bacteria and disease: 'Bacteria are tiny animals that make you ill. They are so small that they cannot be seen by the eye.' We teach them to clean vegetables before they eat them, to wash their hands and their faces, and to cut their nails. We show them various posters and pictures and try to inculcate good habits of hygiene. In the lower classes, we usually go round and inspect the children to see that they are clean and newly washed. In the upper classes this is not necessary. There the class is itself responsible for the pupils' cleanliness.

But country children are robust. They are seldom ill. If any child is away ill for any length of time, we go to its home and work with it in the cave. They don't like being at home. 'It's deadly boring not going to school.'

In the two highest classes, the children often ask for permission to help the family. But they are not usually granted it. We talk with them and query whether it really is absolutely necessary. We suggest that they help their fathers on Sundays, instead.

People say of Chi Chung-chou: He is a good teacher. The older ones say that he loves children and understands them. His colleagues say that he works very well. He has already had three distinctions for good work as a schoolmaster. He is a merit worker. The children are said to set store by him.

Tables

The Staff of Liu Ling Basic School
I   Educated in a higher training institution
II   Educated in a normal school, medium level
III Educated in a normal school, basic level
P   Party member
U   Member of League of Youth

	Name	Sex	Age	Years' service	Wage	Remarks
I	Han Ying-ling	M	28	10	49·50 Y	Headmaster P
II	Chi Chung-chou	M	24	2	43·00	In charge of Pioneers P
II	Li Juei-chen	M	21	3	43·00	Deputy head
I	Wu You-yün	F	25	2	47·00	P
I	Kou Chao-lan	F	25	1½	35·00	U
III	Chang Chang-li	M	21	3	37·00	Administration U

	Name	Sex	Age	Years' service	Wage	Remarks
III	Ho Kai-chuan	M	19	1	35·00 Y	U
III	Chang Chung-fang	F	24	6	43·00	Staff repre-sentative
III	Ho Hsiu-chen	F	25	7	35·00	Freshly ap-pointed, 1962

Assistant employed to help the teachers in their further education, paid by Liu Ling School:

	Name	Sex	Age	Years' service	Wage	Remarks
II	Lu Huan-ping	M	23	4	47·00	U

There is also a cook who is paid 43 Y a month

Pupils from Liu Ling Village in Liu Ling Basic School, autumn term 1962, and their grading, spring term 1962.
Grading is from 1–5. 1 and 2 do not pass.

Beginners from Liu Ling village in first class of Liu Ling Basic School, autumn term 1962:

Name	Sex	Age
Li Ai-ping	M	8
Liu Yuan	M	8
Li Ai-shen	M	9
Jen Chiu-yen	F	8
Li Shi-ming	M	7

Pupils from Liu Ling Village who left Liu Ling Basic School in the calendar year 1962:

Name	Sex	Age	Reason for leaving
Li Shuei-ming	M	12	Under-developed. Unable to follow
Li Shang-wa	F	16	Left to run the home
Li Ai-liang	F	17	Transferred to Yenan Middle School

Pupils from Liu Ling Village in Yenan Middle School, autumn term 1962:

Name	Sex	Age
Li Chi-shen	M	17
Yen An	M	17
Li Ta-min	M	15
Li Ai-liang	F	17

Class	Name	Sex	Age	Chinese Language	Mathematics	Counting on the Abacus	Natural Science	Geography	Agricultural Theory	Drawing	Gymnastics	Music	Member of the Young Pioneers
6	Tsao Ming-wa	M	15	4	5	5	4	4	3	4	3	5	Yes
6	Tsao Shi-lien	F	17	3	2	3	4	4	3	3	3	5	Yes
5	Chang Niu-ming	M	14	2	4	4				4	4	4	Yes
5	Li Shuan-tsai	M	12	2	3	2				3	5	5	Yes
4	Chen Nü	F	11	5	5					4	5	5	Yes
4	Li Shung	F	12	5	3					4	4	4	Yes
3	Liu Lan-shuan	F	10	4	3					4	3	4	No
3	Tsao Shan-nü	F	9	3	4					3	4	4	Yes
3	Tuan Shao-tang	M	11	5	5					5	4	5	Yes
3	Li Shung-chen	M	11	2	3					5	3	4	No
3	Tung Er-wa	F	10	3	3					3	4	5	Yes
3	Li Yun-shen	M	12	2	2					3	3	3	Yes
2	Mau Ying-shin	M	8	2	3					2	3	4	No
2	Chang Shun	M	9	2	2					4	4	4	No
2	Hu Yen-ching	F	9	3	3					3	3	4	No

Part XII

Lao Dung

'By the intellectuals observing the four "with's":
Live with the masses
Eat with the masses
Work with the masses
Discuss problems with the masses,
they will transform themselves until they have acquired
the working people's attitude to life.'

Ching Chi and lao dung: how physical work taught her the proletarian attitude to life, aged 29

IN 1953 I joined the League of Youth, and, in 1956, I became a member of China's Communist Party. My work is that of secretary in Intourist in Sian. I earn seventy-four yuan a month, am married and have two sons, one of eight and one of five. I did thirteen months' lao dung, from the spring of 1959 to the spring of 1960, that is voluntary physical work. I did this in Liu Ling.

I come from a milieu that is not proletarian. We have always been well off. My father is a doctor, and when I was small he was in charge of a clinic in Szechwan. My mother went to college. My father was a Christian. He despised traditional medicine, which he called quackery. What he thinks about it now, I don't know. I expect he was reformed after the liberation, along with the rest. At the moment he is in Moscow studying neuro-surgery. I don't know whether or not he is still a Christian. I was sent to a school run by Canadian nuns. They taught me to play the piano. We used to sing psalms.

Life was never difficult for us, nor were we ever short of food. My father loved cleanliness above all else. I was forbidden to go out to the kitchen; if I did so despite this, then I was beaten. He would give me ten strokes. This was because in Szechwan food is cooked over wood fires, and I could have made myself grimy. I looked down on our servants. They were dirty. I grew up thus and became lazy. I could not use a broom or even wash myself. Those were not things that I needed to do. After 1949, I became a bit better, perhaps. At school I was on my own and had to wash and dress myself; but my sentiments were far from being those of the workers. I knew nothing of the seriousness of life either. I did not know where the food that was set on my table came from. Nor did I bother about it. After the liberation, I learned a lot about how the proletariat felt, it is true, but actually I myself looked down on the poor, because they were uneducated and uncouth and filthy.

I know that I was always saying: 'The farmers are good. The working class and the poor farmers are the leading classes. All honour to work. All honour to the workers. Physical labour is the highest.' I often said that at meetings, but I didn't mean anything by it. I really thought the working class and the poor farmers an uneducated, dirty lot, and even though I did in a way believe what I said—in that I believed in the liberation of the Chinese people—I was only paying lip-service by saying that. I considered it to be our, the intellectuals', job to be the leaders. Which we have always been. I had no contact with working people. As far as I was concerned, this business of class and class struggle was something quite abstract. Those were just words.

But after the liberation, I did at least start washing myself. Before, I had had a servant to do that for me. In 1953, when I was twenty, I got married. But I did no housework, and I did not run the house. My mother-in-law did that. When I had my first baby, I just lay in bed. I did not bother about doing anything. My mother-in-law saw to everything and looked after the baby for me.

In 1958, the party exhorted all young ganbus to do their share of physical labouring and go out among the people. We decided that all the ganbus in our organization must go and spend a year in the country.

I was a town girl and had never lived in the country, nor even been in a village, and I volunteered in 1958. But I wasn't accepted that year. It was not till 1959 that I was selected to go on one year's lao dung, voluntary physical work. I was in the third group to be sent out from our office. As it is, half of our ganbus have done their lao dung. At the moment the fifth group is out doing it. Each group consists of eight to ten people and is away one year. Our office comprises the following organizations: Intourist, Sian Hotel, Sian Representative of the Protocol Department of the Foreign Ministry, and the local Sian section of the Chinese People's Society for Cultural Relations with Foreign Countries.

There were nine of us in the group I was in.

We were to be re-educated and given a proletarian attitude to life. We were to fortify our physique and help the people's commune, to which we were sent, in its work. We were five women and four men. I had discussed all this with my husband. Of course, it was a pity being unable to be together for a year; but we had discussed it all thoroughly and come to the conclusion that one year was not of such great significance in a whole life. It was important to do one's share of physical work and also necessary for me, if I was to be a true revolutionary woman. My mother-in-law promised to look after the baby, which she loves dearly, and my husband said he would write to me often. In general, he is inclined to be lazy, but where I am concerned he has always been most punctilious. We love each other. People say of us Chinese girls that we are cold, just because we don't go about kissing and holding hands in the street and that sort of thing, but that isn't true.

We are like blast-furnaces: we may be cold outside, but we are red-hot inside. So we decided that a year was not such a long time, and that it was important for me to counteract my laziness and become a better person. My husband works at the university. He teaches Russian. He was going to use this year for further study.

So we took the train to Tungchwan, where we changed to the bus. We were very excited to see where we were being stationed. All that we knew was that we were going to the Yenan district. We reached Yenan on 28 February 1959. It was cold and snowing, and we were frozen. We were quartered in the hotel, where many groups from Sian, which were also going out to do lao dung, were staying. We stayed at the hotel for a few days, while the hsien authorities discussed where we were to be sent. Finally, my group was attached to Liu Ling People's Commune. The commune decided that we should join Liu

Ling Labour Brigade, so all nine of us drove out to Liu Ling. That was on 2 March 1959. It was a warm afternoon, and the Old Secretary, Li Yiu-hua, was sitting outside the cave here, smoking. He gazed at us for a while, then he said: 'I know that most of you have never done any real work before in your lives. We will try to help you. You won't have to do too much to begin with. I shall try to find simple jobs for you at first, so that you can accustom yourselves to working with your hands. The best thing, perhaps, will be for you to start by trundling up dry dung and helping to carry soil. After that, we shall see.' Two in our group had done physical work before, but the other seven of us had never done a thing. The first fortnight was difficult for all of us. We ached all over and fell asleep the moment we lay down. But at least nobody laughed at us. Then, little by little, things began to go better. But even the two who said they had done physical work before were as tired as the rest of us, although we were only doing the lightest jobs, the sort of things that otherwise were only given to the old men, and to the women whose feet had been bound, to do.

We had two caves, one for women, one for men. The women's cave was the one Tsao Chen-yung lives in now. We had a man who cooked for us. He cooked for his family at the same time. We were still paid by our office and got the same salary as we had had in Sian. Twice a week I got a letter from my husband. We helped build the collective dining-hall behind here, which they were going to use at harvest-time. Sometimes we would show a film there in the evening.

In July, I was chosen to lead the women's group. We held the meeting on the open space in front of the cave here. We held meetings once a month to discuss our work and plan the next month's work. The brigade leader had had a talk with me, at which he said: 'The women's group needs your help. There are now three work leaders among the women here and not one of them can either read or write. Your job is not only to lead the work, but also to teach the other leaders to read and write. You'll have six months in which to do it.' I said to him: 'If it really is so that the women are relying on me and have chosen me themselves, of course I shall do my best.' At the meeting, I was elected. I was very happy that the women believed in me. That was my first position of trust. At first, I was a bit scared by the job, because, after all, I was a town girl, so how could I take charge of things in the country? Everything there was so different. But after a month I had become one of the group. Actually, I am from Hopeh, though I was born and grew up in Szechwan. I had lived for more than ten years in Chengtu. Well, when I left Liu Ling, at least one of the women labour leaders was able to read and write sufficiently well to be able to keep a work daybook and calculate the day's work. Before, they had had to go to the book-keeper every day and ask him to make the entries. That had been a lot of trouble both for him and for them.

Well, after that I worked all the time. I ploughed and I weeded. I dug and I sowed. I had to learn everything. Every Monday and Tuesday evening, I went to the three leaders of the women's group and taught them reading and writing. Otherwise, when off duty, I went round visiting the families. I was supposed to be on the look-out for difficul-ties, such as a child ill or anything else. Where there were any, I would help the women in the cave or try to find some other woman in the vicinity who could come and help her. But it was out in the fields that I talked most with the women. We have occasional rests, and then the women sit and chat.

At the same time, I worked at my own ideological re-education. I had, you see, to transform myself from a bourgeoise to a human being. This was done partly by physical work and partly by reading. I read a book called *Steel Yourself in the Fight with a Hundred Thousand Difficul-ties*. I read Liu Shao-chi's *How to Become a Good Communist*. I read a variety of articles. We had a leader of our group. He had been chosen even before we left Sian. At first, we all found it very difficult. Even the two who came of farming stock found everything primitive and difficult, but in our second month we had grown accustomed to the work and had adjusted ourselves. We tried to spend as much time as possible with the people of Liu Ling. We were not going to huddle together or make a sort of urban clique. We were to learn from the people and become one with them.

We paid nine yuan a month for our food. We ate a lot because, of course, we were now doing physical labour. Before we went out to the fields in the morning, we helped the families where the husband was working in the town or elsewhere. The women in such families had a hard time of it. We fetched water from the well for them, and we also swept up outside their caves. We helped the women wash the clothes and make quilted winter coats. We also tried to help the women to learn a few characters. What we did was to draw a picture of some-thing, a pig for example, and write the character for pig beside it. We gave ten such pictures to every woman who was interested, and they put them up on the walls of their caves, so that they should have them in front of their eyes all day long. After a week, they were supposed to exchange pictures with each other. The schoolchildren also helped in this voluntary study. But it did not work as well as we had hoped. There are very few women in the village of Liu Ling who can read or write. It is much more difficult to learn to write our characters than you imagine. It is especially difficult for adults. But it is also true that they are much more beautiful than letters.

After the winter harvest was in, that was December 1959, there was less work in the fields. That is the time of year when life in the country quietens down and people occupy themselves with minor jobs. We then embarked on serious criticism and self-criticism. For two months we kept at this and held discussions about it. We went through each one's faults and judged whether they had corrected them and how. We probed into ourselves and examined each other and tried to get to the bottom of all our personal problems and each of our incorrect attitudes to life and work. Sometimes, these meetings lasted half a day, and we went on day after day. Altogether we had seventy or more meetings. This meant that each of us in the group was analysed and corrected for anything up to fifty hours. These meetings were attended by the different ganbus in the village. Li Yiu-hua spoke at them, and so did the different leaders of the brigades and the labour groups and the party organizations. Even the villagers got up one after the other and told us what they thought about us and our work.

This was very important. You know that most of us come from non-proletarian milieux, in which we never come in for harsh, caustic criticism. In the old days, one never told people the truth to their faces. In my home we had always to be polite. It was not fitting to criticize another person. It was only servants one could tell off properly. But these farmers spoke frankly to us. Of course, we were doing lao dung in order to be transformed. Often enough this criticism hurt, but it helped. The village women considered that one of the girls in the group was arrogant; but they talked her out of it. You know, the old person has to go, so that the new can emerge and take her place. I was told I had said that I would teach the leaders of the women's group to write and read, but when it came to it, I had only been able to teach one of them to read.

All that winter we went through our work and our behaviour in this way. Afterwards, there was not much left that we had not analysed and criticized. When you go on as long as that, you have no possibility of hiding behind fine phrases. Then, after thirteen months of lao dung, the time came for us to go home. I felt torn in two. On the one hand, I was longing dreadfully for my husband, but on the other hand I felt fearfully unhappy at having to leave Liu Ling. I had grown to the place and become part of it.

I shall never forget the morning we left. People had come down to the flat here to say goodbye. The women and I were in tears. They begged us to stay. Then they gave us eggs and pumpkin seeds, which are lovely. I wept very much. You see, I had been working with the women's group and now I was having to leave them. I knew all the women and had associated with them all the time and knew them better than I had ever known anybody in my life before. I had never been so close to people before. In my home, one did not behave like that. Then the car moved off and we drove away from Liu Ling.

I believe I learned a lot during those thirteen months. I became a different person. I had acquired a fundamentally proletarian attitude to life. For example, before, in the summer, if I thought it too hot, I used to hope it would rain, without stopping to think whether the rain would be good for the harvest or not. I can never do that again. Now, I automatically think first how the weather will affect the harvest. That year also gave me self-confidence. I learned to rely on myself and on my own capabilites. I am young and actually rather strong, and always have been; yet, before, I could scarcely even wash myself. When first we were told that we were to break new ground up on the hillside, I stood down there in the valley and looked up and almost burst into tears, because it all seemed so impossible. It was so high up and far away and the ground so hard. But there was nothing else to do but to climb up and start work. There was no way of my getting out of it. It was so hard, and it looked so hopeless. But then I noticed that we were making progress, and that I could work. And in the end I realized that nothing was impossible, and that it had only been my bourgeois up-bringing that had prevented me from relying on myself. The work went ahead quicker than the Old Secretary, Li Yiu-hua, had expected.

Yes, that year gave me the working people's attitude to existence. I became a completely different person. I had learned to work, and, when I returned home to my husband, he too thought I had changed. Since leaving Liu Ling, I have written to them all the time and heard from them too, and I am so happy to have been able to come here with you.

I have longed for this the whole time. I have put my name down as a volunteer for another year's physical work, but they haven't given me much hope. First, I must do my work in Sian and make use of all the education I have had. And I cannot expect to be sent out for a second year's lao dung until all the others who have not yet been have done their year. Then it is possible that I may. But I'm told that society has invested a lot of money in my education, and that I must exploit it.

People say of Ching Chi: She is healthy and strong and gay. She loves eating and chattering, and she can get through a lot of work. She loves to talk and laugh and is always helpful. At first, when she came here in 1959, she was like most town girls, but after only a few months she had become a thoroughly ordinary person. She is like one of the village's own daughters. She has no town airs left, and she does not behave in the least as if she were an intellectual. She likes best to sit with the women eating and talking about having babies and men and that sort of thing, like all the rest. But she is a sensible girl, too, and knows what she wants.

Part XIII

The Party

The Communist Party of China

Has twenty-three members in Liu Ling Labour Brigade.

Li Yiu-hua is secretary of the party association in Liu Ling Labour Brigade.

Li Hsin-min is party secretary for Liu Ling People's Commune.

Thirteen members of the party live in the village of Liu Ling:

Li Hai-kuei, leader of Liu Ling Village Labour Group's party group, member of the committee of Liu Ling Labour Brigade's party association

Li Kuei-ying, leader of the women's group. Member of the committee of Liu Ling Labour Brigade's party association

Li Hai-ching

Tsao Chen-kuei

Mau Ke-yeh, member of the committee of Liu Ling Labour Brigade's party association

Li Hung-fu

Fu Hai-tsao, president of the party group of the labour group for vegetable cultivation

Ma Chen-hai

Liu Ching-tsei

Liu Chen-yung

Ma Hai-hsiu

Li Yiu-hua, secretary of the party association of Liu Ling Labour Brigade

Yang Fu-lien

China's Communist League of Youth

Has twenty-four members in Liu Ling Labour Brigade.
Lo Han-hong is secretary of the League of Youth in Liu Ling Labour Brigade
Nine members of the League live in the village of Liu Ling:
Tsao Chen-hua
Tsao Chen-yung
Chiao Kuei-lan
Chi Mei-ying
Wang Fung-li, member of the youth association of the Liu Ling Labour Brigade
Ma Hung-tsai
Ma Tsuei-chang
Ma Ping
She Shiu-ying, member of the committee of the youth association of the Liu Ling Labour Brigade
One member of the League of Youth has moved from Liu Ling to Seven-mile Village:
Li Kuei-lien in charge of the women's group.

Li Yiu-hua, the Old Secretary, aged 57

IT is possible that I may be mistaken in my dates occasionally. You see, I cannot read; farmers of my generation cannot read or write. Not that my sons have been properly to school, but they have learned to read and write. So have their wives. This was the cause of considerable difficulty for us when we formed our first labour group for mutual help and the early farmers' co-operatives. None of the farmers could read or write, and therefore nobody could keep books or a work daybook, and often the children had to keep our books for us. In the old days, it often happened that there was not anyone able to read for several villages around, and so, if one received a letter, one went from village to village searching for someone to read it for one. But even though I cannot read properly and cannot always remember calendar dates accurately, there is nothing wrong with my memory, and I remember all that has happened to me in life.

I, too, am from the north. From Hengshan hsien. There were eleven of us children, eight brothers and three sisters. We were half-brothers and half-sisters, because we had different mothers. I was the eldest child of Father's second wife. I had a younger brother and a younger sister. Father was a tenant farmer. He used to say: 'Your great-grandfather lost our land.' My great-grandfather had owned a lot of land in Yangchiakoushan, but he was a bad farmer and also a lazy man; then he gambled all our land away on some gambling game, so Grandfather had to move to the village of Yuehyoushan, where he became a tenant of the local landowner, Yang Shen-you. I can remember Yang Shen-you; he was very old. Father died when I was eight, and then my eldest brother, Li Fong-hua, Li Hai-ching's father, became head of the family. But he didn't do well. He took to gambling and lost a lot, and several of the brothers had to go out as day labourers.

Then my eldest brother took the family and moved to the village of Hsiaotuwa, where he rented land from a man called Tung Shen-chi. We rented roughly twenty mu, for which we paid about 2,000 jin of corn a year in rental. Besides this, there were various taxes: I cannot now remember them all in detail, but we paid tax every month, and, once the rent and the taxes had been paid, there wasn't much left, and in springtime we went hungry. It was especially bad when my eldest brother had been out and gambled the family's money away. Gambling was a real curse up here in the old days. We were a big family of twenty. But my eldest brother managed things badly and, when I was thirteen, I had to go out as a day labourer. When I was sixteen, Mother died. Life became more and more difficult. The six older brothers were now married; the two younger ones bachelors. Now, we divided up the family possessions, and, since I had neither wife nor child, all I got was myself. The others had more mouths to feed and they shared what there was.

What happened was that every year we had run out of corn and had had to borrow from the landlord, paying the loan back after harvest. The interest varied a bit from year to year, depending on what sort of harvest it had been. The lowest interest was when we borrowed 300 jin and repaid 390, the highest when we borrowed 300 and paid back 450. The worse things were for us and the worse the crop, the higher interest we had to pay. In that way, the landlord always gained, whether the harvest was good or the crop failed. He always won. When we had paid the rental, our debt and the interest on it and the taxes, there was not a great deal left. We had to borrow money for clothes and tools. In the beginning, the interest on money was around three per cent a month, but then it rose to five per cent a month and finally it was up at ten per cent a month. We could not always pay it, and our debts grew with interest being charged on the interest. When we divided up the family possessions, we had a debt of 400 silver dollars and assets of 6,000 jin of grain, plus various small possessions. Being unmarried, I was excluded from the distribution, so that my older, married brothers each took a share both of the debt and of the grain. I, of course, got no grain, but on the other hand I was free of debt. My younger sister was already married then. I was sixteen and able to look after myself, so I went to Yaping, a village thirty li away.

There I took a place as farmhand with a landowner called Chang Ming-liang. I intended to work hard, save money and so gradually get enough to enable me to marry and found a family. We of northern

Shensi have always worked hard. We have a saying that in northern Shensi one lives on a pig's fodder and works like a horse. In the old days, under the old society, there was a small group that lived in luxury, but not even they had brocades or silks or that sort of thing. The rest of us had to live on bran and chaff and wild herbs for six months of the year. Now, life is better, but it is still hard and far from what we want it to be. But work we have always done. And it has been an honourable thing to work, too. A person known to be able to work hard has always been held in honour. When people from lower Shensi come to us here on lao dung, for example, we notice that. Even if they were farmers down there, they don't understand what we mean by work up here in northern Shensi. They just cannot work as we do.

Well, I began as farmhand with Chang Ming-liang. I had said to him: 'I intend to work hard, but I shan't take any wages until I marry. I want twenty silver dollars a year plus food and lodging.' He agreed to that. I worked in that way for four years, and as I did so much, we had no quarrels. When I was twenty, I became engaged. I was on my own, of course, and so I arranged my own marriage. I married when I was twenty-one. I then had eighty silver dollars lying with Chang Ming-liang, but I needed a hundred dollars to marry; so I borrowed twenty dollars from him. He did not charge me interest. 'As you didn't take interest from me for the money you did not draw, I shan't charge you interest on the loan,' he said. I went on working as his hand till 1934. There were now two of us and I took my wages in both cash and corn. My employer took a couple of silver dollars a year to pay off my debt. I was known as a good worker and a couple of other landowners came to me and offered me a higher wage to go to them. When my employer heard this, he was afraid to lose me and increased my wage. In the end, I was foreman and got thirty silver dollars a year. You see, it was the same in the old society too; a person who worked properly was respected, even if he was just a farmhand or a day labourer.

But a lot had happened in those years, too. It had been a hard time: 1928–9 was a period of famine. The 1928 harvest was bad and, in the spring of 1929, the slave dealers began coming to the villages of northern Shensi. They were out to buy children, and many were sold then. Children from northern Shensi were usually sold to Shansi and Hopeh. The boys went to childless families which wanted their name to continue, and the girls were sold as brides or to the towns. When girls were sold, the slave dealers just took them away, and we did not know what happened after that. Most were never heard from again. There was just silence. There are several here in Liu Ling who have experienced that. Two of Ching Chung-ying's younger brothers were sold to Shansi, and Chia Ying-lan was himself sold to Hopeh, and it was not till after the liberation that he got in touch with his sister and turned up again. Later that spring, people were dying of starvation.

The landowners were inhuman and cruel. They themselves had grain enough. They had big stores of grain. But they did not let those who had no land to pledge have any. They demanded security for a loan. They did not worry about people's distress. I worked hard, and we two managed all right. But then there were just the two of us. Yet, if Chang Ming-liang had sold his corn at normal prices, no one in our village would have starved to death. He had a big enough store. We thought he had, even then, during the famine, and later, in 1935, when we expropriated him during the revolution and examined his stores, we found a big hoard of grain dating back to before 1929. But he was a landowner.

The first time we heard any mention of the revolution was in 1929–30. People said then that the landowners' property was all going to be shared out, and that the poor farmers would have the power; but at first we just thought it a joke. At that time, we had not even heard of Sun Yat-sen and the K.M.T. That came later. And then people were also talking about someone called Chu Mao. He was supposed to be a general away down in the south. We thought then that it was just one person.

Later, there was a lot of talk that the students in the cities were demonstrating and saying that the land ought to be divided up equally, and that the students would serve the people. We thought that sounded fine. But it sounded mostly to be just a lovely dream. We thought it would be pretty difficult to put into practice. I don't remember now who it was told me about this. It was mostly just general talk. What the students were saying in the cities made a great impression on us, as did the fact that there was a revolution in the country, led by General Chu Mao among others, and that the revolution was dividing up the land and giving it to the poor, and that all people were equal. All that made a great impression. It was about 1930 that people in the villages were talking of this. It was not till many years later that I realized that General Chu Mao was really General Chu Teh and Chairman Mao Tse-tung, and that they were the leaders of the communists.

In 1934, I went back to Yuehyoushan and worked there for our old landlord's son, Yang Kung-shan. The thing was that I had worked for Chang Ming-liang for a long time and in the end had become fed up with him and no longer liked him, so that when young Yang came and asked me to come back and told me how well off I should be, I thought that I might as well go back to Yuehyoushan. I took out half my wages in cash and half in grain. My brothers had moved away to different villages. Our life was the same as ever, poor people remained poor people. A quilted coat had to last you ten years. You washed it every year and patched it, till it was nothing but patches. One day, when I was sitting having supper, Yang Shen-hsi came to me. He was the old land-lord, Yang Shen-you's brother. He had just come from the town. He said to me: 'My friend, there's a lot of talk now of revolution and that you are going to divide up the landowners' land. So you wait, and before long you'll be sharing out our land and our goats.' Then he laughed, because he thought it a great joke. But I thought: 'But this is quite possible. And it would be a good thing, if it did come.'

After that, people began talking about the Red Army. I was working from sunrise to sunset and did not have much time for talking, but I listened to what people said about the Red Army. It was led by Liu Chih-tan. He divided the possessions of the rich among the poor. The landowners were no longer joking about this. Instead, they began coming to us and saying: 'The communists are only wanting to take your wives and share them with each other. Because the communists share everything. They also share their wives with each other.' We wondered how much of this was true.

In March 1935, the first propagandists from the Red Army began to arrive. But they did not come to our village, because that was where the landowner himself lived. They kept to the other villages. That summer, in June and July 1935, the landowner began to feel afraid. He dug caves into the hillside and hid his possessions away and kept a watch at night. People said that he was afraid, but he said that it was because there were so many bandits about those days. Then everyone said: 'He's afraid of the Red Army.' Now, all the surrounding villages were doing what the Red Army said. The landowner, Yang Kung-shan, himself went to the Red Army and said: 'I believe in the revolution. I want to follow the Red Army.'

But he only just said that. Actually he hated the Red Army and was afraid and wanted to run away. To me he said: 'It's a pity the Red Army is so persecuted. I shall help them.'

But nobody bothered about him, and then the propaganda started among us, his dependants. He was quite hemmed in and had to pretend to be Red. He began saying that all people were brothers. There were only seven families in our little village, besides the proprietor and his family, and we all worked for Yang Kung-shan. Now, when the propaganda became stronger, we farmhands stopped working for the landowner and revolted.

Then he tried to run away. He wanted to get to Yulin, 240 li away, or to Hengshan, 120 li away. He had managed to remove a good deal of his possessions to the town earlier on, and he now came to me and said: 'Come along with me. As long as I have corn for myself and my family, you and your family will have enough to eat.' But I thought: 'Why should I go along with you any longer?' At that time, I had three children, and I did not want to go with him. Then he said: 'As you will. Stay here then. My corn is stored. You will be responsible for it. See that my cave is kept in repair and that it doesn't collapse.' 'Yes,' I replied. Then he left.

He set out that evening and hoped to reach Hengshan before it grew light. Most of the households in our village went with him. They were related to him and did not dare do otherwise. They thought he was more powerful than the Red Army. My family and I were the only ones to stay behind in the village. When the villagers in the other villages round about heard that he had fled, they took up the chase; but they did not succeed in catching up with him. Just as they had sighted him, he reached a K.M.T. post forty li away, and after that, they could not catch him, but had to turn back. They came back then to our village, and at dawn began dividing up his corn. They were all his tenants. Now, too, the landless farmhands and day labourers from the surrounding villages came and joined the revolution. We shared the land and the grain. I got 300 jin of corn, and I thought: 'Corn I can eat and then no one can take it from me. But what about the land?' There was no detachment of the Red Army in the neighbourhood when we made our revolution. There were only Red Guards with spears from the neighbouring villages.

We now had to register for land. Each got as much land as he could till. The rest was set aside to be cultivated by the Red Army. That was our form of grain tax during the revolution. It was organized by the president of the people's militia in our district. He was called Sháng Wen-zu. I don't know what happened to him afterwards. He stayed on in his village after the power of the people was broken, and I have not heard anything of him since.

Now a lot of propagandists and ganbus were coming to the village, sent by our government. They used to spend the night in my cave. One day, a ganbu called Chang came. He was the battalion leader of the Red Guard, and he had a talk with me and said: 'The revolution is for the poor. In our revolution, the poor must themselves take power. You shall be responsible for setting up the Red Guard here.' I had seen this Chang before. He was from a village a bit farther on. We trusted each other, because we came from the same district and we were all poor. One of the things that made our revolution possible was that we always talked to the poorest. Another thing that had a lot of significance was that we heard of the revolution from members of our own family. We had most trust in the family, and when the family started saying that the revolution was necessary, this was better propaganda than anyone coming from outside to talk to us. An uncle can say things that an outsider cannot say.

I now had thirty mu of land. It was the first time I had had my own land, and it was good land. I had chosen it myself. My wife said nothing. That was still in the old society, in which women did not talk about such things. Now that I was in charge of the Red Guard in our village, I took part in the distribution of land in other villages. When we went to those villages, we first got in contact with any we had known for a long time and had a serious talk with them. I took part in the distribution of land in Yaping. I was a platoon commander, and we of the Red Guard came to Yaping armed with spears. We had arranged this with the leader in Yaping. We had walked all night and got there in the morning. We came from a number of villages, as we always did. Hundreds and hundreds of poor farmers and tenants and day labourers and farmhands, all with spears, came from all the villages of the neighbourhood. By the morning, we had all arrived and then we accomplished the revolution.

Three hundred men were assembled in the village of Yaping. The propagandists went up to the landlord, Chang Ming-liang, and talked sense to him. He saw that all resistance was hopeless and he acquiesced in his land being divided up without more ado. He himself shared out his grain and his land and his tools, and then became just one of the ordinary village farmers. He talked with me as with an old acquaintance, but he did not let on that he was against the distribution of land. He behaved well. Later, he fell ill and died, but his son continued to cultivate his land and he never mentioned the dividing up of it, but was an ordinary villager. Most of the landowners were sensible. They accepted the inevitable. Some fled. Yang Kung-shan, who had fled to Hengshan, later went on farther to Yulin, when we were approaching Hengshan. Then, when the counter-revolutionaries defeated us, he returned; but that is another story.

After that, we kept this whole area as a liberated area for two years. If the counter-revolutionaries had not attacked, all the farmers would gradually have got land and oxen, and corn enough to eat their fill every day of the year. During these two years we carried our revolution through at the same time as we were growing grain. Half the time we spent out and about fighting in the revolution, and the other half of the time we were at home cultivating our fields. In those days we had enough corn.

In every village there was a leader of the Red Guard and a president of the Poor Farmers' Union. He was responsible for the grain and for Red Army men being quartered, if any came to the village. The grain we expropriated was shared out among the farmers, except for a small part which was kept for the Red Army. The president of the Poor Farmers' Union was responsible for the grain store. We elected him at a meeting, and this was our first bit of independent administration. Life became easier for us. We had no rents to pay, no taxes, no interest, all we had to do was to work and eat. At that time we paid no grain tax on our production. There were so few Red Army men, and only a couple of ganbus running the entire administration. We had a small plot that we cultivated for the Red Army. The farmers paid nothing whatsoever. The only impost we had, apart from cultivating the plot, was that every woman had to make one or two pairs of shoes a year for the Red Army.

We held lots of meetings. Everything had to be decided in open assembly. Small things as well as big. As soon as a matter cropped up, we arranged for a meeting. Then, the Red Guard in the village had its own meetings, and there were youth meetings and women's meetings. And the communists used to meet at night in some old temple or other, because no one had time by day. At first, things went rather slowly at our meetings. Nobody dared say what he really thought. Naturally, it

341

was difficult at first, for we were only farmers and had never held meetings before or voted or held discussions or made decisions.

We did not hear much about what was being done in the cities, but there was a lot of talk about which areas had now been liberated in northern Shensi and what Liu Chih-tan and Hsien Tse-chiang had said. We also heard about other liberated areas and about Mao.

We used to talk about how big and powerful our Red Army in northern Shensi was. You see, in 1935 and 1936, no one ever thought of the K.M.T., and it never occurred to us that the landlords would come back, or that the counter-revolution would be victorious and defeat us. When Liu Chih-tan and Hsien Tse-chiang led the Red Army against Hengshan, I was there making a delivery of grain. We were besieging Hengshan then, and it was the first time I had seen an army of that size. They had weapons and uniforms. We had come with the grain carts and, when we had delivered the grain to the army, we stayed on for the rest of the day and ate in the mess. As we sat there eating, Liu Chih-tan came in. He walked right past me, but he did not speak to me. He had great responsibilities then, as commander of the Red Army. But I had at least seen him.

Our government was in Anting—the town is now called Tsechiang —and all the villagers were talking of how our army exercised there and how strong it was. We held a lot of political mass meetings at that time. We had meetings about the Soviet Union, and at these, ganbus came and told us that we had learned from its experience how to make a revolution. The Soviet Government had also begun with only a few rifles. We had meetings at which we talked of how all humanity was to be freed of all oppression and all misfortune and need, and how all peoples were to become brothers and live as equals all over the world. We had meetings about imperialism and what the imperialists had done in China. There were different sorts of meetings, and we talked about the three mountains that weighed on the people of China. These three mountains were bureaucratic capitalism, the feudal landowners and the foreign imperialists. We had all to help and topple them over.

We often held our meetings on the tops of hills, and then we had flags with us and posted Red Guardsmen with spears round about as guards. And we had red streamers fixed to the spears. At the start of the meeting we sang. We sang lots of songs and both men and women sang. We all sang together. There were great differences between our life then and what it had been before. The greatest difference was that all landlords, despots and bureaucrats had disappeared and the land been divided up, and that the farmers were free. We never saw a single tax collector those years. Before, the dogs used to come every month, and, even if one paid the tax, they would say: 'But I have walked such a long way, I must have some journey money for myself too.' If one had no money to pay the tax with, they hit one with chains. But in those years the dogs never came near us.

The women too were liberated. The three mountains may have weighed heavily on the people of China, but they had weighed most heavily on the women. A woman's sufferings were unspeakable. When she was fourteen or fifteen she was married off to someone twenty years her senior. Many girls committed suicide then. Their feet were bound. No one would marry a 'big foot'. None dared cut her hair. They all wore theirs in a bun on the nape of their necks, as my wife still does today. When a young girl's feet were bound, the bindings were pulled so tight that she could not walk. It hurt so much that she could not stand. But she was forced to get up and walk; she was hit with a broom till she did so. And this was not done because people were evil. They only wanted what was best for the girl. Nobody wanted to hit their child, but if her feet weren't bound, she would have such an unhappy life that one was compelled to be hard for her own sake. At first, after having their feet bound, girls just stumbled about.

Now, after our revolution, all the women's feet were to be freed. We removed the bindings from the feet of all little girls. Many women took part in our discussions and meetings. Women were elected to different committees and different posts in the villages. The women also formed their own propaganda groups. Then we sang about women's emancipation. I can still remember many of the songs of those days about women's rights. We made propaganda for the equality of women and free choice in marriage. There were lots of divorces in those days, for most people's marriages had been arranged for them and they did not care for each other. We held meetings about love then. Most did not go back to their former marriage partners, but looked for new ones with whom they would be happier. The class enemy then slandered us and flung mud at us, saying that we had no morals. But we wanted everyone to be free and equal, and the new marriages were both happier and more enduring than the old. The upper classes still tell lies about us.

But this new equality certainly was a problem. Li Hai-fu's first

343

wife left him in 1935. She went off with a troupe of women propaga-gandists. She was going to make propaganda for the revolution. Her father-in-law was still very feudal in his attitude. He said: 'Do you want to run away? Then I'll break your leg so that you won't be able even to limp along.' Then I told him: 'If you break her leg, you will regret it. How could you even think of such a thing?' 'She wants to run away from us,' he said. 'She isn't running away,' I said. 'She's trans-ferring to different work.' He had to give in. The power of the people would not let him break her leg and she went with her propaganda troupe. She did a good job for the revolution. Later, when the K.M.T. came, she was taken prisoner and badly tortured. We succeeded in free-ing her in the end, but she died soon afterwards. Her son is grown-up now.

In July 1935, I joined the party. It was very simple. The party was holding a meeting in the old temple above the village. There were four people there. Two party members came and fetched me and took me to the meeting. There we discussed revolutionary work, after which they said to me: 'Are you prepared to become a member of the Communist Party of China?' 'Yes, I am,' I said. That was how I became a party member.

Right up to the end of May 1937, when the enemy attacked us from Hengshan, we had no idea that they were going to launch an attack. The enemy's troops reached our village in September. They rounded up us farmers and made us build fortifications in the hills. There had been many fights in the years before this, but in the great attack of 1937 the Red Guard could not do much against the enemy's troops. We had knives and spears and muzzle-loaders, but they came with machine-guns and cannon and modern weapons. There were many enemy troops. They were advancing the whole time. They advanced ten li, then they compelled the villagers to build them a fort, and, when it was finished, they advanced another ten li. Our guerrillas were retreating the whole time. We never saw the Red Army. When we farmers saw the enemy's troops coming, we said: 'We are helpless. There's nothing we can do.' We could not even defend ourselves when the enemy rounded us up to build forts for them. While we were working on the forts, we kept asking each other: 'When will our government come back? When will our Red Army come? If only we could hear from them, and if only we knew where they are now, so we could work for them.' But however much we asked, nobody knew where our government had gone or where the Red Army was, and we never heard from the party and just wondered. We could not do anything. We were conscript labourers and were beaten by the K.M.T. soldiers while we were building fortifications for them, and the poor people suffered.

Now, too, the owner of the land, Yang Kung-shan, returned. The year before, 1936, when we still were in power, he had led an enemy force to the village of Shiwan, forty li away, and there had stolen goats and corn and plundered us, but on that occasion we had been able to drive him off. The enemy was always bloodthirsty. In November 1935, the enemy had gone to Yushomou, where my sixth brother, Li Shu-hua, Li Hai-chun's father, was president of the Poor Farmers' Union. They cut off my brother's head and those of eleven other poor farmers that same night. When enemy troops re-entered the village in 1937, they cut off the heads of five farmers and one ganbu from the district administration who was in charge of youth matters. I knew them all, because we were neighbours. But of us brothers, it was only the sixth who had his head cut off. The landowners wanted their revenge. They had good relations with the K.M.T. and dragged the farmers before their courts and said: 'This peasant has done this and this.' At first, that was quite enough. But afterwards the K.M.T. came to see that it would be dangerous to cut off too many people's heads.

So, when Yang Kung-shan came back and took me prisoner and hauled me before the K.M.T. court in Shiwan in 1937, he said: 'He has eaten up my corn and divided up my possessions.' Then I replied: 'I was not the only one to make revolution. We all did so and it was your own fault. You weren't worth anything better.' Yang Kung-shan wanted them to cut my head off, but they didn't. They just beat me till I lost consciousness and then poured water over me to bring me round and then beat me again. They kept on with that for a bit. The enemy had a special committee called 'Committee for Quelling the Revolution', and after being thus tortured, I was brought before their committee. There they interrogated me to find out if I was a communist. Then they tortured me again. I never told them anything, and they got nothing out of me, and in the end they put me in prison and left me there. Then friends in Shiwan stood guarantee for me and so got me out of prison. I had been tortured so much that I was unable to walk, and they had to hire a donkey to transport me home. There I lay on my kang for three months unable to get up.

But Yang Kung-shan did not like my being released. He would have liked to have me condemned to death and my head cut off. Not only because he disliked me, but because he would then have been able to sell my widow and my children and in that way get his money back. He never forgave me for having helped to divide up his property. I had scarcely got on my feet again before he had me in prison a second time. Then people in the villages round about said that they had all helped to make the revolution, and not just me, and that it was unfair to treat me in that way. If Yang Kung-shan wanted his money back, he could demand rental for those years from me in the ordinary way, but he could not just have them cut my head off and take my family as pledge. The K.M.T. authorities had now become more circumspect. They wanted the district to be calm and quiet, so the officers just said to me: 'It doesn't matter now you being in the Red Army. Just confess and get it off your chest. We only want to help you become a better person.' But I didn't confess anything and people stood guarantee for me and I wasn't even tortured, but released again. Yang Kung-shan could not endure that and, having twice failed to get my head chopped off, he now drove me out of the village and refused to let me live there any longer.

So I moved to the village of Yuanmukou, which was fifteen li farther on. My employer's name was Ma Tse-yuan. He owned his land. He had been in Shiwan when I was in prison there the first time. I worked for him as a farmhand for two years, 1938 and 1939. All cash I earned I had to pay to Yang Kung-shan; the children were growing up and there were many mouths to feed.

I used to wonder where the Red Army had gone. Some said that it had taken itself down to Yenan, others did not know. We tried to get in contact with the party, but could not do so. Now and again a few of us used to meet in secret, but we had no regular activities and we did not dare meet too often, because we were all poor and all members of the party and all suspected of being so. There were very few members left. Only a few in every other, or every third or so, village.

It was difficult to get into contact with Yenan. Our village, of course, lay inside K.M.T. territory. But some of my family had moved down there long before, before our revolution began in northern Shensi. You see, in those days one was moving the whole time hunting for land and better conditions; and in the old Yenanfu, all ten hsiens were short of people, and so people were always moving. The old people said that famine and wars and revolts under the Ching dynasty had depopulated the area. In October 1939, I went down to Yenan to see if there was work for a farmhand there. My sister, Li Fong-lan, who is Tung Yang-chen's grandmother, was living in Liu Ling, and she said: 'We need someone to work for us.' Then I went back to our village and stayed there for the winter. When we had eaten up our corn, we all went to Liu Ling.

That first year, I worked for Tung Yang-chen's family. I was the only worker there. I got one jin for every ten I harvested for them. In 1940, the harvest was good and we had lots of food. Tung's family had good land down in the valley and they harvested 300 jin per mu. They had a good ox too. But then Tung Yang-chen's mother married and so brought a pair of hands into the family again, so I began working for Li Hsiu-tang's family. I worked there for a year. When I began working for him, I had to borrow 300 jin. I repaid 600 jin. I worked in his fields with his ox, and we divided the harvest fifty-fifty.

I'd known Li Hsiu-tang since he was very young. I know him inside out. His father owned half the valley and many shops and houses in the town here. Li Han-hua, who was Li Hsiu-tang's brother-in-law, owned the west half of the valley and the Date Garden, where the Central Committee had its headquarters. You could almost say that Li Hsiu-tang's brother-in-law has been Mao Tse-tung's host. But he was a very reluctant host. Li Han-hua was a very dangerous man. He was rich and powerful, and he commanded the armed combat forces of the landowners. He had many people's blood on his conscience. Yenan's third big man owned even more. He was the richest of the three. But Li Hsiu-tang's father was one of the three big men of the old Yenanfu. Now, we are trying to bring his children up to be good citizens. They are so young that they have no experience of what used to be.

The Red Army was down here in Yenan, of course. It was called the Eighth Route Army. Here, too, there was the Communist Party and its central committee and the government of the Shensi-Kansu-Ningsia Frontier Region. In 1942, the Central Committee proposed a big production campaign, and then I organized and led a labour exchange group. This consisted mostly of my relatives. Those who had come down here earlier had been given good land in the distribution, and they did not want to join in any sort of co-operative cultivation. But we, who had come here later, had to be content with the hill land

and that called for co-operation. So I went up to Hengshan and fetched more of my relatives and started a labour exchange group. It was the first permanent labour exchange group in the Shensi-Kansu-Ningsia Frontier Region. It had no special name. It consisted of eight families: I, the organizer and leader; Li Hai-fu; Li Hai-kuei; Li Hai-chun, who works now in the people's commune; Li Hai-chen, who also works in the people's commune now, and three families from Hengshan who fled from Hu Tsung-nan back to Hengshan and are still there. We worked one day for one family, the next day for another family, and so on. We broke new ground and cleared fields, and we worked well together. All the fields you see up there on the hillside on the other side of the valley are ones we cleared. We did it all by hand: we had no oxen, just mattocks.

The other farmers in the valley had good land and they did not co-operate. That came much later. But we co-operated. We had to co-operate, if we were to get on. We had discussed it thoroughly in our group. 'Our land is poor,' we said. 'We have no level ground, we have no oxen, but we can work.' At the end of the year we had a lot of corn, and it had all been harvested on the fields we had cleared. As, after this harvest, we all had enough to eat, we bought pigs. Two families clubbed together to buy the beasts, and that winter the group owned six. So we worked on till the winter of 1946–7. By then, every household in the group had animals and a store of corn. I had three beasts and a donkey. I thought the whole time that organization meant strength. The more people, the greater the labour force. In some few short years we had all achieved prosperity through hard work and co-operation. The others down in the valley said: 'They work very hard and they get incomes out of it. They are doing well.'

When I went down to Yenan, our party group had lost contact with the party, as I said. At first, I did not get into touch with the party in Yenan either. I never thought there was anyone to contact. I had no connexions there, you see. Things were different here in Yenan than they had been with us. The Central Committee was here, though, and the government and everything, and one could not just go up and talk with them. But when I was working for Li Hsiu-tang, I was responsible for public safety in the village. Then I organized the labour exchange group. After that, the party got in touch with me and asked me if I would be willing to start working for the revolution. We had many talks, and, in 1945, I joined the party again.

When I was in Hengshan, even in the latter part of my time there, it was very little we knew about the outside world. For example, we had not heard of the war with Japan, even in 1939. I never heard of it till I came down to Yenan.

A lot has happened in Liu Ling in these years. When I came here, there were only a few households and a few caves in the hillside. Then the co-operative built its centre down by the well, and had its big shop on the other side of the river. That was the Southern District's Sellers' and Consumers' Co-operative. All the farmers had shares in it. The co-operative developed very quickly. In 1942, it built a number of proper houses and big sheds. Its employees lived here in long rows. Chiang Kai-shek was trying to blockade the frontier region, so Mao said: 'We must create plenty with our own hands.' By 1943 the co-operative had 800 transport mules. The communist party was poor in those days and had no motor-cars. The mules fetched salt from Ting-pian. Most of the villagers were members of the co-operative, and we elected representatives. Each member had one vote irrespective of the size of his share. Little by little the people had to learn to be masters of the country. It was not easy to begin with. The co-operative was a school in which we learned how to run a business with elected delegates and how to run the country with popularly elected power.

We had our difficulties too. In 1942, the river flooded. The old people said that it was the worst flood in living memory. The co-operative shop was under water and even some of the ganbus lost all hope, but Liu Chien-chang, president of the whole of the Southern District's Sellers' and Consumers' Co-operative, said: 'A single-storey house can be flooded; so we shall have to build two-storey houses.' And we did. We also built an assembly hall and many other buildings. So, gradually, things went better and better for the co-operative. The transport of goods and salt gave it a big income. The dividend on the shares rose to five times the shares' value. Some people—those who were hard up—took out their money, but most people left their money in the co-operative. Five shops were opened and we built workshops, where we produced wine and oil and Chinese bean pudding. We were beginning to put Li Hsiu-tang's mill out of business, by starting a lot of other small co-operative mills, which were driven by donkey power and which charged the farmer less than Li Hsiu-tang did.

But exploitation still existed in those days. There were many who lived wholly or partly on other people's labour. But we controlled this exploitation and kept an eye on it. Those who had been given land, when it was parcelled up, had got very good land. They had valley land and too much of it for a family to be able to cultivate alone. So they had begun hiring hands and day labourers during the busy season. In this way, some farmers, who before had been poor, now became exploiters; or, rather, they were beginning almost to be exploiters. This was the way things went, for example, with Tung Yang-chen and Ma Hai-hsiu. Their family's labour force was too small and so they employed others. In this way, class differentiation was starting again after our land reform. If this had gone on, there would have been new landlords and new big farmers in the valley here. I thought a lot about this at the time. We were up on the hill there breaking new ground. I felt that it was essential to get co-operative farming, if we were not to get a new rich class.

At that time, then, we had our relics from the old days, people like Li Hsiu-tang, who still lived on part of his land and lived on income that he didn't work for. But after our land reform, we had three different tendencies of development among the ordinary farmers: *nouveaux riches* farming on their own, people who had been given good valley land and were beginning to employ day labourers and farmhands and thus starting to live in part on other people's labour; the sellers' and consumers' co-operative, and the labour exchange group working up on the hill land. Li Hsiu-tang and similar relics still fulfilled a certain function.

The winter of 1946–7 was marked by preparations for war. Evacuation was planned and the authorities made propaganda to encourage the farmers to evacuate the valley. All corn was to be buried and all tools hidden. 'The enemy is going to attack and will occupy this area, that much is certain,' we were told. As early as October 1946, ganbus began coming to us telling us that the enemy was going to attack. Then more and more was said about Hu Tsung-nan's coming attack. The ganbus told us to hide our corn, so that we should have it once the enemy had withdrawn, and to prevent it from benefiting them. But I thought: 'Surely Yenan is the headquarters of the Central Committee? How can it be abandoned? And how could the Central Committee ever come back here after having fled?'

In January 1947, a representative of the government came to the village to try to get us really to hide everything. A great deal of propaganda was now being made. The ganbus told us that Mao had said that the enemy was going to capture Yenan, and not just the town but the whole of the surrounding countryside as well. In fact, the whole frontier region would fall to the enemy. Mao was also supposed to have said that if we wanted to lose Yenan, we should defend it. Mao had also said that Hu Tsung-nan would be in Yenan seven or eight months, or a year at the most. I thought that the propagandists must have heard wrong. It couldn't be true. The Central Committee and Chairman Mao had been in Yenan for many years. Why, then, was the Central Committee going to run away from the enemy?

The farmers were not good about hiding their corn. What was hidden was only hidden because a government representative stood over them to see it done. In February, the propagandists were saying: 'Don't be afraid. You will manage under the enemy. Just don't have a change of heart.' Then they went away and our troops marched off northwards. I had sent my children to Ansai, and there was only my wife and I left. Certain families, which came from Michi and Heng-shan, went back to their home country, including three of the families in our labour exchange group. But as we had no land up there, we stayed where we were. The Southern District's Sellers' and Consumers' Co-operative had 800 mules. These were loaded up and driven to Wayapo. After that, the farmers began digging pits to hide their grain in and, by the time the enemy marched in, we had gone up into the hills.

We were living in a little village. When the enemy came, it was with thousands and thousands of men. They marched in and swept the valleys and the branch valleys and the hills clean. There was a couple of households here who thought that the communists had been defeated for good and all, and they hurried to offer the K.M.T. troops boiling water, and to show them the way into Yenan town. They were so impressed by the K.M.T.'s good weapons that they went over to them entirely. Li Hsiu-tang and Tuan Fu-yin did that. After our victory, we re-educated them and they are now treated kindly.

The K.M.T. began making its old propaganda, saying that the communists were evil and that the K.M.T. wanted to save us farmers from their clutches. But nobody believed them. 'We are the troops of the Central Government,' they said. 'We have crushed the communist bandits, and now we are going to see that you live well.' But at the same time as they said this, they were plundering the farmers. Where their troops had been, you would not hear a hen cackle, nor find a pig left. They even dragged the shoes off people's feet. They plundered Li Hsiu-tang's and Tuan Fu-yin's caves just as thoroughly as all the others. It made no difference to the soldiers whether they had gone over to the K.M.T. or not.

We were profoundly depressed when we saw the K.M.T. troops. They were so heavily armed, and they had weapons we had never even seen before. Our soldiers in the Eighth Route Army had nothing similar. I stayed up in the hills for a fortnight, but the enemy was roaming about up there too and, when those who had gone back to Liu Ling came up and told us that it would be all right to go back, we did so. When we got back, we heard that not a single shot had been fired in the valley. Our men had retreated without a fight. But lots of graves were being dug on the hills, and they were being made out to be those of Eighth Route Army men. This was because the K.M.T. needed a victory.

Many of these graves were dug, especially on Lokoushan. We did not properly understand the enemy's purpose in digging them. After the liberation, when we ploughed up the ground there, we examined all the graves before ploughing them, but did not find a body in any of them. They were just bluff.

When I returned to Liu Ling, half the village had been destroyed. The enemy had plundered it most thoroughly. Yet, at the same time, the K.M.T. tried to organize the people into groups and sections. They chose various people and gave them various posts, but those they chose had all had something to do with the K.M.T. before. In Liu Ling, the K.M.T. appointed Tuan Fu-yin its group leader. They appointed a section leader in Seven-mile Village. This was Tuan Shi-tsai. He had been a pedlar. He worked as informer for the K.M.T. He, of course, was from the district and he went round pointing out communists and communist sympathizers to the K.M.T.'s secret police. He was arrested after the liberation, and we re-educated him through work. He got three or four years. He returned to Seven-mile Village in 1954 or so.

Most of the young people of the village were out with the guerrillas. No one from this village fell in the fighting. The guerrillas fought when they were able to defeat the enemy, but otherwise they kept clear and hid from the enemy. Hu Tsung-nan held this area occupied for thirteen months. In March 1948 he had to withdraw. Everything had been destroyed by then. The co-operative had had eighty buildings in its premises in the village, and they had all been pulled down and destroyed. They had stood where the school is now. We had no corn to eat and no seed to sow. When the enemy had been driven out, we had to begin at the beginning all over again. Despite the destruction, however, we were glad to be rid of the K.M.T. The authorities now organized farmers to carry seed-corn from Lochuan, where there were stores of grain. I acted as porter then. We each carried seventy to eighty jin in two sacks on a carrying-pole. It took us roughly a week to walk to Lochuan, get the corn and walk back. Your back ached, life was bitter and I wanted to cry, because everything was so smashed and ruined; but at least the enemy had been sent headlong. We had to work hard to get going again.

All labour was mobilized and organized at the time. Certain of us had the job of fetching corn from Lochuan, others stayed at home in the village. We had almost no animals. The young men had to draw the plough and the women ploughed. Now Li Hsiu-tang emerged once more. He is very sly. He applied for membership of the militia again, just as if nothing had happened; but we would not have him. His hopes were vain. We gave him an official refusal.

Mao got to Peking in 1949. He never returned to Yenan and still has not been here again. But, in 1949, the whole country was in the process of being liberated. He then sent us in the old liberated areas telegrams, exhorting us to organize our work and heal the wounds of war. We were to increase production. Then we began to recall that Mao had been right in saying that the enemy would hold Yenan occupied for about a year, and so we felt that we could rely on the Central Committee and Mao. In Liu Ling, we called a meeting to discuss Mao's telegram and to organize ourselves for production.

That year we set up four labour groups for mutual help, which included every household in the village of Liu Ling. They built on the experience we had gained with ours, before the occupation. I was in charge of the first labour group for mutual help, which had the same members as before the occupation, with the exception of the three families which had moved back to Hengshan and now did not wish to return. Also Li Hai-yuan joined it. We took the land we wanted upon the hills on the other side of the valley. I had chosen this area right from the beginning, because there is good water there and it is easy to get fuel up on the hills, nor was the soil so bad either. We had five beasts.

The second labour group for mutual help was led by Ma Juei-ching. The third was led by Jen Huai-wan, Jen Teh-wan's son, who is now party secretary at the pottery in Yenan. Fu Hai-tsao was in charge of the fourth labour group for mutual help.

But there were certain difficulties in running this kind of co-operative work. When there were eight households working jointly in a labour group for mutual help, it meant that one of the households had its land sowed roughly eight days earlier than the last household's. That involved a financial gain for the one and a financial loss for the other. This led to a lot of discussion. We had lively discussions of the whole question in our group and finally we said: 'Let us try cultivating it all together and then just sharing the produce.' That was in November 1949, after the harvest. But we had no knowledge of how a co-operative farm should be run. We did not even know that we were a co-operative farm. We did not know how we were going to calculate a day's work or how each person's work was to be assessed. But we were not all agreed. Li Hai-fu and Li Hai-kuei refused. They took out their two beasts and went and joined Fu Hai-tsao's labour group for mutual help. That left only four families of us, and we had three beasts.

But I still thought that we ought to try. To start with, we did not have work units, but each of us had a certain labour value. We did not assess the actual work, but the worker in person, acting on the assumption that each of us would always do his best. We were all good workers. We had difficulty over the book-keeping. We were all uneducated and had no one who could keep accurate notes.

Li Hai-chun and Li Hai-chen were the ones who had to do our book-keeping. They had the head for that sort of thing, and both have since transferred to administrative work. It was I who led the discussions in November 1949, and I was able to force the change through, partly because I was leader of the labour group and partly because the members were all my relations and, I being one of the older generation in the family, they had respect for me. I told you before that the ties of family have been of great significance in our revolution. It wasn't so strange that Li Hai-fu and Li Hai-kuei did not want to be in on this. They lived on this side of the valley and they had beasts. We, on the other hand, had nothing but hillside fields on the other side of the valley and so had to join forces. Of those who remained and built up the first farmers' co-operative, Li Hai-chen and I were the better off. I had an ox and Li Hai-chen had two beasts. The other households had nothing but their hands. They owned nothing. But Li Hai-chen and I had been to many meetings and taken part in lots of things, and we were more aware and decided to help the other two families. The Party was interested too. The Party secretary for Yenan hsien came out in person to listen to our discussion. But at that time he only listened. He didn't say anything.

There was no great enthusiasm for our work that first year. The 1950 harvest was good, it is true, but our method did not work. We had decided that every worker had a certain value. A good worker had ten points, a not-so-good worker, like my young son who was not then yet fully grown, was given five points. At the end of the year, when we shared out according to this system, the shares were not related to the work actually done. We did not yet know how to keep books with actual work reckoned in days' work.

We had a very serious discussion after the harvest in 1950. The income per household was big, it is true, but when we examined the distribution of income more closely, we found that there still was exploitation in our co-operative. The oxen were exploiting the people. Each ox brought its owner 900 jin of corn a year, but its feed came from the co-operative.

Even so, despite the fact that our system was a bit lame, people thought that the co-operative was a good idea. That autumn, we acquired two new members. Li Hai-fu came back to us after a year in Fu Hai-tsao's labour group for mutual help, and he brought his ox. Then a family, Ma Chan-wan, came from Hengshan. They moved back to Hengshan some years later. So now we were six families and four oxen. We decided then to value the oxen. We valued the three at 200 Y, that was roughly 3,000 jin of corn. This was to be paid to the owners over five years. Li Hai-fu's ox was valued in the same way. The other families were not so well situated, so the payment period was made longer. We had no dividend on land in our co-operative, because all the land was newly cleared, and we were clearing more the whole time collectively.

In November 1951, I was chosen to attend a conference for merit workers in agriculture being held in Sian. I was to report on our work. The provincial Party authorities heard me before the meeting and decided that what we had actually made was a co-operative farm. We were the only one in Shensi at the time. They also said that we must have a name and gave us mine, calling us Li Yiu-hua's Farmers' Co-operative. I was not quite sure that that was the right thing to call it:

the name might not go down in Liu Ling, but I gave the conference a report on how to organize a labour group for mutual help and how to found a farmers' co-operative. I was given a diploma for good work on the agricultural front and a money prize of sixteen yuan, and, in addition, I was chosen to attend a conference for merit workers for the whole North-western District. There, too, I reported and there too I was given a diploma and a money prize of 200 Y. It was unusual to get such big money prizes. With the 216 Y I bought two oxen, so that now we had enough draught animals. We also bought a donkey.

Now we went over to a better system of book-keeping and, instead of putting a value on the individual, we valued each job and reckoned incomes in days' work performed per year. We were now well off for labour and also for animals. We had six oxen and a donkey. But the land was poor. Down there in the valley were the labour groups for mutual help and, if we were to beat their production, we had to work harder and organize our work better than they.

In April 1952, we were able to borrow forty goats from the hsien authorities. We were to look after them, and half of the kids were to belong to the state and half to us. We also bought another donkey. Our production now increased considerably. The three labour groups for mutual help had not been able to increase the numbers of their stock, nor had they increased their production of grain, so that we did better than they, despite their having the good land. In October 1952 a calf was born increasing our stock to 7 beasts, 2 donkeys and 120 goats, 40 of which belonged to the state.

At the same time, Ma Juei-ching's labour group decided to form its own co-operative. They had good land and thought that what we had done they could do too, and even better, and with less work because of their good land. Then the Party committee of Yenan hsien intervened. It organized a little propaganda troupe to help us and this stayed in Liu Ling for twenty days, and we had great discussions about forming a proper big agricultural co-operative. Ma Juei-ching said: 'We are not going to join Li Yiu-hua's co-operative farm. We can organize one of our own. We have better land.' That was because our fields lay rather far off, well up on the hillside. The other two labour groups were still keeping out of it. Ma Juei-ching's labour group was the only one that had already decided to form a co-operative farm.

With the help of the Party group, we now reported to the others

356

the lessons we had learned and emphasized that it was a question of organization. Better organization gave a greater return. Ma Juei-ching agreed with this, but he refused to join our co-operative. I had always thought it bad policy to give our co-operative farm my name, and now this was proving of considerable significance emotionally. This was exactly what I had feared when I had first discussed it all with the provincial committee in Sian. There was also another matter: who should be elected in future to the various posts in the farmers' co-operative. I now had a frank talk with the responsible comrades from Yenan hsien's Party committee and said: 'If you want us to incorporate the other labour groups into our farmers' co-operative, then we must first change its name from Li Yiu-hua's Co-operative Farm to Liu Ling Co-operative Farm. In addition, there must be guarantees that all posts will be occupied by actual members properly elected. We must introduce real democratic principles into the farmers' co-operative.' The ganbus from Yenan hsien accepted this. When this had been done, many households joined our co-operative.

But Li Hai-yuan said: 'If they come in, I go out. If they come, I'd prefer to be on my own. And I'll never come back. Never.' Then he left us. To get the others in, we also had to put through certain other organizational and financial changes. The organization of the Party association was strengthened. We elected a proper management committee for Liu Ling Co-operative Farm. As the new members had good land and were worried in case they lost it, we had to switch over to paying dividends on land. The previous owners were to be paid ten jin of grain per mu of valley land and three to four jin of grain per mu of hillside land. This was to be done annually. Donkeys were also to remain private property. The new members were to keep their donkeys as private possessions. This was, in a way, a retrograde step, but it was necessary in order to expand the co-operative and include more members. If the collective had need of the donkeys, it was to pay the owners so much a day.

As both Ma Juei-ching and Jen Huai-wan, who were both leaders of a labour group for mutual help, had gone in with us, Li Yü-teh became leader of one labour group for mutual help, and Fu Hai-tsao remained leader of the other. These two groups which had not joined the farmers' co-operative together comprised less than twenty households. We now had two-thirds of the valley land, and sixteen households were members. Ma Chan-wan was homesick for Hengshan and left us. When we got home, he led a movement to organize a farmers' co-operative in his own village there. We bought a horse and a cart, and all went well for us. In November 1954, we again began considering taking in more members. This time we had no need of outside help. It was all voluntary, and we made our own propaganda. In January 1955, people began applying for membership. Then all the households joined Liu Ling Farmers' Co-operative. There was one exception, Li Hai-yuan, who said that he did not want anything to do with us. He was now farming on his own and intended to go on doing so. He was pig-headed.

Our success in 1954 had been so great that it did not need much propaganda to convince people of the advantages of the farmers' co-operative. They could see them themselves. There were now thirty-two households in the co-operative. We had divided ourselves into two labour groups. Li Hai-kuei was leader of the one, and Li Hung-fu deputy leader. Ma Juei-ching was labour leader of the other, and Fu Hai-tsao deputy labour leader.

In October–November 1955, we turned the whole thing into a higher agricultural co-operative, forming the East Shines Red Higher Agricultural Co-operative. This included Liu Ling Co-operative Farm, Wangchiakou Co-operative Farm, Hutoma Labour Group for Mutual Help, and Erchuankou Labour Group for Mutual Help, as well as those who had still been farming on their own. Now, at last, Li Hai-yuan joined again. He was the last in the entire district to go in for collective farming. We now comprised a total of 104 households.

We now also carried out great changes. All cattle and other animals were owned collectively. We arranged this in the same way as we did when we first pooled our animals. That is to say, we valued them and the owners were paid over five years. In addition, we abolished dividends on land. It was to be actual work that brought in the income. But we also, for the first time, brought it in that families which had no member able to work should receive help from the co-operative. This was something quite new. We had never had any definite rules and regulations as such, and we did not draw up any now. That wasn't usual out in the country. After all, we were just ignorant farmers; we had no education, and it was simpler for us just to decide how we were going to have things. We only made the decisions that we thought right. So we did not write down any rules and regulations.

I became party secretary of the East Shines Red Higher Agricultural Co-operative. It is, of course, through the Party that everything is discussed, and it is the Party which draws up the aims of future development.

It was in August 1958 that we began preparing the formation of a people's commune. This was discussed at various levels. We had the decision of the Central Committee to go by, of course. The people's commune was set up on the basis of the Great Leap and the need to increase capital investment. Before the people's commune was set up, we had begun building a dam that was to serve three different improved agricultural co-operatives. But it had been difficult getting them to collaborate. The people's commune made it possible to systematize joint effort. We needed a larger unit in order to be able to carry out the big works required.

We had always had a hsien administration before, one with many employees. In the people's commune we fused our economic organization with the state power. This entailed a big saving, and made it possible for us to get rid of several ganbus from each area and gave us greater possibilities for collaboration and rational working without unnecessary loss of time. In our people's commune we have constantly stuck to the socialist principle 'To each according to his work', and we have never departed from it. In addition, we introduced certain social benefits and also a certain amount of social welfare. The people's commune also acquired a repair workshop of its own, which is now beginning to grow into almost a little factory.

Personally, I consider that the advantages of the people's commune are that it makes it possible to make better use of labour power during the dead season. At those times, the brigades can exchange days' work and carry out big undertakings. There is unified management. There were several other brigades that helped us carry out our terracing work. Though latterly we have not done so much in that direction.

We grow a lot of millet up here. Half a jin of millet will satisfy a man, but after a jin of wheat he will still be hungry. Our revolution was victorious on millet and rifles. China's farmers have liberated themselves by revolutionary struggle and fighting for their emancipation. I have always hoped that all the farmers of the world should be freed and achieve socialism. We Chinese farmers started from a bad initial position: we were oppressed and poor, and our oppression was great. In your countries, the farmers are in a much better position. After all, you are living under capitalism. But we lived under feudalism. I have often thought about this. Our fight was such a difficult one. We had no weapons. But the bureaucrats and the landowners and the warlords had armies and weapons. It was very difficult for us.

Liu Hsin-min, young ganbu, aged 32

I WAS born in Twenty-mile Village. Apart from the time of Hu Tsung-nan's occupation, I have lived in the new society for as long as I can remember. My father was made chairman of Liu Ling hsiang in 1939, under the Shensi–Kansu–Ningsia Frontier Region. I began school in 1943. After Hu Tsung-nan's withdrawal, my father remained chairman of Liu Ling hsiang for one year, then he transferred to the bank. I stopped school that same year. I never joined the Young Pioneers. Nor was I ever in the League of Youth. I did farmwork till I joined the revolution in October of 1952, when I became chairman of Liu Ling hsiang and thus a ganbu. In June 1957, I joined China's Communist Party. That was the first organization I had been in. When Liu Ling People's Commune was set up in 1958, all paid posts in the hsiang administration were done away with, and I then became president of

Liu Ling People's Commune instead. In April 1961 I became party secretary in Liu Ling People's Commune.

Liu Ling People's Commune was formed in September 1958, when eight higher agricultural co-operatives, comprising a total of thirty-nine labour groups, sent their representatives to a constituent assembly. After that, the higher agricultural co-operatives became labour brigades within the people's commune. Since then, there has been a certain amount of administrative re-organization and, today, Liu Ling People's Commune consists of eighteen labour brigades, comprising a total of fifty-seven labour groups. Liu Ling People's Commune has 1,401 households with 5,039 individuals, of which 2,461 are men and 2,578 women. Of these, 1,938 are fully able-bodied, 1,194 being men and 744 women. The people's commune comprises 360,000 mu, and of this 30,027 are cultivated; 2,124 mu are on the valley floor and 27,903 hillside land. The animals collectively owned comprise 933 oxen, 403 donkeys, 20 mules, 30 horses and 816 goats. I have no figures for the numbers of privately owned goats, but there are 850 pigs in private hands and 6,564 head of poultry privately owned.

Like all other people's communes throughout China, Liu Ling's People's Commune was set up in accordance with the general party line and with the advice of the Central Committee and Chairman Mao.

The people's commune is based on the triumph of collectivization. At the beginning of 1943, Chairman Mao exhorted the people to organize exchange labour groups. These were then formed in our area on both a bilateral, as well as a multilateral, basis. In 1950, the party and Chairman Mao exhorted the people to organize, to help each other and to co-operate. Then, we here formed 45 labour groups for mutual help comprising 431 households, amounting to 46·5 per cent of the total number of households. Then, in the spring of 1950, the first farmers' co-operative was formed. It was run by Li Yiu-hua and comprised four households, which had pooled their land and animals. In its first year, it had a record harvest, cropping an average of 131·2 jin per hillside mu. That was 53·6 per cent more than what the labour groups for mutual help were getting. People now saw the advantages of collectivization and actively asked to join the farmers' co-operative. After that, farmers' co-operatives were set up one after the other, in a string.

In 1953, the party made four resolutions on the organization of agricultural co-operatives. This was a demand from the broad mass of the farmers. That year, 632 households were organized, comprising 65·2 per cent of the total number of households. Of these, 295, that is to say, 46·7 per cent of the organized households, joined the seven farmers' co-operatives that were set up then.

In 1955, Chairman Mao wrote his report on co-operation in agriculture, and, therefore, the winter of 1955–6 saw a flood of collectivization. Labour groups for mutual help were transformed into farmers' co-operatives, and farmers' co-operatives into higher agricultural co-operatives. After these changes, we had, in 1956, eight higher agricultural co-operatives with a total of 958 households. That is to say: 96·3 per cent of all the households in Liu Ling hsiang were organized in higher agricultural co-operatives. That year, the average production of the higher agricultural co-operatives was 107·8 jin per mu more than the return per mu of the farmers' co-operatives in 1954, and 27·4 per cent more than what the labour groups for mutual help had obtained in 1951.

Then came the year 1958. That was the year of the Great Leap and it was then that the broad masses of the farmers saw the necessity of co-operation in order to master the forces of nature, expand production and raise the standard of living. So, on the basis of the higher agricultural co-operatives, collaboration between agricultural co-operatives was organized. They required unified management, and their big investments of capital also called for a unified plan. Work was exchanged between agricultural co-operatives on a basis of equal value and mutual advantage. Then, that summer, the Central Committee passed its resolution to set up people's communes in the countryside. This met with warm support from the farmers, and so, in September, we set up up Liu Ling People's Commune on the foundation of the improved agricultural co-operatives. During the four years that have passed since then, we have done much to perfect our people's commune.

We have striven to overcome nature's catastrophes and achieve record crops. We have had great results in our efforts to expand the collective economy, and we have carried out comprehensive water-regulation works. The people's commune is now an entrepreneur, carries out afforestation and herds cattle.

In 1959, it had 18,015 mu under corn, and the average crop per mu was 146 jin: the total harvest was 2,630,248 jin, 35 per cent more than in 1957.

In 1960, it had 19,832 mu under corn. Owing to a severe drought, the average crop was 123 jin and the total harvested 2,439,336 jin.

In 1961, the area under corn amounted to 29,183 mu and the average yield was 147·5 jin per mu, the total harvested being 4,304,483 jin.

The 1962 plan is for an average yield of 150 jin per mu. I have no figures concerning the number of mu put down to corn and have no knowledge either of the size of the total crop. I seem to remember that we were going to increase production somewhat. There must be a plan, but I do not have it.

As production rises, the members' incomes go up.

Income per head in 1959 was 80·20 Y in cash and 642 jin of grain; figures for 1960 were 84·72 Y and 519 jin, and for 1961 92·00 Y and 720 jin. I have no comparable figures for 1958, nor for the time before the formation of the people's commune.

We have also carried out big water-regulating works. At the end of 1957, we had only 30 mu of irrigated land. Since then we have built 5 dams, 3 canals and 400 mu of terraced fields, and in 1962 the total irrigated land amounted to 8,320 mu. We have been continuing with this work all the time. I do not have the figures for how much has been done each year.

Since the formation of the people's commune, we have had workshops run by the commune, and this has solved the farmers' repair problems. We repair carts and tools and semi-mechanized implements. This workshop was started in 1959, when the blacksmiths came to us with their tools. We then borrowed 5,000 Y from the bank. This was repaid in 1961. We are expanding now and planning to be able to produce motors, turbines, etc. In general, our products are sold within the people's commune, but outsiders can, of course, buy if they wish. But we are far too short of agricultural implements to sell any of these, so that if others than members of the people's commune make use of our workshop, it is for repair work; 85 per cent of the workshop's income goes on wages and materials, and 15 per cent to the people's commune. The monies invested in the workshop came from the commune. The labour brigades have different workshops of their own.

By 1962, we had nine basic schools in the area of the commune. Four of these are state schools, and five are run by the labour brigades jointly with the hsien authorities. The labour brigades in these cases pay for them out of their welfare funds. Proportions in the different schools vary. In 1957, we had 375 pupils, and this year we have 592. Now, in 1962, fifty-eight per cent of those over school age, but still under forty, can read at least 1,000 characters. They can thus read *The Yenan Daily* and make notes. I do not know how many were able to read in 1957.

In 1957 we had a small clinic here, but now the people's commune has a hospital, a clinic and five health centres. Eighteen of the labour brigades are on the telephone network. These costs have been paid by the labour brigades themselves. They have paid all the cost of the wire and posts and that sort of thing in their area. I believe the people's commune did make a certain contribution, but I don't know what, and I do not have any figures available. Sixty-three households in Liu Ling Village and Seven-mile Village have got electricity. This has been paid for by the labour brigade.

Here, in Liu Ling, we have always had private plots of land. This helps the collective economy and the country's supplies. We have never made any departure from this policy and have never made any changes.

We have carried out a lot of ideological work to strengthen the farmers' proletarian class-consciousness and their socialistic sense of collective thrift. Since the formation of the people's commune, we have made great progress under the party's leadership and with the 'three flags'—the party's general line, the Great Leap and the people's communes—before us. But we have no experience of how to run and administer a people's commune. Agriculture is still backward. We have no machinery and the yield per mu is low. Because of various natural disasters, our agricultural production has not been steady from year to year, but we believe that, with the guidance of the party and Chairman Mao, this backwardness will disappear and grain production will be stabilized. We are not content with our progress, but want to achieve more.

Our preliminary calculation is that, after a further three five-year plans, we shall have achieved a stabilized yield of 180 jin of grain per mu. Our income then will be twice what it was in 1961. That is to say that we are reckoning on a *per capita* income of 180 Y cash and 920 jin of grain in fifteen years' time. The area used for industrial purposes is to be increased from 423 mu this year to 1,321 mu. The afforested area is to be doubled to become 8,000 mu. We are to get up to a collective stock of animals corresponding to two oxen and seven goats per household and a privately owned stock of two pigs and two hens or ducks per head.

We are convinced that, led by the Central Committee of the party and Chairman Mao and with the 'three flags' before us, we shall by the work of our own hands, with industry, thrift, hard work and a simple way of life, be able to achieve this.

The turn of the year 1958–9 saw us busy making iron by the age-old methods. We used our own ore and, for four months, from October 1958 to January 1959, we had 67 men employed on this. We expended a total of 8,040 days' work at 1·10 Y, so the wage costs amounted to 8,844 Y. We used 150 tons of twenty per cent iron ore, which we quarried ourselves. We bought in 78·6 tons of coke at a price of 25 Y a ton. We spent 340 Y on special bricks and 498 Y on tools, and a further 143 Y went on various administrative costs. The total expenditure on iron production was 11,790 Y.

We produced a total of 39·3 tons of iron. The cost per ton amounted to 300 Y. At the time, we could buy iron in the shop for 289·40 Y a ton. This meant that we were producing our iron at a cost 10·60 Y above the shop price; or, in other words, that every ton of iron we produced involved us in a loss of almost ten days' work. We decided, therefore, to stop the experiment. At the same time, it must be said that our people learned the technique, which has a certain value, and also that at the turn of the year 1958–9, which was during the Great Leap, it was difficult to buy iron. At the meeting at which we discussed the question after this first experiment, the main argument was that we were then able to buy iron once more and thus were able to use our labour in agriculture, where we could make better use of it.

The people's commune receives no administrative fees from the labour brigades. Its administration is paid for by the state. We, of course, fulfil the functions of the state. Every year we send in a budget to the hsien authorities for our administrative costs. Our finances are supervised by the supervisory committee of Liu Ling People's Commune and that of Yenan hsien. In addition, auditors may be sent by the province or the central government without prior notice, and if leading comrades from the provincial capital or from Peking come, they too can have a look at our accounts.

The following expenditure is covered by the states' administrative grant: (a) wages of the ganbus of the people's commune. There are ten of us and our cook. The highest wage is 62 Y a month and the lowest 37·50 Y a month. We are not entitled to our own plot of ground. If we do voluntary manual work, we are not paid for it. The introduction of the people's commune meant a saving to the state. Prior to that, there had been fifteen ganbus in the hsiang administration. This meant a reduction in the amount spent on wages of more than thirty per cent. The five who had to leave went to other areas; (b) postage, telegrams and similar administrative expenditure; (c) various journey allowances, mostly for the Liu Ling People's Commune's representatives and the party conference of Liu Ling People's Commune. Those attending these get an allowance of 0·30 Y a day. This is paid out of the state grant to the administration.

In 1961, we received 8,154 Y from Yenan hsien. We spent 7,875 Y and transferred 279 Y to the 1962 budget. For 1962 we have had 8,925 Y from Yenan hsien.

In addition to this budget, we send Yenan hsien bills for day allowances paid to delegates from our commune attending meetings in the commune called by state authorities. These receive 0·20 Y a day from us. For meetings called by the Yenan hsien authorities within Yenan hsien, but outside Liu Ling People's Commune, delegates receive 0·30 Y a day direct from Yenan hsien.

The income of the people's commune comes from the workshop it runs, Liu Ling People's Commune's Agricultural Implement Factory. This factory's costs amount to 85 per cent of its income. The remaining 15 per cent is taken by the commune. In 1961, the 15 per cent amounted to 5,600 Y. Of this, 5,000 Y was re-invested in the factory. The commune bought a truck for the factory. For 1962 we reckon to receive 6,000 Y and re-invest 4,200 Y in the factory. We have already had 2,000 Y. The surplus goes to the investment fund. This is looked after by the finance and credit department, and the representatives of the people's commune decide on the use to which such means shall be put. It can be used to buy tractors, trucks, cattle, film projectors, etc. At the moment, the fund has about 15,000 Y.

On the recommendation of the management of the commune, short-term, interest-free loans can be made from this fund to a labour brigade, labour group or factory. But this applies only to short-term loans. For proper loans, they have to go to the State Bank. For these, a recommendation from the commune's management is also needed.

In a way, the factory can be said to be a labour brigade. But it does not have the same authority to control its economy as the labour brigades have. The workers in the factory can elect their own book-keeper and their president of the factory management committee and also their representative on the people's commune, but they cannot decide about the factory's finances and economy. That is a matter for the commune's management. On the other hand, the factory pays no taxes.

In 1961, the grain tax paid by Liu Ling People's Commune amounted to 135,250 jin. That is an average of 4·6 jin per mu. This tax was fixed after the land was divided up. It is based on a certain percentage of the 1948 harvest. It has been calculated for each individual field. There is no tax for the first three years after ground is first cultivated. In our commune, we have not changed the grain tax since the commune was formed. That is to say that it is based on the ground that was under cultivation in 1955. This is an incentive to increased production. In this way, the proportion of the total production going in tax is decreasing the whole time. This does not mean that the grain tax has been exactly the same all the years that the people's commune has been in existence. It has fluctuated a few hundred jin, because we have exchanged certain fields with neighbouring communes in order to obtain a more uniform area and to straighten out our boundaries.

We also pay a tax on stock, that is on sheep and goats. This amounts to two per cent of the animals' value. We usually take the declared value of a sheep at eight yuan and that of a goat at six yuan. There are, in addition, certain registration fees for horse-drawn vehicles, ox-carts and bicycles. These could be called a road tax. The people's commune hands all this over without deduction direct to the authorities concerned in Yenan hsien. Before the people's commune was set up, the tax from the improved agricultural co-operatives was paid to the hsiang administration and this handed the money on without deduction to the administration of the hsien.

The credit department acts as a farmers' exchequer. The members of the labour groups elect representatives, and these, in turn, elect a management committee. The chairman of this committee is at the same time responsible for the commune's credit department. At the same time a supervisory committee of its own is elected for the credit department. Li Yiu-hua is chairman of this committee. In addition the State Bank and the management of the people's commune inspect the credit department. This deals with savings and loans. On 8 September 1962, the last day for which we have a report, the savings of the labour groups in the credit department amounted to 10,358 Y, and the private savings accounts totalled 19,485 Y. The total of loans was some few thousands of yuan. Assets are lodged with the State Bank in the credit department's account there. I don't know what interest the bank pays. Nor do I know what interest the labour groups receive. I don't know what interest private savers receive. During 1961 and the first eight months of 1962, the following loans have been made to individuals in Liu Ling:

5 May 1961. Chen Chung-yuan for purchase of sucking pigs, 15 Y. Interest 0·6 per cent a month. This was repaid on 7 September 1961 with 15·37 Y.

20 March 1962. Li Hai-yuan for purchase of sucking pigs, 50 Y. Interest 0·6 per cent per month. This was repaid on 22 August 1961 with 51·53 Y.

Individual loans are not granted for expenditure on consumer goods, but for various forms of investment. We do not encourage extravagance. But if anyone should want a loan to provide a worthy funeral, that would be considered in order. Normally, this does not happen, for it is the custom for neighbours and relatives to contribute. But there have been cases in the commune.

The party committee of Liu Ling People's Commune consists of eleven members, one of whom is a woman, and five ganbus employed full time. There are 196 party members in Liu Ling People's Commune, of whom seventeen are women, and there are four who are still only candidates for membership.

The management committee of Liu Ling People's Commune consists of seventeen persons. Six of these are ganbus. There are ten ganbus in the whole of Liu Ling People's Commune, that is, persons wholly employed in the revolution. I am on both Liu Ling People's Commune Management Committee and Liu Ling People's Commune's Party Committee. That is why we have five ganbus in the party committee and six ganbus in the management committee, but only ten ganbus in the whole commune. The management committee of the commune corresponds to the old hsiang administration. We have all its state duties, plus the additional duty of being in charge of production. Our duties are thus:

To manage the economy. In actual fact, this means that we do the work of planning. We draw up a plan for production in accordance with the objectives set us by the state and the proposals received direct from the labour groups. We also run the factory and manage its economy. We do this absolutely. We have to decide absolutely about its investments and production.

To inspect that the work being done in the territory of the commune is performed in the correct way.

To ensure the supply of agricultural implements, insecticides, artificial fertilizers and good seed. From January 1961 to September 1962 we supplied the labour groups with 5,527 agricultural tools, 5,162 jin of artificial manure and 1,987 jin of insecticide.

To popularize new agricultural methods and to spread agricultural knowledge.

To run social life; to see to matters of public health; to protect public order and local security; to mediate in disputes between members of the commune, and where possible, get them amicably settled.

We are thus a comprehensive economic organ of state management at local level.

At the organizational level of the people's commune there are two supervisory committees, that of the party organization, consisting of seven members, who have the task of watching over the finances of the party organizations and their work, as well as the work and party behaviour of the members of the party; and Liu Ling's supervisory committee, which has nine members and which has to supervise the finances and work of all organs of the commune from commune level down to labour group level. In addition, they are to watch that no one's rights are infringed and that the liberties and rights of citizens are protected. It has thus four specific duties:

(1) To supervise the carrying-out of the party line and of the resolutions of the representatives of the commune.

(2) To see that there is no breach of the country's laws and/or of the liberties and rights of citizens.

(3) To watch that revenue and expenditure are justified and that they are correctly entered in the books, and that there is no breach of financial regulations.

(4) To watch that there is no waste of public means, and that no sabotage of economic policy or destruction of public property takes place.

Every private member of Liu Ling People's Commune has the right to lay complaints before the supervisory committee, and it is incumbent upon the latter to investigate every such complaint. The committee has the right to examine all books, to attend all meetings and to question any person elected to a position of trust. Its members, however, are not allowed to be on other committees or themselves have any function in the management of the commune or of any of its organs. Nor has the supervisory committee any authority to investigate or interfere in the private life of individual members. The members of the supervisory committee are elected by the representatives of Liu Ling People's Commune at its annual meeting and the committee reports to it then.

Similarly, a mediation committee of nine members is elected. Its duty is to mediate in any dispute between citizens. The most usual is for them to have to mediate between husband and wife. Before the courts can consider an application for divorce, the mediation committee must have tried to mediate between the two partners and to get them to continue their life together on a new and firmer basis. The mediation committee also has to mediate between neighbours. But it has no right of decision and cannot impose any punishment or fine. It can merely advise and try to get the parties to agree. It has no right to prevent any-one from going further, to the court, and suing his or her partner; the committee can merely dissuade.

The Committee of the League of Youth in Liu Ling People's Commune consists of thirteen members. The league has 198 members in nineteen groups. Its tasks are: (1) to train the young people ideolog-ically; (2) to encourage and organize the young people to fulfil the production plan; (3) to direct study activities; (4) to develop the League of Youth, both organizationally and ideologically; and (5) to run the Young Pioneers.

The women's committee of Liu Ling People's Committee con-sists of nine members. It has to organize the women in production, help the women to study the techniques of farming, help them run their homes, contribute to their ideological and political development. This women's committee does not represent any special women's organiza-tion, but has to work among all the women in the commune.

As part of the health work, 1,300 people have twice been vacci-nated against smallpox and had injections against typhus. These dis-eases have now been eradicated. We had 5,300 consultations in 1961. The most common ailments have been influenza, stomach trouble and pneumonia. In 1957, seventy-five children were born, while five children under the age of one and twenty between the ages of one and six died. In 1961, 250 babies were born and seven children under one year of age and twenty-three between the ages of one and six died.

The people's militia has three duties:

(1) To take part in production and protect its fruits.

(2) To guard the public safety and be on the watch for thieves, robbers and secret agents.

(3) To be ready to join up with the Chinese People's Liberation Army and support the front in the event of attack from abroad and, in the event of occupation, continue the fight as armed guerrillas till the enemy has been destroyed.

In principle, all men between sixteen and forty-five and all women between sixteen and thirty-five should belong. Membership is voluntary. Exceptions are those whose health is bad or who have been landowners or counter-revolutionaries.

In 1960, 100 hours were spent in training to shoot. 111 persons took part and their results were: excellent 67, good 35, and pass 9.

In 1961, 100 hours were spent in shooting-training and thirty people took part. We see that this training does not take place during working hours or at times which could be used for productive work. It is not often that the people's militia is called upon to act. We have had extremely few cases. But in June this year a criminal escaped from Matunchun. They rang us up and we mobilized the people's militia. Fifteen men captured the runaway down in the valley at Shiaoyuan-chikyou. We then sent him under guard to the Office of Public Safety in Yenan. We also captured a thief from one of our own labour brigades in 1961. This was Chiang Tsung-chen from Beikou Labour Brigade, who had stolen a two-wheeled cart and was captured by the people's militia in Liu Ling. He was taken to the office of the people's commune, and there we had a serious talk with him. He was severely criticized and also criticized himself. After that he signed an undertaking that he would never do such a thing again and was then allowed to go home. We never let such matters go up to Yenan. We can deal with them ourselves. On the whole, we have never had any crime here and the only person we have ever sent up to Yenan after the campaign against counter-revolutionaries many years ago was that runaway. Whatever happens is just minor stuff. Last year, the militia caught a man cutting firewood in the plantations. He was taken to the commune's office; we criticized him and he was allowed to go home after signing a paper in which he promised not to do this again. We read it out to him, and he put his fingerprint on it.

We elect one of our ganbus to be responsible for the commune's department of public safety and the armed forces. But this is not the same person elected to be regimental commander of the people's militia. The person we have elected to command the regiment is the chairman of the management committee of the people's commune.

In 1961, we received from the social welfare fund of Yenan hsien 710 Y for distribution in social welfare grants within the commune. This year we have already paid out 480 Y; but this will go up a bit in the winter. Last year, there were thirty-seven households comprising 141 persons who received social grants from this fund. This year money has been given to thirty households comprising 136 persons. Three households in the commune receive regular monthly allowances. They get twenty-nine yuan a month. These allowances are outside the scope of this fund. In addition, five households comprising fifteen persons have been credited with a total of 640 days' work as assistance.

Larger undertakings, such as water-regulation works, etc., have to be carried out by several labour brigades collaborating. The work is then managed by a work committee which has its office at the site. The chairman of this committee is always the chairman of the management committee of the commune, while the deputy chairman, who is the one who must always be present at the site, as well as the different labour leaders, are chosen by the labour brigades. Before work begins, the size of each participating brigade's share in the result in the work is fixed. That is, how much of the advantage from the work is for their benefit. In 1958, three labour brigades, Liu Ling Labour Brigade, Kaupo Labour Brigade and Chungchuan Labour Brigade, jointly built the Kaochinko dam. Liu Ling invested 1,900 days' work; Kaupo 1,100; and Chungchuan 890.

As Liu Ling Labour Brigade benefited most by the dam, it transpired at the settling up that Liu Ling Labour Brigade owed the other two labour brigades a total of 494 days' work: 394 to Kaupo Labour Brigade and 100 to Chungchuan Labour Brigade. Liu Ling Labour Brigade repaid this by helping in terracing the fields of the other two labour brigades.

In the winter of 1959–60, Liu Ling Labour Brigade carried out a very big water-regulation project. This cost a total of 14,772 days' work, of which Liu Ling Labour Brigade itself contributed only 4,172. Liu Ling Brigade first repaid a total of 1,568 days' work to the other two brigades which had collaborated, Chungchuan Labour Brigade and the Sun Rises Labour Brigade. They got roughly 800 days' work each.

After that, however, it became difficult to repay in days' work, and, after lengthy meetings and much discussion, we agreed that Liu Ling Labour Brigade could pay in cash. Negotiations took a long time. In the end the parties agreed that payment should be at 0·80 Y per day's work performed. That was roughly 0·30 Y below the current valuation of a day's work. It was a matter of a total of 8,532 days' work. Since then, no labour exchange project of this magnitude has been carried out between brigades.

Where free food is concerned, we felt that the system would not suit us, for several reasons. This is a poor and hilly part of the country; nobody would want free food; it would have meant altogether too much trouble arranging dining-halls and seeing that everybody got food. Therefore, it was never discussed. Neither we nor the farmers thought it at all a good idea.

PICADOR

This outstanding modern international series now ventures into the realms of non-fiction on subjects suited to contemporary tastes.

THE MOUNTAIN PEOPLE *by* Colin Turnbull   75p

One of the most remarkable and acclaimed works of contemporary anthropology, this is a devastating portrait of the *Ik*, a black African tribe, in the final stages of decline and dissolution.

'I might compare the book to *The Godfather* if Turnbull's study were not more gruesome, more frightening in its implications for us all. Within the Mafia, after all, there is a morality. The *Ik* have none . . .' ROBERT ARDREY

BOUND FOR GLORY *by* Woody Guthrie   75p

Bound for Glory, first published in 1943, is the autobiography of Woody Guthrie, the founder of modern American folk music. It is a funny, cynical, earthy and tragic account of his life in an Okie oil-boom town, of the Depression that followed, and of his subsequent travels in, on and under trains, in stolen cars, and on his feet, round an America going rotten from the top downwards.

Woody writes as he spoke, and his voice is the voice of Kerouac, Corso, Dylan and Brautigan.

REAL TIME *edited by* John Brockman and Ed Rosenfeld

'Reality is a man-made process. Our images of the universe, of ourselves, are in part the models resulting from our perceptions of the techniques that we generate as products'

Key extracts from the works of Konrad Lorenz, R. D. Laing, Isaac Asimov, Noam Chomsky and many others suggest and outline new and essential ideas in communications, human systems, mind, science and technology. They present a wide range of ideas and activities indispensable to the perception of the 'real' world which exists not in some fixed place or time but in the continuing process of describing the models that tell us who, what, and where we are.

SIDDHARTHA *by* Hermann Hesse   40p

Siddhartha, son of a Brahmin, finds the Buddha but fails to find contentment as his disciple.

He takes the long and tortuous road in search of his destiny. It leads him through a season of passionate love in the arms of a beautiful courtesan, through the temptations of wealth and success, and through emotional conflict with his own son, before he reaches his final renunciation and ultimate self-knowledge.

This timeless story, the odyssey of a man in search of himself, is the perfect expression of Hesse's genius. Written in prose of biblical simplicity, *Siddhartha* is Hesse's great love story, a book that future generations may well call his masterpiece.

'A novel of great beauty . . . subtle distillation of wisdom, stylistic grace and symmetry of form' SUNDAY TIMES

Also available in PICADOR:
KNULP   40p
IF THE WAR GOES ON   50p
KLINGSOR'S LAST SUMMER   50p
ROSSHALDE   40p

If you have any difficulty in obtaining Picador books please send purchase price plus 7p postage to PO Box 11, Falmouth, Cornwall.
While every effort is made to keep prices low, it is sometimes necessary to increase them at short notice. The publishers reserve the right to show new retail prices on covers, which may differ from those previously advertised in the text or elsewhere.